THE RELATIONSHIP BETWEEN THE CHURCH AND THE THEATRE

Exemplified by Selected Writings of the Church Fathers and by Liturgical Texts Until Amalarius of Metz — 775-852 A. D.

Christine Catharina Schnusenberg

UNIVERSITY
PRESS OF
AMERICA

LANHAM • NEW YORK • LONDON

Copyright © 1988 by

University Press of America,® Inc.

4720 Boston Way
Lanham, MD 20706

3 Henrietta Street
London WC2E 8LU England

All rights reserved

Printed in the United States of America

British Cataloging in Publication Information Available

Library of Congress Cataloging in Publication Data

Schnusenberg, Christine.
  The relationship between the Church and the theatre.

Translation of: Verhaltnis von Kirche und Theater.
  Bibliography: p.
  1. Liturgics—History.   2. Liturgy and drama—History.
3. Theater—Religious aspects—Christianity—History of
doctrines.   4. Amalarius, Archbishop of Lyon,
ca. 775-ca.   850.   I. Title.
BV178.S3613   1986   246'.7   86-24637
ISBN 0-8191-5733-3 (alk. paper

All University Press of America books are produced on acid-free
paper which exceeds the minimum standards set by the National
Historical Publications and Records Commission.

DEDICATION

This work is dedicated to the memory of Jackie H. Y. Liu, a very talented young Chinese student in mathematics at the University of Chicago, whose high academic goals could never be achieved because of tragic, cross-cultural circumstances.

PREFACE TO THE ENGLISH TRANSLATION

This work is a corrected, slightly enlarged and revised version and English translation of my doctoral thesis.[1] It is not perfect since unclarities inherent in this complex and vast interdisciplinary subject will, for the time being, have to remain as they stand.

I have not translated the Latin quotations. Their content, however, is expounded in the discussions preceding and following the cited passages. It is hoped that these citations will help bringing home to the reader the power of the allegorical sign and symbol embedded in a complex world-view and expressed in a dramatic-liturgical language, reminding him that this symbolic-allegorical language, as intricately interwoven with the liturgical act, was, for nearly two millennia, an active element in the shaping of Western culture and civilization.

I am indebted to Professors Mircea Eliade and Paul Ricoeur for their interest in the progress of this translation and its publication. I would like to thank Professor James Luther Adams for reading the manuscript, for his criticisms and suggestions for stylistic revisions.

I am grateful to Richard Adamiak and Michael Steinberg for their helpful discussions in bringing about clarity of certain passages and to Katrina McLeod for her criticism and editing of the greater part of the manuscript. I wish to thank Janice Gilmore for her painstakingness in the typing of this large project.

It is hoped that despite remaining imperfections--which are my sole responsibility--this work will provide a useful working tool for English-speaking scholarship and will help to further discussions on this fascinating problem of the development of Christian liturgical drama and its relationship to the Roman theatre.

University of Chicago   C.C.S.
July 24, 1986

Footnotes

[1] Christine C. Schnusenberg, "Das Verhältnis von Kirche ud Theater: Dargestellt an ausgewählten Schriften der Kirchenväter und liturgischen Texten bis auf Amalarius von Metz: 775-852 A.D." Ph.D. Dissertation, The University of Chicago, 1976.

——————— *Das Verhältnis von Kirche und Theater:* Dargestellt an ausgewählten Schriften der Kirchenväter und liturgischen Texten bis auf Amalarius von Metz: A.D. 775-852. (Bern-Frankfurt am Main-Las Vegas: Peter Lang, 1981. (Europäische Hochschulschriften, Reihe Theologie, Vol. 141.)

PREFACE TO THE GERMAN VERSION

I am greatly indebted to the members of my dissertation committee: Professor Kenneth Northcott, Department of Germanic Languages and Literatures, whose seminar on medieval drama gave impetus to my thesis; Professor Bernard McGinn of the Department of Church History in the Divinity School who provided invaluable guidance to Patristic Studies and an indispensable bibliography; and Professor Samuel Jaffe of the German Department for his consultation and encouragement. Furthermore, I would like to thank Professor Braxton Ross of the Department of Classics for his useful introduction to the study of Palaeography in a cultural context and Professor Langdon Gilkey of the Divinity School for his introduction to the history of dogma. I am grateful to Professor James Luther Adams of Harvard University, as whose research assistant I had the opportunity to work; his useful suggestions regarding the sociological aspects of my investigation broadened its scope. I would like to express my indebtedness to Professors Mircea Eliade and Paul Ricoeur for their stimulating seminars in the History of Religion and Hermeneutics which gave a new impetus, new insights and further direction to my research. I was fortunate to have been able to participate in a seminar on the history of the Syriac Church conducted by the Syriologists, Professor Arthur Vööbus of the Oriental Institute and the Lutheran School of Theology at Chicago. I appreciate the kindness and helpfulness of the librarians at Regenstein Library of the Univeristy of Chicago, the Newberry Library and the Lutheran School of Theology at Chicago. I acknowledge with gratitude a scholarship of the University of Chicago.

I enjoyed the various cross-cultural discussions with many of the international students at International House of the University of Chicago where I resided during the years of my graduate studies; these discussions were an enrichment in the process of my thesis.

The academic "Sitz im Leben", however, can become interwoven with those acute or ordinary circumstances of everyday life in an institutional setting either promoting or inhibiting scholarly processes. I would like to take this opportunity to express my thankfulness to Professor Paul Meier of the Department of Statistics, for his sincere and constant interest in problems as they emerged in the student-life sector and for his efforts to bring about clarification and amelioration of such problems.

I wish to extend my appreciation to the Jesuits of Creighton University in Omaha, Nebraska, to Dr. and Mrs. Albert B. Lorincz, and to Mr. and Mrs. William R. Hood, Bellevue, Nebraska for their friendship and constant interest in my work.

It is only proper to express on this occasion a deep gratitude and sincere appreciation to the late Professor Dr. Georg Raederscheidt, the long-time director of the Landjugendakademie, Fredeburg, Germany. In his tireless and unselfish efforts and concerns for the Bildung and growth of that generation of German youth who grew up during the Second World War and post-war period, he was an unceasing inspiration.

And finally my deeply-felt gratitude goes to my parents, my sisters and brothers, my uncles of the Franciscan Order, the late Fr. Alfons Schnusenberg and Fr. Angelus Aschoff, and to all those of Gut Gewekenhorst in St. Vit-Wiedenbruck, Nordrhein-Westfalen, Germany, who provided and cultivated the rich soil which nurtured the growth and dreams of my childhood and early adolescence.

TABLE OF CONTENTS

ABBREVIATIONS

BKV	Bibliothek der Kirchenväter
CC	Corpus Christianorum seu nova Collectio
CPh	Classical Philology
CR	Classical Review
CSCO	Corpus Scriptorum Christianorum Orientalium
CSEL	Corpus Scriptorum Ecclesiasticorum Latinorum
DACL	Dictionnaire d'Archéologie Chrétienne et de Liturgie
DVJS	Deutsche Vierteljahresschrift für Literatur-wissenschaft und Geistesgeschichte
FMST	Frühmittelalterliche Studien
JbLw	Jahrbuch für Literaturwissenschaft
JEGP	Journal of English and Germanic Philology
LThK	Lexikon für Theologie und Kirche
LQ	Liturgiegeschichtliche Quellen
Mansi	J. D. Mansi, Sacrorum Conciliorum, Nova et Amplissima Collectio
MLR	Modern Language Review
PG	J. - P. Migne, Patrologiae Cursus Completus: Series Graecae.
PL	J. - P. Migne, Patrologiae Cursus Completus:

Series Latina.

RAC	Reallexikon für Antike und Christentum
RB	Revue Bénédictine
RGG	Die Religion in Geschichte und Gegenwart
RThAM	Recherches Théologique Anciénne et Médiévale
TAPA	Transactions of the American Philological Association
ZfkTH	Zeitschrift für katholische Theologie
ZfwTh	Zeitschrift für wissenschaftliche Theologie
ZfdA	Zeitschrift für deutsches Altertum und deutsche Literatur
VC	Vigilae Christianae
WW	Wirkendes Wort

INTRODUCTION

This study has grown out of an inquiry into the negative attitude of the Church Fathers toward the Roman theatre and into the apparent disappearance of the theatre for approximately 400 years; that is the period between the end of organized Roman theatre (ca. 530 A.D.) and the manifestation of the Quem quaeritis tropes (ca. 930 A.D.).[1] While recent scholarship has centered anew around the phenomena of liturgical drama on the one hand and the attitude of the Church Fathers toward the theatre on the other, no inquiry has been made into the cultural and religious theological causes which gave rise to the most intense polemics of the Patristic age, namely those against the theatre, or into the simultaneous rise of Christian liturgical drama which developed out of the Eucharistic act--the Last Supper--and the Biblical plot centering around the figure of Jesus Christ. This study moves between these two polemical poles--the Roman theatre and Christian liturgical drama-- connecting rather than separating them. The historical-methodological point of departure in our study is therefore the Roman theatre and Roman culture of which the theatre was an essential expression; in addition, Judaeo-Christian cult forms which were also part of that same culture were analyzed. The Quem quaeritis tropes which appeared much later are not included in our research.

The result of my initial research, a textual examination of the documents of ecclesiastical synod and council decrees up to about 750 A.D., confirmed the existence of the official negation of the Roman theatre by the Church and raised the question of the causes of such negative attitudes. This research led finally to the analysis of selected Patristic texts. It soon became obvious, however, that in order to understand and clarify this problem, the study of Patristic theology and that of the cultural context in which these conflicts were carried out, would be necessary. Furthermore, it became clear that an examination of the different cult forms which grew out of Christianty itself, was necessary in order to understand the complex phenomenon of Christian liturgical drama. This ensuing research led me beyond the limits of the Fachgebiet of Germanic studies into the fields of Church history, history of religions, hermeneutics, exegesis, history of art and culture, as well as sociology and anthropology; it became an interdisciplinary endeavor.

xix

Taking the thesis of Hardison as a point of departure, one can say that he bases his arguments concerning the dramatic qualities of the liturgy on the Poetics of Aristotle and justifies them on the grounds of the works of Amalarius of Metz. I therefore turned my attention to the texts of this Carolingian writer. At first the meaning of these texts seemed obscure. It was only after a contextual and hermeneutical approach to complicated and often paradoxical textual material such as that cited below that the works of Amalarius became elucidated. A liturgical drama of aesthetically beautiful form began to emerge which reflected a mysterious world of intrinsically harmonious motion, a world which in its own form had been nourished not only by Roman culture and Patristic traditions but also by a Germanic world view embedded in mysterious signs and runes.

The tension of this inquiry is derived from two problematical poles: on the one hand, from the conflictual situation of the world of Romanitas and Christianitas and on the other, from the world of Amalarius of Metz of the Carolingian period searching for new forms. It is anticipated that the results of this inquiry have made a contribution to the clarification of the problem regarding the apparent disappearance of the Roman theatre the period of which had for so long a time remained in obscurity. It is also hoped that this study will lead to a greater appreciation of liturgical drama as a unique aesthetical form. I should stress that liturgical drama not be considered as an isolated phenomenon but rather that it be viewed in the context of and in relation to other literary, theological and historical texts and art forms. For example, future research which were to examine the interrelationships of the texts of Amalarius of Metz, the fragments of Old-High-German literature, the fully developed genre of Otfried von Weissenburg's Gospel Harmony (Evangelienbuch), the works of John Scotus Eriugenae as well as their respective sources could yield fruitful and interesting results.

The final conclusion of the results of this research has led to further questions: What is the nature of drama and where are its origins? For this reason a brief analysis of the dramatic genre seems to be necessary.

The world drama, as it is understood today in literary criticism of Germanic studies, originated no later than the mid-

18th century. Until that time all performances had been designated as <u>Schauspiel</u> or as <u>Spektakel</u>. In Old-High-German literature, written during the period which is of greatest interest to us in our present study, the word <u>drama</u> does not occur but rather the word <u>spil</u> which is derived from <u>spectaculum</u>, <u>ludus</u>.[2] But that would lead us to assume that the conception of <u>Spiel</u> or <u>Schauspiel</u> would be more appropriate for a description of the performed action of the plot than the word drama which was borrowed at a much later time. On the other hand, the Greek definition of <u>drama</u> ($\delta\rho\alpha\mu\alpha$) comes close to the conception of <u>liturgia</u> ($\lambda\epsilon\iota\tau o\upsilon\rho\gamma\iota\alpha$) because both refer to a public act or a special performance.[3] In the light of these semantic relations, the meaning of drama and of liturgy do not have to be contradictory. In the framework of this dissertation, drama is understood to be "an activated plot in mimetic representations with possible epic insertions which include persons, objects and spectators whose interactions and subtleties of their inner relationship vary from plot to plot". Such a definition stands in contradiction neither to the <u>Poetics</u> of Aristotle nor to Brecht's <u>Little Organon</u>.[4]

The selected texts here might give the impression of a compendium. But this careful selection of texts should be taken as testimony of the unity of a complex problem as well as of a continuity of the tradition of liturgical drama, especially as it developed from the First Liturgical Act of Jesus. The complexity of Christian liturgical drama and its characteristic <u>Vielschichtigkeit</u>--various layers of multiple meaning--needs further study and interpretation. For instance, it seems to me that the integral <u>Vielschichtigkeit</u> of liturgical drama stems from the overlappings of the temporal and spatial dimensions both of which are inherent in the four senses of Scripture within which Christian liturgical drama is molded. These aspects have hitherto not been examined in those studies dealing with liturgical drama. Our present study is only an initial attempt in this direction. Further research and deeper penetration into and reflection about these aspects would be a challenging task.

Another problem which needs to be mentioned is that of the condition of the examined texts themselves. For example, text-critical complications arose from the Byzantine and Gallican texts because their authors and dates are perhaps not correct. Critical editions and translations would therefore be a valuable task for future scholarship. We are fortunate to have Father[6] Hanssens' critical edition of the works of Amalarius of Metz. This work is an indispensable source of meticulous information. Irregularities in orthography which were indicated by their editor appear unchanged in all of my citations. Other variants are not elaborated. Bibliographical sources which are indicated in my citations are placed in parentheses of their respective footnotes of this work. The critical editions of other primary sources are only cited in footnotes when clarification seemed necessary or when their commentaries have shed light on our problems. In all other cases they are cited only in the selected bibliography at the end of this work.

FOOTNOTES

[1] See especially: O.B. Hardison, Jr., <u>Christian Rite and Christian Drama in the Middle Ages: Essays in the Origin and Early History of Modern Drama</u> (Baltimore: The Johns Hopkins Press, 1965); Fletcher Collins, Jr., <u>The Production of Medieval Church-Music-Drama</u> (Charolottesville: University of Virginia Press, (1972); David M. Bevington, comp. <u>Medieval Drama</u> (Boston: Houghton Mifflin, 1975); Werner Weismann, <u>Kirche und Schauspiele im Urteil der lateinischen Kirchenvater unter besonderer Berucksichtigung von Augustin</u>, Cassiciacum, Nr. 27 (Wurzburg: Augustinus Verlag, 1972) Additional material is listed in the bibliography.

[2] Kluge <u>Etymologisches Worterbuch</u>, 20. Aufl., s.v. "Drama"; Lewis and Short, <u>A Latin Dictionary</u>, 1966 ed., s.v. "drama"; Graff, <u>Althochdeutscher Sprachschatz</u>, 1963, reproduction, s.v. "spil"; Grimms <u>Deutsches Worterbuch</u>, 1862, ed., s.v. "Spiel".

[3] Liddell and Scott, <u>A Greek-English Lexicon</u>, 9th ed. s.v. $\delta\rho\alpha\mu\alpha$ and s.v. $\lambda\epsilon\iota\tau\sigma\upsilon\rho\gamma\iota\alpha$.

[4] Aristotle <u>Poetics</u> 6.2 and Bertholt Brecht, <u>Kleines Organon</u>, par. 60, 65, 70 and epilogue.

[5] The German word <u>Vielschichtigkeit</u> can, in my view, best be rendered into English in a circumscribed form, <u>i.e.</u>, as "various layers of multiple meanings". Because of its significance for our study, the German term "<u>Vielschichtigkeit</u>" will be retained in most instances.

[6] A translation of Amalarius works would be a great contribution to the scholarship of Western culture.

CHAPTER I

RELIGIOUS ASPECTS OF ROMAN CULTURE[1]

Cult of Gods and Emperor

The cult of gods and Emperor was essential to life in the Roman Empire. These cults were the inner components of the Roman state religion intimately related to the myth of Rome. From Romulus to Diocletian and to Symmachus, the tripartite gods Jupiter, Mars and Quirinius were the source of faith in Rome's prosperity and fame. The erection of the Altar of Victory by the Emperor Augustus around 29 B.C. gave evidence of this faith in the historicity of the gods. It also gave witness to Rome's self-awareness of victory. The Altar therefore was Rome's very symbol of itself, rooted in the mos maiorum and pax deorum. These ideal values which resulted from the interplay between religion and the affairs of the state are especially expressed by the Roman poets and writers around the turn of the millennium. Cicero emphasizes the sacred religion of Rome when he writes:

> . . . mihique ita persuasi Romulum auspiciis.
> Numam sacris constitutis fundamenta iecisse
> nostrae civitatis, quae numquam profecto sine
> summa placatione deorum immortalium tanta esse
> potuisset.[2]

The continuous well-being of the state also depends on the protection of the immortal gods. Cicero refers to this in another text:

> . . . deos denique immortales huic
> invicto populo, clarissimo imperio,
> pulcherrimae urbi contra tantam vim
> sceleris praesentes auxilium esse
> laturos.[3]

This conception of the supremacy of the gods is also expressed in the writings of Livius:

> Deserta omnia, sine capite, sine

1

viribus, dii praesides ac fortuna
urbis tutata est.[4]

Livius further maintains that the gods do not desert the state
but rather that they will preserve its harmony and prosperity, a
belief which he expresses as follows:

Nunc dii immortales, imperii Romani
praesides. . . iidem auguriis auspi-
ciisque et per nocturnos etias visus
omnia laeta prospera portendunt.[5]

The vision of Rome's eternal value, however, is especially
expressed by Vergil in his national epic, the Aeneid where
Jupiter assures Venus that he has freed Rome from all spatial
and temporal boundaries: ". . . his ego nec metas rerum nec
tempora pono; imperium sine fide dedi."[6] This poetic vision of
Vergil expresses the deeply rooted belief in the gods of the
Roman Empire. It was after Vergil that Rome was envisioned as
the "Eternal City". This belief finds expression again in the
dispute surrounding the Altar of Victory. In his struggle for
the preservation of the belief in the Roman gods, the aged Roman
citizen Symmachus points in his third Relatio to the many
victories which the Roman goddess Victoria has bestowed upon the
Empire:

Multa Victoriae debet aeternitas vestra
et adhuc plura debebit. Aversentur hanc
potestatem, quibus nihil profuit, vos
amicum triumphis patrocinium nolite
deserere![7]

Thus the Altar of Victory expressed in spatial form the Roman
tradition of victory as protected by the gods, and therefore the
Altar belonged to the scared custom of Rome for which the Romans
had great deference. Symmachus expressed this Roman attitude
most appropriately as follows: "Consuetudinis amor magnus
est."[8]

Closely interwoven with this self-awareness of triumph and
victory and with the cult of which was the figure of the
Emperor. As pontifex maximus he became the deputy of the gods

and protector of the mos maiorum. The triumphal processions of the Roman Emperors were a result of this intertwinement of belief in the gods and the affairs of the state. These processions objectified the res publica as it were from the basis of the mos maiorum renewing itself in constant self-confirmation through the pax deorum. During the time of these processions of victory and their related festivals, the Emperor became the center around which the powers of the Empire converged. The Roman theatre, an essential component of this cult, was of great religious and liturgical significance and therefore vitally important within the structure of the Roman state.

The origin of the Roman theatre was, so it was thought, to be sought in dance performances in connection with the liberalia and lupercalia in honor and for the appeasement of the gods at the outbreak of a pestilence in 364 B.C.[10] Thus, the theatre was from the beginning closely connected with the mos maiorum and pax deorum. After the first public performance the theatrical dances and plays took place at an open wooden stage, often associated with the circus. But there were also performances, as Hanson has shown, near sacred places and particularly in connection with temples. Thus, performances took place in the presence of the gods, i.e, in conspectu dei.[11] In 58 B.C., the first wooden theatre was erected in Rome and three years later Pompeii built the first enlarged permanent theatre of stone, which was not only closely connected with the temple of the goddess Venus but was, moreover, also dedicated to her.[12] Thus, through the erection of special buildings the theatre was not only assigned a permanent and official place in Roman society but through its relation to the temple of Venus its meaning slowly found expression in additional theatre buildings throughout the Roman Empire.[13] In 135 A.D. for instance, the Emperor Hadrian had a theatre built in Jerusalem. Side by side these massive architectural expressions other illuminating confirmations relating to the theatre can be found in other forms of art. For example, the shapes of small cakes which were distributed during festivals in honor of the gods and the Emperor, contained representational scenes of the plays which were to be performed at particular festivals. Such images are also found in reliefs; they have furthermore been captured in pottery and are expressed in mosaics. Chairs and pillows are similarly decorated with figurative shapes of the gods. In most cases, these images deal with scenes from tragedies and comedies as well as with representations of gods and victory parades of the Emperors.[14] Such representations, however, are by no means a shallow ostentation but rather they signify the actual presence of the gods represented in those figurative forms and images during the performances and festivals.[15]

The Educational Function of the Stage

The substantive material of the scenic representational forms is an expression of the Roman tradition and fulfills an essentially educational purpose. The sources of Lactantius and Augustine are especially informative regarding the educational function of the theatre. Lactantius points out that the Romans received knowledge about their myths through the stage. He says:

> . . . quomodo se rapinis et fraudibus abstinebunt qui Mercuri furta noverunt docentis non fraudis esse decipere, sed astutiae? quomodo libidines cohercebunt qui Iovem Hercules Liberum Appollinem ceterosque venerantur, quorum adulteria et stupra in mares et feminas non tantum doctis nota sunt, sed exprimuntur etiam in theatris atque cantatur ut sint omnibus notoria?[16]

According to this view, it is not merely the learned class of society which understands the content and meaning of the myth but it is rather a collective participation of all strata of society. Through dramatic and scenic configurations on the stage the myth is made intelligible to all classes of Roman society. In the following citation Lactantius stresses particularly the cultic purposes of the stage when he emphasizes the mimesis of the god as the highest religious cultform:

> . . . Possuntne inter haec iusti esse, homines, qui etiamsi natura sint boni,

4

> ab ipsis tamen diis erundiantur ad in-
> ustitiam? ad placandum enim deum quem
> colas iis rebus opus est, quibus illum
> gaudere ac delectari scias. sic fit ut
> vitam colentium deus pro qualitate numinis
> sui formet quoniam religiosissimus est
> cultus imitari.[17]

This same creative combination of cult form and forms of
representation in the vital figurativeness of mimesis one can
observe conspicuously manifested in later Christian liturgical
drama.[18]   Most interestingly, Augustine, too, points out that
the Romans had become familiar with Vergil's national epic, the
Aeneid, mainly through the stage rather than through the reading
of this text. He refers to this practice in one of his Easter
sermons:

> . . . nostis enim hoc prope omnes,
> atque utinam pauci nossetis. Sed
> pauci nostis in libris, multi in thea-
> tris quia Aenas descendit ad infernos,
> et ostendit illi pater suus animas Roma-
> norum magnorum venturas in corpora. . .[19]

In addition to making reference to such performances from apparent observations, Augustine relates in other writings that he
knew the stage from his own experiences.[20]

Excessive Performance and Licentiousness

In addition to its liturgical and educational significance
the theatre also fulfilled the function of entertainment. With
its excessive performance it degenerated into base demoralization. This was offensive to the sacred mos maiorum of the
Romans. Tacitus laments that the erection of a permanent theatre
building in Roman society caused the old laws, which had been
enacted for the prevention of idleness and excessiveness, to be
neglected, and that consequently this neglect had not only
endangered Roman youth but had also led to the demoralization of
whole social classes. In his Annales, Tacitus summarizes this

situation as follows:

> Nerone quartum Cornelio Cosso consulibus
> quinquennale ludricum Romae institutum est
> ad morem Graeci certaminis, varia fama, ut
> cuncta ferme nova. quippe erant qui Gn.
> quoque Pompeium incusatum a senioribus
> ferrent quod mansuram theatri sedem
> posuisset. nam antea subitariis gradibus
> et scaena in tempus structua ludos edi solitos,
> vel si vetustiora repetas, stantem populum
> spectavisse, ne si consideret theatro, dies
> totos ignavia continuaret. spectaculorum
> quidem antiquitas servaretur, quoties prae-
> tores ederent, nulla cuiquam civium necessi-
> tate certandi. ceterum abolitos paulatim
> patrios mores funditus everti per accitam
> lasciviam, ut quod usquam corrumpi et
> corrumpere queat in urbe visatur, degeneretque
> studiis externis iuventus, gymnasia et otia et
> turpis amores exercendo, principe et senatu
> auctoribus qui non modo licentium vitiis
> permiserint sed vim adhibeant ut proceres
> Romani specie orationum et carminum scaena
> polluantur. quid superesse nisi ut corpora
> quoque nudent et caestus adsumant easque pugnas
> pro militia et armis meditentur? an iustitiam
> auctum iri et decurias equitum egregium iudicandi
> munus expleturos, si fractos sonos et dulcedinem
> vocum perite audissent? noctes quoque dedecori
> adiectas ne quod tempus pudori relinquatur, sed
> coetu promisco, quod perditissimus quisque per
> diem concupiverit, per tenebras audeat.[21]

Perversion of the old laws and excessiveness are the main
complaints of Tacitus. Other classical writers express the same
concerns; for example, Juvenal describes this condition best
with his notorius saying about "panem et circenses" which he
summarizes in his tenth satire:

> . . . nam qui dabat olim imperium fasces

legiones omnia, nunc se continet atque
duas tantum res anxius optat, panem et
circenses.[22]

Further proof of this development can be found in a calendar which was composed by the calligraph, Furius Dionysius
Philocalus.[23] In this calendar the state festivals are recorded
as they were celebrated in Rome and Constantinople. Müller
gives the following summary:

Im ganzen werden 175 Spieltage aufgeführt.
Das ist reichlich 10 Prozent mehr, als zu
Marc Aurels Zeit üblich waren . . . Von
jenen 175 Spieltagen entfallen nun 10
auf Gladiatorenkämpfe--munera--64 auf
circensische und 101 auf szenische Spiele
--ludi--und von den 165 ludi gelten der
Feier glücklicher Ereignisse 54, Geburts-
tagen von Kaisern 19, Regierungsantritten
2, während zu Ehren heidnischer Götter an
90 Tagen teils Zirkus--, teils Bühnenspiele
veranstaltet werden.[24]

This analysis indicates that the Roman calendar officially
designated about half of the entire year for the performance of
theatre plays. The sponsors were generally Emperors, praetors,
wealthy citizens and priests.[25] We know from Symmachus that in
addition to performances in both capitals, plays were also
performed throughout the provinces of the Roman Empire. In his
sixth Relatio in which he addresses the Emperors Arkadius and
Theodosius, Symmachus asks them to keep their promises to send
theatre troupes in order not to disappoint the populace. He
describes the joyful expectations of the citizens:

. . . orat igitur clementiam vestram,
ut post illa subsidia, quae victui
nostro largitas vestra praestavit,
etiam curules ac scaenicas voluptates
circo et Pompeianae caveae suggeratis.
his enim gaudet urbana laetitia, cuius
desiderium pollicitatione movistis.

7

expectantur cotidie nuntii, qui pro-
pinquare urbi munera promissa con-
firment.[26]

The Roman people were, according to these sources, driven
by a strong desire for entertainment[27] which had degenerated
into idleness and excessive theatre performances and
attendances; therefore the theatre had become an offense against
the mos maiorum; such an offense, it was thought, would be
disapproved by the gods and would stir their anger. It should
also be mentioned that besides these theatrical performances
there was a fully developed mimus which had often the dimensions
of a whole drama; this, too, in addition to the general
performances of the theatre was greatly enjoyed.[28] Thus, there
was always something to be looked at in the Roman world which
was a world of the concrete.

In the above discussion, I have attempted to sketch the
complex background of Roman state religion, the cultic order of
which developed from its innermost component, namely, its god
and Emperor cult of which the Roman theatre was an essential
part. From this basic religious meaning of the Roman state and
its affairs, we should try to understand not only the polemics
of the Church Fathers against the Romans but also the Romans and
their defense of their religious beliefs for it involves a
matter of religious experience. This was in short, a conflict
between Romanitas and Christianitas. One of the greatest
testimonies of this conflict is the struggle surrounding the
Altar of Victory (354-396 A.D.) which, as a symbol of Roman
self-understanding and of the power of Roman victory, was rooted
in the belief in the gods. The climax of this genuine conflict
is recorded in Symmachus' third relatio and in the 17th, 18th
and 57th Letters of Bishop Ambrose of Milan. Since the polemics
against the theatre can be better understood within the context
of these sources we would like to conclude our limited
discussion about the religious aspects of Roman culture with
quotations from these texts. In his third relatio Symmachus is
asking the Emperors Valentinianus, Theodosius and Arkadius to
reinstate the old Roman religion because it had been so
beneficial to the state for such a long time. He says:
"Repetimus igitur religionem statum, qui rei publicae diu

8

profuit. "[29] He invokes the image of the goddess Roma in order
to let her plead for the old custom of the Roman Empire:

> Romam nunc potemus adsistere atque his
> vobiscum agere sermonibus: Optimi
> principum, patres patriae reveremini
> annos meos, in quos me pius ritus
> adduxit! Utar caerimoniis avitis; neque
> enim paenitet. Vivam meo more, quia
> liber sum! Hic cultus in leges meas orbem
> redegit, hac sacra Hannibalem a moenibus,
> a Capitolio Senonas reppulerunt.[30]

These sentences bespeak a universal vision which after
Constantine became the inheritance of the Church and which
Symmachus expressed once more in the third relatio:

> Ergo diis patriis, diis indigetibus pacem
> rogamus. Aequum est, quidquid omnes co-
> lunt, unum putari. Eadem spectamus astra,
> commune caelum est, idem nos mundus involvit.
> Quid interest, qua quique prudentia verum
> requirat? Uno itinere non potest perveniri
> ad tam grande secretum. . .[31]

The vision of Symmachus could however not be realized in the
Roman world where "heretical" Christianity had just begun to
breathe and where the gods of the Romans were denounced by the
Christians as apostatic angels. The representatives of the
Roman state religion and of the Christian religion confronted
each other without compromise. This situation is exemplified in
Letter 17 of Ambrose, Bishop of Milan, where he specifically
says:

> Cum omnes homines, qui sub dicione
> Romana sunt, vobis militent, impera-
> toribus terrarum atque principibus, tum
> ipsi vos omnipotenti deo et sacrae
> fidei militatis. Aliter enim salus
> tuta esse non poterit, nisi unuquisque
> deum verum, hoc est, deum Christianorum,
> a quo cuncta reguntur, veraciter colat;

> ipse enim solus versus est deus, qui
> intima mente veneretur. <u>Dii enim gentium</u>
> <u>daemonia</u>, sicut scriptura dicit.[32]

This summary reflects the essence of the conflict out of which
developed the tenacious polemics of the Church Fathers against
the theatre, in the West as in the East of the Empire. This
conflict must be understood as the background of the relentless
battle against the theatre by the Church Fathers if justice is
to be done to the interpretation of these circumstances. Below
we shall analyze a cross-section of texts relevant to the
ecclesiastical polemics which constituted part of this conflict.

The Theatre in the Literature of the Church Fathers[33]

The Apostolic Church Fathers

The literary sources for the time of these Church Fathers
cover the period from approximately 96 to 140 A.D.[34] This era
which succeeded the Apostolic period is mainly to be understood
in the sense of a primitive kerygma around which a new community
with predominantly eschatological orientation began to be
formed. One of its initial forms of expression was the liturgy.
Gradually, however, particularly as a result of the conflict
with Gnosticism, it became necessary for this Christian
community to publicly identify itself.[35]

With the Christians, however, a new form of community had
developed in the Roman Empire whose God could not easily be
integrated with the other gods.[36] Their resistance to comply
with the cultic order of the state offended not only the <u>mos</u>
<u>maiorum</u> of the Romans but was also a threat to the <u>pax</u> <u>deorum</u>.
With such a refusal they inevitably were to be seen as heretics
and a danger to the Roman state.[37] The order of the Roman state
was on the other hand an expression of a culture which the
Church could not accept because of <u>idololatria</u>. <u>Idololatria</u> was
a main focus of attack for the Church and her polemics
intensified more and more around this point. With the writings
of the Apologists an official polemic began to be formed which
rejected the cultic order of the Roman state because the gods of

10

the Romans were for the Christians by no means dead objects but rather apostate angels who, it was thought, had deceived and mislead poets, mythologists and rulers and had perverted the whole order of creation. Daemonology began to be an important issue in Patristic thought and dogma. The uncompromising attitude of the Church Fathers towards the theatre will have to be understood in the context of this view of daemonology.[38]

The Apologetes[39]

The first extant Apology of Artistides (117-138 A.D.) addressed to Emperor Hadrian[40] and Justin's Apology (146-161 A.D.)[41] are generally believed to be the earliest sources expressing a conflict with idololatria. The writings which follow testify already to the special attack against the theatre. Tatian, a pupil of Justin, is one of the fircest and most elaborate of the polemicists. In his Oratio contra Graecos, which was written about 177 A.D., he describes the theatre as belonging to the devil, and he criticizes particularly the actor.[42] Athenagoras sharply criticizes in his work Legatio (177 A.D.), the brutality of the actors.[43] And Theophilus condemns in his Ad Autolycum (180-181 A.D.) the false pomp of the theatre which can only be corrected through the Christian truth.[44] After the middle of the century a dialectic of falsehood and truth slowly emerged in the battle about idololatria. This dialectic gave rise to a conception of a theatre of the daemons on the one hand and a theatre of Christ the manifestations of which took shape in ever greater dimensions in liturgical drama on the other.[45]

The Alexandrians

Clement of Alexandria (150-215 A.D.), who was a Christian gnostic, saw in the gospel a powerful medium of transformation through which the deceitful world could be renewed. In the Proteptikos he tried to convince the Alexandrians about the nonsense and emptiness of the fables contained in their myths and history. He warned them that their deceitful mysteries and dramatic compositions would lead only to human misery. He elaborates the argument that Cithaeron and Helicon and with them

the dramatic plays of the drivelling poets in connection with
Bacchus, as well as the whole interrelated service of the devil
had been overcome by Christ. Now, Christ, the Logos of eternal
truth, was the "real athlete, who was being crowned in the
theatre of the universe."[46] In his other work, Paedagogos,
Clement criticizes especially the luxurious material conditions
of the Alexandrians and in particular their theatre. He tells
the Christians that their teacher, Christ, had not led them into
the theatre, which as the seat of evil, was a meeting full of
confusion and wickedness where everything was directed against
Christ. And since the Christian could not serve two masters, he
ought to maintain his distance from the theatre which did not
serve Christ.[47] It seems obvious that with Clement there begins
to emerge the view of a Christian meeting place which is seen as
a contrast to the poisonous pagan meeting of the evil ones
gathered in the theatre; furthermore, the concept of a Christian
"counter-mystery" is beginning to form in contrast to the pagan
mysteries.

With Origen (185-254 A.D.), a pupil of Clement, we find an
especially sharp polemic against idololatria and the Emperor
cult which derives from the daemonology of his teleological
world-view about the fall of the material world. In his
disputes with Celsus, Origen denounces the worship of the gods
and the Emperor as idololatria on the following basis:

> . . . But in our opinion, all daemons have
> fallen from the way to goodness; and pre-
> viously they were not daemons; for the
> category of daemons is one of those classes
> of beings which have fallen away from God.
> That is why no one who worships God ought
> to worship daemons......................
> That is the reason why we have decided to
> avoid the worship of daemons like the
> plague. And we maintain that all the
> supposed worship of gods among the Greeks
> with altars and images and temples is a
> worship to daemons.[48]

Thus, the pagan gods are for Origen powers and principalities

12

which have fallen away from the truth. In this connection he
refers to Celsus who sacrifices with good intentions, but
erroneously, to the gods because he does not know the truth. In
this connection he writes:

> . . . For reasons of this kind, Celsus,
> as one who is ignorant of God, may ren-
> der the offerings of thanksgiving to
> daemons. But we give thanks to the
> Creator of the universe.[49]

At this point a dialectic between truth and falsehood emerges
most obviously. The Emperor cult for Origen, too, is rooted in
this daemoniac perversion. He says:

> . . . and the rulers and emperors among
> men, since not even they hold their
> position without the might of the dae-
> mons . . . Or if, as some think who say
> that people who swear by the genius of
> the Roman emperor are swearing by his
> daemon, the co-called genius of the
> emperor is a daemon, in this case also,
> we ought rather to die than to swear by a
> wicked and faithless daemon . . .[50]

In such a world, therefore, which is saturated with daemonic
fabrications of lies, the baptismal formula of renunciation
develops into an especially active part of the baptismal vow.
This formula includes the statement "to renounce satan and all
his pomp".[51] Daemonology was the groundwork from which the
polemics against <u>idololatria</u> derived which was most fiercely
expressed in Tertullian's rhetoric against the theatre.

The Church Fathers and Other Writers of the West

Tertullian (160-230 A.D.)

As the First Latin Church Father, Tertullian is of key
importance in the Western Church. In his writings <u>Apologeticum</u>,

<u>De Spectaculis</u>, and <u>De Idololatria</u>, Tertullian expresses at
length the normative position of the Church towards the Roman
state. In this context he expresses his own position toward the
Roman theatre. These works are therefore an invaluable source
of information for our study. For this reason and for the very
reason that Tertullian's view of the perverted theatre has for
centuries influenced scholarship of different disciplines--<u>i.e.</u>,
history, church history, ecclesiology, the history of the
theatre, as well as the theory and theology of the theatre--we
shall deal with these texts in more depth.

   <u>Apologeticum (197 A.D.)</u>: In this work, addressed to the
vice-counsel of Africa, it is evident that Tertullian still
belongs to the group of apologetes who justify the existence of
Christianity and the conflict between Romans and Christians.
Tertullian justifies Christianity in the Roman state from the
ethical point of view and on the basis of truth, arguing that
the Christians, just as the vice-counsel himself, are also human
beings:

> Vociferatur homo: "Christianus sum".
> Quod est dicit: tu vis audire quod non
> est. Veritatis extorquendae praesides
> de nobis solis mendacium elaboratis
> audire . . . .
> Homo est et ipse, quod et Christianus.
> Qui non potes facere, non debes credere.
> Homo est enim et Christianus, et quod
> es tu.[52]

   Tertullian continues to argue that it could not be proved
that the Christians would be harmful to the state. Since their
motives spring from higher morals, they are, on the contrary,
much better citizens than the pagans. Tertullian contrasts most
vividly the virtues of the new community based on the new law of
Christ with the vices of demoralization and the worship of the
gods of the pagan citizens. Entreatingly he also asks the Roman
Senate, to adhere to the old laws which had been issued in order
to restrict luxury and ostentation; here Tertullian already
polemicizes sharply against the existence of permanent theatre

14

buildings which, coupled with demoralization, had in his view
secured a safe place for idololatria in Roman culture. He says:

> . . . Quonam illae leges abierunt
> sumptum et ambitionem comprimentes . . .
> quae patricium, quod decem pondo
> argenti habuisset, pro magno ambi-
> tionis titulo senatu submovebant,
> quae theatre stuprandis moribus
> orienta statim destruebant, . . .
> Video et theatre nec singula satis
> esse nec nuda. . .[53]

Here Tertullian concurs in his polemics about the degeneration
of the theatre with such classical pagan writers as Tacitus. It
should also be noted that Tertullian in this context is in fact
defending laws which are rooted in the beliefs of the gods of
the Roman state which indicates that he is caught, as it were,
in a conflict, but that he does not blindly condemn all
institutions of the Roman state although the circumstances are
paradoxical. Tertullian's further polemics are directed against
the persecutors who accuse the Christians for not worshipping
the Roman gods or for not sacrificing to the Emperor:

> "Deo", iniquitis, "non colitis et pro
> imperatoribus sacrificia non pen-
> ditis," . . . Itaque sacrilegii et
> maiestatis rei convenimur. Summa haec
> causa, immo tota est . . .[54]

Tertullian justifies this heretical behaviour on the basis that
the Christian had looked through the deception of the images of
the gods as objects of perversion and since these objects were
tools of the devil, this insight and understanding alone
justified the refusal to sacrifice and worship with the pagans.
In the text of the Apologeticum, the entire tension in which
Tertullian, and Christianity as a whole, find themselves, is
most obviously expressed. Here, the conflict, embedded in the
world of the text, becomes especially alive for the reader.

De Spectaculis (197-200 A.D.): This work which is

primarily concerned with the question of the theatre is directly addressed to the Christians. It is an official accusation of the frequent visits to the theatre by the baptized Christians. For Tertullian this corresponds to the recognition of the pagan, that is, of diabolic values. He defines _idololatria_ as a perversion of the true world and this perversion must be considered as the greatest insult of the creature toward his creator:

> . . . Proinde aurum aes argentus
> ebur lignum et quaecumquae frabican-
> dis idolis materia capiatur quis in
> saeculo posuit nisi saeculi auctor
> deus? et numquid tamen, ut haec
> adversus ipsum adhorentur? atquin
> summa offensa penes illum idolo-
> latria.[55]

To go to the theatre is therefore an abuse of creation by the creature; it is, moreover, apostasy.

There were Christians who would agree on the basis of Scripture and particularly from the point of view of the Ten Commandments that it would be necessary to renounce the gods and the Emperor cult but who could not agree that on the basis of the same commandment they should also renounce the theatre. They argue that such laws were not explicitly formulated in Scripture. Tertullian, however, argues against this objection as follows:

> Quorandam enim, fides aut simplicior
> aut scrupulosior ad hanc abdicationem
> spectaculorum de scripturis auctoritatem
> exposcit, et se in certum constituit,
> quod non significanter. neque nominatim
> denuntietur servis dei abstinentia eiusmodi.
> plane nusquam invenimus, quaemadmodum aperte
> postitum est: "non occides, non fraudum
> admittes", ita exerte definitum: non
> ibis in circum, non in theatrum agonem,
> munus non spectabis.[56]

16

Tertullian has a further citation from the Old Testament at hand
with which he objects to frequenting the theatre:

> Sed invenimus ad hanc quoque speciem
> pertinere illam primam vocem David:
> "felix vir", iniquit, "qui non abiit
> in concilium impiorum et in via pecca-
> torum non stetit, nec in cathedra
> pestium sedit."[57]

As previously with Clement of Alexandria, here too, the theatre
is compared with a diabolic and unclean meeting. Tertullian
goes still further and adds that if in Scripture a "handful of
Jews" is being designated as a "godless gathering" then how much
more must this large meeting place for pagans be defined as
such:

> . . . Minus impii ethnici, minus pecca-
> tores, minus hostes Christi quam tunc
> Iduaei? quid quod et cetera congruunt?
> nam apud spectacula et in cathedra sede-
> tur et in via statur; . . .[58]

For those Christians, who are still not convinced that they
should stay away from the shows, Tertullian has at hand the
baptismal seal with which they themselves had renounced the
devil and all his pomp.[59] Especially dependent on Varro,
Tertullian then goes into the origin and liturgical significance
of the theatre. The ludi, he says, had originally been dances
and plays in honor of the gods which proves how deeply the
theatre is rooted in idololatria. Even the different plays
themselves had been named after the gods, as for example, the
liberalia according to Liber (bacchus) or the Consualia after
Neptune. In this description of the sacred signifance of the
theatre which was erected by Pompeius, Tertullian's polemic
reaches its height:

> . . . a loci vitio theatrum propris
> sacrarium Veneris est. hoc denique
> modo id genus operis in saeculo eva-
> sit. . . . itaque Pompeius Magnus solo

17

theatro suo minor cum illam arcem omnium turpitudinum extruxisset, veritus
quandoque memoria suae censorian ani-
mad versionem. Veneris aedem super-
posuit et ad dedicationem edicto populum vocans non theatrum, sed Veneris
templum nuncupavit, cui subiecimus,
inquit, gradus spectaculorum. ita dam-
natum et damnandum, opus templi titulo
praetexit et disciplinam superstitione
delusit. sed Veneri et Libero convenit. duo iste daemonia conspirata et
libidinis. itaque theatrum Veneris
Liberi quoque domus est. . . et est
plane in artibus quoque scaenicis
Liberi et Veneris patrocinium.[61]

Tertullian interprets the theatre of Pompeius, and with that the
theatre as a whole, as a dwelling place of the gods Venus and
Liber and therefore as a place where idololatria and
lasciviousness come together publicly and without any inhibi-
itions. He sees in this a double conspiracy of the daemons.
From such a theology it can be deduced that the daemons by no
means were considered as theological abstract speculations but
rather that they were perceived as real and visible powers which
saturated the every-day Roman world.

    It must be mentioned, however, that Tertullian did not
reject the theatre as such. This attitude could already be
observed when he did not completely reject the laws of the Old
Testament or those of the Roman Senate; he admits that the
theatre, too, just as the whole of creation, had good and
beautiful ideas, but had then become, together with the rest of
the world, perverted by the daemons. It is, therefore,
important for Tertullian, that the whole created world be
considered not only in the sense of its true order and harmony
initially assigned to it by its creator, but it is equally
important for him to consider this world also in its daemonic
perversion.[62] He says:

        Sint dulcia licet et grata et

18

simplicia, etiam honesta quaedam.
nemo venenum temperat felle et
elleboro, sed conditis pulmentis
et bene saporatis, et plurimum
dulcibus id mali inicit. Ita et
diabolus letale quod conficit
rebus dei gratissimis et accept-
issimi imbuit.[63]

Against this background of the perverted pagan world as
expressed in the Roman theatre, Tertullian holds the spectacle
of creation and the Church: the world as God created it; the
course of time, the change of seasons, the great spectacle of
the end of the world to come, the expectant theatre and the
glory of the Last Judgment, the literary and poetic creations of
the Church herself, all of which could delight the Christians.[64]

De Idololatria (200-211 A.D.): In this work it becomes
especially evident that the major contention of polemics against
the theatre had its grounding in idololatria. At the beginning
Tertullian defines idololatria as the capital crime of mankind--
principale crimen--which includes all other sins such as
adultery, fraud, drunkenness, fornication. The following key
text is significant regarding Tertullian's theological position
toward idololatria:

Principale crimen generis humani,
summus saeculi reatus total causa
iudicii idololatria. nam etsi suam
speciem tenet unumquodque delictum,
etsi suo quodque nomine iudicio de-
stinatur, in idololatrae tamen cri-
mine expungitur at enim idolatria
fraudem deo facit, . . . ut fraudi
etiam contumeliam coniungat at enim
idololatria in illa etiam vanitas,
cum tota eius ratio vana sit. in
illa mendacium, cum tota substantia
eius mendax sit. ita fit, ut omnia
in idolatria et in omnibus
idololatria deprehendatur. . . .[65]

19

Idololatria as it is defined in the above text thus signifies
the very self-betrayal of man and cooperation with the apostate
angels--fraudem deo facit--a participation which in itself
is apostasy. Since the theatre is essentially connected with
and even an expression of idololatria--and there is only one
idololatria--Tertullian is unrelenting in his demand to avoid
the theatre.[66] This particular polemical argument of Tertullian
against the theatre can only be properly understood when one
tries to see it in the context of which was a result of the
constant tension existing between Christianity and the Roman
state--between Romanitas et Christianitas.

Tertullian's Theological Basis.

     Tertullian understood salvation history and redemption in
the legal sense. Lex, satisfactio, meritum was the three-fold
basis of his soteriology which became normative for the West.
The relationship between God and man was considered from a legal
point of view, that is to say, it resulted from the fear of God
whereby the fear of man became in turn the glory of God. In
order to understand this disposition, Tertullian's theology of
sin and baptism will have to be considered briefly at this
point. In his work, Adversus Marcion (208-208 A.D.), Tertullian
categorizes, on the basis of Scripture, the seven deadly sins as
follows: worship of the pagan gods, cursing, murder, fornication, fraud, and false witness[87] This category of sins is
unforgivable, i.e., there is no penance or reparation after
baptism through a special act of grace. The possibilities of a
second opportunity for reparation after baptism is, according to
this theology, no longer possible, as for instance, it is the
case with venial sins.[68] Therefore, baptism shall not be
received lightly without a remorseful and long preparation. Man
shall not be baptized so that he may give up sinning but rather
he shall receive baptism because he is no longer sinning.[69]
After baptism, however, the Christian should keep the commandments to give adequate satisfactio through obedience[70] in order
to merit the grace of God which was understood as meritum;
but if that is not the case, then man is acting against the will
of God; he ceases being a Christian, and thus will fall under
the wrath and punishment of God from which no good works and

20

merits can free him.

If one considers Tertullian's position towards the theatre from this point of view, then his uncompromising position falls into a different perspective. He understood _idololatria_ as a capital crime, _i.e._, an accumulation of several deadly sins. Therefore, a single visit to the theatre, which indeed equalled _idololatria_, amounted to an accumulation of several deadly sins; it was deadly poison for the baptized Christians because the theatre belonged to the pomp of the devil which the Christians had renounced out of their free will at baptism.[71] Baptism could not be repeated and forgiveness through merit and exertion of man was from this point onward no longer possible. That meant, however, that the Christian who went to the theatre, could not be an official member of the Christian community from his own free will and decision. A visit to the theatre under these conditions was _idololatria_, that is, open apostasy and a free voluntary decision against God because for Tertullian man was still free after the Fall. Thus, with his visit to the theatre the Christian participated freely in apostasy.

Tertullian's polemic will have to be understood in the light of this general conflict that took place in late antiquity and particularly from his theological standpoint. Classical writers had already criticized the decline in morals and want of moderation of the stage as a violation of the Roman _mos maiorum_.[72] But excessiveness and licentiousness were only one of Tertullian's targets because they were as such contained in the capital crime of _idololatria_ itself. _Idololatria_ corresponded to the entire image of the world of daemons--it was not understood as religious experience. It was worship of apostate angels and participation in an act of perversion in the sanctuary of Venus, _i.e._, in the theatre of Pompeius, and it was therefore understood as an act against the Creator. It was the point of departure of a sharp religious conflict which, from a dramatic point of view, could dialectically only be solved through a drama or theatre which grew out of the Church's own world-understanding, namely, through the dramatic re-enactment of the New Creation.[73]

Tertullian's Influence on Theatre Criticism.

Tertullian's "theology of the theatre", if we may so call
it in this discussion, became the rule for the Church of the
West. His theology did not differ from that of the Fathers of
the East. It was rooted in the entire conflict which was
carried on between the Roman state and the Christian Church.
Unfortunately, this theology was later not only accepted without
re-examination of the earlier issues involved by generations of
theologians and ecclesiastical dispositions and decrees, it was
also accepted by theatre and literary critics and historians who
most often built their entire argument of the negative attitude
of the Church against the theatre around one sentence of
Tertullian, such as was particularly the case with the great
historian Gibbon.[74] For this reason, our rather elementary
introduction and discussion of the basic conflicts involved
seemed to be desirable in order to provide a better and new
understanding of the problems surrounding the issue of
ecclesiastical polemics against the Roman theatre.

Cyprian (200-250 A.D.) and Novatian (210-258 A.D.).

After Tertullian, Cyprian was the most influential Church
Father of Latin Christendom until Augustine. His works are
greatly influenced by Tertullian. Especially in his letters
Cyprian condemns the theatre but at the same time he sees in the
Church an institution in which a Christian would find true
joy.[75] The schismatic and first anti-pope Novatian, who entitled
his De spectaculis after Tertullian's work, designates
idololatria as the mother of all spectacles: "Idololatria. . .
ludorum omnium mater est."[76] He too gives a description of that
spectacula which is so much greater and awaiting the Christian
in the natural beauty of the world and which is also unfolding
for him in Scripture: a spectacle so much greater and so much
more beautiful than that of the Roman state: "Habet Christianus
spectacula meliora si velit . . .," he exclaims.[77] With these
two authorities of the Church, we again can observe that
simultaneously with the polemics against the Roman theatre, a
new understanding of a theatre of the Church begins to emerge--a
theatre which would reflect the true beauty of the works of God
in contrast to the daemonic pomp of the pagan stage.

Arnobius (300 A.D.) and Lactantius (260-340 A.D.)

The reorganization of the Roman state into a tetrachate under Diocletian (284-305 A.D.), was accompanied by a renewal of the Roman state religion. Dependence on the protection and the support of the gods in Roman history was again emphasized during this period. During this renewal of religious fervor, the two augusti, Diocletian and Maximian, were deified and were placed under the special protection of Jupiter and Hercules of whom they were the earthly deputies. At the time of this Roman religious renewal, the Christians were increasing in number in the higher social strata, i.e., in the army and in the Roman Senate. Thus, they constituted an ever increasing heretic danger who threatened the pax deorum of the Roman state.[78] The two apologies of Arnobius and Lactantius are a product of this period.

Arnobius was at first a zealous opponent of Christianity but he was converted to the Christian religion late in life. After his conversion he wrote an apology entitled Adversus Nationes (ca. 300-303 A.D.). In the seven books of this work he defended the Christians against the accusation that they had brought the wrath of the gods over the Roman state. His polemic was especially directed against the Roman myth of origin, polytheism, theatre, temple, as well as against the entire cult of the state. After an attack on the origin of the Roman name, he criticized in particular the institution of the Roman theatre: its spectators came from all strata of society, it provided therefore a special and favorable ground for the activity of the daemons to exercise their influence on them. In an especially elucidating passage, Arnobius gives this description:

> Sed poetis tantummodo licere voluistis
> indignas de dis fabulas et flagitiosa
> ludibria comminisci? quid pantomimi
> vestri, quid histriones, quid illa mi-
> morum atque exoleti generis multitudo?
> . . . sedent in spectaculis publicis
> sacerdotum omnium magistratumque

23

collegia, pontifices maximi et maximi
curiones, sedent quindecimviri laureati
et diales cum apicibus flamines, sedent
interpretes augures divinae mentis et
voluntatis, nec non et castae virgines,
perpetui nutrices et conservatrices ignis,
sedet cunctus populus et senatus, con-
sulatibus functi patres, diis proximi
atque augustissimi reges: et quod ne-
farium esset auditu, gentis illa gene-
trix Martiae regnatoris et populi pro-
creatrix amans saltatur Venus. . .[79]

Arnobius describes here the whole hierarchical order as being
rooted in myths and where the persons of this hierarchy even pay
tribute to the gods in the theatre. The only solution for this
idolatrous act is for Arnobius the destruction of the theatre
and the burning of books because he says:

. . . dissolvere theatra haec potius,
in quibus infamiae numinum propudiosis
cotidis publicantur in fabulis. Nam
nostra quidam scripta cur ignibus
meruerunt dari?[80]

This Apology corresponds to the circumstances of the renewal of
the myths and is not to be understood simply as a replica of the
earlier Greek apologies although it stands in their tradition.
This aspect, so it seems to me, deserves great attention because
it refers to an intensive religious renewal within the Roman
state shortly before the conversion of Constantine.

With Lactantius we find a similar polemic. He was a pupil
of Arnobius and he too was called by Diocletian to the court of
Nicomedia as a teacher of rhetoric. During this time at the
court of Diocletian he converted to Christianity and he subsequently vigorously polemicized in his apology Divinarum Institutiones against the pagan state religion. Here again we are able
to grasp the Christian interpretation of the theatre. It too
gives evidence that Christian polemics are not primarily
directed against demoralization but rather against a theatre

rooted in <u>idololatria</u>. In relation to this, Lactantius writes:

> . . . Vitanda ergo spectacula omnia,
> non solum ne quid vitiorum pectoribus
> insidat, quae sedata pacifica esse
> debent sed ne cuius nos voluptatis con-
> suetudo deleniat, et a deo atque a bo-
> nis operibus avertat. [81]

Both apologies evidence a lively theatre attendance at the
beginning of the fifth century which would also be important for
the further development of the liturgy and its forms of representation. [82]

At the beginning of the fifth century, following the
conversion of Constantine, a Christian culture slowly began to
emerge which was manifested in art, literature, and Christian
architecture. In this "double culture" which, as we suggested
earlier, particularly in relation to the Altar of Victory, [83] was
by no means without conflict and the Roman theatre remained a
deeply rooted and problematic phenomenon for the early Church.

Ambrose (339-397 A.D.) and Prudentius (348-410 A.D.)

Ambrose, the Bishop of Milan, deplores the Christians' frequent attendance at the theatre. He writes:

> Utinam hac interpretatione possi-
> mus revocare ad diversa circensium
> ludorum atque theatralium specta-
> cula festinantes. [84]

His remarks, however, indicate that the Roman theatre is still
flourishing during that time. Similarly, there is a description
of an active theatre in the Christian allegorical poetry of
Prudentius:

> "Dicis licenter haec poetas fingere;
> Sed sunt et ipsi talibus mysteriis
> Tecum dicati quodque describunt colunt

Tu cur piaclum tam libenter lectitas
Cur in theatris te vidente id plauditur?

"Cygnus stuprator peccat inter pulpita,
Saltat Tonantem tauricornem ludius
Spectator horum pontifex summus sedes
Ridesque et ipse, nec negando diluis
Cum fama tanti polluatur numinis.

"Cur tu, sacrate, per cachinnos solveris,
Cum se maritum fingit Alemenae deus?
Meretrix Adonem vulneratum scaenica
Libidinoso plangit adfectu palam,
Nec te lupanar cypridis sanctae movet?[85]

For the purpose of our study, Prudentius seems particularly
important because he is an example of a poet who uses biblical
material for the shaping of poetic and imaginative works but
condemns at the same time Roman dramatic poetry and mocks its
entire culture on the grounds of idololatria.

Augustine (354-430 A.D.)

The fall of Rome terrified pagans and Christians alike in
the Roman world. On both sides this catastrophe was given
religious interpretation: while the Romans made the accusation
that the Christians' refusal to sacrifice to the gods had
brought the wrath of the gods upon Rome, the Christians saw the
cause for this disaster in the basic daemonic foundation of the
Roman Empire itself. For the Christian the destruction of Rome
was the punishment of God for the idololatria of the pagan
Romans. This paradox of reciprocal accusation on religious
grounds, points again to the deeply rooted conflict which was
played out at that time. Augustine's comprehensive work De
Civitate Dei is another great polemic against the pagan cult as
well as against the entire Roman culture. Augustine polemicizes
especially against the theatre. Since the Roman theatre
originated in connection with a pestilence, he compares that
theatre itself with a spiritual pestilence. Because of its
significance for our study, we shall cite below the text which
summarizes Augustine's polemics:

. . . ludi scaenici, spectacula turpitudinum et licentia vanitatum, non hominum
vitiis, sed deorum vestrorum iussis Romae
instituti sunt. tolerabilius divinos
honores deferretis illi Scipioni quam
deos huius modi coleretis. Neque enim
erant illi dii suo pontifice meliores. . . .
Dii propter sedandam corporum pestilentiam ludos sibi scaenicos exhiberi iube-
bant: pontifex autem propter animorum
cavendam pestilentiam ipsam scaenam con-
stitui prohibebat . . . Neque enim et
illa corporum pestilentia ideo conquievit,
quia populo bellicoso et solis antea
ludis circensibus adsueto ludorum scae-
nicorum delicata subintravit insania;
sed astutia spirituum nefandorum prae-
videns illam pestilentiam iam fine de-
bito cessaturam aliam longe graviorum,
qua plurimum gaudet, ex (hac) occasione
non corporibus, sed moribus curavit in-
mittere, quae animos miserorum tantis
obcaecauit tenebris, tanta deformitate
foedavit, ut etiam modo (quod incredibile,
forsitan erit, si a nostris posteris
audietur) Romana urbe vastata, quos
pestilentia ista possedit atque inde
fugientes Carthaginem pervenire
potuerunt, in theatris cotidie certatim
pro histronibus insanirent. [86]

The origin of the gods and the theatre are for the Bishop of
Hippo "deadly poison" and a "crazy institution". Augustine
directs his arguments particularly against the cult of the gods
which is rooted in demoralization and licentiousness and thus it
has, as he himself had experienced, a dangerous influence on
Roman youth. [87] His polemics become almost ironic at this point:

. . . Caelestia virgini et Berecynthiae,
matri omnium. . . Quae si inlecta

27

curiosita adesse potui circumfusa
saltem offensa castitate debuit abire
confusa. Quae sunt sacrilegia, si illa
sunt sacra? Aut quae inquinatio, si illa
lavatio? [88]

Even the destruction of theatre buildings is for Augustine the
consequence of idololatria. He writes:

> . . . nisi forte hinc sunt tempora mala,
> quia per omnes paene civitates cadunt
> theatre. . . cadunt et fora vel moenia,
> in quibus demonia colebantur. Unde
> enim cadunt, nisi inopia rerum quarum
> lascivio et sacrilego usu constructa
> sunt. [89]

Basically here too it is the concept of a vivid daemonology
which Augustine tries to fight on theological grounds as we
could observe earlier with Origen, Ambrose and Tertullian or
Arnobius and Lactantius. But Augustine does not condemn the
theatre quite as harshly in spite of his polemic because he
knows how to differentiate and distinguish between higher and
lower forms of the theatre which were applied in the curricula
of the schools for educated youth of his time. [90] His positive
attitude towards the dramatic arts and the role of the actor can
further be shown from his work De Doctrina Christiana. In his
long explanation about res and signum which, he argues, are
necessary for the understanding of Scripture as well as for the
representation and explanation of that which had been
comprehended, Augustine mentions the actor who, by means of his
bodily movements, particularly his limbs and his eyes, is trying
to give signs to those who can understand him. Augustine's
informative statement regarding the significance of the actor,
is as follows:

> Signorum igitur, quibus inter se homi-
> nes sua sensa communicant, quaedam per-
> tinent ad oculorum sensum, pleraque ad
> aurium, paucissima ad ceteros sensus. . .
> et quidam motu manuum pleraque signi-

ficant: et histriones omnium membrorum
motibus dant signa quaedam scientibus,
et cum oculis eorum quasi fabulantur. . . . [91]

This positive attitude of Augustine toward the dramatic arts as
such contributes to the better understanding of liturgical drama
which later developed in the West, as a means of representation
and Bildung of a newly perceived reality. [92]

Salvianus of Marseilles (400-480 A.D.)

The literature which evidences an existing theatre becomes
very rare after Augustine. In his word De Gubernatio (440
A.D.), Salvianus describes once more the moral conditions of
Rome, the worship of the gods and the service of the devil in
the theatre in which the Christians obviously still
participated:

> . . . nam per turpitudines criminosas
> aeterna illic salus Christianae plebis
> exstinaguitur et per sacrilegas
> superstitiones maiestas divina violatur.
> dubium enim non est quod laedunt deum,
> utpote idolis conscratae. Colitur namque
> et honoratur Minerva in gymnasiis, Venus
> in theatris, Neptunus in circis, Mars
> in harenis, Mercurius in palaestris et
> ideo pro qualitate auctorum cultus est
> superstitionum. . . Alibi est impudi-
> tia, alibi lascivia, alibi intemperantia
> alibi insania, ubique daemon, immo per
> singula ludicrorum loca, universa dae-
> monum monstra,. . . [93]

Salvianus' argument at this later date is still against
idololatria as embodied in the theatre of the pagans.

The Theatre in Gaul

Literary evidence of the existence of a theatre in Gaul can
be found in the poetry of Sidonius where a theatre in Narbonne

is mentioned in connection with the cultural splendor of this city.[94] Furthermore, the <u>Vita Hilarius</u> reports the dismantling of a theatre in Arles the remaining parts of which were probably used for the construction of a basilica:

> Qui basilicis praepositus construendis,
> dum marmorum crustas et theatri pro
> scenia celsa deponeret, fidei opere nu-
> dans loca luxuriae, quod sanctis para-
> bat ornatibus, subito molarum funibus
> ruptis impetus desuper marmoris venien-
> tis stantis pedem cum extrema digi-
> torum. . .[95]

Thus, the transformation of the theatre was beginning to be spatially visible. The sermons of Bishop Caesarius of Arles (470-543 A.D.), however, still point to an existing pagan theatre because he warns the faithful of his flock as follows:

> Noveritis nos tristes esse vel anxios,
> et ideo venite, dissimulemus nos, aut
> ad circum aut ad theatrum euntes, aut
> ad tabulam ludentes, aut in aliquibus
> nos venationibus exercentes. . . ac si
> si dum de crudelissimis theatris ad
> crudeliores conscientias quasi de
> malis ad peiora redeunt, requiem in se
> habere non pussunt.[96]

For Caesarius too the theatre is a tool of the daemons and therefore it cannot bring peace of heart to the Christians.

Cassiodorus (487-585 A.D.)

The letters of this Roman statesman belong to the last documents about an outgoing theatre in Rome. He still describes the <u>tribuni voluptatem</u>, a municipal civil servant, who administrates the affairs of the stage.[97] This however indicates that the theatre of the old order no longer exists. He states:

> Quamvis artes ludricae, honestis mori-

bus sint remotae et histrionum vita
vaga videatur efferri posse licentia,
tamen moderatrix providit antiquitas,
ut in totum non effluerunt, cum et ip-
sae judicem sustinerent. Administran-
da est enim sub quadam disciplina ex-
hibitio voluptatum. Teneat scaenicos
si non verus, vel umbratilis ordo iu-
dici. [98]

Since Cassiodorus withdrew around 530 A.D. into a monastery, it
is most probable that this description refers to a situation
before that time.

Isidore of Séville (ca. 560-633 A.D.)

With the Spanish doctor of the Church, the theatre is
already described as belonging to the past:

Theatrum est quo scena includitur,
semicirculi figuram habens, in quo
stantes omnes inspiciunt. Cujus for-
ma primum rotunda erat, sicut et amphi-
theatri, postea ex medio amphitheatro
theatrum factum est. . . [99]

A further rather technical description is also given in the
imperfect tense:

. . . Scena autem erat locus infra
theatrum in modus domus instructa
cum pulpito quod pulpitum "or-
chestra" vocabatur; ubi cantabant
comici, tragici, atque saltabant histriones et mimi. [100]

Isidore too emphasized in another part of his writings that the
wickedness of the stage should not be blamed on men but on the
daemons because they had initiated the theatre. He makes the
following remark:

31

> . . . Haec quippe spectacula crude-
> litatis . . . non solum hominum vitiis, [101]
> sed de daemonum jussis instituta sunt.

On the basis of these statements it can be assumed that the
Roman theatre, as it had existed under the protection of the
gods since 346 B.C., no longer existed in the West around 600
A.D., the time which coincides with the Pontificate of Pope
Gregory the Great. We shall now briefly examine the texts of
the Fathers of the Eastern Church.

The Theatre in the Writings of the Eastern Church

The Fathers of the Eastern and Western Church proceeded
independently of each other in equally sharp public polemics
against the theatre. As we discussed earlier, the Greek
apologetes had already used idololatria as the point of
departure of their attack against the theatre. Similarly,
idololatria continued to be the basis of the struggle against
the theatre with other Syriac and Greek Fathers of the Church.

Cyril of Jerusalem (315-396 A.D.), criticizes and denounces in
his mystagogical catechism the theatre as diabolic and calls it
madness. He advises the Christians to stay away from the
theatre because of its diabolic pomp. [102] That there was still
a theatre in Jerusalem at the time of Cyril, is verified by the
church history of Sozomen. [103]

Gregory of Nazianzen (325-390 A.D.). Gregory gives in his
apologetic writings an insight into the conditions of the stage
as it was used as a means for the persecution of the Christians.
In particular he mentions the demoralization of the theatre and
the mockery of the Christians in dramatic representations
performed by the Romans. [104]

Gregory of Nyssa (331-394 A.D.) emphasizes the didactic sense of
the myths and he polemicizes, as John Chrysostom does, [105]
particularly against the delusion and masks of the stage.

John Chrysostom (354-407 A.D.) is the sharpest and most
elaborate in the tone of his polemics because in Antioch as well
as in Constantinople, the excessiveness of theatrical
performances reached its peak. His sermon Adversus eos qui
ecclesia relicta ad circenses ludo et theatre transfugerunt [106]
is especially informative. He describes the theatre as a house
of sin and perversion and directs his polemics especially
against the Christians who leave the church after the sermon in
order to go to the theatre not only on Sunday but even on the
Feast of Easter; thus, they become captives of the devil even on
the very feastdays of the Church herself. The tone of his
polemic is similar to that of Tertullian:

> . . . tunc tu, relicta et sacrificio
> spirituali, fratrumque coetu atque. . .
> jejunii gravitate, captivus a diabolo
> ad illud spectaculum abductus es?
> Haccine feranda? Haccine toleranda? [107]

While Chrysostom intends to excommunicate those Christians who
are going from the church to the theatre, he simultaneously
describes the liturgy itself as a theatrum non-fictitious et
spirituale. [108] The liturgy is, in other words, the true and
spiritual theatre. With this key definition of the liturgy by
the doctor of the Church of Antioch and patriarch of
Constantinople the idea of a concrete "double theatre"--a
theatre of Christ and a theatre of the daemons--is
confirmed. The earlier texts which were examined in our study,
already indicated such conceptions with the Fathers of the
Western Church.

Narsai (339-502 A.D.).

The Liturgical Sermons of Narsai: Narsai, a Syriac doctor
of the Church, [109] denounces in his sermon about baptism the
theatre as an evil mystery, and in his most vivid and figurative
language he describes the work of satan among men as follows:

> . . and let us turn away our
> faces from their mysteries which
> are full of wickedness. Full of

33

wickedness is the invention of the
Evil One and of them that listen to
him; and diseases of iniquity are
hidden in the error of his craft. His
inventions are the circus and the sta-
dium and the theatres, and the riotous
sounds of the songs which he has composed and written. His errors are
soothsayings and witchcrafts of all
sorts: eye-winking and ear-tickling
and street-accosting. These things
the disciple of the truth renounces
when he becomes a disciple . . .[110]

In an equally figurative and lively dictum Narsai describes
later that mystery which is given visible expression in
Christian liturgical drama.[111]

Jacob of Serugh (451-521 A.D.). The sermons of the Bishop of
Batna (518 A.D.) point also to an active theatre.[112] His main
attack is directed against its mythical origin; he further
polemicizes particularly against the transformation which the
actor is undergoing in his roles. These sermons however are of
great value for our study because they contain additional
descriptions of the theatre itself. Jacob relates that the role
of women is represented by male actors,[113] that the stage on
which the actors perform their dances is made from stone,[114]
that the exposition of the myths which are portrayed by the
actor, is accompanied by a chorus.[115] And moreover, against
the theme of transformation by the actor and through dancing, he
puts forth the scene of the resurrection of Lazarus.[116]
Nevertheless, those Christians who prefer to go to the theatre
answer the bishop that they are not going to the shows in order
to believe but rather in order to laugh because they themselves
are not deceived by the fabrications and delusions of the myths
displayed on the stage by the daemons.[117] However, despite
these arguments, Jacob of Serugh continues to preach: "Let they
meeting place be here (in the Church)."[118] It is, however,
significant to observe that especially in Mesopotamia and East
Syria an elaborate form of dramatic representation of liturgical
drama was developed in order to render visible the story of

salvation. [119]

The Theatre According to the Ecclesiastical
Councils and Synod Decrees until 742 A.D.

The attitude of the Church Fathers toward the theatre was also exactly formulated and officially adopted in the ecclesiastical decrees. An examination of the synod and council documents has shown that the number of decrees which canonically established the position of the Church can be documented most numerously between 272 and 445 A.D.

Around 300 A.D., the Council of Eliberitanum summarized in its definition (can. 1), idololatria as crimen principale; it is formulated as follows:

> Placuit inter eos, qui post fidem
> baptismi salutaris, adulta aetate,
> ad templum idololatraturus accesser-
> it et fecerit, quod est crimen prin-
> cipale (quia est summus scelus) pla-
> cuit e nec in fine eum communione
> accipere. [120]

A summary of essential formulations of ecclesiastical decrees up to approximately 700 A.D. which are important for our study is given below as follows:

> 269 A.D.: Concilium Antiochum:
> Eos vero qui non lauderent, nec, ut
> in theatris fieri solet, oraria con-
> cuterent, necque una cum fautoribus
> ipsius, viris ac mulierculis inde-
> core auscultantibus exclamarent atque
> exsilirent; sed cum gravitate ac mo-
> destia sicut in domo Dei decet audi-
> rent, increpabat et contumeliis afficie-
> bat. [121]

314 A.D.: Concilium Arelatense, Can. 5:
De theatricis, et ipsos placuit quamdiu
agunt a communione separari. [122]

325 A.D.: Concilium Nicaenum, Can. 10:
Verum invidiae probitatis hosti . . .
omnisque impietatis fautori diabolo
nequaquam harum rerum spectaculum tole-
randum videbatur . . . [123]

343-381 A.D.: Concilii Laodiceni, Can. 54:
Quod non oporteat sacerdotes aut cleri-
cos quibuscumque spectaculis in scenis
aut in nuptiis interesse, sed antequem
thymelici ingrediantur, exurgere eos
convenit, atque inde discedere. [124]

The Council of Carthage in 397 A.D. in which Augustine, Bishop
of Hippo, also participated, speaks of "transferri devotionis",
which implies an "exchange visit" by Christians between theatre
and church. This text reads as follows:

397 A.D.: Concilium Carthage (Novatia-
norum), Can. 61: Necnon & illud peten-
dum ut spectacula theatrorum, cetero-
cumque ludorum die dominica vel ceteris
religionis Christianae diebus celeberri-
mis amoveantur; maxime quia sancti
paschae octavarum die populi ad circum
magis quam ad ecclesiam conveniunt,
debere transferri devotionis eorum dies
si quando occurrerint, nec oportere
etiam quemquam Christianorum cogi ad
haec spectacula; maxime, quia in his
exercendis quae contra pracepta Dei
sunt, nulla persecutionis necessitas
quoquam adhibenda est; sed, uti, oportet,
homo in libera voluntate subsistat sibi
divinitus concessa. Cooperatorum enim
maxime periculum considerandum est, qui

contra praecepta Dei magno terrore
coguntur ad spectacula convenire. [125]

This text is particularly informative because a transference of
religious experience seems to be evident here, the implications
of which, however, cannot be dealt with within this study.
Another African Council, also under the influence of Augustine,
forbids the visit to the theatre on the grounds of blasphemy:

419 A.D.: Concilium Carthagenese: Can. 15:
Placuit, ut filii sacerdotum spectacula
saecularia non tantum non exhibeant, sed
nec expectare eis liceat; hoc semper
christianis omnibus interdictum sit, ut
ubi blasphemiae sunt omnino non accedant. [126]

In the Apostolic Constitution the synagogue as well as the
Roman theatre are designated as seats of evil:

ca. 380 A.D.: Constitutiones Sanctorum
Apostolorum: Can. 60: . . . in eorum
agitandis festis, ac celebritatibus non
interponunt moram, sed eis student, & in-
serviunt, non solum qui sunt eius loci,
sed etiam qui procul habitant, & in ipsis
theatris omnes tanquam in synagoge quadam conveniunt: similiter qui nunc
vano nomine Judaei appellantur . . . [127]

In the same text there is also the formulation of "ecclesia
malignantium" the conception of which was expressed in the
earlier texts which we examined from the early apologets onwards
to Clement of Alexandira and Origen to the other Fathers of the
Church, both in West and East. This text reads:

Can. 61: . . . Sin vero aliquis eam
despexerit, & in fanum profanum Gentilium intraverit, vel in synagogam
Judaeorum, vel haereticorum, quid iste
in die judiciie apud Deum excusabit?
quid dereliquit verba Dei viventis, quae

37

vivunt & vivificant, quaeque ab aeterno
supplicio liberare possunt, & se con-
tulit ad aliquam aedem daemoniorum, aut
ad synagogam eorum, qui Christum occi-
derunt, aut "ad ecclesiam malignantium
& cum inique agentibus non introibo:
non sedi cum concilio vanitatis, &
cum impiis non sedebo . . ."[128]

The fact that God and the devil are irreconcilable is the basis
of the polemic against the diabolic pomp of idololatria. This
again summarizes a polemical tradition which hitherto we have
studied throughout our sources. The Apostolic Constitution
continues:

Can. 62: Cavete igitur ne ferias cum
perditis hominibus, id est, cum syna-
goga Gentilium in errorem & interitum
vestrum agatis, "nulla", namque, "Deo
cum diabolo communio", (Cor. 6), qui
enim tunc cum illis congregatur, qui
ea sapiunt quae diaboli sunt, unus ex
iis ipsis numeratibur, & vae erit haere-
dita eius; fugite demum turpia spectacula, theatra dico, & Gentilium pompas,
incantationes, divinationes, vaticinia,
expiationes, auguria, auspicia, necro-
mentias omia . . . quamobrem oportet
fidelem devitare conventus Gentilium, &
Judaeorum reliquorumque haereticorum;
ne ferias cum eis communes habendo,
animas nostras laqueis irretiamus; &
ne si diebus eorum festis, quos ipsi
in honorem daemonum agitant, cum ipsis
versemur, impietatis eorum socii, &
partiticipes simus . . . Abstinente
igitus ab omni idolorum pompa,
praestigiis, mercatu, conviviis,
monomachia, et ab omni spectaculo
daemoniaco.[129]

38

In the year of 693 A.D., the Concilium Toletanum seems to summarize once more all earlier formulations but referring also in particular to the mimes. [130] The Concilium Germanicum under Boniface in 743 A.D., no longer mentions the theatre but it polemicizes instead against songs and incantations which were a most indigenous trait of the Germanic peoples. [131]

Later the Council of Quirzy in 838 A.D. condemns under the influence of the School of Lyons, the dramatic-allegorical liturgy of Amalarius of Metz. [132]

Summary

The results of the preceding examination of a cross-section of texts justify the conclusion that the ecclesiastical polemics surrounding the Roman theatre and lasting for nearly 500 years, were part of a deep religious conflict. From 364 B.C. to 600 A.D., the Roman theatre was performed in conspectu dei; its sacredness was stressed by its connection with the temple of Venus.

In the discussion which then followed it was shown that the gods of the Romans were for the Fathers of the Church not only false gods or dead objects but were understood to be living daemons, i.e., apostate angels using the Roman stage to penetrate and pervert the entire world of the Roman Empire. The figure of the Emperor was considered to be a special instrument of the daemons. The uncompromising negation of the Roman theatre by the theologians in the Eastern as well as the Western part of Christendom was a result of the struggle against idololatria, the latter signifying rebellion of the creature against his Creator. This entire conflict concentrated especially in the struggle surrounding the Altar of Victory.

The "theatre-theology" of Tertullian I analyzed in more detail because he stood, on the one hand, at the end of the apologetic tradition and because on the other, he was leading the way for a "theatre-criticism" during the time of the Church Fathers as well as for the critics of the theatre of centuries to follow; he did this not only for theologians and ecclesiastical authorities of later times but also for historians and literary critics who accepted or rejected his point of view without further re-examination of the issues involved centuries before.

We saw that in the Church of the Near East the theatre was designated as an evil mystery. A vivid imagery of religious metaphorical language was particularly evident in the polemics of the Syriac Fathers. However, we could observe that side by side with the negative attitude towards the theatre, a vision of a new theatre began to emerge and soon the Church was seen as a counterpart of the pagan meeting place. Such a vision, for

40

example, had already been expressed in the writings of Clement of Alexandria. While Tertullian and Augustine conceded that there were also positive sides to the pagan drama, John Chrysostom described the liturgy itself more specifically as a "theatrum non fictitium et spirituale". This view formed a positive counter image of the existing theatre which was thought to be of diabolic origin.

An examination of a cross-section of writings starting with the earliest liturgical texts of the Church, which will be dealt with in chapter two, will confirm that the Church herself began to develop a representational dramatic liturgy from the Urstoff, i.e., the basic mythological elements of the Bible, centering around the dramatic nucleus of the Passion of the protagonist Jesus Christ. Similarly, the Heilsgeschichte, as it developed from the doctrinal teachings of the Church, brought into visual focus the entire configurations of salvation history, both in its cosmological and eschatological orientations.

FOOTNOTES

[1]The summary in this chapter of the religious aspects of
Roman culture is based on the following works: Franz Altheim,
Römische Religionsgeschicte, 2 vols. (Baden-Baden: Verlag für
Kunst und Wissenschaft, (1951-52); Norman H. Baynes, Byzantine
Studies and Other Essays (London: The University of London, the
Athlone Press, 1960), pp. 116-143, 226-239; Peter R. L. Brown,
The World of Late Antiquity, A.D. 150-750, History of European
Civilization Library (New York: Harcourt: Brace Jovanovich;
paperback, 1971); Charles N. Cochrane, Christianity and
Classical Culture: A Study of Thought and Action from Augustus
to Augustine 4th. ed. (First printed at Oxford: paperback,
1968), pp. 1-176; Georges Dumézil, La Religion Romaine
Archaïque, Bibliothéque Historique Collection les Religions de
l'humanité (Paris: Payot, 1966); Clifford Geertz, The Interpretation of Cultures: Selected Essays (New York: Basic Books,
1973), pp. 87-125, 126-141; A. H. M. Jones, The Later Roman
Empire: 284-602, A Social, Economic and Administrative Survey, 3
vols. (Oxford: Basil Blackwell, 1964); Arnaldo Momigliano, The
Conflict between Paganism and Christianity in the Fourth
Century: Essays (Oxford: At the Clarendon Press, 1963).

[2]Cicero De Natura Deorum 3.5. in part cited by Richard
Klein, Symmachus, Impulse der Forschung Nr. 2 (Darmstadt:
Wissenschaftliche Buchgesellschaft, 1971) p. 19.

[3]Cicero In Catilinam 2.19., cited in part by Klein,
Symmachus, p. 20, n. 11.

[4]Livius Ab Urbe Condita 3.7.1., in part cited by Klein, p.
20, n. 11.

[5]Ibid., 26.41.

[6]Vergil Aeneid 1.255ff., cited by Mircea Eliade, Myth of
Eternal Return or, Cosmos and History (transl. from the French
by W. Trask. First published (Paris: Librarie Gallimard, NRF,
1949) Bollingen Series No. 46; (Princeton: Princeton University
Press, Bollingen paperback, 1971), p. 135.

42

[7]Symmachus _Relationes_ 3.3., cited after Klein, _Der Streit um den Viktoriaaltar: Die dritte 'Relatio' des Symmachus und die Briefe 17, 18 und 57 des Mailander Bischofs Ambrosius_. Texte zur Forschung, No. 7 (Darmstadt: Wissenschaftliche Buchgesellschaft, 1972). p. 100.

[8]Ibid.

[9]One should note here that the earliest extant plays of the Egyptians had an essentially liturgical function. See for example: Kurth Sethe, _Dramatische Texte zu alt-ägyptischen Mysterienspielen: Das Denkmal Memphitischer Theologie und ein Spiel zur Thronbesteigung des Königs. Untersuchungen zur Geschichte der Altertumskunde_, No. 10 (Leipzig: J. C. Hinrich' sche Buchhandlung, 1928).

[10]J. H. Waszink, "Varro Livy and Tertullian on the History of Roman Dramatic Art," _VC_ 2 (Jan. 1948): 227-32. Regarding the origins of drama see now also Ernest Theodore Kirby, _Ur-Drama: The Origins of the Theater_ (New York: New York University Press, 1975), pp. vii-xvi, 1-32, 90-140.

[11]John Arthur Hanson, _Roman-Theater-Temples_, Princeton Monograph in Art and Archaeology No. 33 (Princeton: Princeton University Press, 1959), pp. 9-26; cf. Dorothy Kent Hill, "The Temple above Pompey's Theater", _The Classical Journal_ 39 (Feb. 1944): 360-365; Catherine Saunders, "Altars on the Roman Comic Stages," _TAPA_ 42 (1911): 91-103 and "The Site of Dramatic Performances in the Times of Plautus and Terence," _TAPA_ 44 (1913): 87-97.

[12]Margaret Bieber, _Die Denkmäler zum Theaterwesen im Altertum_ (Berlin und Leipzig: Walter de Gruyter & Co., 1920), p. 95.

[13]Hanson, _Theater-Temples_, pp. 59-77 and Appendix: Illustrations.

[14]Margaret Bieber, "Kuchenformen mit Tragödienszene," _Programm zum Winckelmannsfeste der Archaeologischen_

<u>Gesellschaft</u>, Nr. 75 (1915): 1-31 with illustrations. (We are dealing here with archaeological findings--of about 400 forms and a number of small wine jars--from the second and third century A.D., which were discovered by Pasqui in Ostia in 1906.) Cf. also Lily Ross Taylor, "The 'Sellisternium' and the "Theatrical Pompa'" in <u>Classical Philology</u>, 30 (Jan. 1935): 122-130.

[15]Hanson, <u>Theater-Temples</u>, pp. 9-25, 81-92.

[16]Lactantius <u>Divinae Institutiones</u>, 5.10: 16-17.

[17]Ibid., 5.10. 17-18.

[18]See for example in respect to <u>mimesis</u> Hans-Georg Gadamer, <u>Wahrheit und Methode</u>, third ed., first edition 1960. (Tübingen: J.C.B. Mohr Paul Siebeck 1972), p. 110. (The problem of <u>mimesis</u> is a fascinating one but cannot be dealt with in this work.)

[19]Augustine Sermo 241.5.5. cited by Heiko Jürgens, <u>Pompa Diaboli: Die Lateinischen Kirchenväter und das Antike Theater</u>. Tübinger Beiträge zur Altertumswissenschaft, Nr. 47 (Stuttgart: Verlag W. Kohlhammer, 1972), p. 246, n.3.

[20]See below, p. 29.

[21]Tacitus <u>Annalium</u> 14.20.

[22]Juvenalis <u>Satyra</u> 10. 78-81. Cf. E.K. Chambers, <u>The Medieval Stage</u>, 2 vols. (Oxford: At the Clarendon Press, 1903): 1:22.

[23]Henri Stern, <u>Le Calendrier de 354</u>. Institut Francais d'Archéologie de Beyrouth. Bibliothéque Archéologie et Historique No. 55 (Paris: Imprimerie Nationale, Librairé Orientaliste Paul Geuthner, 1953), p. 116.

[24]Albert Müller, "Das Bühnenwesen in der Zeit von Konstantin d. Gr. bis Justinian," <u>Neue Jahrbücher für das klassische Altertum</u> 23 (1909): 36-37.

[25]Ibid., p. 36.

[26]Symmachus Relatio 6. cited by H. R. Barrow, Prefect and Emperor: The 'Relations' of Symmachus, A.D. 384 with translation, introduction and notes (Oxford: At the Clarendon Press, 1973), pp. 56-57.

[27]For an overview see especially Jones, Roman Empire, see above p. 43, n. 1.

[28]Hermann Reich, Der Mimus, 1 vol. in 2 pts. (Berlin: Weidmann'sche Buchhandlung, 1903), vol. 1, pt. 1: Die Theorie des Mimus, pp. 1-80. Cf. Heinz Kindermann, Theatergeschichte Europas, 3 vols. (Salzburg: Otto Müller Verlag, 1957), I: Das Theater der Antike und des Mittelalters, p. 129. See also Tacitus, Annalium. 4.14.

[29]Symmachus Relatio 3.3. cited after Klein, Viktoriaaltar, p. 100.

[30]Ibid, 3.9., p. 104.

[31]Ibid., 3.10. Klein, pp. 104-106.

[32]Ambrosius Epistula ad Valentinianus 17.1. cited after Klein, Viktoriaaltar, p. 116.

[33]Werner Jaeger, Early Christianity and Greek Paideia (Cambridge: Belknap Press of Harvard University Press, 1961). W. Krause, Die Stellung der frühchristlichen Autoren zur heidnischen Literatur (Wien: Verlag Herder, 1958), pp. 7-53. Berthold Altaner und Alfred Stuiber, Patrologie, 7th newly edited and expanded edition (Herder: Freiburg, 1966), pp. 43-58, 79-82.

[34]The following works belong to the most important literary sources of this epoch: Clement of Rome, The Epistle to the Corinthians ca. 96 A.D.); The Pastoral Book of Hermas (ca. 150 A.D.); Barnabas of Alexandria, The Epistle of Barnabas (ca. 96-98 A.D.); Didache (ca. 140 A.D.); Ignatius of Antioch, Seven Epistles (ca. 110 A.D.); Polykarp of Smyrna, The Epistle to the

<u>Philippians</u> (ca. 156 A.D.).

[35]Cf. Goethe, <u>Römische Elegien</u>, 4. 3-4.

[36]Oscar Cullmann, <u>Urchristentum und Gottesdienst</u> (Basel: Verlag von Heinrich Mayer, 1944), pp. 42, 46-47; John N.D. Kelly, <u>Early Christian Creeds</u> (London and New York: Longmanns Green and Co., 1950), p. 3.

[37]See also John Helgeland, "Christians and Military Service" (Ph.D. Dissertation: The University of Chicago, 1973), pp. 109-126; H. Gregoire, <u>et</u> <u>al</u>., <u>Les Persécutions dans l'empire romain</u>, 2nd rev. et augm. Lettres et de sciences morals et politiques. Memoires, Académie Royale de Belgique (Bruxelles: Palais des Academies, 1964), pp. 1-22, 78-88; J. Vogt, "Zur Religiösität der Christenverfolgung im Römische Reich," <u>Sitzungsberichte der Heidelberger Akademie der Wissenschaften</u>. Phil. hist. Kl. (Heidelberg: Universitätsverlag C. Winter, 1962), pp. 28-30.

[38]Regarding the sociological consequences and formations of this daemonology see Ernst Troeltsch, <u>Gesammelte Werke</u>, I: <u>Die Soziallehren der christlichen Kirchen und Gruppen</u>. 2nd ed. of the edition published in 1922 by J.C.B. Mohr (Paul Siebeck). (Aalen: Scientia Verlag, 1965), pp. 1-178, esp. pp. 99-105.

[39]Robert M. Grant, "The Chronology of the Greek Apologists," <u>VC</u> 9 (1955): 25-33.

[40]Aristides <u>Apology</u> 3.13.

[41]Justin Martyr <u>Apology</u> 1.

[42]Tatian <u>Oratio contra Graecos</u> 22. Otis C. Edwards, Jr., "Barbarian Philosophy: Tatian and the Greek Paideia" (Ph.D. Dissertation, University of Chicago, 1971), pp. 218-221.

[43]Athenagoras <u>Legatio</u> 35. 4-5.

[44]Theophilus <u>Ad Autolycum</u> 2.36; 3.15.

[45] Heinrich Wey, _Die Funktion der bösen Geister bei den griechischen Apologeten des zweiten Jahrhunderts nach Christus,_ (Winterthur: P.S. Keller, 1957); A. Kallis, "Griechische Väter" s.v. "Geister" (Dämonen). In _Reallexikon für Antike und Christentum,_ edited by Theodor Klauser et al,. (Stuttgart: Hiersemann Verlag GMBH, 1050-), vol. 9 (1974-75): 700-715, and P.G. van der Nat, "Apologeten und lateinische Väter," s.v. "Geister" (Dämonen), 9 (1974-75): 715-761. After this cited as _RAC._

[46] Clement of Alexandria _Proteptikos,_ Book 1.

[47] Clement of Alexandria _Paedagogus._

[48] Origen _Contra Celsum,_ translated with an introduction and notes by Henry Chadwick (Cambridge: At the University Press, 1953), book VII, 69, p. 452. (In the German version of my dissertation I used the volume of the Bibliothek der _Kirchenväter_ for the citations in German).

[49] Ibid., book VIII, 33, p. 476.

[50] Ibid., book VIII, 63, pp. 500-501.

[51] Hugo Rahner, "Pompa diaboli: Ein Beitrag zur Bedeutungs-geschichte des Wortes πομπη _pompa_ in der urchristlichen Taufliturgie," _ZkTh_ 55 (1931): 239-273, esp. 255-264.

[52] Tertullian _Apologeticum_ 2.13 and 8.5.

[53] Ibid., 6. 2-3.

[54] Ibid., 10.1.

[55] _De Spectaculis_ 2.9.

[56] Ibid., 3. 1-2.

[57] Ibid., 3. 3. Ps. 1.1.

[58] Ibid., 3. 4-5.

[59]Ibid., 4., Cf. also Joseph Köhne, "Die Schrift Tertullians über die 'Schauspiele' in kultur- und religionsgechichtlicher Beleuchtung" (Ph.D. Dissertation, Breslau, 1929) and also Rahner, Pompa, pp. 255-264.

[60]De Spect. 5-9. Cf. Waszink, "Varro," p. 231.

[61]De Spect. 10. 3-8. Cf. above, p. 16.

[62]Ibid., 2.

[63]Ibid., 27. 4.

[64]Cf. E. Nöldechen, "Tertullian und das Theater," ZfKTh 15 (1895): 161-203, and "Tertullian und das Spielwesen," ZfwTh 37 (1894): 91-125.

[65]De Idololatria 1.

[66]De Spectaculis 6.

[67]Adversus Marcium 4.9. Cf. also 1 Cor. 5-6; Ga. 5:21; 1 John 5: 16-17.

[68]De Puditia 19.

[69]De Baptismo 18.

[70]De Paenetentia 6 (Cf. this with the decrees of the Synod of de lapsis in 254 A.D.)

[71]Cf. above, pp. 2f. and Rahner, "Pompa," pp. 255-264.

[72]Cf. above, pp. 1-4.

[73]Cf. below, chapter II.

[74]Gibbon's criticism in this regard is as follows: ". . . The ties of blood and friendship were frequently torn asunder by the difference of religious faith; and the Christians, who, in

this world, found themselves oppressed by the power of the
pagans, were sometimes seduced by resentment and spiritual pride
to delight in the prospect of their future triumph. "You are
found of spectacles," exclaims the stern Tertullian, "except the
greatest of all spectacles, the last and eternal judgement of
the universe. How shall I admire, how laugh, how rejoice, how
excult, when I behold so many proud monarchs, and fancied gods,
groaning in the lowest abyss of darkness; so many magistrates,
who persecuted the name of the Lord, liquefying in fiercer fires
than they ever kindled against the Christians; so many sage philosphers blushing in red-hot flames with their deluded scholars;
so many celebrated poets trembling before the tribunal, not of
Minos, but of Christ; so many tragedians, more tuneful in the
expression of their own sufferings; so many dancers . . . But
the humanity of the reader will permit me to draw over the rest
of this infernal description, which the zealous African pursues
in a long variety of affected and unfeeling witticism." (De
spect. 30). Edward Gibbon, The Decline and Fall of the Roman
Empire, 2 vols. (London: W. Strahan and T. Cadel, 1776-1778 in 6
vols. New York: The Modern Library, n.d.), vol. 1: 15. 406-407.
Cf. also E. K. Chambers, The Medieval Stage, 2 vols. (Oxford: At
the Clarendon Press, 1903), 1: 22. Although both of these works
are outdated with respect to some of their views, they remain,
because of their rich source material, indispensable tools.

[75]Cyprianus Epistola 1. 7-16.

[76]Ps. Cyprianus (Novatian) De spectaculis, 4.

[77]Ibid., 9.

[78]Cf. here especially Helgeland, "Christians and Military
Service," pp. 87-135; Vogt, "Religiösität der Christenverfolger," pp. 28-30; Gregoire, et al., Persécutions, pp. 1-22,
78-88; C. E. Brand, Roman Military Law (Austin: University of
Texas Press, 1968), pp. 83-98, 91-109.

[79]Arnobius Adversus Nationes 4.35.

[80]Ibid., 4.36.

[81]Lactantius *Divinae Institutiones* 6.20.

[82]Cf. chapter II.

[83]Cf. above pp. 1-2, 9f., and P. R. L. Brown, "Aspects of the Christianization of the Roman Aristocracy," *The Journal of Roman Studies* 51 (1961): 1-11.

[84]Ambrosius *Expos. ps. 118.* 5.28

[85]Prudentius *Peristephanon* 10, 216-226.

[86]Augustinus *De Civitate Dei* 1. 32.

[87]*Confessiones* 1.10; 3.2; 4.1,2,3,4; 10, 35.

[88]*De Civitate* 2.4.

[89]*De Consensu Evangelistarum.* 1.33.

[90]*De Civitate Dei* 2.11,13.

[91]*De Doctrina Christiana* 2.3 (4).

[92]Cf. below, pp. 167-247.

[93]Salvianus *De Gubernatione Dei* 6.11. 59-61.

[94]Sidonius *Carmina* 23.40

[95]*Vitae Sanctorum Honorati et Hilarii, Episcoporum Arelatensium*, ed. Samuel Cavallin. Skrifter Utgivna av Vetenskaps-Societeten Lund 40 (Publications of the New Society of Letters at Lund). (Lund: C. W. K. Gleerup, 1952), 10.12, p. 97. Cf. also Jurgens, *Pompa*, p. 204.

[96]*Caesarius de Arles Sermones* 61.3.

[97]Cassiodorus *Variarum* 7.10.

[98]Ibid.

[99] Isidore de Séville _Etymologiarum_. 18.42.

[100] Ibid., 18.43.

[101] Ibid., 18.59.

[102] Cyrilus de Jerusalem _Catechesis_ 19 1.6.

[103] Sozomenus _Ecclesiastical History_ 4.25.

[104] Gregorius Nazianzenus _Orationes_ 2.84.

[105] Gregorius Nyssenus _Epistola_ 9.

[106] Johannes Chrysostomus _PG_ 56: 263-270.

[107] Ibid., pp. 264-65.

[108] Ibid., and pp. 98-142; see also Georgios J. Theodaris, "Beiträge zur Geschichte des Byzantinischen Profantheaters im 4. und 5. Jahrhundert, hauptsächlich auf Grund der Predigten des Johannes Chrysostomus, Patriarchen von Konstantinopel." (Ph.D. Dissertation, München, 1942).

[109] See below, pp. 79-86.

[110] _The Liturgical Homilies of Narsai_, translated from the Syriac by Dom H. R. Connolly with an Appendix by Edmund Bishop. Texts and Studies 8.1. (Cambridge: At the University Press, 1909), pp. 37-38.

[111] See below, pp. 80-84.

[112] C. Moss, "Jacob of Serugh's Homelies on the Spectacles of the Theatre," _Le Muséon. Revue d'Études Orientales_ 48 (1935): 87-112.

[113] Ibid., pp. 103-104.

[114] Ibid.

[115]Ibid., pp. 105-106.

[116]Ibid., pp. 107-108.

[117]Ibid.

[118]Ibid., pp. 105-106.

[119]See below, pp. 70-79.

[120]J.D. Mansi, Sacrorum Conciliorum Nova et Amplissima Collectio. 60 vols. (Paris: 1899-1927, vol. 2: 5-6. After this cited as Mansi, and Carl Joseph von Hefele and Henri Leclercq, Histoire des Conciles. Nov. trad. corrige et augm. 11 vols. (Paris: Letouzey et Ane 1908-1952), vol. 1, part 1: 212-264. After this cited as: Hefele Leclercq.

[121]Mansi. 1: 1097; Hefele-Leclercq: 1.1: 195-206.

[122]Ibid., 2: 471; Ibid., 1.1: 275-283.

[123]Ibid., 2: 779; Ibid., 1.1: 335-632.

[124]Ibid., 2: 582; Ibid., 1:2: 989-1028.

[125]Ibid., 3: 767; Ibid., 2.1: 125-126.

[126]Ibid., 4: 427; Ibid., 2.1: 190-196.

[127]Ibid., 1: 367; Ibid., 1.2: 1047-1070.

[128]Ibid., 1: 369-370.

[129]Ibid., 370-371.

[130]Ibid., 12: 59-88.

[131]Ibid., 12: 365-370.

[132]See below, chapter IV., pp. 167-247.

CHAPTER II

THE LITURGICAL TRADITION[1]

The Meaning of Liturgy

The concept of liturgy will be outlined in the following
study from three different points of view: 1. as an act of
public worship; 2. as an educational means; and 3. as
literature.

The Liturgy as an Act of Worship

The word liturgy ($\lambda \epsilon \dot{\iota} \tau o \nu \rho \gamma \iota \alpha$) is of Greek origin and was
generally understood to be a public service carried out for the
welfare of the Greek polis in the field of education, in
entertainment or warfare, as well as a religious-ritual act.[2]
The Hellenistic Jews adopted this concept with their translation
of the Septuagint. As a result of this, the concept underwent
further transformation until in the theocratic state of Israel
its significance became restricted to the act of worship, i.e.,
the liturgy became a public act in honor of Yahweh.[3] With the
Israelites, however, the liturgy was viewed in close relation to
the concept of ecclesia ($\epsilon \kappa \kappa \lambda \epsilon \partial \iota \alpha$), whereas in the Greek
polis the term liturgy had referred to a certain popular meeting
of political democratic character. Thus the Jews changed this
concept to the exclusive meaning of worship.[4] Liturgy and
ecclesia understood in this way embraced the entire life of the
people in its religious, cultural, social and political
dimensions.[5]

The Liturgy as a Means for Education

While the meetings of worship of the early Church were
connected with baptism and the proclamation of the good news,
the liturgy had, from the beginning, didactic significance. The
teachings of the primitive kerygma were, at first, limited to
the Lord's Prayer and the profession of faith.[6] With the
expansion of Christianity as well as with the deepening of faith
and the development of dogma, the educational function of the

Church expanded. The liturgy developed and thereby expanded into an educational instrument of particular significance for the transformation from a pagan to a Christian culture.[7]

The Liturgy as Literature

With Christianity a new world view began to be formed which naturally also sought expression in literary and artistic works. The abundance of early Christian literature in its different genres testifies to this new perception of reality and to the existence of a creative imagination at work in the production of this new literary and artistic corpus,[8] whereby the Biblical material--the teachings of Jesus Christ and with that the whole vision of salvation history which developed out of this material--takes on objective configurations in liturgical-dramatic representations. In this section we are faced with the task of working out, from a cross-section of liturgical texts, the dramatic structure of the liturgy.

The Liturgy in Chronological Sequence

The Jewish Tradition

The Christian liturgy has its roots in the Jewish tradition and has taken over its fundamental components. The Jewish synaxis consisted of Old Testament teachings, exegesis, psalms and prayers.[9] The interpretation of Scripture had a special significance. In this order of worship the Jews differentiated between Temple, Synagogue and family liturgy.[10] Jesus taught daily in the Synagogue and prayed in the Temple.[11] The Feast of the Unleavened Bread was primarily a family liturgy which was celebrated in homes.[12] Within this traditional liturgy, at the time of the First Liturgical Act of Jesus during the Last Supper, Jesus spoke the words of the New Covenant in which were simultaneously concealed both the promise of a heavenly banquet and a new reality.[13] After the Passion and Resurrection of Christ, the breaking of the bread became the symbol of the Resurrection in the early Christian community.[14] The breaking of bread, symbolizing both the Resurrection and the Passion, added a new dimension to this first Christian liturgy. After the first Pentecost, baptism and a sermon developed into essential components of these gatherings of worship of the growing Christian community.[15]

With these new forms, the traditional liturgy was broken up and slowly the Christian community began to separate itself from the Jewish Synagogue and Temple worship. Another introduction was the transfer of worship from the Sabbath to Sunday or the Day of the Lord because this day signified the Resurrection of Jesus Christ. Joy at the Resurrection, thanksgiving, and eschatological expectation, which are documented in the Book of Revelation,[16] characterize this new liturgy. After the expansion of Christianity, the conversion of Saul to the Apostle Paul, and the subsequent incorporation of the pagans into the kerygman as well as with the event of the destruction of Jerusalem, independent Christian communities gradually began to be formed in the Roman Empire the liturgy of which became slowly stable in structure and visibly distinct from Jewish worship as well as from the Roman state and mystery cults. Although synaxis and communion were the kernels of the Christian liturgy, the total structure remained flexible enough in order to assimilate new cultural forms and world views.

Liturgical Sources until the Second Century A.D.

Scattered traces of information about liturgical gatherings are found, aside from the New Testament, in early Christian writings.[17] A non-Christian source is preserved in a letter of Pliny to the Emperor Hadrian in which the gatherings of the Christian sect are mentioned.[18] The Didache (ca. 140 A.D.) can be designated as the first liturgical document. It gives insight into the liturgy around the first half of the second century which is on the one hand still dependent on Jewish custom and indicating a local rural environment.[19] On the other side, in the Apology of Justin Martyr (ca. 141-161 A.D.), there are traces of a liturgical scheme and regular Sunday gatherings are mentioned. Justin polemicizes at the same time against the errors of similar pagan mystery cults, particularly against those of Mithra, which indicates his familiarity with them.[20] In Adversus Haereses by Irenaeus of Lyons (ca. 202 A.D.), the liturgy already begins to show cosmic-universal dimensions which seem to break the rather narrow frame of a community circle.[21]

With Clement of Alexandria the liturgy receives an expansion in meaning in the sense of a great divine mystery and he invites the people of this great cultural center of Alexandria, to leave the pagan songs and mysteries to the Maenads and to participate in the great Christian mysteries.[22]

In the second century there slowly begins to emerge a certain structure with local imprints as exemplified in the Syriac Didache. At the same time, the liturgy undergoes a cognitive expansion and receives a meaning as mystery as we could observe with Justin and Clement or a cosmic-universal dimension as with Irenaeus of Lyons.

The Liturgy of the Third Century A.D.

The Church Orders.

In the third century the Church no longer lived with the immediate memory of the life of Jesus or with immediate eschatological expectations but became more conscious of her Apostolic tradition. During this time the literary genre of Church Orders came into being the beginnings of which seem to be manifested in the Didache. They are of Syriac origin and the Eastern Church remained their most fertile soil. Their imaginative pseudo-origin goes back to the apostles themselves.[23] In their form they are a kind of pastoral handbook which mainly contained guide lines for the life of the Christian community in distinction to Jewish and pagan gatherings. With these Orders, so it seems, signs of a public self- and group-consciousness as belonging to the Apostolic tradition were manifested.

The Apostolic Tradition of Hippolytus (ca. 217 A.D.). Hippolytus was a Presbyter of Rome and his work constitutes the first complete form of the genre of the Church Orders. Hippolytus seems to have been the first writer to draw on a somewhat completed form of the Church at the beginning of the third century; he makes particular reference to the tradition of the apostles. The liturgical forms which are dealt with in this work are flexible and not fixed. The forms also contain directions as to how the Church should deal with actors: they are to give up their profession or they are to stay away from

the meetings of Christian worship.[24]   The Syriac <u>Didaskalia</u>
<u>Apostolorum</u> appears around 250 A.D.   This work makes the
fictitious claim to have come directly from the hands of the
apostles themselves.   There is an elaborate polemic against the
theatre and the dialectic of both communities, the pagan, <u>i.e.</u>,
Roman, on the one side, and the Christian, on the other, becomes
even clearer in this work.[25]   The <u>Testament of the Lord</u> (ca. 350
A.D.) deals with directions which Christ Himself apparently had
given to the apostles during the time between the Resurrection and the Ascension.   These apparent orders of the Risen Lord
Himself also forbade the idolatrous visit to the theatre.[26]   The
<u>Statua Ecclesia Antiqua</u> (ca. 398 A.D.) are a product of the
Syriac character of the Gallican Church.   Here too, neophytes
are forbidden to go to the theatre.[27]   The end-products of this
genre are the compilations of the <u>Apostolic Constitutions</u> (ca.
380 A.D.) where the threads of the different <u>Church Orders</u> seem
to become interwoven.   This compendium is of Syriac origin and
claims to have been drafted at the first Apostolic Council of
Jerusalem.   These compilations probably point to an older
liturgical custom which is indicated by the liturgy of Clement
contained in the eighth book of this work.[28]

With the <u>Apostolic Tradition</u> and the <u>Church Orders</u> a
gradually structured systematic development as well as an
expansion of an organized public life of the Church can be
observed.   The liturgy of this Church will become manifested in
richer dramatic forms throughout the following centuries.

The Liturgy in the Fourth and Fifth Centuries.

Constantine's conversion to Christianity changed the
conditions of Christian life in the fourth century.   Until that
time the Church had been suppressed and persecuted in an alien
culture and it now became recognized as an official public
institution.[29]   At the same time, however, the Church found
herself accepted in a culture which she could not in principle
affirm because of the phenomenon of <u>idololatria</u>.   With the
erection of basilicas and churches, spatial visibility of a
manifested Christianity was achieved[30] while at the same time
these buildings constituted "spiritual counter-places" to the
Roman temples or theatre buildings which were considered to be

dwelling places for the daemons.[31] How significant these
spatial manifestations were in the entire conflict within the
Roman Empire is signified by the conflict surrounding the Altar
of Victory[32] as well as by the destruction of pagan temples and
theatres by the Church on the one hand and Christian churches by
the Romans on the other. This constant tension between pagan-
Roman and Christian forms of expression led to a slow and
dynamic process of transformation which reached deeply into the
symbolic structures and which was probably in cases of mass
conversions of a long and slow duration.[33] The objective forms
of liturgical-dramatic representations were interconnected with
these external manifestations of Christian architectural art
which were considered to be an expression of true beauty, a
projection of the true creation by the Creator in contrast to
the pagan perversions and false pomp of the daemonic cult in
Roman theatrical ostentations, as the Church Fathers called
them. The bishops and doctors of the Church themselves came
from this pagan Roman culture, and thus, they played a decisive
role in the execution of the educational program of the Church.
The liturgy, because it was especially capable of adaptation,
remained thereby a valuable educational instrument. It was
Baumstark who in particular called attention to this capacity
for adaptation of the liturgy. He wrote:

> It seems to be the nature of the liturgy
> to relate itself to the concrete situa-
> tion of times and places. . . we should
> expect a priori analogous relations be-
> tween the evolution of the Christian lit-
> urgy and the forms of the ancient cults. [34]

Such a capacity for transformation anticipates a vitality and
flexibility which do not necessarily lead to the renouncement of
one's own values but rather to their deeper understanding.
Liturgical scholarship[35] distinguishes in general between a
basic unity of all liturgical families resting upon the basic
structure of synaxis and Eucharistic celebrations, as well as
between improvisations and variations which are grouped around
this unity and which give the total structure a certain
flexibility. Such a flexibility makes room for creative work of
the most various kinds of imagination in the context of which

the liturgy on the one hand is able to unfold to a representational dramatic configuration and on the other to an
efficacious center of Christian teaching.

The Liturgical Centers

Since the fourth century, the large number of texts which
have survived point to an active life of the Church expressing
itself in manifold forms.[36] Specialists have tried to organize
this abundance into four great liturgical families, i.e.,
Antioch and Alexandria in the East, Gaul and Rome in the West of
the Church. However, the influential liturgical centers of
Syria, Edessa and Nisibis, are of utmost significance for the
understanding of the development of Christian liturgical drama.
In this study, therefore, these centers will be dealt with as
equally important.[37]

The Eastern Church

The Syriac Church with Jerusalem and Antioch in the Western
and Persia and Mesopotamia[38] with Edessa and Nisibis in the
Eastern part of Syria are of special importance because here one
can grasp relatively easily the shaping of a rich imaginative
liturgy especially in its dramatic representations. Alexandria
was a great center of education and culture in Asia Minor where
movements of Hellenism, Judaism and Christianity met and
merged.[39] The center of Egypt's liturgy, which also includes
Ethiopian and as well, at least in part, the Greek liturgies,
was in the midst of Alexandria. Neo-Platonism as well as
allegorical Biblical exegesis, the expressions of which were
later assimilated to the liturgical representational forms,
emerged from this great center. The Byzantine liturgy of Constantinople and Ravenna stands between the most different
movements and can, therefore, from the beginning be defined as a
mixed liturgy.[40] The Syriac liturgy seems to have been of
greatest influence on the liturgy of Byzantium primarily,
perhaps, because doctors of the Church such as Chrysostom and
Gregory of Nazianzen were patriarchs of Constantinople[41] and
were thus able to exercise their influence on the shaping of
this liturgy. Jerusalem, the historical place of salvation and
consequently a leading center of piety, also had great influence

61

upon the Byzantine liturgy of Constantinople--the "second Rome" in the Eastern part of the Church.

The Dramatic Shaping of the Liturgy.

A cross-examination of liturgical texts of the most different genres reveals, from the fourth century onwards, an abundance of dramatic evidence which clusters on the one hand around the theme of the Incarnation and on the other around the Passion and Resurrection of Jesus. Structurally, this means that the synaxis of the Mass of the catechumens, as well as that of the offertory are dramatically expressed. This literary genre of the Mystagogical Catechisms[42] which concentrate their dramatic figurative explanation around baptism and the Eucharist confirm such a development. The explanatory letters and sermons also testify to such a structure. With the examination which follows, it is as well to remember that these new creative forms of expression did not rise in a vacuum but rather in a situation of conflict in which the main source of contention was idololatria.[43]

Jerusalem:

In the fourth century, Jerusalem, as the original place of the historical events of the Passion, Death and Resurrection of Jesus, became a center of Christian piety where the liturgy had expanded[44] to commemorative representations, especially during the Passion Week. As Dix has shown, however, it was also in Jerusalem[45] where a solid liturgical structure developed. This structure as well as the heightened dramatization is evident in the following documents:

Cyril of Jerusalem (315-396 A.D.): The Mystagogical Catechism (348 A.D.) of the bishop of Jerusalem is an explanation of the mystery of Baptism and Eucharist in a structured liturgy. The renouncement of the diabolic pomp of the theatre[46] belongs essentially to the initiation into the vision of the world which is created in baptism.[47] A cosmological image with reference to the allegorical exegesis betrays the influence of the School of Alexandria which implies that these philosophical and theological tendencies also blend with the liturgy of Jerusalem.

Peregrinatio Aetheria (ca. 389 A.D.): A particular
revealing document of the dramatic liturgy of Jerusalem is the
report of a Gallican pilgrim, who described her observations
during Holy Week in Jerusalem. In the text which follows, the
representations of the entry of Jesus into Jerusalem on Palm
Sunday is described as:

> Hora ergo septima omnis populus ascendet
> in monte Oliveti, id est Eleona, in eccle-
> sia; sed et episcopus, dicuntur ymni et
> antiphonae apte diei ipsi vel loco, lec-
> tiones etiam similiter . . . Et iam cum
> coeperit esse hora undecima, legitur ille
> locus de evangelio, ubi infantes cum ramis
> vel palmis occurrerunt Domino dicentes:
> "Benedictus, qui venit in nomine Domini."
> Et statim levat se episcopus et omnis
> populus, porro inde de summo monte Oli-
> veti totum pedibus itur. Nam totus po-
> pulus ante ipsum cum ymnis vel antipho-
> nis respondentes semper: "Benedictus,
> qui venit in nomine Domini." Et quot-
> quot sunt infantes in hisdem locis, us-
> que etiam qui pedibus ambulare non pos-
> sunt, quia teneri sunt, in collo illos
> parentes sui tenent, omnes ramos tenen-
> tes alii palmarum, alii olivarum et si
> deducetur episcopus in eo typo, quo tunc
> Dominus deductus est.[48]

This dramatization of the entry of Jesus into Jerusalem on Palm
Sunday which includes people from all over the world at the
historical place is later integrated into the structure of the
different liturgies but most obviously so at Byzantium. The
historical places themselves reappear in a transposed allegorical-dramatic form outside of Jerusalem.

Antioch:

   The liturgy of this center can partly be grasped from the
sermons of Chrysostom, a doctor of the Church of Antioch.[49]   Of
particular interest for our examination is the sermon In illud
vidi Domini where Chrysostom criticizes theatre manners during
the hours of the liturgy.   On the other side, this description
presents a counterpart to the dramatization of Jerusalem which
indicates that the liturgy in Antioch was conceived by the
faithful people of the Church themselves as dramatic and also as
a counterpart of the Roman theatre, in existence in Antioch.

   Chrysostom: This Church Father gives the following
description of the situation in his church:

> . . . quam lymphati, toto corpore tumul-
> tuantes ac circumacti, moresque prae se
> ferentes a spirituali statione alienos. Mi-
> ser et infelix! . . . tu vero mimorum et
> saltatorum mores huc inducis, dum inde-
> center manus factas, pedibus subsultas,
> totoqua circumageris corpore . . . Non
> cogitas ipsum hic invisibiliter adesse
> Dominum, . . . verum tu ista non cogitas,
> quoniam ea quae in theatris audiuntur,
> quaeque spectantur, mentem tuam obscura-
> runt; et ideo quae illic geruntur in
> Ecclesia ritus inducis. . . Quomodo igi-
> tur audes angelorum Deus glorificantium
> hymnis daemonum admiscere ludrica?[50]

This vivid description indicates that the image and experience
of a Roman theatre must have been deeply rooted in the
consciousness of the people and was obviously transferred to the
Christian liturgy by the newly arrived catechumens.   According
to such descriptions, however, the liturgy itself must have
resembled the theatre and its performances.   Chrysostom also
described a world of beauty, which will lead to the joy of the
angels, that is to say, to pure and refined expressions of joy
and not to the rude manners of the theatre inspired by the
daemons.[51]

Alexandria:

The abbreviated liturgy[52] of the Cappadocian, Basil the Great (325-375 A.D.), belongs to the later form of the Byzantine mixed liturgy. This is particularly informative because in the structure of this liturgy new spatial and temporal dimensions are noted which reflect, on the one hand the Neo-Platonic cosmos (of Plotinus) and, on the other, a spiritualized counterpart of the universal Roman Empire.

Basil the Great opens the liturgy with a song of praise to the Lord of the Universe which is repeated time and again throughout the whole liturgy. This can be demonstrated from the following quotations:

> Te glorificamus, opifex et rex omnium,
> et adoramus ineffabile et venerandum
> nomen tuum . . . Iterum precemur omni-
> potentem et misericordem Deum, Patrem
> Domini, Dei et Salvatoris nostri Jesu
> Christi . . . Memento Domine pacis,
> sanctae, unius catholicae et apostoli-
> cae tuae Ecclesiae. Domine, qui es, Deus,
> veritatis existens ante saecula et reg-
> nans in saecula . . .[53]

These spatial and temporal dimensions—which are simulta- neously an irruption of the spaceless and timeless into the dramatic liturgy—constitute the background for the stage of this liturgy. This deserves our attention because these dimensions later become essential components of the liturgical drama as a whole; they are also given expression in the architectural structure of the basilicas as well as in the liturgical forms of representation. It is in part a counter- image of that Roman universal image of which Symmachus as well as Ambrose gave an expression.[53a]

65

<u>Edessa and Nisibis</u>.

These two centers belong to the most important and influential ones of East Syria and the Eastern Church in general. From here originated the impetus of theology, asceticism and the creative abundance of Christian liturgy.[54]

<u>Tatian (d. ca. 180 A.D.)</u>. Jerusalem had, on the one hand, been a place of historical reality and therefore a special point of departure of the dramatization of the real events of the life of Jesus, particularly of the Passion Week, within the liturgy.[55] Tatian's <u>Diatessaron</u>--a gospel harmony--(ca. 170 A.D.) however seems, on the other hand to have had great influence upon the poetic and dramatic shaping of the Biblical material, particularly at first in Syria. Syria had an extensive system of pericopes which was greatly influenced by Tatian's <u>Diatessaron</u> and which, in its multi-layered structure allowed also non-Biblical material to be incorporated and harmonized with the Biblical stories.[56] Such a structure leaves within itself enough room for creativity and the insertion and assimilation of different materials. The hymn-like sermon of the Syriac Church, which is particularly suitable for incorporation into the entire liturgical structure, was of great importance[57] in this context. After Tatian, Ephraim was of great significance for the Syriac Church and his poetic vision influenced the development of its liturgical drama.

<u>Ephraim the Syrian (ca. 306-373)</u>.[58] Emphraim was a deacon and doctor of the Church. His works were, until Theodore of Mopsuestia, in usage in the School of Edessa. He was one of the most imaginative Christian poets and an erudite scholar. He reshaped most aesthetically the story of the life of Jesus. His hymn-like sermons, for example, evidence his poetic creativity. Ephraim's <u>Commentary on Tatian's Diatessaron</u>[59] is especially important for our study. In my search for the source of the dramatic figure of Joseph of Arimathea, which was conspicuous in many sources in connection with the burial scene of Jesus and which later also occurs in the works of Amalarius of Metz, I came upon the following text by Ephraim:

Maria per Evam, et Joseph per Josephum
(celebratur). Nam et illi "petiit corpus
eius" (sc. Domini) Josephi nomen erat. Et
ille prior (tam) "iustus erat", ait, "ut, non
traduceret" Mariam, et alter adhuc iterum
"iustus erat", quia "non fuit consentaneus in
consiliis et in operibus eorum", cum detractoribus,
ut manifestum fieret (Dominum) nomini illi cui
confisus erat prius, cum nasceretur, concessisse
iterum ut involveret eum in morte hac sua, ut
acciperet hoc (nomen) mercedem perfectam,
quia fuerat servus (et) minister nativitatis
eius (sc. Domini), in specu illo, et corporis
eius in sepulcro hoc.[60]

Ephraim creates here imaginatively a counter-figure to Joseph of
Nazareth, the foster-father of Jesus, in order to unify birth,
death and life through two corresponding figures having the same
name and enacting them dramatically. While the theme of the
Annunciation to Mary by the Angel and with Joseph of Nazareth in
the background was often dramatically represented during the
synaxis in connection with the sermon, especially so in the
liturgy of Byzantium, the burial in the garden of and by Joseph
of Arimathea with its complex positional symbolism and
allegorical implications constituted a source for the imagination and was reshaped anew by constantly new visions and
variants from the offertory onwards throughout the final act of
the liturgical drama, the benediction. Thus, the figure of
Joseph of Arimathea became a connecting link between rebirth
through death on the Cross, and to life through the Resurrection. From this intricate dialectic relationship between
life-death, death-rebirth, the figure of Joseph of Arimathea received its special symbolic-allegorical significance and it soon
developed into a typus or topos.[61]

This burial scene with Joseph of Arimathea developed into a
more and more complicated topos of the entire Passion- and Re-
surrection-narrative and belonged in addition to positional
symbolism and the representations of the Last Supper to the
earliest renactment of liturgical drama which can be

demonstrated with the documentations which follow.

The Liturgy of Clement. As was mentioned earlier, the
Apostolic Constitutions (ca. 380 A.D.)[62] were of Syrian origin.
In the Liturgy of Clement of this compilation, the offertory
procession is by explicit directions clearly linked to the
Eucharist, whereby the Last Supper is made present by a
positional symbolism as follows:

> Let the deacons bring the gifts to the
> bishops at the altar, and let the Pres-
> byter stand on his right and his left, as
> disciplines assisting their master. Let
> two deacons on each side of the altar hold
> a fan of thin membrance or of peacock feath-
> ers or of linen and slowly drive away lit-
> tle insects flying around that they may
> not fall into the cups.[63]

In this configuration of the Last Supper, the celebrant personifies Christ and the priests standing beside him, represent the
apostles. The deacons hold fans made from linen or peacock
feathers. These fans seem to serve in this liturgy a rather
practical purpose, namely the chasing away of insects--although
it should be mentioned here that peacock symbolism was also
associated with early Christian baptistries.[63a]

In the Fragments of the Persian Anaphora, however, the
peacock fans represent the wings of angels and therefore
indicate a transcendental order:

> . . . and the bishops shall stand at
> the altar, and the deacons shall be
> around him and shall fan with fans and
> linen like the wings of the cherubim
> and the presbyter standing with him and
> so the whole clergy in their order.[64]

Here the fans carried by the deacons transform into wings of
cherubim which, in turn, simultaneously indicate the relation
between deacons and angels. The fans could also signify a

representation of the cherubims as they are presented at the Jewish altars[65] thus transposing a figure of the Jewish temple or synagogue to the Christian liturgical drama embedding it with new religious meaning. Attention should also be drawn to the manifestation of a double-layered positional symbolism of the Last Supper which in this Persian Anaphora implies already on the one hand a hierarchical order within the Church structure but which on the other also signifies in connection with the wings of angels a transcendental order.[66]

In a letter of Isidore of Pelusium (360–440 A.D.), Explicato ecclesiasticae initiationis, however, there is a specific description of the burial scene with a certain dramatic meaning of the linen cloth of the altar and the figure of Joseph of Arimathea in connection with that linen. Isidore gives the following vivid description:

> Pura illa sindon, quae sub divinorum donorum ministerio expansa est, Joseph Arima-thensis est ministerium. Ut enim ille Domini corpus sindone involutum sepultu-rae mandavit, per quod universum morta-lium genus resurrectionem percepit eodem modo nos propositionis panem in sindone sanctificantes, Christi corpus sine dubi-tatione reperimus, illam nobis immortali-tatem fontis in modum proferens, quam Sal-vator Jesus, a Josepho funere elatus, posteaquam a morte ad vitam rediit, lar-gitus est.[67]

From this description it follows that the white linen cloth --sindon--represented the shroud of Christ and that the figure of Joseph of Arimathea belonged to the special forms of representation which carry over to the Resurrection scene and receive from there their dramatic significance.

According to these three literary sources which describe the public custom of the liturgy in the fourth century, the following belong to the means of dramatic representation: the personification of Jesus and the apostles, positional symbolism

of the Last Supper implying also a hierarchical order, the fans
which represent the wings of the angels, and the white altar
linen (sindon) which symbolizes the burial linen of Christ.
With Theodore of Mopsuestia and Narsai the configurations of the
dramatic representations became more complex and dense in their
various layers with multiple meanings (Vielschichtigkeit).

Theodore of Mopsuestia (350-428 A.D.). This Syrian was an
influential and significant theologian of the time of the Church
Fathers. He was a close friend of John Chrysostom. His
abundant literary output was translated into Syriac by Quiore of
Edessa (ca. 437 A.D.). It became thereafter the standard text
of this educational center, replacing the works of Ephraim.[68]

In Theodor's Commentary about Baptism and Eucharist, the
liturgy expresses in all detail a drama and a "terrible
mystery". The function of the "church-crier", which is a figure
taken over from the theatre, is a particular feature of this
Syriac dramatic liturgy. This role is taken over by a deacon
who each time announces the specific acts, gestures and
positions. Theodore specifically states:

> . . . announced beforehand in the loud
> voice of the deacon, who, as we ought to
> know, explains the sign and the aim of
> all things that take place. The cere-
> monies that are to be performed by all
> those present are made known by the pro-
> clamation of the deacon, who orders and
> reminds every one of the statutory acts
> that are to be performed and accomplished
> by those who are assembled in the Church
> of God.[69]

This situation especially includes the Christian community in
its active role in the liturgical drama. At the same time, the
objective configuration of the liturgy is emphasized and
includes the Christian community. Although in the liturgy of
Eastern Syria, the constellation of the Last Supper is displaced
by the positional symbolism of the tomb and burial, the sacrifice stands at the center of the liturgy of Theodore; it has for

him the meaning of a public sacrifice. This meaning is
elaborated by the "church-crier":

> . . . while the church crier, that is to
> say, the deacon, whose voice is a clear
> indication of what the congregation has to
> do while following the priestly signs . . .
> first shouts: "Look at the oblation."
> In this he exhorts every one to look at
> the sacrifice, as if a public service
> was about to be performed and a public
> sacrifice was about to be immolated, and
> a public sacrifice was about to be offered
> for all, . . .[70]

Whether this counterpart of a public sacrifice refers to a
Syrian custom or to a rite of a Roman Emperor or cult of the
gods must be examined in a further study.

The celebrant is introduced as the figure of Christ in whom
are concealed the essential elements of the history of
salvation:

> Because Christ our Lord offered Himself
> in sacrifice for us and thus became our
> high priest in reality, we must think that
> the priest who draws nigh unto the altar
> is representing His image, not that he
> offers himself in sacrifice, any more than
> he is truly a high priest, but because
> he performs the figure of the service of
> the ineffable sacrifice (of Christ) and
> through this figure he dimly represents
> the image of the unspeakable heavenly
> things and of the supernatural and in-
> corporeal hosts.[71]

It is most interesting to observe here that the hierarchical
transcendental order of the world of angels is only suggested
but that instead a description and representation of angels as
biblical figures, mingled with daily existence, is coming more

to the fore. Theodore's extensive elaboration of the angels is
instructive for a better understanding of these liturgical
dramatic figures. He says:

> Indeed, all the visible hosts did service
> to the Economy which trancends our words
> and which Christ our Lord accomplished
> for us. . . Incidents in the Gospel show
> also events that happended through them,
> whether it be through those who at the
> birth of our Lord sang. . . or to those
> who at His resurrection revealed to women
> what had occurred or through those who at
> His ascension explained to the Apostles
> that which they did not know.[72]

The angels become a special link to the Birth and Resurrection
of Christ and since they share the free service in Christ with
the deacons, the angels are represented by the deacons:

> It is necessary, therefore, that here
> also, when this awe-inspiring service
> is performed, we should think that the
> deacons represent an image of the service
> of these invisible spirits . . . This name,
> however, is especially applied to those
> who perform this ministry, and are called
> by all "deacons" as they are alone appoin-
> ted to perform this ministry and represent
> a likeness of the service of the spiritual
> messengers and ministers.[73]

To the special symbolic representation of service in freedom as
opposed to service in slavery belong the vestments of the
deacons, which seem to correspond to a local domestic attire,
and which is furnished with a free-moving stole. This most
informative description is as follows:

> They have also an apparel which is con-
> sonant with their office, since their
> outer garment is taller than they are,

72

as wearing such an apparel in such a way
is suitable to those who serve. They
place on their left shoulder a stole,
which floats equally on either side, for-
wards and backwards. This is a sign that
they are not performing a ministry of
servitude but of freedom, as they are
ministering unto things that lead to freedom. . .[74]

From the above description it can be inferred that the exact
placement of the stole is as important as the vestment itself
because it is differentiated from the garment of a slave as well
as from that of an earthly freeman. Theodore describes the
stole as follows:

They do not place the stole on their neck,
in a way that it floats on either side but
not in front, because there is one serving
in a house who wears such an apparel; it
is only those who are masters of themselves and remote from servitude of any kind
wear it in this way, but the deacons place
it on their shoulders because they are
appointed for service. The stole is their
only sign of that freedom to which all of
us, who believe in Christ, have been called.[75]

The exact placement of the stole, which provides for free
motion, is essential for the symbolic significance and is an
example of the subtle nuances which characterize the allegorical liturgical drama.

The offertory procession becomes, with Theodore, a representation of the handing-over of Jesus whereby the role of the
community is changed to that of the passive spectator:

It is the deacons who bring out this
oblation--or the symbols of this ob-
lation--which they arrange and place
on the awe-inspiring altar (an obla-

tion) which in its vision, as represented in the imagination, is an awe-
inspiring event to onlookers.[76]

Hereafter follows the representation of the Passion through
movements, symbolic gestures and positional symbolism. Now the
following configuration emerges before our eyes:

> We must think of Christ being at
> one time led and brought to His Passion,
> and at another time stretched on the al-
> tar to be sacrificed for us. And when the
> offering which is about to be placed (on
> the altar) is brought out in the sacred
> vessels of the paten and the chalice,
> we must think that Christ our Lord is
> being led and brought to His Passion,
> not, however, by the Jews--as it is
> incongruous and impermissible that an
> iniquitous image to be found in the sym-
> bols of our deliverance and our salva-
> tion--but by the invisible hosts of
> ministry, who are sent to us and who were
> present when the Passion of our Salvation
> was being accomplished, and were doing
> their service.[77]

Through the representations of the offertory gifts, through a
few gestures and movements, the entire passion comes figuratively into being. Christ is being led to his sacrifice and
is as if stretched out on the cross. At this point, Theodore of
Mopsuestia makes a significant statement which is essential for
the understanding of Christian drama and Christian art as well,
namely, that an image may only be represented through that which
it resembles. An example of this is the personification of
angels by the deacon whereas the Jews are, as it were, made
present through their absence.[78] Thus, we notice that the
presence of the angels, who consoled and strengthened Christ in
His Agony and Passion, become, in imagination and representation, more and more intensified around the altar. In
particular Theodore elaborates the support of the angels during

74

the Passion by comparing their sustenance with persons who encourage the athletes.[79] Then, by recourse to the offertory, by means of a turn, a gesture, a change in position, the altar becomes transformed and assumes the configuration of the burial site of Christ.[80] Corporal, fans, and the position of deacons indicate thereby the tomb of Christ with the corpse of Christ which is signified especially by the following passage:

> This is the reason why those deacons who
> spread linens on the altar represent the
> figure of linen clothes of the burial (of
> our Lord). Sometime after these have been
> spread, they stand up on both sides, and
> agitate all the air above the holy body
> with fans, thus keeping it from any de-
> filing object.[81]

Although the altar linens retain the meaning of the shroud of Christ, the figures of Joseph of Arimathea and Nicodemus are completely absent here. The fans appear again in their practical although dramatic significance. The air is being fanned in order to protect the body of Christ from soiling particles. Thus, by way of the connection with local burial rites the tomb of Christ is being projected into the local vicinity. The following description gives an impression of local burial customs:

> They make manifest by this ritual the
> greatness of the body which is lying
> there, as it is the habit, when the
> dead body of the high personages of
> this world is carried on a bier, that
> some men should fan the air above it.
> It is, therefore, with justice that the
> same thing is done here with the body
> which will very shortly rise to an
> immortal nature.[82]

Most obviously, Christ becomes here identified with a local and worldly personage. By way of complicated and subtle gestures and positional symbolism, as well as elaborate depiction of the local rites of "lying-in-state", the following image of the dead Christ, "lying-in-state" emerges:

> It is on all sides of this body that
> persons, who are especially appointed
> to serve, stand up and fan. They offer
> to it an honour that is suitable, and
> by this ritual they make manifest to
> those present the greatness of the sa-
> cred body that is lying there. It is
> indeed clear to us from the Divine Book
> that angels sat upon the stone near the
> sepulchre and announced His resurrection
> to the women, and remained there all the
> time of His death, in honour of the One
> who was laid there, till they witnessed
> the resurrection, which was proclaimed
> by them to be good to all mankind, and
> to imply a renewal of all the creation
> . . . Was it not right, therefore, that
> here also (the deacons) should repre-
> sent as in an image the ministry of the
> angels? It is in remembrance of those
> who constantly came to the Passion and
> death by our Lord, that they also stand
> in a circle and agitate the air with fans,
> and offer honour and adoration to the
> sacred and awe-inspiring body which is
> lying there. In this they make manifest
> to all those present the object that is
> lying there, and induce all the onlookers
> to think of it as awe-inspiring and truly
> sacred, and to realize that it is for this
> reason that they kept it from all defiling
> things, and do not even allow the dirty
> tricklings of birds to fall upon it and
> come near it. This they do now according
> to their habit in order to show that

76

because the body which is lying there
is high, awe-inspiring, holy and truly
Lord through its union with the Divine
nature, it is with great fear that it
must be handled, seen and kept.[83]

Most conspicuous in this configuration is the double role
of the deacons, which seems to refer to certain local guardians
of a death-watch. Subsequently, this scene of a death-watch
becomes transposed into the historical burial scene of Jerusalem, and the role of the deacons changes over into that of the
angels at the tomb whereby the historical scene again takes on
local dimensions. This constant intersection through subtle
gestures, movements and positional symbolism which characterize
the extensive mobility and subtlety of liturgical drama seems to
interweave here a local death cult with the Resurrection of
Christ. After the depiction of this burial scene, fear and
silence of the present, terrible mysterium overlap with fear and
the silence of the tomb of Jerusalem whereby the role of the
congregation as spectators blends now with that of the
frightened apostles and the silence of the angels:

. . . When our Lord also had died the
Apostles moved away and were in the house
in great silence and immense fear; so
great indeed was the silence that over-
took everyone that even the invisible
hosts kept quiet while looking for the
expected resurrection, until the time
came and Christ our Lord rose, and a
great joy and an ineffable happiness
spread over those invisible hosts.[84]

At the end, movement and silence mix in a strange paradox
which refers, on the one hand, to the walking of the women and
to the running of the apostles to the tomb of Jesus in Jerusalem, and on the other hand, to the mystical silence of the
actual mystery present:

And the women who came to honour the
body received from the angels the new

77

message of the resurrection that had
taken place, and when the disciples
also learnt through them what had occurred they run together with great
zeal to the sepulchre. We are drawn
now by similar happenings to the remem-
brance of the Passion of our Lord, and
when we see the oblation on the communion
table--something which denotes that
it is being placed in a kind of sepulchre after its death--great silence
falls on those present . . . We remember . . . the death of our Lord in the
oblation because it makes manifest the
resurrection . . . [85]

Theologically speaking, the consecration becomes for Theodore
the actualization of the Resurrection.[86] Silence and fear seem
to introduce the act of communion and seem to remain the
inherent characteristics of the Resurrection.

The representation of the Passion and burial through
subtle, allegorical movements and gestures, interwoven with
local customs of burial rites, personfication of angels by the
deacons, characterize this liturgical drama of Eastern Syria.
The theory of Christian representational art, that an image
should only be represented by an equivalent image, is elaborated
in detail by Theodore in the representation of the angels by the
deacons whose garments were given complex symbolic-allegorical
significance. On the other hand, this theory is also exemplified by the absence of the Jews. Whereas the positional
symbolism of the Last Supper is absent, the sacrifice of Christ
in connection with local public sacrifices is placed into the
foreground. The altar stands at the center, where, interwoven
with local customs and mystical silence, the Crucifixion and
burial of Christ are actualized by means of complex allegorical
configurations and gestures. The expectation of the Resurrection finds expression through silence blended with fear and
the silence of the tomb of Jerusalem. The figure of Joseph of
Arimathea is completely missing probably in favour of the
influence of local customs.

Personification, gestures, movements, the altar, the linen (sindon), the fans, positional symbolism, change of place and role, as well as silence belong to the liturgical means of representation of Theodore of Mopsuestia. While with Theodore the concrete local vicinity plays a significant role, with Narsai the liturgical drama gives the impression of a spiritual transformed landscape of the Resurrection which again concentrates around the altar.

Narsai (399-502) A.D.) was a doctor of the Church and director of the School of Edessa and later, after the culmination of the Nestorian controversy, was directing the educational center of Nisibis. Narsai was an extremely gifted poet and writer, so that his contemporaries called him the "harp of the Holy Spirit".[87] The greater part of his writings belongs to didactic poems which have been combined into collections of memra. His creative work, however, also belonged to cult and history. The sources of his imaginative power were the Biblical traditions from which he combined the different themes of the gospel.[88] His writings are very instructive for our study because here the formation of dramatic liturgy can be grasped in a state of near-perfection. Furthermore, with Narsai particularly the tension among theatres--i.e, the "daemonic" theatre of the pagan culture and the theatre of the world of the new creation of the Christian Church--becomes very tangible. In his sermon about baptism these two world views are given expression in vivid metaphorical language. He says:

> The Evil One he renounces as an evil one,
> and his angles as haters of the word of
> truth. The Evil One and his adherents
> hate the word of truth . . .[89]

Then the daemonic gathering is contrasted with a heavenly assembly:

> The assemblies of the height he makes
> to rejoice by the words of his faith. . .[90]

In Narsai's sermons about the mysteries of the Church and
baptism, Christ is represented as the new artist who is creating
a new world:

> Cunningly He mixed the colours for the
> renewal of our race, with oil and water
> and the invincible power of the Spirit,
> a new art the Chief Artist put forth;
> . . . It is altogether a new thing, and
> great is the lesson given therein.[91]

When the neophyte has in baptism renounced the visible and
tangible works of Satan, he is expected by a world which has
been unlocked for him in baptism. In his sermon about the
priesthood, the church, as a temple, becomes a counter image of
the heavenly kingdom in the world of a new creation; but it also
becomes a counter image of the diabolic theatre:

> A holy temple the Creator built for them on
> earth that in it they might offer the wor-
> ship of love spiritually . . . He fash-
> ioned a sanctuary on earth and holy of
> holies in the heavens above . . . two . . .
> institutions he made in His incomprehen-
> sible wisdom; and He filled them with
> temporal and everlasting riches.[92]

The shaping of this new world of creation unfolds for us in
Narsai's Exposition about the Mysteries in constantly becoming
and ever more subtle forms. He begins his description with the
offertory procession, which, as it did with Theodore of
Mopsuestia, represents the handing-over and passion of Jesus.
Here, too, the handing-over is enacted by deacons who represent the angels, and not by the Jews:

> In that hour let us put away from us anger
> and hatred, and let us see Jesus who is
> being led to death on our account. On the
> paten . . . and in the cup He goes forth
> with the deacon to suffer. The bread
> on the paten and the wine in the cup

are a symbol of His death. A symbol
of His death these (the deacons) bear
upon their hands; and when they have
set it on the altar and covered it they
typify His burial; not that these
(the deacons) bear the image of the
Jews, but (rather) of the watchers
(i.e., the angels) who were ministering
the passion of the Son. He was minis-
tered by the angels at the time of
His passion, and the deacons attend
His body which is suffering mystically.[93]

In this representation of Narsai a mystical deepening dominates
the liturgical drama in contrast to an almost tangible corporality which was evident in the offertory procession of Theodore
representing the handing over of Jesus.[94] Here too the Passion
is introduced in which the angels are personfied by the deacons
and the Jews are indicated by their absence but here, as the
Passion is introduced, the altar begins to take on the contours
of the tomb. Narsai begins to describe the imagery and representational forms of a new configuration, pregnant with rich
metaphors and symbols which grow into the representation of a
whole new vision the image of which appears as if intricately
interwoven of passion and glory. The world of this text is
unfolding thus:

The priests now come in procession into
the midst of the sanctuary and stand
there in great splendour. . . The priest
who is selected to be celebrating the
sacrifice, bears in himself the image
of the Lord. . . All the priests who
are in the sanctuary bear the image of
those apostles who met together at the
sepulchre. The altar is the symbol of
our Lord's tomb, without doubt: and the
bread and wine are the body of our Lord
which was embalmed and buried. The
veil also which is over them . . .
presents a type of stone sealed with the

ring of the priests and executioners . . .
And the deacons standing on this side
and that and brandishing (fans) are a
symbol of the angels at the head and at
the feet thereof . . . And all the deacons who stand ministering before the
altar depict a likeness of the angels
that surrounded the tomb of our Lord.
The sanctuary also forms a symbol of the
Garden of Joseph, whence flowed life for
men and angels. In another order it is
the type of that Kingdom which our Lord
entered, and into which He will bring
with Him all His friends. The adorable
altar thereof is a symbol of that throne
of the Great and Glorious, upon which He
will be seen by watchers and men on the
day of His revelation. The apse . . .
typifies things below and above; it calls
to mind the things that have been and
those that are to be it typifies spiri-
tually.[95]

This complex, dense and fascinating image with various layers of
multiple meanings emerges through the allegorical significance
of the sanctuary: it is transformed from the tomb of Jesus to
the Garden of Joseph of Arimathea which, at the same time, is
symbolizing the Garden of Eden in Paradise and which then
simultaneously is representing the kingdom of those eternal
heights where Christ is now abiding upon the throne of glory.
The deacons personify the angels, the fans having here purely
spiritual-symbolic significance. With the apses which signify
the division of the visible and invisible world image, a further
allegorization of the inside of the church emerges.

Before the trisagon takes place, there is, as it were, an
actualization of mystical silence, which includes the whole
church and which represents the radiating altar in an almost
anthropomorphisized configuration of kingly majesty and dignity.
This description is as follows:

82

All the ecclesiastical body now observes
silence, and all set themselves to pray
earnestly in their hearts. The priests
are still and the deacons stand in silence, the whole people is quiet and still,
subdued and calm. The altar stands
crowned with beauty and splendour, and
upon it is the Gospel of life and the
adorable wood . . . (sc. the cross). The
mysteries are set in order, the censers
are smoking, the lamps are shinning, and
the deacons are hovering and brandishing
(fans) in likeness of watchers. Deep
silence and peaceful calm settles on
that place: it is filled and overflowed
with brightness and splendour, beauty
and power.[96]

In this paradisical image which emerges out of the Garden of
Joseph, there is the presentation of the mystic-invisible realm
which was initiated by the passion the presentation of which
began at the offertory.

At the end, the majesty of the Risen Lord is drawn together
and objectified, as it were, in a solemn procession which moves
onward into the Church nave for the distribution of communion
and which is depicted as follows:

The Sacrament goes forth on the paten . . .
and in the cup with splendour and glory,
with an escort of priests and a great
procession of deacons. Thousands of
watchers and ministers of fire and spirits go forth before the Body of our Lord
and conduct it. All the sons of the
Church rejoice, and all the people, when
they see the Body setting forth from
the midst of the altar; and even as the
apostles rejoiced in our Lord after His
resurrection, so do all the faithful
rejoice when they see Him.[97]

83

Here a counter image emerges to the triumphal procession of the Emperor in which a multitude of heavenly hosts (ministers of fire and spirits) will overcome satan and his angels.

With Narsai the realities of the Passion and Resurrection have become a fused aesthetic representation which includes the subjective experience of the participants because they themselves belong to the objective representation of the entire "representational image". The themes which begin to unfold here represent the spiritualized triumph and splendor of the Risen Lord in the eternal heights above as well as in the Church below awaiting the Christian who has renounced at baptism the pomp and handiwork of the daemonic cult.

While the offertory with the handing-over of Jesus points to Theodore of Mopsuestia and the imagery of the burial scene with the Garden of Joseph indicate the influence of Tatian's Diatessaron and Ephraim's Commentary, the allegorical significance of the apses seems perhaps to be connected with the Neo-Platonic world view of Pseudo-Dionysius whose work originated at about the same time.

Pseudo-Dionysius the Aeropagite (ca. 500 A.D.)[98] projected in his work on the Heavenly and Ecclesiastical Hierarchies the structure of the hierarchical cosmos based on his symbolic-rational-mystical theology. Dionysius, whose writings were of long-lasting influence, based the two hierarchies on the spiritual-corporal nature of man, on the basis of which the ecclesiastical hierarchies would be formed according to the same basic laws as those of the heavens. This view, therefore, fits as it were, into the Weltanschauung of the dialetics of the two theatres which we discussed earlier.

About a hundred years later, the Byzantine Maximos Confessor, combined the method of the allegorical exegesis of the Alexandrian School with the negative theology of Pseudo-Dionysius and transferred it to the interpretation of the liturgy. This could, of course, indicate that the liturgy because of its complex and dense structures with figurative

84

representations, had itself become in need of interpretation.

The Byzantine Liturgy.

Constantinople and Ravenna[99] with their majestic basilicas developed into ecclesiastical-political centers where the liturgies of Jacob-Basileios-Chrysostom were the basis of this complicated Byzantine worship which in turn was based on imperial theology.[100] Their representations were in accordance with the imagination of a universal dominion under Christ, their allegorical-mystical imagery and figurativeness, however, particularly in relation to the Resurrection, seem to have been nourished by Syria. For the examination of this liturgy, four texts have been selected because they are very instructive regarding structure and representations, as well as about the Resurrection theme with the figures of Joseph of Arimathea and Nicodemus.

Gregory of Nazianzen (325-390 A.D.) is one of the great Cappadocians and later Patriarch of Constantinople. He presumably is the author of the work Christos Paschon, a drama in the form of Euripides, consisting of 1640 iambic verses.[101] According to structure and theme, this interesting work corresponds to a solid liturgical scheme. Such an analogous structure, however, shows not only the relationship of the liturgy to drama but reveals the dramatic structure of the liturgy.[102] At the center of this drama stand Mary, the mother of Jesus, in all her sorrow and who, in one scene is even contemplating suicide, the choir (or chorus), the dying Jesus and John the theologian. The other key figures, which are of interest to us here, are Joseph of Arimathea and Nicodemus who concern themselves for over 680 verse lines with the deposition from the cross.[103] The drama closes with several Resurrection scenes, which, according to Scripture, correspond to the appearances of Christ. This drama interests us particularly because of its fully developed scenes with the dramatic figures of Joseph of Arimathea and Nicodemus. These scenes and figures appeared first in the very earliest manifestations and compositions of the Syriac liturgy[104] and also play a key role in the other Byzantine texts which we have studied. But most important, they appear later also in the work of Amalarius of Metz.[105]

Maximos Confessor (580-662 A.D.). This Byzantine doctor of
the Church combined the method of allegorical exegesis with the
negative theology of Pseudo-Dionysius and applied it systematically to the liturgy.[106] His interpretation of Scripture and
liturgy is essentially anagogical. According to his theory,
Scripture refers to the word, whereas nature and liturgy express
the works of God. According to this, the other signs of creation
and liturgy become, as the letter of Scripture, the corporal
veil with a hidden meaning. For Maximos, the Church becomes a
typus, eikon, and eidei schemati of the word and works of God.[107]
Ecclesia Dei typus continentis omnia is his over-all
definition of the Church. Only the anagogical sense of
Scripture is able to penetrate into this hidden spiritual
meaning of the archetypus, figures, images and schemata.
Maximos gives the following description of Church and liturgy:

> Rursusque solius mundi qui in sensum
> cadit secundum se, ac seorsim spectati,
> symbolum esse aiebat sanctam Dei Eccle-
> siam, ut quae coelum quidem, divinum
> sacrarium; terram autem, templi decorem
> obtineat. Similiter autem etiam mundum
> esse Ecclesiam, qui coelum quidem, sacra-
> rio simile, terrae autem ornatum, templo
> affinem habeat.[108]

In his work, Quaestiones ad Thalassium, Maximos deals especially
with the hermeneutical questions of Scripture and cultic representations. He concentrates mainly on the anagogical sense:

> . . . corporale scilicet legis cultum in
> umbris ac figuris constitutum, secundum
> instabilem ac viaticam, velut in via po-
> sitam, traditionem, ac quas transeuntibus
> figuris caeremoniisque dedita esset . . .
> Deo potibus animi affectum exhibentes,
> quam hominibus exteriori cultu similacro
> constantem morum speciem.[109]

This manner of interpretation which refers to the liturgy, may

have emerged from a cosmic vision. However, it seems to pre-
suppose a liturgy which is in need of interpretation and which
seems to have its allegorical-poetic source in Syria.

Maximos deals intensively with the structural scheme of the
liturgy but not, however, with individual dramatic figures.
Through the constellation of the _introit_ he is casting the
entire cosmic background as follows:

> Primum igitur pontificis in ecclesiam
> introitum, cum sancta synaxis celebran-
> da sit, primi ejus adventus, quo Filius
> Dei ac Salvator noster Christus per car-
> nem in mundum istum intravit, typum prae-
> ferre docebat ac imaginem . . . A quo
> deinceps adventu, ejus in coelus ac super-
> coelestem thronum ascensus postliminoque
> restitutio, per ingressum pontificis in
> sacrarium, ac quo sedem sacerdotalem in-
> scendit, symbolic figuratur.[110]

The entrance of the pontiff is the representation of the
Incarnation of Christ at His entrance into the world. Through
this, the liturgical drama receives cosmic dimensions and
becomes spatially related. The entrance of the faithful congregation into the basilica signifies the turning away from the
world of sin and error. The kiss of peace, the _pax_ before the
gospel, symbolizes the turning away from the world of daemons
and movement towards union with the angels. Whereas in the
works of Maximos the manner of interpretation and a structural
scheme of the dramatic liturgy are predominant, in the texts
which are ascribed to the Patriarchs Sophronios of Jerusalem and
Germanos of Constantinople, the dramatic-allegorical
significance of the sanctuary, of the liturgical objects and
vestments, and of the dramatic-liturgical figures, are most
conspicuous.

Sophronios, Patriarch of Jerusalem (560-638 A.D.) was a
contemporary of Maximos, and the _Commentarius Liturgicus_ attributed to him elucidates the _Jacobian-Basileios-Chrysostomus-
Liturgies_.[111] The most obvious point about this commentary is

the allegorical-dramatic significance of the historical places
of the life of Jesus which around this time had been transformed
and transposed into the basilicas and liturgies. The complex
and subtle relations of the Incarnation, Passion and Resurrection themes are allegorically implied in an internally
moving, multi-layered configuration of objects and figures. The
inner structure of the church with all its details, particularly
that of the sanctuary, is assigned a historical meaning which
refers to Jerusalem and Bethlehem as well as to the allegorical-
symbolic significance of the heavenly Jerusalem. This spatial
relationship with the irruption of the timeless seems to be an
essential mark of the Byzantine liturgy. Of the allegorical
objects, the concha signifies the stable and manger of
Bethlehem, a synthronus, the seat of God the Father and Son, the
sancta prothesis symbolizes Calvary, the altar the tomb of
Christ and the myax the vault of the firmament.[112] While on the
one hand the altar primarily represents the tomb, and the linen
cloth of the altar the burial shroud of Jesus, the ambo on the
other signifies the rolled-away stone from which the angel
proclaimed the message of Easter. The steps of the ambo receive
a mystical significance because they represent the ladder of
Jacob--gradus autem ambonis scalem Jacobi commemorant.[113] These
steps also represent the relationship between the visible and
invisible worlds as well as the Old and New Testaments. The
hierarchical order is represented through personification and
positional symbolism whereby the pontifex represents Christ, the
ruler, who is enthroned above all angelic powers. The priests
are assigned the place of the chorus, the cherubim and seraphim,
while the deacons personify those angelic powers which are ready
to serve Christ. The figures of Joseph of Arimathea and
Nicodemus appear again in connection with the burial and the
sindon.[114]

Germanos, Patriarch of Constantinople (635-737). In the
text of Historia ecclesiastica et Mystica Contemplatio[115] which
has been attributed to Germanos, we have a clear dramatic structure before us the significance of which is the intersecting of
various levels with multiple meaning. At the center is the
altar which in itself implies such multi-layeredness which, in
the course of the liturgical drama, begins to unfold. Germanos
states this explicitly:

88

Conchae autem altaris, translatio est
crucis, turres vero, signa: idcirco
utraque rationabiliter ponantur in facie
sacrificantium. Sancta mensa est vice
loci sepultarae, in quo positus est
Christus, in qua proponitur versus et
coelestis panis, quod est mysticum et
incruentum sacrificium... Est quoque
ipsa Dei sedes, in quo supercoelestis
Deus qui super Cherubim vehitur . . .in
qua mensa ut etiam in mystica illa sua
caena, in medio apostolorum suorum sedens
et accipiens panem et vinum, dicit suis
discipulis et apostolis: "Accipite,
manducate, et bibite . . ."[116]

The concha, the symbol of the manger, is at first related to the
Cross, whereby the altar itself receives the meaning of
sacrifice and birth. Then, almost immediately, the meaning of
the sacrifice becomes transposed into the figurative image of
the tomb, whereby simultaneously the image of the throne of the
Most High arises and again, with a movement backward into time
and forward into the present, the altar becomes the table of the
Last Supper where the words of the First Liturgical Act were
spoken and are again pronounced. Thus, through the altar, the
anagogical sense receives corporal significance, which becomes
extended through further objects and personification. The ambo
is, as the symbolic tombstone and place of proclamation,
directly connected with the altar, and thus, the meaning of the
word: ambo, and act: altar becomes intricately interwoven as a
representational entity. The ambo is further interpreted as a
connective link between sanctuary and the nave of the church,
that is to say, between fallen mankind and Christ. This can be
demonstrated from the following text:

Cancelli, locum orationis designant,
quousque extrinsecus populus accedit,
intrinsecus autem sunt Sancta sanctorum,
solis sacerdotibus pervia . . . Ambo
figuram lapidis sancti monumenti designat:

quem angelus cum evolvisset ex ostio monumenti, proclamabat resurrectionem Domini unguentiferis mulieribus.[117]

Here again the spatial concept present in the church structure
is most conspicuous. Whereas the Passion is more or less
circumscribed with reference to Calvary, the burial scene in the
Garden of Joseph receives on the other hand much greater and
more detailed description and a dense meaning. He continues as
follows:

Armarium, ubi praesentatio perficitur,
pro Calvariae loco est. Corporale sign-
nificat sindonem in qua involutum est
Christi corpus cum e cruce descensum est,
et in monumentu collocatum. Et superius
disci velamen, indicat sindonem qua in-
volverunt corpus Domini. Disci velamen-
tum est pro sudario quod erat super facie,
circumtegens illam in sepulchro. Velum
sive aer, est et dicitur esse vice lapidis,
quo munivit Joseph monumentum, quod ob-
signavit tabella custodiae.[118]

The sindon receives its earlier allegorical-dramatic
significance of the shroud of Jesus; this was particularly the
case also in the Syriac liturgy. It refers here not only to the
burial but also to the deposition from the Cross where both
Joseph of Arimathea and Nicodemus seem to receive growing significance. The discus (patena) seems, in this way, to have new
importance. Germanos states as follows:

Discus lectia est in qua corpus Domini
componitur a sacerdote et diacono, qui
sunt Joseph et Nicodemus . . . .
. . . .
Discus est vice manum Joseph et Nicodemi,
qui funus Christo celebrarunt. Discus est
autem, ubi Christus infertur. . .[119]

Germanos describes then once more the scene of the burial in connection with the altar:

> Est autem sancta mensa ad imitationem
> sepulturae Christi, qua Joseph sublato
> corpore de cruce, involvit sindone munda,
> et aromatibus et unguentis ipsum unctum
> exportavit cum Nicodemo. et sepelivit ip-
> sum in monumento novo exciso ex petra:
> quod est exemplum sancti monumenti illius,
> altare et catathesium, in quo positum est
> sanctum . . . corpus quae est sancta
> mensa.[120]

The Garden of Joseph is not mentioned here, but the sanctuary
with its allegorized tombstone in the form of an ambo and with
its spatial dimensions seems to include the topos of the Garden.

The offertory procession, also called the Great Entry, when
the gifts are brought to the altar, represents the entry of
Jesus into Jerusalem but in relation to the Cherubicon it
receives immediately anagogical meaning:

> Sacrorum translatio a prothesi, corporis
> . . . Dominici et sanguinis et eorum in-
> gressus ad altare, et Cherubicum a Betha-
> nia in Jerusalem Domini introitum signi-
> ficat. Tunc enim plurima turba et Hebrae-
> orum pueri tanquam regi et victori mortis
> hymnum referebant sensibiliter: spiritua-
> liter autem angeli cum Cherubim, ter sanc-
> tum reddiderunt hymnum ac sceptra ac
> rhomphaes at insignia regis proferunt
> diaconi.[121]

Thus, the hierarchical orders of the corporeal and spiritual
world find expression in the two orders of songs as well as in
the regal insignia which are carried by the deacons.[122]

The spatial interrelationships of the corporeal and
spiritual worlds find full expression in the dramatic liturgy of
Germanos and make for an extraordinary complexity of the dra-

matic-symbolic-allegorical configurations. This interrelationship is also expressed in the external architectural
structure and the allegorical-symbolic potential of the interior
structure of the church; this interaction of external and
internal structure of the church is further intensified by the
interrelationships of the manifold significations of objects,
figures and gestures. In the liturgy of Germanos, the songs
also express a certain representational dramatic meaning and
form, particularly during the offertory, indicating two hierarchical orders. The configurations of the deposition from the
Cross and the burial scene with Joseph of Arimathea and
Nicodemus become more complex, and the gestures of the celebrant
and the deacons thus attain highly dramatic significance. The
patena also assumes symbolic-dramatic function.

Summary

The examination of a cross-section of liturgical texts of
the Eastern Church has led to an abundance of dramatic evidence
which has grown out of the first liturgical act of the Last
Supper around which the plot of the Life-Passion and Resurrection of Christ was grouped. Structurally this plot is
enacted in synaxis and offertory, each one corresponding accordingly to the Mass of the catechumens and the celebration of the
Eucharist. For Jerusalem the Catecheses of Cyril of Jerusalem
as well as the peregrinatio of Aetheria are proof of dramatic
historical forms of representation at the place of the historical occurrence, particularly during Holy Week and the week following Easter. The sermons of Chrysostom indicated that in
Antioch the theatre manners were transposed into the Church
which points to a relationship in the representational form of
the "pagan-diabolic" theatre and the Christian "theatrum non
fictitium", as Chrysostom called it. Tatian's Diatessaron forms
the basis of the Syriac pericope-system which, within itself,
particularly in connection with baptism, makes room for movement
and imagination. In Ephraim's Commentary, Joseph of Arimathea
becomes a poetic dramatic counter-figure of Joseph of Nazareth,
the foster-father of Jesus, closely interrelated with the burial
scene which represents the transition from death to life and
which develops henceforth into a topos. With the liturgy of
Clement of the Apostolic Constitution, the Last Supper is

represented by positional symbolism while in the Persian Anaphora, the fans, which are held by the deacons, indicate a spiritual order. With Isidore of Pelusium, the figure of Joseph of Arimathea in connection with the shroud (sindon) of Jesus seems to have assumed a stable dramatic significance of the liturgy. With Theodore of Mopsuestia the story of the Passion and Resurrection becomes increasingly dramatized and enacted by way of subtle gestures, manifold positional symbolism and suggestive movements as well as the personification of the deacons representing the angels. In this liturgy, especially through the compression of time, change in location, and the incorporation and transformation of local cult customs, the spatial and temporal realms intersect and complex representational configurations emerge. The figures of the angels correspond with Theodore mainly to the Biblical story and do not, as is the case with the Byzantines, represent a hierarchical order. In Narsai's liturgy, a mystic-spiritual world of the Resurrection comes into being saturated with metaphors, symbols and allegorical meaning, triumphing over the world of daemons. Although locality and temporality are intersecting here, out of this representational form speaks a certain density and mystical silence, from which flow new images and visions. The liturgical drama lacks the spatial vastness and objectivity of the Byzantine liturgy which was already expressed in the universal vision of Basil, influenced by Alexandrian trends. The mystical trend of Byzantine liturgical drama is kept at a greater latitude with eschatological dimensions, the representations of which are more interrelated among themselves whereby the intersections of space and time becomes more and more dense and multilayered.

The means by which the Biblical material is represented and which justify the Eastern liturgy as drama can be summarized as follows: personification, positional symbolism, subtle gestures, movements, songs, silence, sindon and linteum with Joseph of Arimathea and Nicodemus, fans, garments, explicit change in locality and condensation of time through implicit concurrent various layers with multiple meaning (Vielschichtigkeit): i.e., the altar represents Jerusalem, the room of the Last Supper, the Cross, the Tomb, the heavenly Jerusalem, the Garden of Paradise, and the Throne of the Most High and Eternal Judge. Spatial relationships of the spiritual and corporeal worlds are its special characteristic whereby on the one hand internal and spiritual processes take on external objective representational forms and on the other, the visible world leads to an invisible one by allegorical and symbolic processes. This intersecting process of the liturgical drama of the Eastern Church constitutes the basis for its internal dynamism. Structurally this Christian liturgical drama seems also to be related to the plays of Euripides. The primary basis, however, of this aesthetic liturgical drama is the plot of the Biblical narrative centering around and interwoven with the first liturgical act and the entire salvation history flowing from it and expressed in objective representational form.

The Liturgy of the West[123]

The manifestations of the Eastern liturgy in its many different literary genres and forms of expression could be grouped around individual centers. A large part of the Western liturgy also belonged to the radius of influence of the Eastern liturgy. This was especially true of the Gallican liturgy although it certainly had its own Western imprint. The following main- and sub-groups are classified by scholars as Western liturgies: The main Gallican group includes: 1. the Ambrosianic (Milan), 2. the Mozarabic, 3. the Celtic-Irish, and 4. the Gallican liturgies. It differs from the other main groups which are sub-divided into African and Roman liturgies, through its flexibility, its elaborateness and possibilities of expression.[124]

The Gallican Church:

The basic features of the Gallican main groups are long prayers, lyrical sonority, meditative fervour, representational dramatic forms, songs, a variety of feasts and an extensive complicated system of pericopes.

The Ambrosianic Liturgy of Milan: The more simple of the four sub-groups differs from the other forms mostly through its more simplified system of readings. The two works of Bishop Ambrose of Milan, De Sacramentis and De mysteriis, belong to the

94

explanatory literature of this liturgy.[125]   In contrast to the
other forms, this liturgy already stands in view of its geographical position, under the greater influence of Rome.   The
Mozarabic liturgy is, of the four variants, more closely related
to the Gallican liturgy; it is essentially intra-cultural.[126]
After the conversion of Ekkehard, King of the Visigoths, to the
Roman Church in 589 A.D., the existing liturgical books were
revised (599 A.D.)[127]   The Fourth Council of Toledo (633 A.D.)
brought about a further revision by Isidore of Séville.   This
trend towards a unity of the liturgical world view in a time of
great anarchy finds also expression with Pope Gregory the
Great[128] as well as with the Byzantine Maximos Confessor[129]   although the motivations for such unified view may
have differed in each case.   The Celtic-Irish liturgy[130] resembles the Old-Spanish as well as the Gallican liturgy.   It is
distinguished by its poetic forms of expression and by its
fervent prayers.   The Book of Cerne is an example of this
liturgy.[131]

    The Gallic Liturgy: A receptive flexibility which is able
to blend its own views with new forms of expression seems to be
the special characteristic of the Gallican liturgy.[132]   One of
the first written witnesses to the Gallican liturgy and the
interrelation between Gaul and Asia Minor are the letters of the
Martyrs of the Church of Lyons and Vienne from the year 177 A.D.
which were directed to the Christians in Asia and Phrygia during
the Christian persecution under Marcus Aurelius.[133]   Such an
interrelation between Gaul and Asia Minor can also be documented
from other sources.   For example, Hilary of Potiérs (315-365
A.D.) wrote his works De Trinitate and Liber Mysteriorum which
were most influential for the Church in the West, during his
exile in Phrygia.[134]   The peregrinatio of Aetheria indicates
parallels between the liturgies in Gaul and Jerusalem.[135]   A
further early document of this interchange is the Gallic Church
Order, Statuta ecclesia antiqua, the literary form of which has
its source in Syria.[136]   Monasticism was probably also of great
importance for this interchange of liturgical traditions.[137]

    The old Roman metropolis Arles was the leading episcopal
seat of the Gallican Church from where, especially under Bishop
Caesarius of Arles (470-543 A.D.), liturgical and ecclesiastical

reforms were initiated.[138] From the historiography of Gregory
of Tours (538-590 A.D.), an active participation of the congregation can be reconstructed.[139] The most valuable documentations of the Gallican liturgy are, of course, the texts
themselves. These texts consist of the Expositio Antiquae
Liturgicae Gallicanae (ca. 570 A.D.) which has been attributed
to Bishop Germanus of Paris,[140] the seven Monemasses,[141] and
the Lectionary of Luxeuil;[142] these are considered almost "pure"
Gallic texts. The Gothicum,[143] and Missale Gallicanum Vetus[144]
and the Missale Francorum might be described as mixtures. The
characteristic features of these three Gallic texts are as
follows: the dramatic shaping in Expositio,[146] the particularly
musical language of the Monemasses,[147] one of which is composed
in pure hexameters, and complex long interconnections of themes
of the Lectionary of Luxeuil, which is closely related to the
Diatessaron[148] and thus it might provide a close link to the
Syriac church.

Expositio Antiquae Liturgicae Gallicanae.[149] This small
work confirms the allegorical-dramatic structure of the Gallican
Mass and betrays a relationship with the liturgy of the East.
However, the eschatological vision brings into focus the Old
Convenant and the Eternal Judge adding thus a new dimension to
this liturgy. Furthermore, it seems to be determined from the
ethical side, that is to say, the moral sense of Sacred
Scripture is prevailing, leading to the performance of perfect
acts of charity. Configurations of the Last Judgement on the
one side and those of salvation history on the other already
determine the Introit:

> (Introitus) De praelegere: Antiphona ad
> praelegendum canitur in specie patriar-
> charum illorum qui, ante diluvium adven-
> tum Christi mysticis vocibus (in) tonu-
> erunt, sicut Enoch septimus ab Adam qui
> translatus est a deo, prophetavit dicens:
> "Ecce venit dominus in sanctis milibus
> suis facere iudicum" . . . Sicut enim
> prophetantibus (patriarchis) venit manus
> domini super arcam, ut indemnatis daret
> reliquias terrae, ita psallentibus cleri-

cis procedit sacerdos inspecie Christi
de sacrario tamquam de coelo in arca domini, quae est ecclesia, et tam monendo
quam exhortendo nutriat in plebe bona
opera et extinguat mala.[150]

Together with the _Introit_ a spatial-cosmic setting for the
liturgical drama emerges. The clerics, representing the invisible church, come in procession out of the sacristy and
personify the patriarchs of the sintflut era, the celebrant is
representing Christ as coming down from heaven, whereas the
church building in its shape and figure symbolizes the arch of
Noah. But with this allegorical-typological representation, the
tropological sense of the liturgy, reminding the Christian
community of the performance of good works, is right at the
beginning, interwoven with this configuration. A further conspicuous phenomenon of this liturgy is a triumphal song which is
interwoven with the whole dramatic configuration, and which on
the one hand could have had a precursor in the Byzantine liturgy
but on the other could easily reflect an essentially indigenous
development among the Gauls and Franks.

The tripartite readings are extremely ceremonial, spatially
oriented and dramatically structured as well as surrounded by
great ritual splendour. The readings are preceded by a silent
recollection which is announced by a deacon.[151] Following this,
the readings are introduced by an _Aius-song_ which corresponds to
a _sanctus_ and this then is followed by a song of the _kyrie-
eleison_, sung by the three boys. With these two layers of songs
--_sanctus_ and _kyrie_--the condition of sinful mankind
and the majesty of God are expressed. The three boys each
personify the three holy languages and the three ages of the
world as is stated below:

> De aius: . . .Tres autem parvuli, qui ore
> uno sequuntur Kyrie eleison (item in specie
> illarum trium linguarum) hebraeae scilicet
> graecae et latinae vel trium temporum
> saeculi, ante legem, sub lege, et sub
> gratia.[152]

The song of Zacharias which is sung in antiphonal voices
after the Kyrie, precedes the readings of the prophets leading
the way to the figure of John the Baptist:

> De prophetia: Canticum autem Zachariae
> pontificis in honorem sancti Iohannis
> baptistae cantatur, pro eo quod primordium
> salutis in baptismi, sacramento consistit,
> quod in ministerium Iohannes deo donante
> suscepit. Et (quia) deficiente umbra ve-
> teris (testamenti) et oriente nova evan-
> gelii claritate Iohannes medius (est) pro-
> phetarum novissimus et evangelistarum
> primus, ante faciem verae lucis radians
> lucerna fulsit: ideo prophetiam, quam
> pater eius ipso nascente cecinit, alter-
> nis vocibus ecclesia psallit.[153]

Then follows a reading of the prophets from the Old
Testament.[154]   Immediately after the kyrie, this part stands
under the sign of penance which through the figure of John the
Baptist, prepares for the coming of Christ of the Gospel but
also for Christ, the Eternal Judge of the Last Judgement. Here
we can observe a certain backward and forward movement in space
and in time creating an interrelatedness which becomes a special
characteristic of liturgical drama.

The second reading which includes the Acts of the Apostles,
the Book of Revelation as well as legends of saints and mar-
tyrologies, is followed again by a long triumphal song. Three
boys personifying the three young men in the furnace sing the
hymn:

> De hymno: Hymnum autem trium puerorum,
> quod post lectiones canitur, in figura
> sanctorum veterum, qui sedentes in tene-
> bris adventum domini expectabant. Sicut
> enim illis silentibus quartus angelus
> adfuit in nube roris et feruentis ignis
> incendia vicit: ita est istis Christo
> praestolantibus ipse dei Filius magni
> consilii angelus adfuit, qui tartaria
> frangens imperia gaudium resurrectionis
> illos liberans intulit, quod evange-
> liste docet.[155]

After this re-enacted triumphal song, the three young men change
their role and represent the innocent children at Bethlehem or
the children during the entrance of Jesus into Jerusalem who are
now triumphing with Christ. Such a change gives constant movement to the dramatic configurations. This change is indicated
as follows:

> . . . ut inter benefictionem et evan-
> gelium lectio (non) intercedat nisi
> tantummodo responsorium, quod a par-
> vulis canitur, instar innocentium, qui
> pressi in evangelio consortes Christi
> nativitatis leguntur, vel eorum parvu-
> lorum, qui properante ad passionem cla-
> mabant in templo: Hosanna filio David . . .[156]

After the song of the three boys there is, immediately preceding
the gospel, another aius-song, which is at this time sung by the
deacons who personify the angels; the image of the triumphant
king introduces this part:

> De aius ante evangelium: Tunc in adventu
> sancti evangelii claro modulamine denuo
> psallit clerus "aius" in specie angelorum
> ante faciem Christi ad portes inferi cla-
> mantium: "tollite portas principes ves-

tras, et elevamini portae aeternales, et
introibit dominus virtutum rex gloriae."[157]

This song, in order to introduce the triumphant entrance of the
gospel, takes up the Christ image of the _introit_ as entering
into the world. Then, in a solemn procession, the book of the
New Testament, which simultaneously personifies here the Risen
Lord and Eternal Judge, adorned with seven burning candles symbolizing the seven gifts of the Holy Spirit, is carried into the
Church. The book of the gospel is placed on the _ambo_ which does
not symbolize here--as was the case in the Byzantine liturgy--
the tombstone of Christ's burial site but rather it is referring
to the figure of Christ enthroned at the right hand of the
Father. Thus, the living Word relates to the Last Judgement.
The deacons who sing the gloria, personify now those angels who
sang the gloria over Bethlehem. The overlapping of these
symbolic representations is expressed in the following citation:

> _De evangelio_: Egreditur processio sancti
> evangelii velut potentia Christi trium-
> phantis de morte, cum praedictis harmo-
> niis et cum septem candelabris luminis
> quae sunt septem dona spiritus sancti
> vel (veteris) legis lumina mysterio cru-
> cis confixa, ascendens in tribunal ana-
> logii velut Christus sedem regni, paterni,
> ut inde intonet dona vitae clamantibus
> clericis: "Gloria tibi domine," in specie
> angelorum qui nascente Domino: "Gloria
> in excelsio Deo," pastoribus apparentibus
> cecinerunt.[158]

Although the themes of Birth, Resurrection and Ascension are
markedly interwoven, the image of the triumphant king and
eternal judge nevertheless dominates the scene. The gospel is
followed by another _sanctus-hymnus_. Here again the deacons
change their role and represent the saints who now triumph with
Christ: either those who are freed out of the limbo or the
triumphing elders of the Revelation of John:

> (_De Sanctus post evangelium_): Sanctus

autem, quod redeunte, sancto evangelio
clerus cantat, in specie sanctorum, qui
redeunte domino Jesu Christo de inferis
canticum laudis dominum sequentes cantaverunt, vel septuaginta quatour seniorum,
quos in apocalypsi Iohannes commemorat,
qui mittentes coronas suas ante agnum
dulce canticum cantaverunt . . .[159]

The dismissal of the catechumens follows after the sermon and
the prayers. The offertory procession which then proceeds is
again accompanied by unceasing songs. The part of the offertory
which is divided into two parts, namely, offertory procession
and offering, is internally related through the theme of Law.
The exit of the offertory procession corresponds to the oblation
of the people according to the Law of Moses:

(De Sono): Sonum autem, quod cantitur,
quando procedit oblatio, hinc traxit
exordium: Praecepit dominus Moysi, ut
faceret tubas argenteas, quas levitae
clangeret, quando offerebatur hostia, et
hoc esset signum, per quod intelligere
populus . . .[160]

The procession toward the altar also represents the handing-over
of Jesus. Although this representation points back to Theodore
of Mopsuestia, it has besides the fulfilling of the Law another
spiritual meaning:

Nunc autem procedente ad altarium corpore
Christi non iam tubis inreprehensibilius,
sed spiritalibus vocibus praeclara Christi
magnalia dulci melodia psallit ecclesia.[161]

The passion which follows is only alluded to but it is at the
same time connected with the triumph of the Risen Lord. The
term turris seems to belong here to the Gallic liturgy because
it is mentioned by Gregory of Tours; it also seems to belong to
the Byzantine liturgy because this term could already be
observed in the liturgy of Germanos namely in connection with

101

the Great Entrance:[162]

> Corpus vero domini ideo defertur in turribus,
> quia monumentum domini in similitudinem
> turris fuit excisum in petra et intus lec-
> tus, ubi pausavit Corpus dominicum unde
> resurrexit rex gloriae in triumphum. [163]

The consecration makes present the Passion as such which then immediately leads over into the burial scene. _Corporale_ and _linteum_ have here retained their earlier allegorical dramatic significance. The _palla_, however, seems to be something new because it represents the garments of Christ. It is thus stated:

> Patena autem vocatur, ubi consecratur
> oblatio, quia mysterium eucharistia in
> commemoratione offertur passionis domini.
> Palla vero linostima in illium indumenti
> tenet figuram, quia in gyro contexta a
> militibus non fuit divisa, tunica scilicet
> Christi. Corporalis vero palla ideo pura
> linea est, super quam oblatio ponitur,
> quia corpus domini puris linteaminibus cum
> aromatibus fuit obvolutum in tumulo. [164]

Although everything points to the burial, the figure of Joseph of Arimathea and Nicodemus are absent here but in their place the undivided garments of Christ play a part. The _alleluia_ which is sung before the kiss of peace and communion reflects the _alleluia_ of the Apocalypse of John, the _alleluia_ after the Resurrection and the angelic _alleluia_ after the Ascension. It signifies also the three ages of the world before the Law, under the Law and under Grace. It thus embraces the entire salvation history:

> Laudes autem, hoc est Alleluia, Iohannes
> in apocalypsi post resurrectionem audivit
> psallere. Idea hora illa (qua corpus)
> domini pallio quasi Christus tegitur coelo,

> ecclesia solet angelicum canticum (can-
> tare): quod autem habet ipsa Alleluia
> primam et secundam et tertiam, signat tria
> tempora ante legem, sub lege, sub gratia. [165]

Significantly, the breaking of bread refers in this Gallic text
to the Crucifixion and not to the Resurrection. With a song of
praise to the Trinity, the trecamus, which seems to be sung here
by the choir while the faithful go to communion, the liturgy is
completed. [166] This Gallican liturgical drama has, despite
obvious Eastern influence, its own theology which has been
shaped by a Western world-view. This liturgy has an orientation towards the law which is also more or less a trend
according to its indigenous Western traits. Not Eastern mysti-
cism but the eschatological images of the triumphant king and
eternal judge are its main aspects. Spatial relationship with
its multidimensional temporal and spatial overlappings
characterize this drama. Personficiation of angels, biblical
figures and objects, songs, movements, and gestures with
allegorical symbolic significance are the dramatic means by
which the biblical material is interwoven with salvation history
and comes to be re-enacted into configurational form. Constant
forward and backward movements in space and in time give this
entire configuration depth-dimensional dynamism.

The African Liturgy is the first Latin liturgy. Although
there are no official liturgical documents, the writings of
Tertullian, Cyprian and Augustine [167] point to a complete liturgy which made necessary the intervention of different
councils. [168]

The Roman Liturgy. Although this liturgy is more sober and
constrained, it too has its own dramatic manner of expression.
The sindon belongs to the dramatic objects of the earliest
liturgies of the pontiffs. Pope Silvester (335 A.D.) gives
dramatic-allegorical significance to the linen of the altar:

> Hic instituit sacrificium altaris non in
> siricum neque in pannum tinctum celebrari
> nisi tantum in lineum terrenum procreatum
> sicut corpus Domini nostri Jesu Christi

in sindonem lineam mundam sepultus est. [169]

As we have shown earlier, however, its allegorical-dramatic significance and function becomes more complex in the other branches of the liturgy.

"Libelli"--Pope Innocent I. One of the characteristics of the early Roman liturgy is a certain flexibility which is documented in the so-called Libelli[170] in which individual mass formulas are loosely drawn together. However, already under Pope Innocent I. (401-417 A.D.), certain regulations can be observed. Papal intervention with the liturgy as it was practiced in Gaul is manifested in a letter to Bishop Gubbio as follows:

> Si instituta ecclesiastica, ut sunt a
> beatis Apostolis tradita, integra vellent
> servare Domini sacerdotes, nulla diver-
> sitas, nulla varietas, in ipsis ordinibus
> et consecrationibus haberetur . . . [171]

This trend towards a unification of the liturgy proceeding from Rome rests upon the claim to the Apostolic tradition.

The First Sacramentaris.

The first Sacramentary, the Leoniamun (599 A.D.)[172] is a collection of libelli and corresponds to a collection of material collated by several compilers. It arranges the mass formulas according to months rather than in agreement with the liturgical year. The place of origin of these classified formulas is the Roman Curia whereby, however, Spanish prayers indicate a connection between Toledo and Rome.[173] The Sacramentary Gelasium[174] which followed is a complex liturgical mixture dating from the sixth and seventh centuries; it also circulated in Gaul.[175] The first great liturgical reform took place under Pope Gregory the Great (604 A.D.) and is formalized in the Sacramentarium Gregorianum.[176]

Pope Gregory's "Dialogues": The real liturgical conception of this Pope, namely, the mystical interpretation, is given in his Dialogues where it is stated:

104

> Hinc ego pensemus quale sit pro nobis
> sacrificium, quod pro absolutione nostra
> passionem unigeniti Filii semper imi-
> tatur. Quis enim fidelium habere dubium
> possit in ipsa immolationis hora ad
> sacerdotis vocem caelos aperiri, in illo
> Jesu Christi mysterio angelorum choro
> adesse, summis ima sociari, terrena cae-
> lestibus jungi unumque ex visibilius atqua
> invisibilius fieri. [177]

Such an interpretation, however, which united the visible and
invisible realms places this Roman Pontiff too in the tradition
of Byzantium, of a Maximos the Confessor or of the Syrians such
as Ephraim, Theodore of Mopsuestia and Narsai. [178] Theodore had
already cited the mystical vision of John the Evangelist in
connection with the offertory and consecration:

> . . . This is also attested by the Lord
> who said: "Hereafter ye shall see heaven
> open and the angels of God ascending and
> descending to the Son of Man." [179]

Such an interpretation surpasses all spatial and temporal
limitations and makes room for further expansion of the
imagination. [180]

Summary

In contrast to some of the Eastern liturgies which we
analyzed, those of the West reflect a certain conflict. While
the Gallican liturgy on the one side stands within the radius of
influence of Eastern liturgies, it corresponds on the other side
to the way of expresssion of the Gauls which soon will stamp its
own indigenous Western mark on it. This liturgy works as a
certain catalyst and absorbs that which corresponds to its own
indigenousness whereas it seems to reject exogenous regulations
which are contrary to its very native mode of being. While the

105

Eastern and Gallican liturgies are creative and eager to shape, to transform new currents thus giving new meaning to forms of expression, the Roman liturgy is more sober although it had in the first centuries more flexible features. Certain differences between the Gallican and Roman world views were already expressed in the letter of Pope Innocent I to Bishop Gubbio and while the sacramentaries show certain regulations of rubrics, the Dialogues of Pope Gregory the Great express a more flexible point of view which, I think, should be regarded as an essential complement to these liturgies.

Conclusion

The result of this examination of liturgical texts which was undertaken in this chapter is really amazing especially if it is considered in relation to the problems raised in our first chapter. In a slow process there developed a Christian drama, that is to say, a representational form of the Life, Passion, Resurrection and Ascension of Christ, grouped around and emerging from the First Liturgical Act of Jesus, the Last Supper. How much the art of narration of the Syrians, not lastly Tatian's Diatessaron, have enriched this representational transformed structure, can for the time being not be examined. It can, however, not be denied that we have here a counterpart of the Roman theatre where a mimesis of the life of the God of the Christians is re-enacted and represented for imitation and re-creation.

Especially informative are the different genres of liturgical-literary expression which have perhaps to be inter-preted anew and have to be seen in a special interrelationship. A good example would be the Expositio Antiquae Liturgicae Gallicanae because it seems to stand in the literary tradition of the Eastern Mystagogical Catechisms. Charlemagne, too, introduced with his reform the expositio--explanations--of truth, faith and rites. But these explanations correspond to a more simple form of expositio.[181] Both of these forms of genre seem to culminate in the great Expositio of Amalarius of Metz. Its great advantage lies in the fact that it allows room for the creative imagination. The more complex allegorical world view is essentially interwoven with that of Amalarius' Weltan-

106

schauung. In order to be able to follow the allegorical-dramatic structure of Amalarius, it will be necessary to give a short introduction to the tradition of the allegorical method in the third chapter.

FOOTNOTES

[1]The concept of liturgy will be defined and dealt with in this study not in the wider sense of the hermeneutics of history of religious but in the more narrow sense implied in the Judaeo-Christian tradition.

[2]Lidell-Scott, Greek-English Lexicon, 1961, s.v. λειτομργια Catholic Encyclopedia, 1910, s.v. "Liturgy" by Adrian Fortescue.

[3]Arndt and Gingrich, A Greek-English Lexicon of the New Testament, 1971, s.v. εκκλεδια

[4]Arnold T. Ehrhardt, Politische Metaphysik von Solon bis Augustin, 3 bd. (Tübingen: J.C.B. Mohr (Paul Siebeck) 1959) 1:117, n. 1, 136-145.

[5]The cultic acts of the Roman affairs of state would also deserve to be considered from this side. See above, pp. 1-10.

[6]A. Wilmart, "Expositio Missae," in Dictionnaire d'Archéologie Chrétienne et de Liturgie, eds. F. Cabrol at H. Leclercq, 15 vols. (Paris: Librarie Letouzey et Ané, 1907-1953), vol. 5, pt. 1 (1922): 1014-1027. After this cited as DACL.

[7]Dom Gregory Dix, The Shape of the Liturgy (West-Minster Dacre Press, 1945), p. 394; Joseph Jungmann, Early Liturgy to the Time of Gregory the Great, transl. by F. Brunner (Notre Dame, Ind.: University of Notre Dame Press, 1959), and The Mass of the Roman Rite, its Origin and Development, transl. by F. Brunner, 2 vols. (New York: Benzinger, 1951-55), 1: 3-37.

[8]Pere Dom Fernand Cabrol, Les Origines Liturgiques (Paris: Letouzey et Ané Editeurs, 1906), pp. 8, 17; J. Danielou, Bible et Liturgie (Paris: Edition du Cerf, 1951), pp. 7-49; Dom Benedict Steuart, The Development of Christian Worship (London: New York: Longmanns Green and Co., 1953), p. 13.

[9]See below, pp. 125-158.

[10]W.O.E. Oesterley, The Jewish Background of the Christian

Liturgy (Oxford: At the Clarendon Press, 1925), p. 113; Ismer Elbogen, Der jüdische Gottesdienst in seiner geschichtlichen Entwicklung, 4th ed. (Hildesheim: Georg Olms Verlagsbuch-handlung, 1962).

[11] Mk. 11:11 and 14:49 (Jerusalem Bible) cited as JB herafter.

[12] Oscar Cullmann, Urchristentum und Gottesdienst, 2nd and augm. ed. (Zürich: Zwingli Verlag, 1950), pp. 13-15. Klaus Gamber, Domus ecclesiae (Regensburg: Pustet Verlag, 1968).

[13] Mk. 14:22-25; Matth. 26:26-29; Lk. 22:13-20. JB

[14] Mk. 16: 14-15; Lk. 24: 30-31; Jn. 21:1-14. JB

[15] Acts of the Apostles. 2:14-47; 1 Cor. 14:26-33. JB

[16] Revelation. 1:10. JB

[17] See above, p. 7, fn. 24.

[18] Plinius Epistula 10.96. Printed by Karl Mirbt, Quellen zur Geschichte des Papsttums, 4th ed. (Tübingen, Leipzig: Verlag J.C.B. Mohr (Paul Siebeck), 1924), pp. 8-9.

[19] Arthur Võõbus, Liturgical Traditions in the Didache, Papers of the Estonian Theological Society in Exile, no. 16 (Stockholm: ETSE, 1968), pp. 9-39.

[20] Justin Martyr 1 Apology, 61-67.

[21] Irenaeus Adversus Haereses 4.17. 5, 18.6.

[22] Clement of Alexandria, The Exhortations to the Greeks, bk. II (transl. G.W. Butterworth) Loeb Classical Library (Cambridge, Mass.: Harvard University Press, 1979), pp. 27-51.

[23] A.F. Walls, "A Note on the Apostolic Claim in the Church Order Literature," Texte und Untersuchungen 64 (1957): 83-92.

[24]The Apostolic Tradition of St. Hippolytus (of Rome), 16.12. Cf. Walls, "Church Orders," Texte, pp. 84-86.

[25]Didascalia Apostolorum 1 et 9. Cf. Walls, "Church Orders," Texte, pp. 87-88.

[26]The Testament of Our Lord, 2.

[27]Statuta Ecclesia Antiqua, can. 24.

[28]Constitutiones Apostolorum 2.57., 8. 5-15.

[29]Eusebius Ecclesiastical History 9; John W. Eadie, ed., The Conversion of Constantine, (European Problem Studies (New York: Holt, Rinehart and Winston; paperback, 1971); H. Doerries, Das Selbstzeugnis Kaiser Konstantins, Abhdl. d.Ak.d. Wiss. in Göttingen, Phil. hist. kl., 3.F., Nr. 34. (Göttingen: Vandenhoeck & Rupprecht, 1954); Robert M. Grant, Augustus to Constantine: The Thrust of the Christian Movement into the Roman World (New York: Harper and Row Publishers, 1970); A.H.M. Jones, Constantine and the Conversion of Europe, rev.ed. (New York: Collier Books, 1962); A. Pigániol, L'Empire Chrétien (Paris: Presses Universitairs de France, 1947); J. Vogt, "Constantin der Grosse," RAC 3 (1956): 306-379, and "Christenverfolgung (historisch)," RAC 2 (1954): 1159-1208.

[30]Dix, Liturgy, pp. 3-5.

[31]See above, pp. 4-5.

[32]Ibid.

[33]This problem of the imagination can only be mentioned in our study but cannot be dealt with in depth at this point.

[34]Anton Baumstark, Comparative Liturgy, transl. from the 3rd French edition by F.L. Cross, ed. by Bernard Botte (London: A.R. Mowbray & Co. Lt., 1958), pp. 18-19; 12. Cf. Peter R.L. Brown, "The Rise and Function of the Holy Man in Late Antiquity," The Journal of Roman Studies, 61 (1971): 80-81, esp. 94-95.

[35]L. Fendt, Einführung in die Liturgiewissenschaft (Berlin: Alfred Töpelmann, 1958).

[36]A. Baumstark, Comparative Liturgy, p. 31; F.E. Brightman, Liturgies Eastern and Western (London: At the Clarendon Press, 1896), p. xviii; Pere Severin Salaville, An Introduction to the Studies of Eastern Liturgies. Adapted from the French with a preface and some additional notes by M.T. Barton (London: Laus & Co., Ltd., 1938), p. 9; F.C. Burkitt, "The Old Lectionary of Jerusalem," JTS 24 (July, 1923): 415-425.

[37]The liturgical texts which we dealt with in this chapter indicate the uniqueness of the rich influence of the Syriac Church. Regarding the results of recent scholarship see especially the works of the Syrologist A. Vööbus, which came to my attention only at the conclusion of this work. See also: Robert Murray, Symbols of Church and Kingdom: A Study in Early Syriac Tradition. (Cambridge, Cambridge University Press, 1975.)

[38]Brightman, Liturgies, p. lxxxvii.

[39]Ibid.

[40]See below, pp. 85-92.

[41]Louis Duchesne, Christian Worship: Its Origin and Evolution. A Study of the Latin Liturgy up to the Time of Charlemagne. Transl. by M.L. McLure, 5th ed. London Society for promoting Christian Knowledge (New York: The Macmillan Co., 1919), p. 71; Salaville, Eastern Liturgies, p. 25; Baumstark, "Denkmäler der Entstehungsgeschichte des Byzantinischen Ritus," Oriens Christianus 3, ser. 2 (1927): 3.

[42]F. E. Brightman, "The Historia Mystagogia and other Greek Commentaries on the Byzantine Liturgy," JTS 9 (1908): 248-65, 387-97.

[43]See above, chapter I.

[44]F. C. Burkitt, "The Old Lectionary of Jerusalem," JTS 24

(1927): 415-424.

[45]Dix, *Liturgy*, pp. 307-308.

[46]See above, pp. 11ff.

[47]*Mystagogische Katechesen*, 13.9.

[48]*Itinerarium Egeria* (*Peregrinatio Aetheriae*): 31.1 (Matt. 21:9).

[49]F. Probst, "Die Antiochianische Messe nach den Schriften des heil. Johannes Chrysostomus dargestellt," *ZfkTh* 7 (1883): 250-303.

[50]Chrysostomus *In illud vidi Domini* 2. (In Oziam). Cf. *In Genesis*, hom. 54.2.

[51]Ibid., 2,3.

[52]Probst, "Die Antiochische Messe," p. 251.

[53]Basileios the Great *Liturgia*. In J.-P. Migne, *Patrologiae cursus completus: Series Graeca*. 162 vols. (Paris: 1857-66), 31: 1630-73. Hereafter cited as *PG*.

[53a] Cf. above, pp. 8-10.

[54]Arthur Vööbus, *History of the School of Nisibis*. Corpus Scriptorum Christianorum Orientalium, Scriptores Syriaci, 266. Subsidia t. 26 (Louvain: Secretariat du Corpusco, 1965). Herafter cited as *CSCO*.

[55]Tatian *Diatessaron*, 51-53.

[56]F. C. Burkitt, "The Early Syriac Lectionary System," *Proceedings of the British Academy* 10 (1921-1923): 301-338; A Baumstark, "Nichtevangelische syrische Perikopenordnungen des ersten Jahrhunderts," *LQ* 3 (1921).

[57]Johannes List, *Studien zur Homelitik Germanos I von Kon-*

stantinopel and seiner Zeit, Texte und Forschungen zur Byzantinisch Neugriechischen Philologie Nr. 29 (Athen: Verlag der Byzantinisch-Neugriechischen Sprache, 1939); M. Carpenter, "Romanus and the Mystery Play of the East," Philological Studies in Honor of Walter Miller, The University of Missouri Studies 11 (July 1936): 21-51.

[58]A. Vööbus, Literary, Critical and Historical Studies in Ephrem the Syrian. Papers of the Estonian Theological Society in Exile, 10 (Stockholm: ETSE, 1958).

[59]Saint Ephrem Commentaire de l'évangele concordant. Editee et traduite par Louis Leloir (Louvain: L. Durbecq, 1953-54). CSCO 137, 145.

[60]Ibid., XXI. 20. (Matth. 27:58., 1:19; Luc. 23:51).

[61]Regarding the influence of Tatian's shaping of the configuration of the Passion on Ephraim, Narsai and Jacob of Serugh, see R. H. Connolly: "Jacob of Serugh and the 'Diatessaron', "JTS 8 (July 1907): 581-590; see also Augustus Carl Mahr, Relations of Passion Plays to St. Ephrem the Syrian (Columbus: The Wartburg Press, 1947).

[62]See above, pp. 58-59.

[63]Apostolic Constitutions 8.12.3.

[63a] This aspect of the peacock symbolism was discussed in Professor Mircea Eliade's seminar on "Symbolism". The University of Chicago, Winter 1981.

[64]Persian Anaphora.

[65]This similarity was brought to my attention by Professor Paul Ricoeur.

[66]Joseph Braun, Der christliche Altar (München: G. Koch & Co., 1924), p. 104. Braun draws attention to the fact that these fans were symbols of cherubim with six wings. Perhaps such images and signs on fans might suggest that the Roman

custom to draw images of gods on pillows, forms of cakes and other possible objects in order to provoke the presence of the gods which they were to present, might have played an influential part for the Christian liturgy in the cultural context of the Roman world. Such observation would, of course, lead to the further exploration and study of interesting problems of symbol transformation and interactions as well as its effects on the imagination. Unfortunately, we cannot pursue this problem in the framework of our present study.

[67]Isidori Pelusiotae Epistola 123, Explicatio ecclesiasticae initiationis. Cited by J. R. Geiselmann, Die Abendmahlslehre an der Wende der christlichen Spätantike bis zum Frühmittelalter (München: Max Heuber Verlag, 1933), pp. 157-160, and PG 78: 264.

[68]Arthur Võõbus, "Theodore of Mopsuestia," Encyclopedia Britannica, s.v.; and "Regarding the theological Anthropolgy of Theodore of Mopsuestia," Church History 33 (1964): 115-24; and "Theological Reflections in Ancient Syrian Traditions," in The Scope of Grace: Essays on Nature and Grace in Honor of Joseph Sittler, edited by Philip J. Hefner (Philadelphia: Fortress Press, 1964), pp. 101-19.

[69]Theodore of Mopsuestia Commentary on the Lord's Prayer and on the Sacraments of Baptism and Eucharist, edited and translated with a critical apparatus by A. Mingana, Woodbroke Studies, no. 6, Christian Documents (Cambridge: W. Heffer and Sons, Ltd., 1933), p. 88. (Hereafter cited as Mingana).

[70]Ibid., p. 95.

[71]Ibid., p. 83.

[72]Ibid., pp. 83-84 (Luc. 2:14).

[73]Ibid., p. 84.

[74]Ibid.

[75]Ibid., pp. 84-85.

[76]Ibid., p. 85.

[77]Ibid., pp 85-86.

[78]Regarding the problem of "absence", cf. Jean-Paul Sartre, The Psychology of Imagination, translated by B. Frechtman, 2nd printing (New York: Washington Square Press, Inc., 1968), pp. 28-31, 71-120.

[79]Mingana, p. 86.

[80]Ibid.

[81]Ibid.

[82]Ibid., pp. 86-87.

[83]Ibid., p. 87 (Matth. 28: 2-10; 2 Cor. 5:17).

[84]Ibid., p. 88.

[85]Ibid.

[86]It is not possible to deal here with Theodore's special theological position which is, of course, also expressed figuratively in these representational forms.

[87]Vööbus, The School of Nisibis, p. 66.

[88]Ibid., pp. 72-76.

[89]Narsai The Liturgical Homelies of Narsai, edited and translated from the Syriac by R. H. Connolly with an Appendix by Edmund Bishop, Text and Studies, v. 8, no. 1 (Cambridge: At the University Press, 1909), p. 36. Cited after this as Connolly. (See also that reference in Chapter I).

[90]Ibid., p. 38.

[91]Ibid., p. 46.

[92] Ibid., p. 62.

[93] Ibid., pp. 3-4.

[94] Ibid., See above, pp. 73ff.

[95] Connolly, p. 4.

[96] Ibid., p. 12.

[97] Ibid., pp. 27-28.

[98] Pseudo-Dionysius der Aeropagite Die Himmlischen und Kirchlichen Hierarchien BKV²; and J. Stiglmayer, "Eine syrische Liturgie als Vorlage des Ps. Aeropagiten," ZfKTh 35 (1909): 383-85.

[99] Otto von Simpson, Sacred Fortress: Byzantine Art and Statescraft in Ravenna (Chicago: The University of Chicago Press, 1948).

[100] Cf. Brightman, Liturgies, pp. 353-411; Salaville, Liturgies, pp. 14-16; Duchesne, Origins, pp. 71-72; Probst, "Die Antiochanische Messe," pp. 250-51; Baumstark, "Denkmaler," pp. 1-32.

[101] Die Tragödie 'Das Leiden des Erlösers' (Christos Paschon) angeblich vom heil. Gregorius von Nazianz. Herausgegeben und aus dem Griechischen ubersersetzt von E. Ellison (Leipzig: Verlag von Otto Wiegand, 1855), pp. 99-151. (The authenticity of author and date have been an issue of scholarly controversy. This however does not diminish the significance of this remarkable work and its meaningful reciprocity both to Greek drama and Christian liturgical drama.).

[102] Perhaps it would be an interesting problem to re-examine the interrelationship between Greek and liturgical drama which seems to be very conspicuous here. The studies by Donald Cornford in The Origin of the Attic Comedy edited with a foreword by Theodor Gaster (Garden City, N.Y.: Doubleday &

Company, Inc., Anchor Books, 1961) and by Gilbert Murray
Euripides and His Age (London: Thornton Butterworth, Lt., 1927)
need perhaps to be carried further.

[103]lines 1135-1815, Ellison, Christos Paschon, pp. 99-151.

[104]See above, pp. 66ff.

[105]See below, pp. 167-335.

[106]Maximos Confessor Mystagogia, PG 91: 658-718.

[107]Ibid., 3. PG, 91: 663. Cf. R. Bornert, OSB,
"Explication de la liturgie et interprétation de l'Ecriture chez
Maxime le Confesseur," Studia Patristica 10 (1970): 323-27.

[108]Mystagogia, 3. PG, 91: 671.

[109]Maximos Questiones ad Thalassium 20, PG, 90: 310.

[110]Mystagogia, 8. PG, 91: 687.

[111]Sophronius (Patriarch of Jerusalem) Commentarius
Liturgicus 1. PG, 87: 3982.

[112]Ibid., 3. p. 3986.

[113]Ibid., 4. p. 3986.

[114]Ibid., 4. p. 3986.

[115]Germanos (Patriarch of Constantinople) Historia Ecclesiastica et Mystica, PG, 98: 383-454.

[116]Ibid., p. 387.

[117]Ibid., p. 391.

[118]Ibid., p. 399.

[119]Ibid., pp. 398-433. Cf. also Amalarius, below pp. 324-
330.

[120]Ibid., PG, 98: 419.

[121]Ibid.

[122]Cf. Gallican Liturgy, above pp. 95ff, and also
Amalarius, below pp. 285ff.

[123]Friedrich Heiler, Altkirchliche Autonomie und Päpstlicher Zentralismus (Munchen: Verlag von Ernst Reinhardt, 1941).

[124]Duchesne, Christian Worship, pp. 86-105; Jungmann, Early Liturgy, pp. 24-25; Steuart, Development.

[125]Ambrosius De Sacramentis et de Mysteriis. CSEL, 73: 1-116.

[126]F. Cabrol, "Mozarabic, "(la liturgie), DACL, 12 (1935): 390-491; Pius Bonifatius Gams, Die Kirchengeschichte von Spanien, 2 vols. (Regensburg: Druck und Verlag von Joseph Manz, 1974); Isidor de Séville Ecclesiastic Offices. (This text is an example of the Mozarabic liturgy); Dom Paul Séjourne, Saint Isidore de Séville, Études de Théologie Historique (Paris: Gabriel Beauchesse, 1929).

[127]Heiler, Altkirchliche Autonomie, p. 58.

[128]Cf. below, pp. 105-106.

[129]Cf. above, pp. 86-87.

[130]John T. McNeill, The Celtic Churches: A History A.D. 200 to 1200 (Chicago: University of Chicago Press, 1974).

[131]Ferdinand Cabrol, "Le Book of Cerne. Les Liturgies celtiques et gallicanes et la liturgie romain," Revue de questions historique 56 (N.S. 32) (1904): 210-222; David N. Dumville, "Liturgical Drama and Panegyric Responsory from the Eight Century? A Re-examination of the Origin and Content of the Book of Cerne," JTS, N.S. 23 (October 1972): 374-406.

[132]Cf. below, pp. 132-133.

[133]Edgar J. Goodspeed, History of Early Christian Literature, rev. and enlarged by Robert M. Grant (Chicago: University of Chicago Press, Phoenix Books paperback, 1966), pp. 26-27; Heiler, Altkirchliche Autonomie, pp. 78-84; William H. Hutton, The Church of the Sixth Century (London and New York: Longmanns Green and Co., 1897); Johannes Quasten, "Oriental Influences in the Gallican Liturgy," Traditio 1 (1943): 55-78; T. Scott Holmes, The Origin and Development of the Christian Church in Gaul (London: Macmillan & Co., 1911), pp. 141-83; E. Griffe, "Aux origines de la liturgie gallicane," Bulletin de littérature ecclésiastique 52 (1951): 17-43.

[134]See below, pp. 132-133.

[135]Peregrinatio.

[136]See above, pp. 58-59.

[137]J. B. Thibaut, L'ancienne Liturgie Gallicane son origine et sa formation en Provence aux V et Vi siecles son l'influence et de Saint Césaire d'Arles (Paris: Maison de la bonne presse, 1929).

[138]A. Malnory, Saint Césaire, évêque d'Arles, 503-543 A.D. (Paris: E. bouillon, 19=894); C. F. Arnold, Caesarius von Arelate und die gallikanische Kirche (Leipzig: J.C. Hinrich'sche Buchhandlung, 1894).

[139]Gregorii Turonensis Historia Francorum 1.48, 10.31.; G. Nikel, Der Anteil des Volkes an der Messliturgie von Chlodwig bis Karl dem Grossen, Forschungen zur Geschichte des innerkirchlichen Lebens, Heft 2. (Innsbruck: Druck und Verlag F. Rauch, 1930).

[140]The question of proper dating and the question of authenticity of the author remain an unsolved problem for continued research the discussion of which cannot be dealt with in this study. Jean Leclercq, "Germain-de-Prés (saint)", DACL VI (1924): 1102-1150 and A. Wilmart, "Germain de Paris", DACL VI (1924): 1049-1102. For further reading see, Klaus Gamber, Ordo Antiqua Gallicanus: Der gallikanische Messritus des 6. Jahrhunderts (Regensburg: Verlag Friedrich Pustet, 1965); P. Rado, "Verfasser und Heimat der Monemessen," Eph. Lit. 42 (1928): 64. Radó supposes that the author might have been Germanos of Auxerre (488 A.D.).

[141]J. Mone, Lateinische und griechische Texte aus dem 2. bis 6. Jahrhundert (Frankfurt, a.M.: C.B. Lizius Verlag, 1851).

[142]Pierre Salmon, ed., Le Lectionnaire de Luxeuil, 2 vols. Collectanae Biblia Latina, 7 et 9. (Roma: Abbaye Saint-Jerome, 1944-53).

[143]Leo C. Mohlberg, ed., Missale Gothicum, Rerum Ecclesiasticarum Documenta. Series Maior: Fontes 5. (Roma: Casa Editrice Herder, 1961).

[144]Leo C. Mohlberg, L. Eisenhófer and P. Siffrin, eds., Missale Gallicum Vetus, Rerum Ecclesiasticarum Documenta, Series Maior: Fontes 3. (Roma: Casa Editrice, 1958).

[145]Leo C. Mohlberg, L. Eisenhöfer and P. Siffrin, eds., Missale Francorum, Rerum Ecclesiasticarum Documenta. Series Maior: Fontes 2. (Roma: Casa Editrice Herder, 1957).

[146]See above, pp. 96ff.

[147]Mone, Monemessen, pp. 3-35.

[148]P. Radó, "Das älteste Schriftauslegungssystem der altgallikanischen Kirche," Eph. Lit. 45 (1931): 9-25, 100-115; O. K. Burkitt, "Early Syriac System," pp. 301-338.

[149]Expositio Antiquae Liturgicae Gallicanae Germano Parisiensi ascripta, editit notisque instruxit Joannes Quasten, Opuscula et Textus: Series Liturgicae (Munster: Aschendorff Verlag, 1934). Hereafter cited as Quasten, Expositio.

[150]Ibid., pp. 10-11.

[151]Cf. above, p. 70.

[152]Quasten, Expositio, p. 12.

[153]Ibid., p. 13. Thibaut has pointed out that the song of Zacharias had been an outstanding trait of the Gallican Church and that it referred to the baptism of Chlodwig at which time the triumphal song was sung. See his Liturgie, p. 13.

[154]Quasten, Expositio, p. 13.

[155]Ibid., p. 14 (Dan. 3:51-90).

[156]Ibid., (Ps. 8:3).

[157]Ibid., (Ps. 8:3).

[158]Ibid., p. 15 (Luc., 2:14).

[159]Ibid., p. 15 (Apoc. 4:10-11). The theme of the harrowing of hell deserves perhaps special attention here; cf. Dumville, "Liturgical Drama," pp. 374-406.

[160]Quasten, Expositio, pp. 17-18.

[161]Ibid., p. 18; also cf above, pp. 73-75.

[162]Cf. above, p. 89 and Historica Francorum, 10, 31; A. Fortescue, "Cheroubicum," DACL 3 (1921): 1281-86.

[163] Quasten, Expositio, p. 18.

[164] Ibid., p. 19

[165] Ibid., p. 20.

[166] Ibid., p. 23, n. 1.

[167] W. C. Bishop, "The African Rite," JTS 13 (1922): 250-77; and Wunnibald Roetzer, Des heil. Augustinus Schriften als liturgiegeschichtliche Quellen (Munchen: M. Hueber Verlag, 1930).

[168] Emmanuel Bourque, Étude sur les Sacramentaries Romains, Studi di Antichita Cristiana, vols. 20 and 25. (Citta del Vaticano: Pontifico istituto di archeologica cristiana, 1949, 1958), vol. 20.

[169] Liber Pontificalis, 1.51. Cf. Geiselmann, Die Abendmahlslehre, p. 158.

[170] Cyrille Vogel, "Le développement historique du culte Chrétien en occident. Resultates et problèmes," in Problemi di stori della Chiesa l'Alto Medio evo (Milano: Vita et Piensiero, Publicazioni delli Universita Cattolica del Sacro Curo, 1973): 73-98.

[171] See PL 20: 551-52. Regarding this problem see also C. C. Flanigan, "The Roman Rite and the Origins of the Liturgical Drama," University of Toronto Quarterly, 43 (1934): 263-84.

[172] Bourque, Sacramentaries, 20: 65-169.

[173] Ibid.

[174] Ibid., pp. 173-298.

[175] Vogel, "Le développement," pp. 73-98.

[176] Bourque, Sacramentaries, 20: 301-91.

[177] Gregory the Great Dialogues, 4.60. Cf. also Hardison, Christian Rite, pp. 36-37, ns. 1 and 2.

[178] Cf. above, pp. 66-92.

[179] Mingana, pp. 84-85. (Joh. 1:51).

[180] For further treatment of the Roman liturgy see below,

pp. 167-173.

[181]See Wilmart, "Expositio," pp. 1014-18.

CHAPTER III

THE TRADITION OF THE ALLEGORICAL METHOD[1]

The Essential Meaning of Allegory

General Introduction

The sharp division which was drawn between allegory and symbol in scholarship of the last centuries deprived the allegorical figure of its inner dynamism and its sign-like nature which it had in Antiquity, in the Patristic Age and in the Middle Ages. Instead, something static and rigid or perhaps even an immovable nature has been ascribed to the allegorical figure. With such a prejudice I also began to analyze the texts related to my research only to be almost overpowered by their inner dynamism and symbolic-allegorical interaction. As I proceeded further in my studies, I began to realize that this symbolic-allegorical interaction also became dramatically expressed. Thus I was led to the understanding that perhaps the essence of allegory or of the allegorical symbol would have to be approached anew, from a different perspective. Proceeding from such an understanding as a point of departure, this study attempts to give only a sketch of the development and widespread manifestation of the allegorical symbol and its method. Methodologically we shall first deal with the Greek, Jewish and Alexandrian allegory until about 50 B.C. After that the allegorical exegesis of early Christianity and the Greek Church Fathers until the outgoing third century will be discussed and finally to conclude with a brief treatment of the way of interpretation of the Latin Church Fathers up to the time of Bede with special consideration of Augustine.

Definition

The word allegoria ($\alpha\lambda\lambda\eta\gamma\circ\rho\iota\alpha$)[2] is a product of the rhetorical school and replaces the earlier uponia ($\mu\pi\nu\circ\iota\alpha$). It comes from the Greek allos ($\alpha\lambda\lambda\circ\varsigma$). Allegory means speaking about the other, that which lies beyond itself from which it receives its veiled significance.[3] But such a related situation presupposes movement, and for this reason it cannot at all be static.

The Greek Tradition.

The beginnings of the allegorical method lie with the Greek philosophers who in their search for the basic ideas thought they would find with the poets, who were inspired by the muses and the gods, those things figuratively alluded to which they themselves had arrived at by way of cognitive method. The stammering of the poets and prophets was for them enigmatic and irrational and was poured into certain signs and myths which[4] served as veils for the truth which was contained in poetry. Allegory was a veil under which the truth was hidden, and therefore a special hermeneutic procedure related to the imagination was perceived to be necessary in order to unlock the deeper and true sense of poetry. From this method of interpretation developed the allegorical method which was widespread among the Greeks around 500 B.C.

The beginnings of the allegorical interpretation go back to the poetry of Homer and Hesiod and there is no agreement among scholars about whether it began with the Grammarian Theagenes of Rhegium (ca. 525 B.C.) or with the philosopher Pherecydes of Syros (ca. 600 B.C.).[5] In general, however, the fifth century B.C. is considered as that point in time when the spreading of the allegorical interpretation became visible with Anagoras who was the first to interpret Homer's writings in terms of virtue and justice. His pupil Metrodorus of Lampsacus expanded this method from the point of view of the natural sciences. Democritus (ca. 460-370 B.C.) also tried to give, in his work About Poetry, an analysis of inspired poetry from the point of view of the natural sciences. Antisthenes (ca. 455-360 B.C.) on the other hand tried to expound the deeper and true sense of Homer in his commentaries.[6] Even in Plato's writings there are passages which resemble the veiling method of the poets[7] as well as allegory which Plato himself applied.[8]

In the third century B.C. the allegorical method received a new impetus from the Stoics. The Stoic Zeno as well as Cleanthes, Chrysippus and Diogenes interpreted the anthropo-

124

morphic figures of the gods which they thought to be blasphemous, in another than literal sense. Cleanthes believed to have found the true philosophy-theology in the veiled language of the poets of primordial time.[9]

The School of Alexandria, a leading cultural and educational center of Hellenistic times where Jewish and Greek intellectual currents converged and from which Neo-Platonism received its impetus, was especially influenced by the allegorical method of interpretation which had developed. During the first two centuries of our era, Cornutus, Heraclitus, Plutarch, Philo and Numenius of Apamea are important for the development of allegorical interpretation.[10] Heraclitus of the first century defines allegory as follows:

> . . . what is called allegory is that which, as the name implies, says one thing but means something other than what it says.[11]

From this inquiry into the veiled language of the poets which concealed the truth, developed the allegorical method of the Greeks. Even the philosophers, above all Plato, expressed their abstract truth in veiled metaphors and allegories. Independent of the Greeks, however, the rabbis too had their free interpretation of Scripture which was not necessarily bound by the understanding of the letter alone.

Jewish Allegory.

The Old Testament was believed to be not merely inspired in part as was the case with Greek poetry but it was considered to be inspired in its entirety. Since it dealt with the Word of God, everything in Scripture had to be justified and explained. In the most obscure passages, in a repetition, the most important message of God could have been veiled to reveal the Word of God in a given situation and reality. Because God has spoken through Moses and the prophets, it was the task of the exegete to interpret this world in relation to Scripture at all times correctly. In order that the Law might be applied effectively to the reality of a given historical situation, the rabbis used new methods of interpretation.[12] It was however through the wisdom and apocalyptic literature that the allegorical method became more and more widespread in Judaism. Since this literature did not refer immediately to the will of God as it was the case with the Law but was expressed in a richer way in symbols, images and metaphors, Hellenistic and Rabbinic exegesis came closer to each other[13] in the interpretation of this literary corpus.

Through the translation of the Septuagint into the Greek language, Greek ideas and concepts had already entered the Biblical text and had brought about a shift in meaning.[14] For example, hand became interpreted as symbolic strength. The first systematic attempts of an allegorical way of interpretation are documented with Aristobolus (200-100 B.C.), a Jewish philosopher, who tried to combine Greek philosophy and Rabbinic theology. Influenced by the Stoics, he fought particularly against the anthropomorphic representations of God in the Bible. In his commentary about the Mosaic Law he is convinced that the Greeks must have had access to the Septuagint because only thus could the many overlappings between the Old Testament and Greek philosophy be explained.[15] The letter of Ps. Aristeas (145-127 B.C.) is of further importance for the significance of an allegorical exegesis because he gives a new interpretation to the regulations[16] regarding clean and unclean animals as certain types of men; this corresponds to the allegorical sense, namely, that which points to another beyond itself.

Philo of Alexandria (20 B.C. - 54 A.D.)

Philo, a Jew educated in Greek classics, was the most significant allegorizer of Hellenistic Judaism. He combined pious Jewish thought with the philosophy of the Greeks, aiming to create a Jewish philosophy. The influence of his extensive allegorizing commentaries and writings on Christian exegesis was considerable. As was indicated above, Philo's exegesis was not new; it differed however from Rabbinic exegesis and the Greek interpretation of texts in that it was more synthesized from a philosophical point of view. Philo subjected philosophy and reason to the revealed word of God as it was manifested in the Bible through Moses and the prophets because the prophets, as direct instruments of God, were of greater significance than the

126

philosophers. He followed Aristobolus in seeing in the Old Testament the source of Greek philosophy.

Philo was the first to formulate precisely the doctrine of the literal and inner meaning of Scripture and to deal with it most extensively and intensively and here lies his particular significance for Patristic exegesis. The teachings of the creation of the heavenly and earthly man was binding[17] for Philo and it is with the body-soul metaphor that he time and again designates the meaning of the inner and outer sense of Scripture. For him, each external act of the Law had also an internal significance, which he formulates as follows:

> We should look on all outward observance
> as resembling the body, and their inner
> meaning as resembling the soul.[18]

Philo differentiates in his exegetical treatment of the Therapeutae[19] and Essenes[20] between the philosophical-mystical and the ethical-tropological direction of allegorical exegesis. This differentiation had already been applied by the rabbis of Hellenistic Judaism and this same approach belonged later essentially to the structure of the Christian allegorical way of interpretation.[21]

Regarding the particulars of the allegorical interpretation of Scripture, Philo came close to the Midrash. According to Philo the exegete should pay particular attention to the following textual difficulties because they most likely have hidden and significant allegories to be deciphered. These aspects are also discussed by Grant and Siegfried and cited as follows:

> Reduplicated expression; seemingly super-
> fluous words; tautologies; contradictory
> expressions placed close together; expres-
> sions apparently out of context; synonyms;
> play on words; seemingly unusual adverbs,
> prepositions, or pronominal forms; compound
> words; ambiguous expressions; words whose
> meaning would change with an accent or

> breathing; strange expressions generally;
> verbs used with inappropriate number of
> tense; verses or phrases in an unusual
> context; numbers, natural phenomena, and
> names which could have a symbolic meaning.[22]

The allegorical method was for Philo not only an instrument of exegesis but also of speculation. It was his goal, on the one hand to combine Greek thought and Jewish piety and on the other to justify the Torah in a Hellenistic world and trying to make it equal, if not superior to the philosophical writings of the Greeks, a problem, of course, with which the Church Fathers had to cope further. His influence upon Christian exegesis was far-reaching while Rabbinic interpreters of Scripture did not draw from his writings.

Early Christianity

Jesus Himself often spoke in veiled and metaphorical language so that not only his apostles and disciplines mis-understood him sometimes when they tried to interpret his words literally[23] but Christian exegetical and hermeneutical inter-pretation has been involved--over the nearly two thousand years of its existence--in an ever new exploration of the deeper meaning of Scripture without perhaps having reached its most profound meaning yet.

For the exegesis of early Christianity and the Patristic Age, Paul and Philo were initially perhaps the most influential sources. The epistle to the Corinthians with the indication that "the letter kills but the spirit gives life"[24] has always provided nourishment for the exegetes. For the typological interpretation--which, for the time being, will here be under-stood as the correlation of the Old and New Testaments--the statement of the Apostle Paul in the letter to the Galatians where Hagar and Sarah correspond to each of the two Testaments[25] has been decisive for the development of this mode of inter-pretation.

In the controversy about the inspiration of the Old and New Testaments, particularly in the polemics with the Gnostics, the allegorical method was not only used as a polemical tool but as a didactic means and for exegetical explorations as well. The letters of Barnabas and Clement[26] belong to the first documents of this struggle. With the Apologists one finds already an abundance of examples of the allegorical method. Justin Martyr in his work <u>Dialogues with Trypho</u> refutes the Jewish interpretation in favor of the Christian interpretation of the prophets.[27]

Theophilus speaks in his apologetic writings of inspiration not only in connection with the prophets but he ascribes it also to the Sybil.[28] Irenaeus of Lyons gives in his <u>Adversus Haereses</u> a systematic refutation of the Gnostics whereby he defends in particular the historical reality of the Old Testament. According to Irenaeus, the application of the allegorical method is already necessary for the proper understanding of Scripture provided that the Christian article of faith and not Gnostic inspiration are its point of departure.[29] As a matter of fact, Irenaeus himself applies the allegorical method of interpretation in his own sermons.[30]

Clement of Alexandria

Faith and gnosis were the dynamic sources in the world-view of Clement of Alexandria. His allegorical conception was influenced by the Egyptian hieroglyphic tradition which veiled the truth in enigmas, symbols and metaphors. These allegorical and figurative signs imitate the cosmos the order of which will finally lead to the full truth.[31] Since this truth—and Christ is the whole truth--is accessible only to the initiates of truth, into the mysteries of Christianity, poets, philosophers and prophets of all times, who were considered the initiates of truth, have used veiled language. For Clement himself, primordial concepts and mysteries belonged to the same branch of speculation. Only with painstaking efforts of interpretation could one pierce the veil which was covering the truth.[32] Although Clement of Alexandria has no exegetical system as such, he arrives at the following schema from hieroglyphic models:

1. epistolographic
2. hieratic
3. hieroglyphic: a. literal (kyriology)
                               b. symbolic:

                                   1) literal
                                   2) figurative
                                   3) allegory-
                                      enigmas[33]

Clement transposes this hieroglyphic scheme to the mysteries of the Old and New Testaments.[34] Thus faith and gnosis are the two trends of epistemology which Clement connects with the literal and spiritual senses of Scripture which in turn lead to the mysteries of truth. In this schema the literal sense corresponds to the faith of the people gathered around Jesus at the Sermon on the Mount whereas the meaning beneath the allegorical sense of Scripture is finally accessible only to the initiates of Mount Tabor.[35] Clement did not develop a systematic method to uncover the hidden meaning of Sacred Scripture. This task was taken up by his great pupil Origen.

Origen

This doctor of the Church developed, from the basic concept of the literal and spiritual sense of Scripture, a certain exegetical method which would enable the exegete, as well as the faithful, to grasp the multiple sense of Scripture according to their capacities. A definite threefold method for the interpretation of Scripture was for the first time worked out by Origen; it corresponded to the <u>physical</u> (body), <u>psychic</u> (soul) and <u>philosophical-spiritual</u> (intellect) divisions in man. According to this division, the physical part corresponds to the body-soul sense and the philosophical part to the spiritual sense.[36] Origen offers proof of his doctrine of the threefold division from Solomon's proverbs. He says:

      And do Thou portray in a threefold manner,
      in Counsel and Knowledge, to answer words

of truth to them who propose them to Thee.[37]

For the Alexandrian Origen, the entire Scripture had a spiritual but not necessarily a literal meaning. He cautions that inversions and text insertions are to be analyzed most carefully for it is possible that beneath such passages a mysterious truth might be hidden. Here the influence of Philo is obvious. Origin proves this method of interpretation again from Scripture itself and summarizes it in the following way:

> . . . And therefore, the exact reader must, in obedience to the Savior's injunction to 'search the Scripture' carefully ascertain in how far the literal meaning is true, and in how far impossible; and so far as he can, trace out, by means of similar statements, the meaning everywhere scattered through Scripture, of that which cannot be understood in a literal significance.[38]

With Origen, the interpretation of Scripture received its own traditional form which was nourished by the tradition of Greek philosophy, rhetoric and Stoicism, Hellenistic-Rabbinic exegesis, particularly Philo, the writings of Saints Paul and John as well as of early Christian exegesis; not least it was influenced by his teacher, Clement of Alexandria. Thus, this new form of interpretation was stabilized in the threefold method of interpretation which was for a long time the standard model of the School of Alexandria.

The Latin Church Fathers

The themes and writings of the Greek Church Fathers were brought into the Western Church by translations and Bible commentaries. But direct interrelationships such as those developed by pilgrimages, diplomatic relationships or exile also contributed to the increase of this knowledge. A special role in the transportation of theological ideas and in the translation of texts was played by the Gallican Bishop, Hilary of Poitiérs, the Presbyter Rufinus, Ambrose, Bishop of Milan and

131

Jerome because they mastered the Greek language and because they also had been in some contact with the Eastern Church. They all accepted the threefold method of Origen and developed it according to their own exegetical insights.

Hilary of Poitiérs (315-365 A.D.)

Hilary was condemned to exile in Phrygia during the conflict with Arianism at the Synod of Béziers in the year of 356 A.D.; he stayed in exile for six years.[39] During these years he learned Greek and he occupied himself with theological questions, particularly with speculations about the Trinity, an issue with which the Greek Church wrestled very much during that time. He penetrated deeply into the works of Origen and he himself wrote several theological treatises, i.e., De Trinitate.[40] These works are an attempt to bring about a synthesis between Eastern and Western theology. This effort towards a synthesis finds particular expression in his work Liber Mysteriorum[41] in which he applies the allegorical method of Origen but in which he re-works the spiritual sense of Scripture in a more simplified, figurative way so that the people of the Church of Gaul would be able to understand Scripture more easily. Hilary was perhaps the first scholar who applied the typological exegesis so extensively and systematically. Augustine and Ambrose have been particularly influenced by this insight of Hilary.[42] Brisson has rightly pointed out that the independent thought of Hilary consisted in his effort to combine the traditional, more subtle exegesis of the School of Alexandria with the more simple interpretation of Scripture which was practiced in the Western Church in order to make it more accessible to pastoral care.[43] Hilary's work is, therefore, an important link between Eastern and Western interpretation of Scripture.

It seems rather significant that the small work of the Liber Mysteriorum, the first systematic document of the allegorical method in the Western Church, is a product of the Church in Gaul from which a certain liturgical impetus continued to proceed. Three particular traits of the Gallican people which will concern us up to Amalarius of Metz, speak out of this work. They are: 1) openness towards exogenous traditions; 2) the

132

ability to assimilate them in given situations; and 3) to transform them according to their indigenous traits and endogenous
traditions.[44]

Rufinus Tyrannius of Aquilaia (345-460 A.D.)

The special significance of the presbyter Rufinus lies in
the fact that he made Greek texts, particularly those of Origen,
accessible to the Western world.[45] He was an enthusiastic
follower of Origen whose threefold interpretation of Scripture
he accepted. His work, De Benedictione Patriarcharum, an allegorical interpretation of Gen. 49:6, is significant for the
transmission of the formulated three-fold sense of Scripture.[46]

Ambrose, Bishop of Milan (339-397 A.D.)

The Bishop of Milan had a special influence upon the tradition and diffusion of the allegorical exegesis. He stands
entirely under the influence of the School of Alexandria and
obviously he was influenced by Philo because he often borrowed
from him verbatim.[47] The concept of the body as a wrapping for
the spirit is particularly pronounced with Ambrose. It can, of
course, be traced back to Philo and his allegorical interpretation of the creation of the earthly man.[48]

Under the influence of Origen, Ambrose accepted the
categories of the threefold sense of Scripture and he himself
gave the following definition:

> Tertia quoque est quam nobis apostoli
> Pauli tribuit auctoritas, qui ait:
> "Illa quae Abraham ut de ancilla susci-
> peret sobolem, in figuram facta sunt, et
> secundum allegoriam dicta, allegoria est
> cum aliud geritur et aliud figuratur.[49]

This formulation, which contains within itself the entire
ambivalence of allegory was taken over more or less by all
exegetes of the Middle Ages. Through allegory the historical
factors of the Old Testament receive a new meaning which points
beyond itself and which the exegete will have to explore.

Ambrose applies this tripartition also to the entire interpretation of Scripture itself. Thus, for example, <u>Genesis</u>,
corresponds to the historical sense, <u>Deuteronomy</u> to the moral
sense, and <u>Liviticus</u> to the mystical sense of Scripture.
Ambrose also divides the book of Solomon in this threefold
manner. His definition is as follows:

> Omnis scriptura divina, vel naturalis,
> vel mystica, vel moralis est. Naturalis
> in Genesi, in qua exprimitur quomodo
> facta sunt coelum maria, terrae et que-
> mad modum mundus iste sit constitutus
> mystica in Levitico, in quo comprehen-
> ditur sacerdotale mysterium. Moralis
> in Deuteronomio, in quo secundum legis
> praeceptum vita humana formatur. Unde
> et Salomonis tres libri ex plurimis
> videntur electi: Ecclesiastes de natura-
> libus, Cantica canticorum de mysticis,
> Proverbia de moralibus.[50]

The influence of this Scriptural tripartition can later also be
observed in Amalarius' allegorical-dramatic liturgy where it is
expressed in the modulation and representational forms of
songs.[51] The typological sense, that is, the inner relationship
of the two Testaments, comes to full expression in Ambrose's
writings; his source was most likely the <u>Liber Mysteriorum</u> of
Hilary.[52] An exclamation of wonder and astonishment about the
mysterious interrelationship expresses his vision:

> . . . O mirandum mysterium! rota intro
> rotam currebat et non inpediebatur
> novum testamentum in veteri. . . erat,
> intra illud currebat, per quod adnuntiabatur.[53]

It was always of great concern to the Bishop of Milan to explore
the spiritual sense and to penetrate to the hidden mystery of
the written word. His exclamation; "<u>Quam profunda latent
mysteriorum secreta in litteris</u>!"[54] permeates his entire
exegesis. From the writings of Augustine it is evident how
effectively Ambrose used his allegorical interpretation in his

sermons and influenced the mind of Augustine to the extent that he overcame his prejudices against the rudimentary expressions of the Bible.[55]

Jerome (340-420 A.D.)

This Church Father was also most significant for the transmission and further diffusion of the allegorical exegesis and interpretation of Scripture. His method is, however, more complicated because he draws from several sources: he was influenced by the School of Alexandria as well as by Rabbinical exegesis. As a philologist he was primarily concerned with the literal sense of Scripture[56] which does not imply, however, that his exegesis was not allegorically determined.

The Ezechielcommentary of Jerome is particularly informative about this threefold method which he also divides into the steps of naturalia-moralia-mystica of Origen whose influence he admits in saying: "...ut scias Origenis opuscula in omnem scripturam esse triplica".[57] Like Origen he too sees the doctrine of the threefold division of Scripture emerging from the structure of the Old Testament itself.[58] Beyond that Jerome gives his own formulation which is as follows:

> Et jubetur nobis, ut eloquia veritatis
> id est, Scripturas sanctas, intelligamus
> tripliciter. Primum, juxta litteram
> secundum medie per tropologiam; tertio
> sublimius, ut mystica quaeque noscamus.[59]

In addition to the application of the threefold exegesis of Scripture, Jerome is the first exegete in the Latin Church to formulate the fourfold sense as he interprets the meaning of the city of Jerusalem in a fourfold way: as a historical city, as a heavenly city, as the Church on earth, and as the faithful soul:

> Quator autem modis intelligi potest Jeru-
> salem: Vel haec quae Babilonio et Romano
> igne succensa est; vel coelestis primiti-
> vorum; vel Ecclesia quae interpretatur visio
> pacis; vel animae singulorum quae fide

135

cernunt Deo.[60]

Cassian adopted this scheme and since then, following him, this interpretation can be found throughout the Middle Ages,[61] particularly in the enactment of the drama of the liturgy.[62]

With the translation of the Greek texts by Rufinus, the synthesized and figurative exegesis of the Bishop of Poitiers, and with the allegorizing of Ambrose and Jerome, the way of understanding Scripture had also become a significant herme-neutical principle in the Western Church. With Augustine, however, a new phase began in the Church in the field of alle-gorical understanding and interpretation which must be considered in relation to Augustine's signum-res-schema. Augustine's ideas are extremely complicated and the sign-schema is particularly difficult to appropriate. In the following examination of texts I will only attempt to give a simple introduction to this complex world view and to make visible the tradition which nourished a new Weltanschauung. It does not pretend to be more than that.

Augustine (353-430 A.D)

Augustine's allegorical interpretation of Scripture cannot be understood without his search for truth, without his intellect trained in rhetoric, and without his theory of signs. Therefore, his epistemological development will be briefly examined up to the time of his meeting with Ambrose in Milan. Here in Milan, the allegorical sense of the sermons of Bishop Ambrose led Augustine to a new and deeper understanding of Scripture resulting in a decisive insight leading to a turning-point in Augustine's life; following this, his theory of signs will be briefly outlined and in the concluding discussion Augustine's understanding of the allegorical method will be dealt with.[63]

Rhetoric and the Interpretation of Scripture: Augustine was an enthusiastic rhetorician and in his Confessions[64] he admits that it had been his greatest ambition to shine in his rhetorical career. When he was eagerly studying the books of rhetoric, Cicero's Hortensius became a turning point in

136

Augustine's thought. He began to be interested in philosophy.[65]
Before he turned to philosophy, however, Augustine studied the
Bible; but his intellect, trained in the art of rhetoric, found
Scripture without taste and without any meaning and disdainfully
he put the Bible aside.[66] Augustine himself admits that his
vision had been caught in the literal sense of Scripture and
therefore he could not have penetrated to the deeper sense.[67]
During his Manichaean period Augustine was a teacher of
rhetoric, first in Thagaste and then in Carthage. He remained
in Carthage until his break with Faustus and his consequent
estrangement from the Manichaeans.[68] After that Augustine went
to Rome in 383 A.D., where he founded a school of rhetoric and
enrolled, at the same time, in the Academy of the Sceptics.[69]
In the year of 384 he applied for a position of rhetoric in
Milan. It was here that Symmachus, the prefect of the city,
introduced him to Ambrose whose rhetorical erudition made a
great impression on Augustine.[70] The spiritual sense of the
allegorical interpretation of Scripture, combined with the
skilled rhetoric of Ambrose, led him away from the Manichaean
point of view and brought him closer to the Christian
teachings.[71] The constantly repeated references of the Bishop of
Milan to the spirit of Scripture referring to the word of St.
Paul impressed themselves more and more upon his memory.
Augustine makes the following statement about this:

> . . . saepe in popularibus sermonibus
> suis decentem Ambrosium laetus audiebam:
> "Littera occidit spiritus autem vivi-
> ficat," cum ea, quae ad litteram perver-
> sitatem docere videbantur, remoto mystico
> velamento spiritaliter aperiret, non dicens
> quod me offenderet, quamvis ea diceret...[72]

The rudimentary expression of Scripture had been a stumbling
block for Augustine but now he could intelligently relate to the
Bible and Augustine began to understand the double sense of
Scripture[73] and, under the influence of Ambrose, he began to
utilize his own rhetorical education for the better understanding and unlocking of Scripture. In that process, the
rhetorical formulas themselves gained a new significance and
meaning through the decipherment of the scriptural senses for

which they were, in a way, an unlocking device.

In De Doctrina Christiana, Augustine had emphasized the significance of rhetoric and schemata for the understanding of the Bible; he further stressed that knowledge of tropes had contributed to the solution and clarification of scriptural ambiguities.[74] Strauss and Mayer, in particular, have worked out this conceptual change in Augustine. Strauss emphasized the view that through the transference of rhetorical schemata to the exegesis of Scripture, it had become possible for Augustine to find beneath each concept and word a possible signifying indication, a signum, which belonged to the intelligible and invisible world, to res.[75] Mayer pointed to the deepening of rhetorical concepts such as allegoria, imago, figura, as signs[76] in relation to a newly discovered spiritual world and cosmos.

In this brief sketch I have attempted to illustrate the extent to which rhetoric had been important for Augustine in order to understand Scripture. Although his rhetorically trained mind found Scripture at first repulsive, rhetoric itself later became for him a means to unlock the word of God hidden in the Bible. He began to devote himself more deeply and intensively to the meaning of the word as such which finds expression in his treatise about the philosophy regarding words as signs. Before we deal with those writings of Augustine which particularly concern themselves with signs, we shall briefly outline the tradition of signs.

The Tradition of the Concept of Signs: The sign in Augustine's work is extremely subtle and complicated. Because of its significance in connection with the allegorical mode, its tradition will be examined from three aspects, namely, 1) from the aspects of deduction, 2) from the aspects of semantics and theory of language, and 3) in the sense of Neo-Platonism. Thereafter, we shall deal with the idea of signs of Augustine himself.

The Sign as Deduction[77]

Aristotle differentiates between mistakable and unmistakable signs as follows:

> . . . for anything such that when it is
> another thing is or when it has come in-
> to being before or after, is a sign of
> the other's being or having come into being.[78]

This sign theory of Aristotle was taken over by the Stoics and Epicurians. According to Sextus Empiricus, the relationship of the sign to that which it designates, is a logical nexus, with the Epicurians on the other hand, the relationship comes from the empirically given.[79] In Roman rhetoric the sign will also be taken over in this sense. Cicero's definition is a combination of Aristotelian and Epicurian theories. He states:

> Signum est quod sub sensum aliquem cadit
> et quiddam significat quod ex ipso pro-
> fecto videtur, quod aut ante fuerit aut in
> ipso negotio aut post sit consecutum, et
> tamen indiget testimonii et gravioris con-
> firmationis.[80]

The sign points beyond itself and is simultaneously in need of verification. Quintillian also deals with signs in the sense of deduction.[81] The grammarian Dionysius Thrax and Donatus describe the sign not as such, but rather, as the process of designation, as for instance with the declination of substantiva.[82] For Varro on the other hand, the sign is again an aliquid significent, that is to say, signifying another beyond itself.[83] Augustine himself a rhetorician and grammarian, must have been familiar with these conceptions. In the Old and New Testaments[84] as well as with the early Christian writers,[85] the sign is understood in the deductive sense. Tertullian also applies it in this sense.[86] With Origen the signs are mainly miracles which point to the Creator. His definition expresses the entire ambivalence which rests within the sign: signum namque dicitur cum per hoc videtur aliud indicatur.[87] Then with

Hilary and Ambrose, the sign undergoes a change in meaning in relation to the typological interpretation of the Old Testament.[88]

In Greek philosophy, with the Romans and with the early Christian writers up to about 200 A.D., there is evidence for the sign concept in the sense of deduction. With the typological-figurative interpretation of Hilary of Poitiérs, there is for the first time a change through the interaction of typology and figurative sign.

The Sign in Semantics and Philosophy of Language.

Markus sees the new dimension in Augustine manifested in the linguistic modification of the sign from the word of Scripture. He states that:

> . . . words are for Augustine, signs par
> excellence, and his theory of signs is
> meant to be, from the start, a theory of
> language as well as of other types of
> sign. In this consists the origina-
> lity of his reflection on meanings...[89]

Jackson on the other hand shows on the basis of textual comparison how Augustine stands linguistically both in the semantic tradition of Aristotle as well as in that of the Stoics. He emphasizes that the originality of Augustine consisted in his application of the traditional theory and language of signs to the interpretation of Scripture. He says in this connection:

> . . . It consists, I suggest, in the
> application of traditional sign-theory
> and sign-language to a new task, the
> interpretation of Scripture. Briefly,
> Augustine's application consists in
> using the technical terms of semantics
> to make distinctions and definitions
> which delineate clearly the problems
> faced by the interpreter of Scripture.[90]

Jackson furthermore calls attention to the fact that the Stoics
had worked out primarily the sense of the semantic meaning of
words which also was later the case with Augustine. It must
also be noted, that the schematic vision with the Stoics was, as
well as with Augustine, a three-fold interrelated situation
which consisted of the sign, the signified and the object or,
respectively, the subject.[91] The essence (eidos) of a sign in
this three-fold-related situation consists, according to this
view, in the fact that it communicates and from this inter-
change--merging from a thing or a situation--it is both
receiving its existence and handing down its becoming. This
however is a situation dynamically in motion, a motion which
Aristotle already discussed.[92] From such a consideration and
understanding, however, the sign would correspond in its essence
with allegoria, that is, it presupposes another.[93]

The Sign in Neo-Platonism

With Plato the material world is a reflection of the world
of ideas which are manifested in the empirical realm. This
Platonic dichotomy of a world vision was taken over by Plotinus
and developed into the Neo-Platonic structure of a tripartite
universe.

Augustine read the writings of Plotinus during his time in
Milan which contributed to his metaphysical break-through and
which moved him to denounce Manichaeanism. It was, however,
only in connection with Scripture, particularly in relation to
the Gospel of St. John and the letters of St. Paul that Plotinus
became more significant for Augustine.[94] At the same time, the
Neo-Platonic ideas which were interwoven with the sermons of St.
Ambrose, probably had influence on Augustine's thought. But the
structure of his vision at Ostia[95] as well as his description of
the Pauline vision in De Genesi ad Litteram[96] which correspond
to the threefold structure of the Plotinic universe, point to
Augustine's independent synthesis of Neo-Platonism.

Although Augustine's Neo-Platonism cannot be dealt with in
the framework of this dissertation, it may be stated, however,
that Augustine's conception of signs is, in part, derived from
his metaphysics--from the two worlds of the Platonic

system, the realm of the invisible and the visible which later culminates in the dramatic world structure of his De Civitate Dei.[97]

I have attempted to show that the traditional concept of signs, as it culminated in Augustine's scheme was derived from the traditions of Greek philosophy, i.e., in the deductive sense, from Roman rhetoric and grammar, as well as from the Old Testament and early Christian literature. The semantic-linguistic tradition beginning with Aristotle up to the Stoics with special consideration of the three-fold sign-related situation was discussed next in order to show how Augustine's sign-scheme via Plotinus and in connection with St. John and St. Paul was rooted in Neo-Platonism which seemed to be the point of departure of his own synthesis. In the following section we shall try to sketch the sign as such in Augustine's own thought.

The Sign in Augustine's Thought.

According to Augustine, a sign may point to things of the visible and invisible world and it can be recognized by two characteristics: first it makes an impression on the senses and secondly it provokes thought. Thereby it is possible that a thing can retain in itself a sign and signify further meanings and realities. Already in his childhood, Augustine had exper-ienced these essential traits of the sign from his own observa-tions.[98] The most extensive treatment of the sign can be found in Augustine's De Magistro (398 A.D.) and De Doctrina Christiana (begun around 387 and completed around 427 A.D.) where he ex-pounds his theory of signs.[99] Therefore these two works will be dealt with briefly.

De Magistro,[100] a dialogue between Augustine and his son Adeodat, is an examination of the semantic meaning of a sign. At the beginning the question is asked why signs are needed. The answer is that teaching is the purpose of all speaking. Christ had not taught words but realities through words and the main purpose of signs (signum) would be to direct the intellect towards things (res). For this reason nothing can be learned without signs. The real meaning of a sign often had to be interpreted and arrived at by way of further signs, that is,

through synonyms, circumscription, gestures, figurative representations or illustrative demonstrations. Augustine also
deals with the signifying and complex gestures of the actor. He
points out:

> Hinc nescio quomodo ad surdos et
> histriones devenimus, qui non sola
> quae videri possunt, sed multa prae-
> terea ac prope omnia quae loquimur gestu
> sine voce significant; eosdem tamen
> gestus signa esse comperimus.[101]

The phenomenon of the gesture of sign language, i.e., miming,
was a frequent pre-occupation of the Bishop of Hippo.[102]

The second part of this work deals with the explication of
signs. Here Augustine argues mainly that the meaning of signs
could not be understood without knowing the realities which are
veiled by the signs. The real value of words, on the other
hand, consists in their challenge to us to search for things
because the things themselves are not immediately presented to
us. Men cannot be reliable teachers of semantics; only the
immanent teacher, who is Christ, is able to shed light upon all
given realities.[103]

If in De Magistro, the inner teacher, Christ, is of importance in order to help to throw light on the meaning, in
Augustine's work De Trinitate, the light itself is a con-
stitutive element of the word and from it, it receives its
metaphysical significance. For this reason only the correct
understanding of sacred Scripture and of the signs will lead to
the source of all light. But this can only take place through
the application of different kinds of approaches.[104]

In De Doctrina Christiana, Augustine tries to work out a
scheme which will lead to the decipherment of Scripture. In the
first four books he deals particularly with the concepts of
signs and things. In the first book he comes back to the theme
with which he dealt in De Magistro. He also points out that
things (res) can only be understood through signs: Res per signa
discuntur.[105] Signs are things which become the signified and

143

thus point beyond themselves: Signa res. . . quae ad significandum aliquid adhibentur.[106] After Augustine has elaborated this essential trait of signs, he distinguishes in the second book between two classes of signs, namely, the signa naturaliter and the signa data.[107] To the first signs, the natural signs, belong signs such as smoke or traces, i.e., signs, which result from the thing itself. On the other hand, signa data or given signs are understood to be signs which living creatures give to each other. Augustine again places the actor among such signs or sign-givers. Such a sign-situation which results from the signa data, is a three-fold-related one because it deals with intercommunication, that is to say, communication between sign-giver, signified and that which is open to the signifying sign.[108]

Augustine divides the signa data into further sub-classes, namely into signs as such--signa propria--and translatable signs--signa translata. The latter have the greater significance because they can conceal a revelation or a mystery. Augustine, in addition, differentiates between signa propria referring to foreign languages and their translation, signa translata, to the veiled discourse of Scripture, which often arises from ignorance and in such a case Augustine recommends the application of the pagan sciences to the interpretation of sacred Scripture.[109] With the greatest care Augustine devotes a whole chapter to the ambiguous signs, signa ambigua. In this chapter, the signa propria refer to grammatical obscurities whereas signa translata contain ambiguities in the figurative sense. These places in Scripture demand meticulous care and perseverance and it must be avoided to interpret figurative expressions in the literal sense,[110] because literal wisdom is for Augustine "wisdom of the flesh" since it does not originate from the truth. This is for Augustine the reason why pagans have fallen into idolatry because they interpreted signs as things themselves.[111] The rabbis too have, according to Augustine, ascribed too much significance to the literal sense.

From this point of Augustine's development it would perhaps be possible to see a connection with his time in Milan because it seems as if his allegorical method is related here with his schema of signs. Perhaps in this connection it is not without

144

significance that Augustine composed his first Genesis-Commentary: De Genesis contra Manichaeos[112] also in the year of 389 A.D. in which he refutes the Manichaeans with an allegorical interpretation of Scripture; this was also the time in which his semantic work, De Magistro appeared. To examine this relationship, however, cannot be the task of our present study.[113]

The Allegorical Interpretation in Augustine.

In his commentaries on Genesis,[114] Augustine deals exhaustively with the allegorical interpretation of Scripture. His world was a hierarchical one, consisting of a manifoldedness of forms which culminated in the transcendental realm. Augustine transfers this manifoldedness of forms to the senses of Scripture. Just as creation in its manifold forms refers back to its Creator, so Scripture narrates in its signs about other signs which then in turn lead back to reality or contain it within themselves. As the literal sense of Scripture was the point of departure for the immanent spiritual realities, so too the material creation was only a figure, the deciphering of which led back to the Creator. Scripture and creation were the garments, the veils of true being, of the Creator. Allegory, too, was for Augustine a signpost leading the way into the transcendental realm. It was filled with the inner dynamism of becoming, presupposing another, as was the case with Aristotle. Or it moved toward the image which at the same time it veiled, as was the case in the cosmos of Neo-Platonism. The world of knowing God which had been lost through the Fall of man could, for Augustine, only be regained by way of allegorical signs-- and it is here, I would suggest, that one can find the uninterrupted juncture which can be illustrated from the texts themselves.

Augustine's first commentary on Genesis--De Genesi contra Manichaeos--was an allegorical dispute of purely literal interpretation of the Old Testament.[115] In De Genesi ad litteram, liber imperfectus, written about 393 A.D., Augustine limits himself to the purely literal interpretation of the Old Testament story.[116] The most elaborate treatment of the account of Genesis is given in De Genesi ad litteram, liber duodecimus

145

which begins with a definition of the four-fold interpretation and which ends with a three-fold Neo-Platonic vision.[117] In the last three books of the Confessions (about 400 A.D.), Augustine gives again an allegorical interpretation of the Genesis account. Here, too, allegory is blending with the concept of signs and with Augustine's metaphysics. He confirms there that the manifoldedness of forms from the world of creation is transferred to the discourse of Scripture. This informative statement reads as follows:

> . . . sed quod ita crescat et multipli-
> cetur, ut una res multis modis enuntietur et
> una enuntiatio multis modis intellegatur,
> non invenimus nisi in signis corporaliter
> editis et rebus intellegibiliter excogitatis
> signa corporaliter edita generationes aquarum
> propter necessarias causas carnalis pro-
> funditatis, res autem intellegibiliter
> excogitatas generationes humanas propter
> rationis fecunditatem intelleximus . . .
> in hac enim benedictione concessam
> nobis at te facultatem ac potestatem
> accipio et multis modis enuntiare,
> quod uno modo intellectum tenuerimus,
> et multis modis intellegere, quod ob-
> scure uno modo enunciatum legerimus.[118]

Neither the manifoldedness nor the interrelatedness from which the polysemous allegorical signs and symbols result could be expressed in a better way. Although there is a certain parallelisation of the two worlds, they flow into each other. But this vision of forms then, an observation which is most interesting for our study of liturgical drama, finds also expression in the form of liturgical-dramatic representational configurations. As we pointed out earlier, this formation had already taken place in the Syriac and Byzantine liturgies.[119] Later, as we shall see, this configurational dramatic form is coming into its own in the liturgical vision of Amalarius of Metz.[120]

Although Augustine formulates a fourfold interpretation of

Scripture, it is very difficult to get a full grasp of his method. Perhaps the reason for this is that his allegorical interpretation corresponds with his understanding of the universe. Augustine is really the first one to formulate a fourfold sense of Scripture and perhaps he comes closest to the hieroglyphic formulation of Clement of Alexandria.[121] His fourfold method of interpretation is elaborated as follows:

> . . . secundum historiam ergo traditur, cum docetur, quid scriptum aut quid gestum sit; quid non gestum, sed tantum--modo scriptum quasi gestum sit. Secundum aetiologiam, cum ostenditur, quid qua de cause vel factum, vel dictum sit, secundum analogian, cum demonstratur non sibi adversari duo testamenta, vetus et novum. Secundum allegoriam, cum docetur non ad litteram esse accepienda quaedam quae scripta sunt, sed figurate intelligenda.[122]

The historical-literal sense refers not only to facts alone but also to probabilities which is not in accordance with the formulations which were previously discussed; that sense which inquires about the origins of things is also a new formulation and so is the analogical relationship of the two Testaments which could perhaps indicate the influence of Hilary; Augustine equates the fourth allegorical sense with the figurative and sign-like forms. Out of his second hermeneutical formula there sparkles the kernel of his ontology--where world and image blend into unity:

> . . . fides rerum temporalium. Et quid intersit inter allegoriam historiae, et allegoriam facti, et allegoriam sermonis, et allegoriam sacramenti. Et quomodo ipsa locuti divinarum Scripturarum secundum cujusque linguae proprietatem accipienda sit. . .[123]

This harmony of the meaning of words and the allegorical sign finds particular expression in his longer treatment of the gestus allegoricus to which Augustine repeatedly refers in connection with the actor and the theatre;[124] this part which is most informative for our study, will conclude our longer treatment about the Bishop of Hippo. It is as follows:

> . . . Ergo venti, animae in allegoria non
> absurde accipiuntur. Videte autem ne pute-
> tis nominata allegoria, pantomini aliquid
> me dixisse. Nam quaedam verba, quoniam
> verba sunt, et ex lingua procedunt, communia
> nobis sunt etiam cum rebus ludricis, et
> non honestis; tamen locum suum habent verba
> ista in ecclesia, et locum suum in scena.
> Non enim ego dixi quod apostolus non dixit,
> cum de duobos filiis Abraham diceret. . .
> Allegoria dicitur cum aliquid aliud videtur
> sonare in verbis, et aliud in intellectu
> significare. Quo modo dicitur agnus
> Christus: numquid pecus? Leo Christus:
> numquid bestia? Petra Christus: numquid
> duritia? Mons Christus: numquid tumor
> terrae? Et sic multa aliud videntur
> sonare, aliud significare; et vocatur
> allegoria. Nam qui putat me de theatro
> dixisse: allegoriam, putet et Dominum de
> amphitheatro dixisse parabolam. Videtis
> quid faciat civitas ubi abundant spectacula:
> in agro securius loquerer; quid sit enim
> allegoria non ibi forte didicissent homines,
> nisi in scripturis Dei. Ergo quod dicimus
> allegoriam figuram esse, sacramentum figuratum
> allegoria est.[125]

The relationship between allegory and dramatic representation, which later has its parallel in liturgical drama, is especially obvious from this part of the text. Furthermore, it shows on the one hand the close connection between word and sign and on the other a Roman public which was essentially adapted to sign and allegory, that is to say, to the mimesis of the gestus allegoricus having polysemous meaning.

148

In the foregoing treatment on Augustine, I have attempted to show the various traditions of modes of interpretating signs and their relationship to the allegorical method. It could be established that Augustine's rhetorical education received a new dimension in connection with the semantic sign-theories of the Epicurians and Stoics. It also became integrated with the cosmos of Neo-Platonic signs. When Augustine applied this newly appropriated body of rhetorical knowledge and signs to the interpretation of Scripture, a new signum-res-schemata ensued. The threefold-related situation of sign-giver, sign and object constituted its inner dynamism. Allegory and sign were blending into each other at this point. One of the most important sign-givers for Augustine was the actor. The allegorical signs of the Roman stage, however, could for Augustine not lead to the truth. Therefore he construed them as parallels with Christian allegorical signs. This conflation was later superseded when in its development Christian liturgical drama had absorbed some of the essential purpose and structure of the Roman stage.

Cassian (360-435 A.D.), Eucher of Lyons (450 A.D.?) and Cassiodours (487-583 A.D.) [126]

These three exegetes were particularly important for the period between Augustine and Pope Gregory the Great. They influenced the subsequent centuries partly because they further elaborated and systematized the meaning of Scripture.

Cassian: With Cassian the main division of the senses of sacred Scripture is twofold: namely, historical and spiritual. By this means he divides the spiritual sense again into three higher senses which really results in the structure of the four senses of Scripture. He elaborates this as follows:

> Theoretica vero in duas dividitur partes,
> id est in historicam et interpretationem,
> et intelligentiam spiritualem. . . Spiri-
> talis autem scientiae genera sunt tria
> tropologia, allegoria, anagoge. [127]

Although his Conlationes complement Augustine's De Doctrina Christiana, Cassian follows Jerome and his fourfold inter-

pretation of the city of Jerusalem which has influenced
hermeneutics and exegesis of the entire Middle Ages and which
was also conspicuously reflected in the representational configurations of liturgical drama. Cassian describes the
following image:

> Igitur praedictae quatour figurae in
> unum ita, si volumus, confluunt, ut una
> atque eadem Hierusalem quadrifariam possit
> intelligi; secundum historiam civitas
> Judaeorum; secundum allegoriam Ecclesia
> Christi; secundum anagogem civitatis Dei
> illa coelestis quae est mater omnium
> nostrum; secundum tropologiam anima
> hominis. . . .[128]

Here the exegetical structure is a result of the allegorical figure of the city of Jerusalem.

Eucher of Lyons: If with Cassian we can observe a certain
blending of Augustine's and Jerome's interpretation of
Scripture, with Eucher and Lyons[129] although he seems to follow
Cassian, we can again notice the dominance of the classical
triad which began with Origen. A significant difference is,
however, that Eucher relates the triad of the senses of sacred
Scripture also to the tripartition of the sciences of classical
learning. His formula in this respect is as follows:

> . . . Quam triplicem Scripturarum regulam
> convenienter observat confessio Trinita-
> tis sanctificans nos per omnia . . .
> Sapientia mundi huius philosophiam suam
> in tres partes divisit: Physicam-ethicam-
> logicam, id est naturalem, moralem, ratio-
> nalem. . .[130]

As can be seen from the title of his work, Eucher has produced
an exegetical handbook which tries to give the allegorical image
of the cosmic structure: concise formulas which express
uncertainty but also some rigidity.

150

<u>Cassiodorus</u>:[131] This learned scholar recommends, as
Augustine did, the application of the secular sciences to
Christian exegesis. His expositions concern themselves mainly
with the exegesis of the spiritual sense and here lies his
significance. He constitutes a certain bridge to Pope Gregory
the Great. Cassiodorus also emphasizes the <u>gestus allegoricus</u>
as follows:

> . . . manibus loquitur et quibusdam gesti-
> culationibus facit intellegi quod vix narrante
> linqua aut scripturae textu possit agnosci. . .[132]

Cassiodorus' works became a source for the educational system of
the West and therefore the radius of his influence was widespread and long-lasting.[133]

Pope Gregory the Great (540-604 A.D.)

With Pope Gregory the Great a new dimension in the allegorical interpretation of Scripture developed. Pastoral work
during the time of the general destruction by the Langobards and
the consequent expectation of the Last Judgment, which was
believed to arrive soon, was the greatest concern of this Pope.
At the center of his exegesis was therefore the moral-spiritual
sense. His orientation is threefold: historical-literal and
allegorical-typological-moral.[134]

Pope Gregory's voluminous <u>Magna Moralia in Job</u>[135] had great
influence on Isidore of Seville and on Bede as well as on the
Carolingians. He deals in particular with the entire work in a
tripartite manner. The first book is based on the first verses
of the Book of Job and is an example of his exegesis.[136]

In an accompanying letter to Bishop Leander which Pope
Gregory sent along with the Job Commentary, he describes the
threefold sense of Scripture in a metaphorical way and compares
it with a building under construction:

> Sciendum vero est, quod quaedam historica
> expositione transcurrimus, et per allegoriam
> quaedam typica investigatione perscrutamur;

> quaedam per sola allegoricae mora-
> litatis instrumenta discutimus; nonulla
> autem per cuncta simul sollicitus exqui-
> rentes, tripliciter indagamus. Nam primum
> quidem fundamenta historiae ponimus; deinde
> per significationem typicam in arcem
> fabricam mentis erigimus; ad extremum quo-
> que per moralitatis gratiam, quasi super-
> ducto aedificium colore vestimus.[137]

Here Pope Gregory groups his exegesis around the dramatic figure
of Job. Thus, his exegesis is determined, as it were, by
mimesis and figurativeness and reaches beyond itself into the
limitlessness of the spiritual sphere.[138]

Isidore of Seville (570-630 A.D.)[139]

Church reform and practical pastoral care were the concerns
of this Spanish bishop. He was, in his moral and spiritual
exegesis, particularly dependent on Pope Gregory the Great.[140]
With Isidore there is again a certain balance in the threefold
senses of Scriptural exegesis. He ascribes greater significance
to the literal sense whereby he is neglecting the moral or
spiritual sense.[141] His definition corresponds again to the
classical tripartite structure of Scriptural meaning. This can
be documented as follows:

> Lex divina triplici sentienda est modo,
> primo, ut historice, secundo ut tropologice,
> tertio ut mystice intelligatur.[142]

The books of the encyclopaedist Isidore of Séville have had, as
compendia and works of reference, great influence upon the
Carolingians and beyond that on the entire Middle Ages.

Bede the Venerable (673-735 A.D.)[143]

Bede belongs to the last Patristic source of allegorical
exegesis. With him one can find again a mixture of the third
and fourth senses. He wrote an abundance of allegorical
commentaries which are an indispensable source of Patristic

material. Because Bede and Isidore of Séville summarized the
Patristic Age and handed it down interdispersed with their own
insights and understanding, they were of great influence for the
early and entire Middle Ages. For our study Bede's work De
Tabernaculo et vasis eius is most important. Through the profound connection of the fourfold exegesis with the altar of the
Jewish Tabernacle in which the legs of the table of the altar of
sacrifice are related to each other and represent the four
senses, Bede expresses visually the interrelatedness of
Scripture and liturgy. At the end of our long journey through
the world of allegorical literature, we shall cite Bede's
summarized formulation:

> . . . Quatour autem pedes habet mensa: quia
> quadriformi ratione omnis divinorum elo-
> quiorum series distinguitur . . . Item
> mensa tabernaculi quatour habet pedes; quia
> verbo coelestis oraculi, vel historico in-
> tellectu, vel allegorico, vel tropologico,
> id est, morali, vel certe anagogico solent
> accipi.[144]

This relationship was in harmony with the allegorical exegesis
and liturgical representations. It was here that Amalarius of
Metz began to connect Eastern and Western liturgical drama.[145]

Summary

From the preceding study it is evident that the allegorical
interpretation presupposed a veiled and invisible reality. The
realities of being in the world were arising in constantly
becoming movements to signs and images of this invisible ground
of all things. Allegory thus points in signs and images beyond
itself to those invisible realities. This seems to be its very
essence. And at this point it is apparent that allegory and
liturgical drama converge and that the heritage of the classical
world and of the Patristic Age blend intricately with the
inheritance of the numinous Weltanschauung of the Germanic
peoples.[146]

It was Amalarius of Metz who brought together in a unique creation of representational configurations of dramatic liturgy that which was flowing together in the liturgical-allegorical traditions. He molded it with his own creative vision and imagination into an aesthetic whole, unlocking new dimensions of depths of the ever new revealing and ever new concealing mystery of the First Liturgical Act of Jesus, followed by His Passion, Death and Resurrection. In the fourth and fifth chapters of our study, we shall try to show the development of the works and significance of Amalarius for liturgical drama in the West.

[1]The following works cited below are invaluable for the
study of "allegory". More work, however, needs to be done to
help differentiating and clarifying this complex area of study.
I have mainly consulted the following works: Henri de Lubac,
Éxegèse Médièvale: les quatre sense de l'Écriture, Théologie 4,
2 vols. (Paris: Aubier, 1959); Beryl Smalley, The Study of the
Bible in the Middle Ages (Oxford: Basil Blackwell & Mott, Ltd.,
1952) paperback, second printing (Notre Dame, Indiana:
University of Notre Dame Press, 1970), pp. xi-xxvii, 1-82;
Robert E. McNalley, The Bible in the Early Middle Ages,
Woodstock Papers, n. 4 (Westminster, Md.: The Newmann Press,
1959); Michael Murrin, The Veil of Allegory (Chicago: The
University of Chicago Press, 1969); J. Pepin, Mythe et
Allégorie: les origines greques et les contestantiones judeo-
chrétienne (Paris: Édition Montaigne, 1958); Frank E. Robbins,
The Hexameral Literature: A Study of Greek and Latin
Commentaries on Genesis. Ph.D. Dissertation, Chicago (The
University of Chicago Press, 1912). A. Fletcher, Allegory: The
Theory of a Symbolic Mode (Ithaca: Cornell University Press,
1964; Cornell paperback, 1970), pp. 1-23; R. Herzog, Die
allegorische Dichtkunst des Prudentius. Ph.D. Dissertation,
Kiel, 1964. Zetamata, Nr. 42. Monographien zur klassichen
Altertumswissenschaft (München: C. H. Beck'sche Ver-
lagsbuchhandlung, 1966); Hans-Georg Gadamer, Wahrheit und
Methode, 3. erw. Aufl. (Tübingen: J.C.B. Mohr (Paul Siebeck),
1972), pp. 66-77; H. Doerrie, "Spätantike Symbolik und
Allegorese," FMST 2 (1968): 67-77; Christel Meier, "Überlegungen
zum gegenwärtigen Stand der Allegorie-Forschung, mit besonderer
Berücksichtigung der Mischformen", FMST 10 (1976): 1-69; Henning
Brinkmann, Mittelalterliche Hermeneutik (Darmstadt:
Wissenschaftliche Buchgesellschaft, 1980); Friedrich Ohly,
Schriften zur Mittelalterliche Bedeutungsforschung, 2. Aufl.
(Darmstadt: Wissenschaftliche Buchgesellschaft, 1983), Paul
Ricoeur, Conflict of Interpretations: Essays in Hermeneutics.
Translated from the French by Kathleen McLaughlin. (Evanston:
Northwestern University Press, 1974); P. Ricoeur, The Rule of
Metaphor: Multidisciplinary Studies of the Creation of Meaning
in Language. Translated from the French by Robert Czerny with

Kathleen McLaughlin and John Costello, S. J. (Toronto: University of Toronto Press, 1977); Mircea Eliade, _Images and Symbols: Studies in Religious Symbolism_. Translated from the French by Philip Mairet. (New York: Sheed and Ward. A Search Book, 1969); M. Eliade, _Symbolism, the Sacred and the Arts_. Edited by Diane Apostolos-Cappadona. (New York: Crossroads 1985), esp. pp. 3-16 and 105-142; and M. Eliade, _Briser le Toit de la Maison: La Créativité et ses Symboles. Les Essais_. (Paris: Édition Gallimard, 1986), esp. pp. 79-216, and Victor Turner, _The Forest of Symbols_, (Ithaca, N.Y.: Cornell University Press, 1967).

[2]Plutarch _de aud. poet._ 4.19e. cited by R. P. C. Hanson, _Allegory and Event_ (London: SMC Press, 1959), p. 39, n. 1; see also Gadamer, _Wahrheit und Methode_, p. 68, n. 1.

[3]Kluge _Etymologisches Wörterbuch_ 20th ed. s.v. "Allegorie"; Lewis and Short, _A Latin Dictionary_, 1966, ed. s.v. "allegoria"; Liddell-Scott _Greek-English Lexicon_, 1961, ed. s.v. αλληγορια Fletcher _Allegory_, p. 2, n.1.

[4]Plato _Apology_ 22[b-c]

[5]J. Tate, "The Beginnings of Greek Allegory," _CR_ 41 (1927): 214-15, and "Plato and allegorical interpretation," _CQ_ (1929): 142-54; 24 (1939): 1-10. But cf. also the _Dervi papyrus_, a commentary on Orphic writings, translated by Larry Jon Aldernick, in his "Crisis and Cosmogony: Post-Mortem Existence in the Eleusian and Orphic Mysteries", Ph.D. Dissertation: The University of Chicago, 1974. (Appendix).

[6]Robert M. Grant, _The Letter and the Spirit_ (London: S.P.C.K., 1957), pp. 3-5.

[7]Plato _Protagoras_ 316[d]; _Republic_ 2. 378[d]

[8]Plato _Timaeus_ 37[c]-40[d]

[9]H. v. Arnim _Stoicorum Veterum Fragmenta_, IV vols. (Leipzig: B. G. Teubner, 1905-1924), I: 274, 486, cited by Grant, _Letter and Spirit_, pp. 7-9.

[10] Harry Austryn Wolfson, _Philo_, 3rd rev. ed., (Cambridge, Mass.: Harvard University Press, 1962), pp. 87-162. Grant, _Letter and Spirit_, pp. 9-30.

[11] Heraclitus _Questions Homericae_ 22 cited by R. P. C. Hanson, _Allegory_, p. 39, n. 1.

[12] See Wolfson, _Philo_, pp. 133-35; Fritz Maas, "Von den Ursprüngen der rabbinischen Schriftauslegung," _ZfkTh_ 52 (1955): 133-35; I. Heinemann, _Altjüdische Allegoristik_ (Breslau: 1936) and Leonard Goppelt, _Typos_ (Gutersloh: Verlag C. Bertelsmann, 1939), pp. 30-31.

[13] Grant, _Letter and Spirit_, pp. 31-40; Wolfson, _Philo_, pp. 148-49; Goppelt, _Typos_, pp. 59-69.

[14] John L. McKenzie, _Dictionary of the Bible_ (Milwaukee: The Bruce Publishing Company, 1965), s.v. "Hand".

[15] Grant, _Letter_, p. 32; Hanson, _Allegory_, p. 43.

[16] Lev. 11: 24-30. _JB_

[17] _De Opificio Mundi_.

[18] _De Migratione Abrahami_ 15. 89-93.

[19] _De Vita Contemplativa_ 3. 28-29.

[20] _Quod Omnis probus liber sit_ 12. 82-83.

[21] See below, pp. 199-206 and pp. 212-218.

[22] Carl Siegfried, _Philo von Alexandrien als Ausleger des Alten Testaments_ (Jena: Verlag von Hermann Dufft, 1875), pp. 168-96, cited by Grant, _Letter_, p. 35.

[23] Joh. 4:32-38; Luk. 22:35-38. _JB_.

[24] 2 Cor. 3:6. _JB_.

[25]Gal. 4:21-31. JB.

[26]See above, pp. 57-59.

[27]Justin Martyr, Dialogues with Trypho, 31, 33, 36, 76, 113, 115.

[28]Irenaeus v. Lyon Adversus Haereses.

[29]Ibid.

[30]Ibid. and The Demonstration of the Apostolic Preaching with an introduction and notes by J. A. Robinson. London Society for the Promotion of Christian Knowledge. (New York: Macmillan, 1920).

[31]Clement of Alexandria Stromata 5.8.

[32]Ibid., 5.5.

[33]Ibid., 5.4.

[34]Ibid.

[35]Ibid. 5.6.

[36]Origenes De Principiis 3.4. (Prov. 22:20-21) Cf. de Lubac, Exègese, vol. 1, pt. 1: 199-207.

[37]Origenes De Principiis 4.1.11.

[38]Ibid., 4.1.19 (John 5:39).

[39]A. Altweiler, "Hilarius, Bischof v. Poitiérs," in Lexikon für Theologie und Kirche, 2nd rev. ed., Joseph Hofer und Karl Rahner, (eds.) 10 vols. (Freiburg, i.Br.: Verlag Herder, 1957-65), 5 (1969): 337-38. Hereafter cited as LThK.

[40]Saint Hilary of Poitiérs: The Trinity, translated with an introduction and notes by Stephen McKenna, C.S.S.R., The Fathers

of the Church, A New Translation (New York: The Fathers of the Church, Inc. 1954), v-xv; see also: Alfred Federer, "Kulturgeschichtliches in den Werken des heiligen Hilarius v. Poitiérs," Stimmen aus Maria Laach 81 (1911): 30-45.

[41]Hilaire de Poitiérs: "Traité de Mystères," texte etabli et traduit avec introduction et notes par Jean-Paul Brisson, Sources Chrétiennes (Paris: Les Éditions du Cerf, 1947), pp. 72-163.

[42]R. A. Markus, "St. Augustine on Signs," in R. A. Markus, ed. Augustine: A Collection of Critical Essay. (Garden City, N.Y.: Double Day & Co. Anchor Books Paperback, 1972), p. 65, n. 16.

[43]Brisson, Hilaire, pp. 7-14, 59-60.

[44]Cf. above, pp. 94ff. and below, pp. 173ff.

[45]F. X. Murphy, "Rufinus Tyrannius v. Aquileia," LThK 9 (1964): 91-92; Altaner-Stuiber, Patrologie, pp. 392-94.

[46]Rufinus Tryannius Aquileia De Benedictionibus Patriarcharum.

[47]McNally, Bible, pp. 53-54; de Lubac, Exegese, 1.1: 200-07, 230-37 and R. M. Malden, "St. Ambrose as an Interpreter of Holy Scripture," JTS 16 (1914-15): 509-522.

[48]Wolfgang Seibel, S.J., Fleisch und Blut beim heil. Ambrosius. Ph.D. Dissertation, Rome, 1955. Münchener Theologische Studien, Nr. 2, Systematische Abt., 14. Bd. (München: Kommissions Verlag Karl Zink, 1958), pp. 7-10.

[49]Ambrosius De Abraham 1.4.28.

[50]Ambrosius Enarratio in psalmum 36, Praefation 1.

[51]See below, pp. 285ff.

[52]See above, pp. 133ff.

[53]Ambrosius Ps. 118.4.28., see also Joseph Huhn, "Bewertung und Gebrauch der Heil. Schrift durch den Kirchenvater Ambrosius," Historisches Jahrbuch der Görresgesellschaft 77 (1958): 387-396.

[54]Ambrosius De Cain et Abel I,4,13.

[55]Cf. below, pp. 136ff.

[56]Smalley, Bible, pp. 10-23; de Lubac, Éxègese, pp. 205-269.

[57]Hieronymus Prologus de Homiliae et Jeremiam et Ezechielem.

[58]Idem, Commentaria in Ezechielem 5.16.

[59]Ibid.

[60]Ibid., 4.16.

[61]See below, pp. 158-59. Cf. also Smalley, Bible, pp. 20-22, 27-28; McNalley, Bible, p. 54 and L. Schade, Die Interpretationslehre des heil. Hieronymus, Biblische Studien Nr. 15 (Freiburg, i.B.: Herder'sche Verlagsbuchhandlung, 1910), p. 110.

[62]Cf. especially Maximos, above, pp. 86-88 and Amalarius, below, Chapters IV and V.

[63]Joseph Geyser, "Die erkenntnistheoretischen Anschauungen Augustins zu Beginn seiner schriftstellerischen Tätigkeit," in Augustinus Aurelius. Die Festschrift der Görresgesellschaft zum 1500. Todestag des Heil. Augustin. Herausgegeben von M. Grabmann und Joseph Mausbach (Köln: Verlag J. P. Bachem, GMBH, 1930), pp. 63-86; Arthur Allgeiser, "Der Einfluss des Manichaismus auf die exegetische Fragestellung bei Augustin" in Augustinus, pp. 1-13; Matthias Korger, "Grundprobleme der Augustinischen Erkenntnislehre. Erläutert am Beispiel von 'De Genesi ad Litteram'," Recherches Augustiniennes 2 (1962): 33-57, and

Vernon J. Bourke, <u>Augustin's Quest for Wisdom</u> (Milwaukee: The Bruce Publishing Company, 1945), esp. pp. 224-47.

[64]Augustinus <u>Confessiones</u> 3.3.

[65]Ibid., 3.4.

[66]Ibid., 3.5.

[67]Ibid.

[68]Ibid., 3.6.

[69]Ibid., 5.8.

[70]Cf. above, pp. 7-10.

[71]<u>Confessions</u> 5.13-14.

[72]Ibid., 6.4. (2 Cor. 2:6).

[73]Ibid., 6.5.

[74]<u>De Doctrina Christiana</u>. 2.37.

[75]Gerhard Strauss, <u>Schriftgebrauch, Schriftauslegung, und Schriftbeweis bei Augustine</u>, Beiträge zur Geschichte der biblischen Hermeneutik (Tübingen: J. C. B. Mohr (Paul Siebeck), 1959), p. 86.

[76]Cornelius Petrus Mayer, O.S.A., <u>Die Zeichen in der geistigen Entwicklung und Theologie des jungen Augustinus</u>, Ph.D. Dissertation Würzburg: Augustin Verlag, 1969), pp. 330-348.

[77]This treatment is based on the following works: B. Darrel Jackson, "The Theory of Signs in St. Augustine's '<u>De Doctrina Christiana</u>'," in: <u>Augustine: A Collection of Critical Essays</u>, ed. R. A. Markus (Garden City, N. Y.: Doubleday & Co., Inc., An Anchor Book, 1972), pp. 92-147 and R. A. Markus, "St. Augustine on Signs," in <u>Augustine</u>, pp. 61-91.

[78]Aristotle _Prior Analytics_ II. 27.70^{a}7; Cf. also Markus, "Signs," in _Augustine_, p. 61f.

[79]Sextus Epicurius _Adversus Mathematics_ 8. 11-12, 13, 177, cited by Markus, "Signs," in _Augustine_, pp. 61-63.

[80]Cicero _De Inv._ i.30., cited by Markus, "Signs," in _Augustine_, p. 64, n. 13.

[81]Quintillian _Inst. Or._ v.9., cited by Markus, "Signs," in _Augustine_, p. 64.

[82]Cf. Jackson, "Signs," in _Augustine_. 118.

[83]Varro _De Lingua Latina_ vii. 14., cited by Jackson, "Signs," p. 118, nos. 72, 73-74.

[84]_Gen._ 17:11., Luk. 2:12, 11:19-20., cited by Markus, "Signs," in _Augustine_, pp. 64-65 and Jackson,"Signs," Ibid., pp. 115-16.

[85]Clement., 12.7. _Didache_ 16.6. Cf. Markus, "Signs," in _Augustine_, pp. 65-75.

[86]Tertullian _Adv. Marc._, 3.13.4., 4.39.16. cited by Jackson, "Signs," in _Augustine_, p. 116.

[87]Origenes _in Joannem_ 13.69., cited by Markus, "Signs," in _Augustine_, p. 65.

[88]See above, pp. 131-33 and 133-36 and Markus, "Signs," in _Augustine_, p. 65, n.16.

[89]Markus, "Signs," in _Augustine_, p. 66.

[90]Jackson, "Signs," in _Augustine_, p. 136.

[91]Ibid., pp. 128-135 and Markus, "Signs," in _Augustine_, p. 74.

[92]See above, pp. 138ff.

[93] See abcve, pp. 123-24.

[94] Confessions, 7.1.

[95] Ibid., 9.10.

[96] "Sancti Aureli Augustine 'De Genesi ad Litteram, Liber Duodecimus,'" edited with an introduction, translation and commentary by John H. Taylor, S. J. (Ph. D. Dissertation, St. Louis University, 1948), pp. xiv-xxx.

[97] See also Heinrich Scholz, Glaube und Unglaube in der Weltgeschichte: Ein Kommentar zu Augustins 'De Civitate Dei' (Leipzig: J. C. Hinrich'sche Buchhandlung, 1911), pp. 65-69.

[98] Confessions 1.8.

[99] See Ulrich Duchrow, Sprachverständnis und Biblisches Hören bei Augustin (Tübingen: J. C. B. Mohr (Paul Siebeck), 1965).

[100] De Magistro.

[101] Ibid., 1.7.19.

[102] Ibid., 3.5.

[103] Cf. below, pp. 145ff.

[104] Augustinus De Trinitate 9.7.12 and 4.2.4. cited by Markus, "Signs," in Augustine, pp. 84-85.

[105] De Doctrina Christiana, 1.2.2. 1f.

[106] Ibid., 1.2.2. 11f.

[107] Ibid., 2.2.1.

[108] See above, pp. 138-40.

[109] De Doctrina Christiana, 2.20.

[110] Ibid., 3.5.9.

[111] Ibid., 3.11.

[112] De Genesi Contra Manichaeos.

[113] Cf. for the interrelatedness of allegory and sign, Duchrow, Sprachverståndnis, p. 155.

[114] Gilles Pélland, S. J., Cinq etudes d'Augustine sur le début de la Genése, Théologie recherches Nr. 8 (Paris-Tournai, 1972).

[115] See above, p. 145ff.

[116] De Genesi ad Litteram, Liber Imperfectus.

[117] De Genesi ad Litteram, Liber Duodecimus, 1. and 30.

[118] Confessiones 13.24.

[119] See above, pp. 66-92.

[120] See below, Chapters IV. and V.

[121] See above, p. 129f.

[122] De utilitate credendi. 1.5.

[123] De Vera Religione 1.50.99.

[124] See above, p. 142f.

[125] Enarratione in Ps. 103. serm. 1.13 (Gal. 4:21-31). Cited by Rudolph Abresmann, "The 'daemonium Meridianum' and Greek and Latin Patristic Exegesis," Traditio 14 (1958): 27-28.

[126] Smally, Bible, pp. 17-32; de Lubac, Éxègese, 1.1. 190-98. Regarding the influence of Cassian on the development of

monasticism in the West, see especially O. Chadwick, John Cassian: A Study in Primitive Monasticism, 2nd ed. (Cambridge: Cambridge University Press, 1968).

[127]Conlationes 14.8.

[128]Ibid.

[129]Smalley, Bible, p. 29.

[130]Eucher, Formulae spiritualis Intelligentiae: Praefatio.

[131]Smalley, Bible, pp. 29-32.

[132]Cassiodorus Variarum 1.20.5. In part cited by Jürgens, Pompa, p. 240, ns. 1-6.

[133]Cassiodorus, Institutiones.

[134]Smalley, Bible, pp. 32-35; de Lubac, Éxègese, 1.1: 185-93. See also D. Hoffmann, Die geistige Auslegung der Schrift bei Gregor dem Grossen, (Münster-Schwarzach: Vier-Türme-Verlag, 1968), pp. 18-21 and René Wasselynck, "Les Morals in Job,' dans les ouvrages de morale de haut Moyan age Latin," RThAM 31 (1864): 5-31.

[135]Gregorius I. Magna Moralia in Job.

[136]Ibid.

[137]Ibid., Praef. Epistula III.C.

[138]Cf. above, p. 105. See also Theodore Mopsuestia's treatment of the dramatic figure of Job in his "In Jobum". See also, Amalarius of Metz and his use of the dramatic figure of Job in his liturgical-dramatic representations. See below, pp. 298-99.

[139]See Smalley, Bible, p. 35; de Lubac, Éxègese. 1.1: 143-49.

165

[140]Wasselynck, "Morales in Job," pp. 5-31 and Ph. Delhaye, "Les idées morales de Saint Isidore de Séville," RThAM 26 (1959): 17-49.

[141]Sister Patrick Jerome Mullins, O. P. The Spiritual Life according to St. Isidore de Séville (Ph.D. Dissertation, The Catholic University of America Studies in Medieval and Renaissance Latin, Languages and Literatures, No. 13 (Washington: The Catholic University of America Press, 1940), pp. 45-59.

[142]Isidore de Séville Sententiae 18.12.

[143]Smalley, Bible, pp. 35-36; de Lubac, Éxègese, 1:1:143-49; B. Thum, "Beda," in LThK 2 (1958): 93-4.

[144]Beda De Tabernaculo et vasis eius 1.6.

[145]See below, pp. 198-208.

[146]Cf. Ursula Fischer, "Karolingische Denkart: Allegorese und 'Aufklärung'. Dargestellt an den Schriften Amalars von Metz und Agobard von Lyons," (Ph.D. Dissertation, Göttingen, 1957), pp. 25.42.

CHAPTER IV

AMALARIUS OF METZ: 775-852 A.D.

Liturgical Reform under Pepin and Charlemagne

After the invasion of the Roman Empire by the Germanic
tribes, after the sack of Rome and the incursion of the Arabs,
the era until about 750 A.D. was marked by political confusion
and general anarchy but, at the same time, also by a slow and
dynamic process of transformation in cultural, social and
political areas where the interactions of Roman and Germanic
worlds contributed to the emergence of a new culture. The
Church stood in the midst of this process of transformation. A
new order had already developed with the Christians within the
old order of the Roman Empire and since the Church disposed in
its expansion on the basis of her constitution over intra-
cultural sources, she had a key position in this great cultural
assimilation at which time the liturgy became an important organ
of renewal; at the same time it remained a vehicle of expression
in and of the new culture and transformed order.[1] The cradle of
this transformation in relation to the liturgy in the West was,
as has been shown, to be found in Gaul and with the Frankish
tribes. In consequence, the Church of the Franks played an
important role in the further cultural development of the West
not least through the forms of its liturgical expression.[2]

Until 750 A.D., the political disorders had also found
expression in the liturgy. In this general religious and
political decadence, initial attempts for a new ecclesiastical
orientation proceeded with the Merovingians under Boniface of
England. Around 742 A.D., Boniface had in his general reform
gained the support of Pepin for his missionary task. When in
754 A.D., Pepin was crowned as king of the Franks by Pope
Stephen II., the Merovingian dynasty was brought to an end; the
beginning of the kingdom of the Franks and its relationship with
Rome was also officially sealed.[3]

The first phase of a liturgical renewal which expressed the
order of the Franks, was started by Pepin when he abolished the

official Gallican liturgy in favor of the Roman liturgy.[4] The driving force of this reform had several sources. Because the indigenous "Gallican" liturgy was, by its very nature, flexible and open[5] to new streams of innovation, it was, for this very reason, in times of anarchy, itself no less prone to anarchy. Furthermore, it will have to be considered that around 750 A.D. the Gallican liturgy had already assimilated aspects of the Roman liturgy. This assimilation had been prompted by the circulation of the <u>Gelasium</u> and <u>Gregorianum</u>; it was also influenced by pilgrims who had been to Rome and through the cult of the apostolic princes, St. Peter and St. Paul.[6] However, the indigenous liturgy remained to be the kernel of this liturgical composite. The tradition of the Gallican liturgy had, however, been fed by the Byzantine-Syriac liturgy which was closely related to it, particularly on the basis of its dramatic figurative structure.[7] Since the Franks, however, considered themselves as a new God-chosen kingdom on earth, and since the relationship to Byzantium was already impeded by the iconoclastic controversy, the new political orientation must be considered as a decisive factor for the introduction of the Roman rite.[8]

The result of Pepin's reform is manifested in the <u>Gelasium</u> of the eighth century which, because it is mainly based on the older copy--Vat. Reg. 316 and on the <u>Gregorianum</u> Pad. D. 47--is an extremely complicated text.[9] The reasons for this were as follows: For the implementation of Pepin's program it was necessary to obtain examples of the Gregorian sacramentaries and antiphonaries from Rome which were sent to Pepin by Pope Paul around 760 A.D.[10] However, even the copies which were kept in Rome were incomplete, and in most cases these were texts which had already been extensively edited. Because of this, the copying which was undertaken by the Franks on the basis of incomplete and defective manuscripts could not result in a "pure Roman" liturgy.[11] As a matter of fact, even the "prototype" was not a unique Roman liturgy but rather constituted extraordinary Papal station-masses which in a certain sense were a framework for rubrics and not flexible enough; as a matter of fact, these texts of the Papal masses themselves were in need of emendations and up-dated editing.[12]

The metropolis of Metz[13] was, because of its cathedral and its central geographical location, of extreme importance for the realization of Pepin's reform program. From this metropolis the impetus of a liturgical Romanization proceeded under the leadership of Bishop Chrodegang. In this endeavor, the songs were at the center of reform. Furthermore, the Roman masses of the Papal stations were imitated in detail which must have resulted in rather rigid liturgical forms. This might have promoted discrepancies which occurred later, particularly if one considers how essential singing had been in the Gallican liturgy.[14] Under Charlemagne and Louis the Pious, Metz had continued to be a leading center and authoriative source because lively liturgical interests were outstanding traits of these Carolingians.

Charlemagne summarized his reform program mainly in the Capitularies[15] where the "explanation" of faith and liturgy--which belonged to the tradition of the expositio--was one of his main concerns.[16] Generally these expositions correspond both to the mentality of the clerics as well as to the receptivity of the faithful in dispersed rural areas among which were also the newly Christianized Saxons. These expositions were therefore, as they related to practical pastoral care, simply written according to the literal sense and differed considerably from the earlier and more subtle and complex Expositio of Germanus of Paris (ca. 500-600 A.D.) which was discussed earlier in this study.[17] It was not until the time of Amalarius that these expositions again became more complex and elaborate.

The beginnings of Pepin's reform were continued by Charlemagne who considered Pepin's sense of liturgical unity to be of great significance. These intentions can be documented as follows:

> Omni clero. Ut cantum Romanum pleniter
> discant, et ordinabiliter per nocturnale
> vel gradale officium peragatur, secundum
> quod beatae memoriae genitor noster
> Pippinus rex decertavit ut fieret, quando
> Gallicanum tulit ob unanimitatem aposto-
> licae sedis et sanctae Dei ecclesiae paci-
> ficam concordiam. . .[18]

Not only universal unity with the Church in Rome, however, was
the intention of the Emperor but he wished even the smallest
discrepancies to be eliminated:

> Quae (sc. ecclesia Franciae) dum a primis
> fidei temporibus cum ea (sc. Romana eccle-
> sia) perstaret in sacrae religionis unione
> et ab ea--paulo distaret--quod
> tamen fidem non est--in officiorum
> celebratione venerandae, memoriae genitoris
> nostri. . .exemplis, qui sanctissimi viri
> Stephani, Romanae urbis antestitis, est ei
> etiam in psallendi ordine copulata . . .[19]

Rome was the great example of unity and tradition. Charlemagne
particularly emphasized the tradition and significance of the
songs and the readings. He says:

> . . . totas Galliarum ecclesias Romanae
> traditionis suo studio cantibus decoravit,
> nos nihilominus solerti easdem curamus
> intuitu praecipuarum insignire serie lec-
> tionum.[20]

Here the anti-Byzantine position of Charlemagne can be grasped
quite clearly because in these parts of the liturgy the Eastern
influence is quite obvious[21] and here the Gallican liturgy
differs remarkably from that of Rome. Songs and readings
remained until Amalarius sensitive constructive parts of the
liturgy because the possibilities of variation, improvisa-
tion, and imaginative creative work were particularly manifested
in singing and reading and consequently it was from these parts
that resistance to uniformity and unity was strongest.[22]

Alcuin was the driving force in the reform program of
Charlemagne. The fact, however, that it was not easy to
transfer the custom of Rome to the liturgy of the Franks is
evident from Alcuin's work and his editing of the sacramentaries. This great reformer of the liturgy was confronted
with the task of composing from the available incomplete copies

of sacramentaries filled with errors and inaccuracies, a uniform
liturgy for the Empire. Because of such inadequacies, Charlemagne had requested through Paul Wanefried an unmixed
(inmixtum) sacramentary from Pope Hadrian (772-795 A.D.).[23]
This order of Charlemagne however could not be completed until
785-86 A.D. because there was most likely no copy in Rome itself
which would have been suitable to comply with the request from
the Imperial Court. Even in Rome itself there was not one pure
copy because the sacramentary which John of Ravenna delivered to
the Emperor's Palace in 785-86 A.D., was a copy which had
already been edited and revised, namely, the so-called Hadrianum. Alcuin recognized however that even this sacramentary in
its stiff format was not sufficient for its use in school or
parish because it lacked the capacity for expression and warmth,
both of which were distinguished traits of the Franks; therefore
he expanded it with his own emendations the end-product of which
became to be known as the Alcuin-Supplement.[24] This supplement
enlarged the framework for the Papal book of the Stations of the
Mass and made room for the official integration of the indigenous liturgy, in this case, the Gallican-Frankish one.

Meyer[25] has especially pointed out that the prayers of the
Alcuin-Supplement have an obvious similarity with the Book of
Cerne which belonged to the Irish-English liturgy and thus was
part of the Gallican liturgical radius. The establishment of
this relationship is important for our study because later with
Amalarius there will be an integration of a much greater extent.

If Pepin in his reform program eliminated the Gallican
liturgy in favor of a universal unity with Rome, then, with the
expansion of the Alcuin-Supplement, a second phase of the reform
program was initiated the manifestations of which were, so it
seems, a reverse process: that is to say, the Papal Stations of
the Mass were emended and supplemented by expressions of the
Gallic-Frankish heart, at first, it is true, only in the form of
a supplement. This Alcuin-Supplement--which was really a
supplemented Hadrianum--provided an official framework
for indigenous expressions of religious experience. Thus, the
supplemented Hadrianum remained during Charlemagne's lifetime in
usage as an exemplary handbook. After the death of the Emperor,
clerical and liturgical anarchy took place to a much greater

extent in consequence of which not only new additions were made but also the blending and mixing of texts was randomly undertaken.[26] This mixture gave the impression as if the entire sacramentary was now really a Massbook of the Pope himself and consequently there was no obstacle to its authoritative usage and at-random copying by the clerus.[27] The results of this condition were a great discrepancy and lingering-on of archaic forms because the attempted Romanization had not been able to extinguish the indigenous liturgy but rather it had invigorated it.[28] These manifold forms can particularly be documented from the works of Amalarius who initiated the third liturgical reform.

In the great confusion at the end of the seventh century, Gregory the Great (590-604 A.D.) had already expressed liturgical uniformity as one of his goals. This desire took form in the Massbook of the Pope, the Gregorianum, which may be designated as a work of liturgical reform based on a mixture of liturgies. In Spain as well, during the third and fourth Councils of Toledo, liturgical uniformity had been the special canon of Isidore of Séville. With the Merovingians the liturgy became Romanized under the influence of Boniface. Pepin tried to introduce liturgical uniformity after his coronation. Nevertheless, Pepin's attempt was doomed to failure for two reasons: first, there existed no faultless exemplars of the Roman liturgy and secondly, the copies which were available were forms of Papal Station Masses which referred to certain church solemnities but did not leave enough room for the expressions of religious experiences of the Gauls and Franks. Although they provided the frame for the rubrics they were neither sufficient for the expression of piety nor were they efficient didactic instruments.

Besides the Hadrianum with the Alcuin-Supplement which was accepted as an official model, the reform program of Charlemagne stood under the sign of the traditional expositio which corresponded to the mentality of the clerics and the faithful and was therefore kept brief and short. The Alcuin-Supplement which was added to the Hadrianum had been a decisive step toward the second liturgical reform phase under Charlemagne and Alcuin because it allowed room for the expression of feeling and piety

172

of the Franks. But the sources of the official frame, the Roman
exemplary models as well as those of the indigenous liturgical
traditions were kept too narrowly and provided not enough room
for further expansion and development which corresponded to
current needs and appealed to the essential traits of the
Franks. Thus it followed that in the end the reform programs of
Pepin and Charlemagne were really not successful. They had,
however, led to the invigoration of the indigenous liturgy which
manifested itself in anarchy or expressions of manifold forms.[29]
It was not until Amalarius that the sources of liturgical traditions were of a wider scope and more room was provided for the
expansion of the imagination of the Franks. For this reason,
the allegorical-dramatic form of the representations of the
liturgy of Amalarius of Metz was successful far beyond his own
time. Amalarius was driven by a thirst for knowledge and by a
desire to discover and penetrate deeper into the meaning of the
sense of the liturgical tradition. According to this tradition
he wanted to draw together the complex, interrelated parts of
the liturgy into a deeper sense of meaning and from this deeper
sense he attempted to shape the liturgy into a new creative and
unifying form. His voyage to and sojourn in Constantinople
which brought him into contact with the Byzantine liturgy was of
decisive significance in this endeavor. Amalarius' own
imaginative and creative powers made an original contribution to
the new shaping of the drama of salvation as expressed in his
liturgy.

Biographical Sketch of Amalarius

Amalarius of Metz belonged to the great reformers and
synthesizers of the Carolingian age. Amalarius'[30] achievements
in the domain of dramatic allegorical liturgy were of equal
importance for the history of drama as Otfried of Weissenburg's[31] accomplishments were in the field of Old-High-German
language and literature and as the contributions of John Scotus
Eriugena[32] were to philosophy and theology during the same
period.

We do not know much about Amalarius. His life had to be
reconstructed from his own writings and from council and synod
documents, annals and registries of the Carolingian epoch. Out

of these sources, however, there speaks an internally and externally active life which reflects the problematics of Amalarius' lifetime. This can be illustrated from an excerpt of one of Amalar's letters to Bishop Hilduin (822-830 A.D.) who was arch-chaplain at the court of Aachen:

> O quam salutiferum et optabile est nautis,
> vallatis procellosis turbinibus et peri-
> culosissimis aequoris, adprendere portum,
> ut evadant loetum. Ita mihi, quotiescum-
> que mentem fragilitatis meae quatiunt fluc-
> tus emergentes novarum rerum, vitale est,
> si potuero transnare ad gremium prudentiae
> vestrae. Hic mihi, portus est de omnibus
> quaestinonibus insperate insurgentibus,
> si videro in eis vestrum intellectum.[33]

With the metaphor of the stormy sea--with which he probably refers to his own stormy sea voyage to Constantinople where he gained new insights into the tradition of the liturgy--Amalarius describes the tension and struggle among the old, traditional and new forms in which he is obviously involved. Out of this tension which resulted from the conditions of liturgical anarchy of that time, as well as from Amalar's newly gained knowledge of other liturgical traditions, particularly that of Byzantium and from his own insights and creative powers, a transformation and synthesis of structure of the liturgical forms emerged. This new liturgical structure took on the shape of dramatic-allegorical representational forms. It marked the point of departure of the third reform movement in the kingdom of the Franks under Amalarius of Metz. This transformation of structure was Amalar's great contribution to the culture of the West.

Amalarius was born around 775 A.D. and although his birthday is not known, it is assumed that his immediate home had been in Metz because he himself refers to this area as "nostrae provinciae", "nostrae regionis", or "nostrae Gallilae".[34] It is certain that Amalarius had been a pupil of Alcuin because he refers to his school time under this erudite Anglo-Saxon as follows:

Audivi illos canere in isto ordine,
quando videbar puer esse ante Albinum
doctissimum magistrum totius regionis
nostrae. Cuius auctoritate delectatus
ac fretus, postquam libertate usus sum
canendi quae congrua mihi videbantur,
coepi illos canere tempore suprascripto,
id est ab octavis pentecostes usque in
kalendas iulii.[35]

Amalarius was not, however, an uncritical disciple of Alcuin but
soon chose his own way. It is probable that he belonged to the
secular clerics, i.e., the "regular canonics" which means that
he was not a monk or abbot.[36] His whole life was closely
connected with the Imperial Palace under Charlemagne and later
Louis the Pious. Already early in his life he was commissioned
by the Palace to participate actively in a liturgical reform
program. When in the year of 800 A.D., Bishop Leidrad of Lyons
(788-814 A.D.) requested help from the Palace to advance his
liturgical reform, Charlemagne sent Amalarius to Lyons in order
to introduce liturgical innovations according to the example of
the Palace School.[37] Following this, Charlemagne called
Amalarius in 809 A.D. to the episcopal chair of Treves which he
held until 814 A.D. This period of his episcopal office which
was filled with significant pastoral activity brought Amalarius
into desolate areas of rural parishes; it also included
ecclesiastical-diplomatic engagements among which were those
which led him to Constantinople. During his episcopate,
Amalarius consecrated the first church in Hamburg.[38] This was
around 811 A.D. On this occasion the Bishop of Treves was
brought into contact with the people of the most northern part
of the Carolingian Empire which most likely will have provided
him with insights into the mentality of the converts of that
remote region as well as with Germanic forms of religious
expressions.[39] An extant correspondence of 812 A.D. between
Charlemagne and Amalarius in connection with his work De
Scrutinio de Baptismo[40] testifies to the leading position which
was assigned to Amalarius in matters of liturgical and
theological queries and developments. Charlemagne wrote:

Sed quamvis sanctitatem tuam in divinis
rebus tota intentione vigilare non igno-
remus, omittere tamen non possumus quin
tuam devotionem Sancto incitante Spiritu
nostris apicibus conpellamus atque commo-
neamus ut magis ac magis in sancta Dei
ecclesia studiose ac vigilanti cura
laborare studeas in praedicatione sancta
et doctrina salutari. . .[41]

After Amalarius had sent him his work, Charlemagne replied with
acknowledgment and praise:

. . . De episcopis suffraganeis ad ecclesiam Treforum in qua, Dominum annuente,
te praesulem esse volumus, sicut antenus
nostram ordinationem et dispositionem
atque iussionem expectasti, volumus ut,
interim quod ad nostrum venias conloquium,
ita expectes, ceteris vero gradibus, id est
presbyteris, diaconibus, et omni clero,
vel plebi tuae tibi commissae, inter tuam
parochiam commorantibus, cum omni devo-
tione praedicare et docere viam veritatis
studeas.[42]

These statements confirm that Amalarius was held in high esteem
in the Imperial Palace because of his theological knowledge, and
his pastoral capacities furthermore indicate that with him, as
with Alcuin, a new leader in matters of church reform had
emerged.

In the year of 813, Amalarius was part of a diplomatic
mission which was sent to Constantinople by Charlemagne in order
to help clarify matters of the iconoclastic controversy; they[43]
were to ratify a peace-treaty with the Emperor Michael.
During his travel through Greece and his extended stay in Constantinople Amalarius had not only the occasion to observe the
Byzantine liturgy in its grandiose display and in its drama-
ization but he himself had the opportunity to celebrate a mass
in the Hagia Sophia on the Feast of Epiphany. On his return

176

journey through Italy he also had the opportunity to participate in a Papal Mass of Pope Leo III.[44] This long journey
during which time Amalarius became acquainted with the different
liturgical traditions had the greatest influence on him and his
subsequent liturgical visions and compositions. During this
journey Amalarius composed his basic liturgical work Missae
expositionis geminus codex,[45] the basic conception of which
presents his dramatic-allegorical interpretation and which shows
obvious resemblance with the Eastern liturgies as well as with
the Gallican forms of representation. A vivid poem, de versibus
marini,[46] describes his adventurous trip to Byzantium from the
beginning to the end. In July 814 A.D., Amalarius arrived again
at the Imperial Palace of Aachen where the delegation received a
festive reception by Louis the Pious.[47] During Amalarius'
absence, Charlemagne had died and the episcopal chair had, in
the meantime, been filled by Bishop Hetti.[48] Being thus
relieved of his episcopal duties, Amalarius was provided with
more leisure during which time he composed his major opus.
Until the appearance of this main work, the Liber Officialis, in
823 A.D., Amalarius seems to have appeared only once in public,
namely in connection with the Imperial Diet of Aachen. Here he
seems to have been one of the editors of the rules of
Chrodegang, De Institutione Canonicorum.[49]

After the appearance of the Liber Officialis, Amalarius was
again assigned ecclesiastical tasks. In 825 A.D. he
participated in the Synod of Paris which dealt with the
iconoclastic controversy[50] and in 831 A.D. he was sent by Louis
the Pious in liturgical matters to Rome to obtain an antiphonar.[51] This stay in Rome brought to his attention particularly
the differences in singing and the different rules of the rubric
which existed between Rome and the Frankish Church. These
observations led him to a composition of his own antiphonar.[52]
In 833 A.D., Amalarius became publicly involved in political
matters of the Empire. Because Agobard, Archbishop of Lyons,
became entangled in the quarrels of the Empire on the part of
Lothar, he had to flee and the vacant episcopal seat was
assigned to Amalarius by Louis the Pious. During this time he
tried to introduce his liturgical innovations in the Dioceses of
Lyons and for this purpose he convoked a regional synod in 834
A.D. His most poignant opponent was the deacon and magister

177

Florus, a passionate proponent of the School of Lyons and a close friend of Agobard. In two letters he polemicized against the heresies of Amalarius in consequence of which the Synod of Diedenhofen in the year of 835 A.D. concerned itself thoroughly with the works of Amalarius. At the Imperial Diet of Quirzy in 838 A.D., Amalarius' writings were condemned.[53] When in 839 A.D. Agobard was reinstituted, he too published polemical writings, most likely composed by Magister Florus, against Amalarius. The first of his works, the Liber contra quattor libros Amalarii abbatis was an attack on Amalarius' main work, the Liber Officialis. In his following works, the Liber de correctione antiphonarii and Liber de divina psalmodia, he argues against Amalarius' reform of songs.[54]

After this it seems that Amalarius' public career had come to an end. His name appears only once publicly before his death and that was after the condemnation of his work in connection with the controversy surrounding Gottschalk. In this controversy which centered around the issue of predestination Amalarius belonged with Scotus Eriugena to a commission of consulting theologians.[55] His work dealing with this controversy, Epistula ad Pardulum Laudunensem episcopum de praescientia et praedistinatione, has not been preserved.

Since the dispute concerning Gottschalk[56] was completed between 849 A.D. and 852 A.D. and Florus refers in 853 A.D. in his work Liber Tribus Epistulis to Amalar's influence saying: ". . . quam omnia scripta ejus saltem post mortem ipsius debuerint igne consumi. . ."[57] Amalar's death is estimated to have been around 850-852 A.D.[58] He was buried in a tomb of the Church of St. Arnold at Metz.

From this brief elaboration it may be concluded that Amalarius was gifted and open-minded, that he was widely travelled, an erudite theologian, closely associated with the ecclesiastical, cultural and political circumstances of Carolingian times. But he was also a poet and writer and a liturgical artist, who, in his creative imagination knew how to combine new insights, knowledge and world views in an aesthetic manner and to expound them in a scholarly way all the same in his works. The span of time in which his creative works appeared was that time in which the imagination of the Germanic heritage became assimilated to liturgical and ecclesiastical forms of expression. Kolping describes Amalarius justifiably as an "exponent of the most inner interests and concerns of his cultural epoch".[59]

In chronological order we shall now examine the works of Amalarius focusing our analysis mainly on his theories, interpretation of traditional materials and general content. In chapter five we will meticulously analyze the texts on the basis of their dramatic structure.

Works

Amalarius carried on his literary activity over a period of about forty years. It can be divided into three working periods: i.e., from 812 to 815 A.D., from 816 to 831 A.D. and from 831 to 851 A.D. His works are mainly of liturgical nature and belong to the literary genre of expositio.[60] To his non-liturgical works belong a poem and the products of his participation in Church council deliberations and decisions.[61]

In the brief discussion of Amalarius' works which will be undertaken in chronological order, we shall try to work out the theories of his dramatic allegorical representational method and its dramatic structure. Since Amalarius' theories and conceptions can be grasped most clearly from his letters as well as from the introductions of his various works, we have in our analysis mostly concentrated on this part of his works.

The Early Works (812-815 A.D.)[62]

The first literary manifestations can be documented from the years of 812-13 A.D., namely, from the correspondence with Charlemagne in connection with the work De Scrutinio de Baptismo[63] which explains the symbolic significance and the meaning of individual baptismal rites in the sense of the Patristic tradition; it is, however, of the more simple form of expositio which was prevalent in Charlemagne's time.[64]

The composition of two of Amalarius' works took place

179

during the voyage to and sojourn in Constantinople. These are
an illustrative poem, de versu marini,[65] which vividly describes
his sea journey and his initial basic liturgical work, Missae
Expositionis, in which he expounds the fundamental conception of
his allegorical-dramatic liturgy. Its structure is similar to
that of the expositio of Germanus of Paris,[65a] that is to say,
of the Gallican liturgy as well as to that of the Byzantine
liturgies.[65b] A brief but informative correspondence between
Amalarius and one of his travel companions to Constantinopel,
Abbot Peter Nonantulanus, is attached to the Codex. We shall
analyze it at the beginning of our study because it obviously
contains Amalarius' essential theories and liturgical concepts
out of which his great work emerged. These letters are dated
about 815 A.D. and that is about a year after their return from
Constantinople.

Epistula Venerabilis Abbatis Nonantulani ad Amalarium.

Abbot Peter N. wished to enrich his church through
Amalarius' liturgy. In a short letter he requests the work
Expositio Missae which Amalarius had composed during his sea
voyage. He says the following in his letter:

> . . . Et obscreamus tuam amabilem et invio-
> labilem caritatem, ut illum expositionis
> codicem quem, dictante Spiritu Sancto cordi
> tuo, in itinere maris exposuisti, nobis
> dirigere ad augmentum et statum sanctae
> ecclesiae nostrae; ut qui legerint et aedi-
> ficati fuerint, pro te, beatissime pastor,
> Domino preces fundant. . .[66]

At the same time, Abbot Peter N. inquires about the exposition
on baptism which Amalarius had written for Charlemagne.[67] These
short statements of the Abbot confirm that Amalarius continued
to have a leading position for two other reasons: First it is a
confirmation of the impression that Amalarius continued his
writings under the influence of the Byzantine experience and
secondly, it is an indication of the "inspiration" of his work.
It should be pointed out here that in connection with an "inspired" work, Amalarius himself fell into the tradition of

exegetes. Consequently, his authority, necessary for exegetical
and theological questions, increased even more. Since liturgical matters are also closely related to exegesis and theology,
Amalarius' "inspired" insights into liturgical-dramatic-alle-
gorical traditions had thus all the more weight. It has to be
taken into consideration that "inspiration" could also have been
a cover for Amalarius's experiences, impressions and insights he
had gained in the Hagia Sophia where the Byzantine liturgy had
become an inspiration, if not a model, for Amalarius. Such a
precaution on the part of Amalarius was understandable in view
of the strained political relationships between the Byzantine
Court in Constantinople and the Carolingian Emperors at Aachen
over the iconoclastic controversy on the one hand, and the
struggle for the position of power between Byzantium, Aachen and
Rome on the other.[68] In his response to Abbot Peter N.,
Amalarius sketches the basic conception of his liturgical views.
His later works are also built on this basis.

Epistula Amalarii ad Petrum abbatem Nonatulanum.[69]

Amalarius proceeded from the essence of his theories and
step by step he is expounding his theories, thus writing:

> Nuperrime suscepi a vestra sanctitate
> directam epistolam plenam caritate et
> humilitate, in qua inter alia contine-
> batur ut meum, non tantum meum, sed et
> vestrum, quamvis parvum, opusculum quod
> inter equoreas comminationes cudimus . . .
> In quo si quid dignum, si quid honestum
> si quid rationale repperitur, non meae
> nempe doctrinae sed vestris merito
> sanctis precibus deputantur. . .[70]

Amalarius wished to penetrate to the true sense of Scripture and
liturgy; therein lies the kernel of his teachings, but since it
is possible to arrive at wrong interpretations (inrationabili-
iter), Amalarius calls upon the authority of tradition as well
as that of the Abbot:

181

> . . . temeritate mea faciente ac stulta prae-
> sumptione, inrationabilitier scriptum est,
> per vestram prudentiam correptionem habere
> mereatur, et nos indulgentiam apud omnes
> doctores.[71]

It is evident from this statement that Amalarius right at the
beginning of his writings refers to his own teachings
(. . . meae . . . doctrinae) which makes obvious that he places
himself into the protection of tradition but not in its shadow.
Immediately Amalarius emphasizes again that he had written what
he thought to be true and right. Scripsi enim quidquid mihi
videbatur iustem et honestum.[72]   In his search he is being
driven by his burning desire "to expose and set free the rays of
light" which lay concealed within the deeper sense of Scripture:

> Non eo animo, ceu valuerim omnem recti-
> tudinem praesumpti operis indagare, sed
> ut tangerem meo incepto vestros industri-
> os, qui facillime possent rei veritatem
> dilucidare eius quam vehementer desidera-
> bam.[73]

This subjective emphasis of his own insight and imagination in
connection with tradition betrays a certain tension in which he
is caught but which lead to new objective forms of expression.

Amalarius' own observation and his searching for the deeper
meaning of the liturgical tradition of the older and more recent
Church Fathers for whom there was never anything without sense
and meaning, is obvious from the following quotation:

> Scripsi, ut nostis, quos illos arbitrabar
> imitari qui in choro stant, et cantant in-
> trante episcopo in ecclesiam, ut postea
> in sequenti opere demonstrabitur; quae con-
> venientia esset nostro toti officio, quod
> agitur in missa, sive in psallendo sive in
> situ, sive in qualitate sive in quantitate,
> cum nostris authenticis quos omnis eccle-

sia colit, reputans apud me nihil statu-
tum esse in ecclesia, neque apud anticos
patres neque apud recentiores, quod ratione
careat.[74]

Out of this dramatic allegorical tradition Amalarius tries to
shape and to represent, and where tradition is not sufficient
there he himself becomes creative and tries to weave the old and
the new into a visible harmonious whole.

Amalarius justifies his own reform program by reference to
the application of the allegorical method which was also a
product of the classical tradition:

Si enim gentiles argumentantur ludos aliquod suos allegorice promere, sicut alea-
tores, qui perhibent tribus tesseris suis
tria tempora significari, praesens, prae-
teritum et futurum, et vias eorum senario
numero distinguunt propter sex aetates
hominum, quanto magis christianam indus-
triam, orationem sibi a Deo concessam,
nullo modo acciderit frustra aliquid
statuere.[75]

He argues that for Christians divine reason would have to be the
source of all things and therefore it must be their task to
search for the deeper sense in all things:

Non ideo exemplum de gentilibus posui,
et eos imitemur. Sed si illi hoc vel
illud argumentantur rationis, quanto
magis totum quod rationes est, christianus sequi debet, qui summae rationi Deo
se sponsorem facit.[76]

The eschatological orientation which characterized the over-all
vision of the liturgy is justified by Amalarius in the sense of
ancient traditions. He points out that if the pagans had
already made provisions for a future life, how much more must

183

the Christians incorporate this vision, whose final goal is God
in eternity. He writes in this respect:

> Non ideo Dominus villicum iniquitatis
> laudatem esse dicit, ut illum imitaremur
> sed si ille ex villicatu iniquitatis pru-
> denter sibi in futurum providit, quanto
> magis oportet christianum ex iustis cen-
> sibus adquirere qui eum recipiant in
> aeterna tabernacula.[77]

In conclusion, Amalarius requests his former travel
companion, Abbot Peter N., to take sufficient precautions so
that his work would not fall prematurely into the hands of
intruders only to be ridiculed by them. He describes himself as
a diligent student searching for the truth and continues:

> Rogo, pater, ut non ad publicas aures et
> libellus noster mittatur, ne intrem dentes
> obstrectatorum, neque cacinni superborum
> per auras resultent de humillima doctrina
> paupertatis nostrae, quoniam non me prae-
> fero magistrum de hac scriptione, sed dis-
> cipulum inquirentem quod diligo scire.[78]

This allusion to a certain opposition refers most likely to the
School of Lyons. Abott Peter N., however, seems to have
followed Amalarius' request because only one manuscript of
Amalarius initial work has been preserved.[79]

It may be inferred from this correspondence that the representational form of the Eastern liturgy at Constantinople was
in its unique and figurative form a source for Amalarius'
imagination and dramatic-liturgical vision. One can also assume
that Amalarius in his search for the deeper meaning, the ratio,
of Scripture and liturgy, was cognizant of his carrying on a
rich tradition to which he could refer and which justified the
meaning of his quest. This was the tradition of the Church
Fathers.

<u>Missae Expositionis Geminus Codex I</u> (813-814 A.D.)[80]

The most conspicuous feature of this liturgical composition is the dramatic structure and the historical-allegorical basic conception of the entire work. It is as if Amalarius had taken the events of Scripture, as well as the teachings of the entire plan of salvation, and woven them into a representational liturgical drama. Furthermore, the structure of the scheme of the Mass consists of four acts with corresponding scenes which refer to 1) the <u>Introitus</u>: the Incarnation with its implicit eschatology; 2) <u>Lectio</u>: the Life of Christ; 3) <u>Offertorium</u>: the Passion of Christ; 4) <u>Confractio/Benedictio</u>: the Resurrection and Ascension of Christ.

Amalarius opens his works with a scheme of the dramatic-allegorical over-all plan in which he briefly explains the individual structural parts. For a better overview and for a better understanding of his works we shall represent this scheme below:

I. <u>Codex seu Scedula Prior</u>.[81]

1. Capitula sequentis opusculi praenotamus, ut si quis forte ignarus extans de ignobilitate operis nostri, aggrediensque illud quasi dignum, ac postea reperiens vile, ne paenitentia ductus dicat apud semetipsum vel apud suos adstantes . . .

2. Illud vero intimadum est, quod ea quae celebramus in officio missae usque lectum evangelium respicientia sunt ad illud tempus quando properabat Hierusalem passurus.

After this general introduction and sketch of the general course, a short interpretation of the dramatic allegorical structure follows:

3. Introitus vero ad chorum prophetarum respicit et merito hos hic tangimus, quod Augustinus ait: "Moyeses minister fuit et veteris testamenti, et prophetae ministri novi testamenti."[82]

185

Kyrieleison ad eos prophetas respicit qui circa adventum Domini erant, de quibus erant Zacharias nec non et Iohannes filius eius.

4. Gloria in excelsis Deo ad coetum angelorum respicit, qui gaudium nativitatis Domini pastoribus adnuntiaverunt.

Prima collecta ad hoc respicit, quod Dominus agebat circa duodecimum annum, quando ascendit Hierosoliman, et sedebat in templo inter medios doctorum, et audiebat illos atque interrogabat.

5. Epistola ad praedicationem Iohannis pertinet.

Responsorium ad benivolentiam apostolorum, quando vocati Domino et secuti sunt.

Alleluia ad laetitiam mentis eorum, quam habebant de promissionibus eius, vel de miraculis quae videbant fieri ab eo, sive pro nomine eius.

De tractu alias dicemus.

Evangelium ad suam praedicationem usque ad praedictum tempus.

6. Deinceps vero quod agitur in officio missae, ad illud tempus respicit quod est a dominica quando pueri obviaverunt ei, usque ad ascensionem eius sive pentecosten.

Oratio quam presbyter dicit a secreta usque, "Nobis quoque peccatoribus," hanc orationem designat quam Iesus exercebat in monte Oliveti.

Et illud quod postea agitur, illud tempus significat quando Dominus in sepulchro iacuit.

7. Quando panis mittitur in vinum, anima Domini ad corpus redire demonstrat.

> Et quod postea celebratur, significat illas
> salutationes quas Christus fecit discipulis suis.

> Et fractio oblatarum illam fractionem significat quam
> Dominus duobus fecit in Emaus.

This panoramic scheme reveals in essence the plot of the drama
of salvation history. The drama of salvation begins with the
representation of the prophets of the Old Testament by the choir
and concludes with a scene after the Resurrection, that of the
breaking of bread with the disciples at Emmaus, represented
respectively by the deacons and subdeacons. In conclusion,
Amalarius ascribes great significance to the individual roles
enacted by the clerics. He says:

8. QUALITER OCCURAT CANTORUM OFFICIUM, QUOD AGITUR AD
   MISSAM, SIVE SUBDIACONI VEL DIACONI, QUOD AGITUR IN
   PULPITO, SACRAMENTO INCARNATIONIS CHRISTI, ANGE-
   LORUM PRAEDICATIONIS, PASSIONISQUE, NEC NON
   ET RESURRECTIONIS.

The similarity of this entire structure with that of the drama
Christos Paschon,[83] the liturgical work of Germanos of Constantinople,[84] and the Gallican liturgy is obvious.[85] Immediately following this summary, Amalarius goes into detailed
explanation of the dramatic structure of the Mass. He discusses
in detail the meaning of the representations as well as the
roles which are assigned to each cleric. Furthermore it becomes
evident that gestures, positions and songs are in constant
interplay with each other whereby the singing in particular
develops dramatic significance. Amalarius makes a significant
statement about the relationship of representational forms and
songs in connection with the Emmaus-scene: ". . . quae ideo,
cantatur, sicut nobis videtur. . ."[86]. His extensive description
refers to the Introit and Lectio, that is, the themes of the
Incarnation, the Second Coming and the Life of Jesus, whereas
the Passion and Resurrection expressed in Offertorio and
Fractione are less extensively dealt with. Most obvious is the
dramatic structure of the Responsorium and Alleluia which is
achieved by means of songs and personification.[87]

187

Amalarius gives only the Old Testament and New Testament
and a short reference to Augustine and Isidore as his literary
sources.[88] However, according to the correspondence between
Abbot Peter N., and Amalarius, and in comparison with the
already examined liturgical texts,[89] the liturgy of Constantinople and the still existing remains of the Gallican liturgy
seem to have been his model, that is to say, that tradition
which fed his own creative imagination since his journey to
Byzantium.

Codex seu scedula altera II.

This composition bears the title De Romano Ordine et de
Statione in Ecclesia. One wonders why Amalarius gave this work
the title "Romano Ordine" because the representational forms as
a whole really bear the characteristic mark of Eastern and
Gallican liturgies. This Codex refers in detail to plot,
gestures and representations until the end of the Gospel-
reading; everything in this part is dramatically accentuated
bearing the stamp of a great symbolic-allegorical display which
is really not a trait of the Roman liturgy. Particularly
striking is therefore the increased dramatization of certain
themes by way of subtle allusions and suggestive gestures as
well as through personifications, as for example, the theme vita
activa-vita-contemplativa, or the scene in the Garden of Olives,
or Christ's calling of his disciples. This Codex closes with
the reading and elaborate display of the Gospel, the evangelium.
The second part of the liturgical drama consisting of the theme
of the Passion and Resurrection does not appear in Codex II.
Are these texts the result of a combinatory process of
Amalarius' immediate impressions he had in Constantinople, of
the Papal Mass the constellation of which he saw in Rome in
connection with his journey, of the integrated texts of the
Gallo-Frankish liturgy, including the Alcuin-Supplement?
Besides Scripture, Amalarius' sources in this part are primarily
the Ordo Romanus II (A.V.), Origen, Bede and Clement of
Alexandria.[90]

<u>Canonis Missae Interpretatio (814-815 A.D.)</u>[91]

This work is a mystical interpretation of the Mass. Here Amalarius discusses exclusively the hierarchical structures of the visible and invisible realms which constitute the liturgy and which time and again, as we shall be able to show later, will take on the shape of configurational structures. The composition of this part is therefore also a most important key for the overall interpretation of the dramatic liturgy because Amalarius deals here in detail and almost exclusively with the spiritual-mystical background together with the deeper unifying sense of the liturgy.[92] As his main literary sources, Amalarius cites Gregory the Great. It will however be noted that the mystical interpretation, in particular the structure of the angelic hierarchy, corresponds to the metaphoric figurative constellations of the Byzantine liturgical drama.[93]

In contrast to the <u>Missae Expositionis I et II</u> of which there is only one manuscript, there are a total of twelve extant manuscripts of this mystical interpretation which indicates its significance and wide distribution.[94]

Main Works

<u>Epistula Amalarii ad Hilduinum Abbatem (822-830 A.D.)</u>[95]

The <u>Liber Officialis</u>, Amalarius' main work, appeared in 823 A.D., nine years after he had introduced his initial works. A letter by Amalarius to Abbot Hilduin which is a discussion concerning questions of the importance of rubrics most likely also falls into the period of the appearance of the <u>Liber Officialis</u>; it provides a good insight into Amalar's own position as well as into the kernel of his ideas and interpretation of liturgical phenomena.

Amalarius opens his letter to Abbot Hilduin with the metaphor of a stormy sea and with that he brings to figurative expression the fermentation and innovation of his time in which he himself was so very deeply involved both in his pastoral, theological and political missions.[96] On his voyage to Constantinople via Greece, Amalarius came across several liturgical

189

regulations, especially in connection with an ordination to the priesthood which can be documented as follows:

> Quando fui apocrisiarius, quamvis indig-
> nus, videlicet minimus a maxima potestate,
> in partibus Grecorum, audivi inter nostros
> id est meos socios et eos qui ad imperium
> Grecorum pertinent, diversa sentire de
> temporibus fixis apud nos sacrorum ordi-
> num. Ut repperi apud quandam archi-epis-
> copum, ipso narrante, de civitate Iadhare,
> sine aliqua observatione nostrae consue-
> tudinis celebrant consecrationem sacro-
> rum. [97]

Without observing the prescribed regulations of the Byzantine Church in Iadhere, Amalarius using his own judgement ordained a deacon to the priesthood according to Frankish-Roman regulations. He gives the following description of this event:

> Retulit quomodo vellet aliquem diaconum
> promovere ad presbiteratus officium in
> vigila paschae; ipso renuente eodem
> tempore, promotus est in festivitate
> sancti Petri. In loco ubi eram, vigi-
> lia memoratae festivitatis sancti Petri,
> erat quidam, ut retulis diaconus nobis-
> cum, qui veniebat a partibus Romae, con-
> firmans se factum diaconum ab aposto-
> lico Leone. Rogavit me ut in illo die
> proveherem illum. Ego ammodum restiti et
> legato, qui me ducebat, et ipsi diacono,
> et vix evasi. [98]

This initiative threw Amalarius into a controversy with his travel companions; he defended himself however by referring to the ecclesiastical regulation of the Frankish Church:

> Socii nostri, Petrus abba et sui
> monachi dissentiebant a meis in ordi-
> natione primi mensis. Dicebant se

> velle habere duodecim lectiones, se-
> cundum romanum usum, semper in prima
> septimana quadragesimae in quocumque
> mense sive tempore mensis eveniret.
> Ego non habebam quid dicerem, nisi quod
> scriptum tenebam in nostris libris:
> "primi mensis prima sabbati". Cogitabam
> et me tenere romanum usum, quia scrip-
> ta quae legi in Frantia, de eodem loco
> cogitavi advolasse.[99]

This seemingly unimportant incident at Iadhere had become the
incentive of a great dispute for and about Amalarius. He states
further:

> Ista praelibata quae in itenere occurre-
> runt, tempus est ut de metatu cogitem.[100]

Amalarius had previously also dealt with the "sense"(ratio) of
the rubrics making the following referene: ". . . quomodo
potuisset fieri quod sine ratione aliqua praefixi essent des-
cripti dies qui vulgo vocantur apud nos quattor temporum".[101]
Amalarius justifies his solution of the problem of the rubrics
in the light of tradition since he is confident that in everything he does he is guided by and is following in the footsteps
of the Church Fathers. He assures that:

> Firme teneo quod nihil subsicivum a
> patribus sanctis constitutum sit, sed
> omnia ratione dignissima, et nihil in
> ecclesia frequentetur, quod non sit
> tritum eorum vestigiis.[102]

Amalarius understands himself as a protector and promoter of
this liturgical tradition in which everything is meaningful and
he will only subject himself to an authority such as Hilduin
himself. His position is as follows:

> Qua de re vestram auctoritatem operior
> de duodecim lectionibus primi mensis, pro
> quibus istae litterae scriptae sunt, ut

191

> ipsa me statuat in portum tutissimum. Pro-
> nam tamen, quamvis praesumptiose, quod mihi
> videtur posse congruere praesenti rationi,
> non praeponendo potiori. Quod si
> probabile est, oro, probetur per vos; si[103]
> corrigendum, corrigatur per vos.

But as previously with his travel companions, Amalarius finds himself again in disagreement about his views, this time with his bishop and in this connection he asks Hilduin for help in solving the argument:

> Absit ut ideo dicam, quasi coner resistere
> ammonitioni episcopi mei in aliquo, vere
> ipse nondum aliquid praecinuit de ieiunio
> memorato, sed familiariter a vobis vestrum
> velle requiro, quia vestrum et omnia inae-[104]
> qualia ad aequitatem reducere.

A response by Abbot Hilduin, in case it existed, is not preserved.

Three points which were already observed in his letter to Abbot Peter N., are again very obvious in this correspondence. It is a confirmation firstly that his trip to Constantinople had intensified his interests regarding liturgical matters and secondly that Amalarius recognized that in his teaching about the deeper sense--ratio--of Scripture and liturgy he was following the tradition of the Church Fathers. Lastly his views and reform activity led to a controversy. This letter also discloses Amalarius' preferene for indigenous customs.

Liber Officialis (823 A.D.)[105]

In 823 A.D., Amalarius published his main work which initially consisted of three books. According to the manuscripts that work was quickly and widely diffused and finally it appeared in three editions.[106]

The first edition of 823 A.D. is preceded by a dedication, Glorissime imperator, addressed to the Emperor Louis the Pious;

the fourth book was added to the second edition which appeared
around 829-830 A.D. and the third edition was published with his
later works written after he returned from his trip to Rome in
831 A.D. and while he was Bishop of Lyons in 835 A.D. To this [107]
last edition the foreword Postquam scripsi was added. The
dedication Glorissime imperator of the first edition sketches
the purpose and conception of the Liber Officialis. As in his
letter to Abbot Peter N. and Hilduin, Amalarius again explains
step by step his motivation and his goals. He makes the
important statement that it is his main concern to penetrate
into the meaning of ratio of the liturgy as it was originally
conceived and celebrated according to old customs of the Church.
The meaning of ratio as it was inherent in old customs is manifested anymore only in dispersed forms of a liturgical anarchy.
He makes the following statement:

> Glorissime imperator et magnificen-
> tissime ac centies invictissime . . .
> Servus ego vester, quamvis minimus om-
> nium, afficiebar olim desiderio ut
> scirem rationem aliquam de ordinae nos-
> trae missae, quam consueto more caele-
> bramus, et amplius ex diversitate quae
> solet fieri in ea, hoc est quod aliquo-
> ties una epistola legitur, aliquoties
> duae, et cetera talia, simulque de
> ceteris officiis. [108]

Here, for the first time, we have a concrete statement which
refers to liturgical discrepancy after ending of the liturgical
reform programs of Pepin and Charlemagne. These discrepancies
presumably become evident in the structure of the reading part
of the liturgical drama. Amalarius places himself in the
tradition of the "inspired" exegete. He states that he had long
struggled with the problem of the underlying unity of the
liturgy and that finally, in the crypta of the Imperial Palace,
the light of the right solution had penetrated his mind.
Notably, here too, Amalarius is writing under the cover of inspiration and does not even mention his trip to Constantinople.
He compares his "inspiration" to rays of light breaking through
a window:

> Praeterita proxima aestate videbatur
> mihi, quasi in crypta posito, fenestra-
> tim lucis scintillas radiare usque ad
> nostram de re quam desiderabam.[109]

Following this description, Amalarius emphasizes immediately
that despite his fear of certain opponents, he had written what
he felt and thought was right, thus fearlessly expressing his
own understanding of the liturgy. Amalarius then stresses that
he had written according to his own insights:

> Longa esurie avidus, non frenum passus
> sum timoris, alicuius magistri, sed, illico
> mente gratias agens Deo, scripsi quod sensi.[110]

Although he has admitted to the freedom of his own views,
Amalarius immediately subjects himself to the authority of Louis
the Pious:

> Dein tractare coepi cui sapientum
> porrigerem ea quae scripsi, ut eius
> auctoritate statuerentur ea quae or-
> dinate sunt scripta, seu corrigentur
> quae inordinate.[111]

After Amalarius had strengthened his position through the cover
of "inspiration", he emphasized the continuity of the primary
liturgical tradition and he assures that with burning zeal he
will try to penetrate into the sense and meaning of the First
Liturgical Act out of which the structure of the liturgy had
developed. He goes on to say:

> Ardor mihi inerat ut scirem quid priores
> auctores haberent in corde, qui nostra
> officiis statuerunt. Sed quia hoc diffi-
> cillimum mihi est affirmare, ut identi-
> dem scripsissem quod illi meditabantur,
> unum tamen suffugium mihi est, si ea
> quae scripsi, videbuntur vestrae pietati
> vita caritatis non excedere.[112]

194

Amalarius stresses that, if this interpretation of the liturgy in which he tries to bring to the fore that which lies mysteriously hidden within it, should be misunderstood, such a misunderstanding had not been his intention. In order to prevent such wrong interpretations of his intentions and for his own protection he relies on the authority of St. Augustine by referring to the Doctrina Christiana as follows:

> Ex libro Augustini de Doctrina Christiana
> defendar ab illis qui me voluerint capare,
> quasi periculose scripsissem, eo quod mentes
> auctorum officii nostri non praesentes
> haberem.[113]

The fact that Amalarius in connection with the interpretation of the liturgy refers to the sign-theory of Augustine presupposes penetration into this tradition. Our treatment of the second book of the Liber Officialis will verify this.

In the foregoing discussion we again were able to show that a certain tension between tradition, the given temporal condition, and his own imagination were the sources of Amalarius' driving force. His burning desire to penetrate into the meaning of the beginnings of the liturgical tradition is also expressed in the foreword to the first book of the Liber Officialis.

Liber I:[114] The foreword to the first book, Ubi sanctus Augustinus, is obviously an acceptance of the Augustinian tradition and here again Amalar's views and theories can be discerned rather easily. Following Augustine, Amalarius too differentiates between voluntas and cupiditas and ratio whereby ratio is the leading principle towards truth and good works (caritas).[115] With the organic metaphor of the tree, Amalarius illustrates how God is the source of all reason--ratio--to whom lastly all searching for truth will have to return. His description is as follows:

> Voluntas quasi quidam stipes est, quae
> a Domino menti datur, cui inhaerent quasi
> quidam rumusculi appetitus, quibus con-

195

iungitur res ab auctore omnium rerum, in
qua aliquid operetur voluntas, cui si assit
ratio, aberit error. Ratio dirigit ra-
dios appetitus ad verum solem Deum, ut
sua luce perspicue et veraciter sciat
quid vel quale sit quod appetit.[116]

Because of the fall of mankind, pure searching is impossible.
Man needs to be enlightened by the Holy Spirit and, referring to
St. Paul, Amalarius argues that each person is capable of re-
ceiving enlightenment which would benefit the common good:
"Uniquique," iniquit, "datur manifestio spiritus ad utili-
tatem"[117] He also uses the following metaphor:

Stomachus est qui diversos cibos recipit,
de quibus solet ructus fieri ad superiora;
similiter quidam venter est mentis, qui
recipit cogitationes. Si his defuerit
res non habent unde ructum faciant. Mihi
peccatori grossa res data est potius ad
indagandum quam exponendum, id est de officio quod continentur in sacramentario et
antiphonario, quae pene omnibus rusticis
nota est. Fiducialiter ago coram Deo,
qui vult ut unusquisque devote in suis
datis ministret pro praemio aeterno . . .[118]

In his search for the deeper meaning and the kernel of the
liturgy, Amalarius again cognizantly knows himself to be on the
traces of the discarded path of tradition. In the spirit of
this tradition he begins his official reform program and again
confirms that:

Ardor mihi inest tritae viae et abo-
litae propter antiquitatem, ut sciam
quid habeat in medulla res memorata, id
est quid in corde esset, primorum dicta-
torum officii nostri et quem fructum
pariat. Itaque mihi prima inquisito
est de septuagesima, cuius finis con-
stat in primo mense.[119]

196

Amalarius assures that he will attempt to penetrate to the central meaning of the liturgical sense: the medulla res memorata. His point of departure is thereby the beginning of the liturgical cycle, Septuagesima, which is culminating in the Holy Week of the Passion and Easter Vigil. He sees his vocation, and his inspiration in the sense of ratio and will try to give sense and meaning to the dramatic liturgy from the roots of this tradition. Amalarius is driven in his search by a burning desire to penetrate into the depth of meaning of the First Liturgical Act and the spoken Words of Christ: ". . . ut sciam habeat in medulla res memorata, id est in corde esset primorum distatorum officii nostri . . ."[120] The significance and depth-dimension of this Act and these Words could not have been better formulated by Amalarius. The entire Christian dramatic-liturgical tradition took its impetus from this new event. Where the existing tradition is no longer sufficient to bring to the fore this deeper meaning, Amalarius begins to work creatively, weaving together old and new forms of liturgical, allegorical traditions. The resulting new representational configurations reflect a vision which is fed by manifold layers of traditions. The dramatic representational configuration follows from Amalarius' vision of the deeper four-fold sense of Scripture combined with the signum-res-schema of Augustine, the Byzantine-Syriac conceptions and from Amalar's own view of the concrete world of the Carolingians which was mingled with a Germanic positive but also rune-like mysterious vision of the world. For Amalarius thus, the dramatic liturgy was a dynamic, constantly expanding and unfolding process which will lead to truth and caritas.

The first book of the LO is very important for our study from two points of view: Firstly from the dramatic representation of the historical event of the Passion and Resurrection of Christ during the cyclical year, the liturgical meaning of which is not only rooted in the Judaeo-Christian tradition but also in the myths of "pagan" societies[121] and secondly, because of the fourfold sense of Scripture which is underlying the dramatic figurative representations in connection with the baptismal liturgy of the Easter Vigil. It is most important to keep these two viewpoints in mind in order to

penetrate into the dramatic-allegorical representations of
Amalarius of Metz. Because of their significance, we shall deal
with them briefly.

1. Dramatic Representation: The first book deals with all
the liturgical details of the entire Easter cycle beginning with
the Sunday of Septuagesima until the Feast of Pentecost which
embraces the temporal and spatial dimensions from the beginning
of the Babylonian captivity of the Old Testament up to the
sending forth of the Holy Spirit at the Feast of Pentecost of
the New Testament. The commemorative character of the
historical events of the Passion Week is particularly obvious.[122]
The Papal Alms Day on the Saturday before Palm-Sunday which
points back to the annointing of Christ by Mary Magdelena of
Bethany, open the events of the Passion Week. With an elaborate
explanation and justification of this part, Amalarius summarizes
the commemorative sense of the liturgy as follows:

> Ubi notandum quod ea quae recolimus
> cultibus ecclesiasticis circa passionem
> Domini et resurrectionem atque ascensi-
> onem in caelos, in memoratione illarum
> rerum quae suo in tempore peractae sunt
> agimus. Unde cotidie dicimus in sacrifi-
> cio missae, "Quotiescumque haec feceritis,
> in mei memoriam facieties." Habemus
> opus praecedens elemosinae praesentis
> sabbati quod imitemur, et ad memoriam
> nostri reducamus.[123]

The dramatic making-present of the historical events is, lastly,
rooted in the pronouncement of the Words of Christ at the
institution of the Last Supper, His First Liturgical Act, out of
which the development of the entire representational forms of
liturgical drama then follows. This, however, signifies that
the meaning or sense (Sinn), the ultimate ratio of the First
Liturgical Act and its representational enactment obtains its
real significance only through its connection with the Spoken
World of this First Liturgical Act, that is to say, in this
case, the Act of Jesus Christ at the Last Supper.

The most obvious aspects of the further dramatic structure and the representations of the variations of themes of the Passion and Resurrection, we shall not discuss at this point but in the following chapter.

In this connection attention must also be given to the organic definition of ecclesia to which Amalarius refers:

> Ac per hoc, quia ecclesia convocatio
> dicitur, homines sunt ecclesia, non
> parietes domus.[124]

The active inclusion of the faithful is a particular concern of Amalarius and in his liturgical drama the ecclesiastical community will play its own representational dramatic role.

2. The Representation of the Fourfold Senses of Scripture: In connection with the instruction of the catechumens which reaches its climax in the baptismal liturgy of the Easter Vigil, Amalarius gives a visual explanation of the fourfold sense of Scripture which is made manifest through positional symbolism as well as through the interchange of songs and readings.

While the candle and light symbolize the transformation of the catechumens from the darkness of human existence to the light of life in Christ, the process of real conversion is represented through the objectivation of the fourfold sense of Scripture. Amalarius says this specifically as follows:

> Lumen ipsius lumen Christi significat,
> quo et praesens nox inlustratur, gratia
> scilicet resurrectionis, et catecumini
> qui venturi sunt ad baptismum. Ipsam
> inluminationem designant lectiones quae
> ante baptismum leguntur, ut in sequenti-
> bus monstrabitur.[125]

Step by step the neophyte is led through Scripture to the full light whereby each scriptural sense indicates a gradual ascension to the light of Christ.

Through Bede, Amalarius makes the connection to Patristic exegesis using the example from the work <u>De tabernaculi et vasis eius</u>.[126] In this work the four legs of the altar of the Jewish Tabernacle are connected with one of the four senses of Scripture which indicates that with this reference to the Mosaic Tabernacle, scriptural exegesis was being linked allegorically directly to the liturgical sacrifice and following that, it takes on concrete representational form.[127] According to Bede's definition the fourfold sense is inherent in the Word of God and in Scripture itself. It belongs to their very essence. Amalarius, following Bede, then states:

> Hanc doctrinam significat mensa in taber-
> naculo moysaico quae habet quattour pedes;
> quia ut Beda in libro de Tabernaculo:
> "Quadriformi ratione omnis divinorum elo-
> quiorum series distinguitur."[128]

Amalarius applies the fourfold sense of Scripture in this manner systematically first to the baptismal liturgy of the Easter Vigil. He says further:

> Hic oro intendatis quam congruentiam
> habeant lectiones quattour et cantica
> et orationes, quae aguntur propter in-
> structiones catecuminorum, cum quattour
> pedibus mensa. Idem qui supra in memo-
> rato: "Mensa tabernaculi quattour habet
> pedes, quia verba caelestis oraculi vel
> historico intellectu vel allegorico vel
> tropologico, id est morali. vel certe
> anagogico solent accipi . . ."[129]

By conflating the table of the Mosaic Tabernacle with the framework of the liturgical drama of the New Testament, Amalarius achieves not only a backward glance into time and space but more important, through the connection of the Tabernacle with the allegorical sense of Scripture, the allegorical <u>Weltanschauung</u> becomes figuratively projected into the beginnings of salvation history of the Old Testament.

Then Amalarius discusses in detail the meaning of the four
senses of Scripture in connection with the four legs of the
table of the altar in the Tabernacle. I shall now briefly
discuss his viewpoints regarding this connection because it is
most significant for the understanding of liturgical drama as a
whole.

That part of the readings of the baptismal liturgy which
refers to the first leg of the table represents the historical
or literal sense of Scripture now being transferred to the
liturgy. It contains the facts of salvation history and its
definition is as follows:

> Historia est namque, cum res aliqua
> quomodo secundum litteram facta sive
> dicta sit, plano sermone refertur.[130]

Significant for our study and for the understanding of
liturgical drama as such is the division of the first reading
because it consists of two readings with a concluding song. The
first reading deals with the historical creation of man:

> Nonne, sicut ibi scriptum est de
> generatione hominis, tenetur secundum
> historiam? . . . Et sicut ibi narratur,
> die sexto credimus hominem factum.[131]

This reading includes the fall of man and therefore points to
man without God. The lack of singing signifies this separation
of man from God. However, the second part of the reading which
concerns the first sense has historical as well as allegorical
meaning:

> Secunda lectio plano sermone refert
> quomodo populos Israhel ex Aegypto
> salvatus sit. quia in superiore lecti-
> one audivit catecuminus suam formatio-
> nem, in ista audiat suam redemptionem
> . . .[132]

The allegorical significance is symbolized through the song

which follows the second reading. Amalarius deals specifically
with this difference because he states:

> Istas duas lectiones unum canticum sequi-
> tur, quia utraque in primo pede stant, id
> est in allegoria, vel ideo priori lectioni
> canticum non sequitur, qui in illa insi-
> nuatur parens in quo omnes peccaverunt.[133]

The motive of salvation is thus inserted by means of songs and
with this addition the entire reading part becomes amplified in
its meaning. The understanding of this amplification of meaning
through the insertion of songs is especially important for the
dramatic interpretation of the subsequent acts and configurations of the liturgical drama.

The second leg of the table refers to the purely
allegorical sense and symbolizes here the sacramental-mystical
character of the Church. This is defined and interpreted
accordingly in the third reading:

> Transeamus ad secundum pedem mensae.
> Idem qui supra in eodem: "Allegoria est,
> cum verbis sive rebus mysticis praesen-
> tia Christi et ecclesiae sacramenta
> signatur."[134]

The interpretation of the allegorical sense leads here to the
initiation of the catechumens into the sacramental and mystical
character of the Church. Amalarius combines this introduction
with the following, typologically complicated allegory:

> Tangamus tertiam lectionem, quae quam-
> vis tertia sit ordine lectionem, tamen
> propter sacramenta quae continet, secun-
> do pedi mensae coniungitur. In ea habe-
> amus sacramenta Christi et ecclesia:
> "Apprehenderunt septem mulieres virum
> unum in die illa, dicentes: Panem
> nostrum comedemus." Secundum historiam
> non legimus illud factum, sed in Christo

202

scimus completum, quem apprehenderunt
septem dona Spiritus Sancti.[135]

This part is an example of allegorical exegesis which has no
historical significance; with its tropological meaning it could
fall into the tradition of Hilary of Poitiérs. The subtlety of
such interpretation is later transposed to the dramatic representations and implications by way of songs and gestures which
contribute to its complexity and manifoldedness.

The third leg of the table symbolizes the tropological
sense and encourages neophytes to the performance of good works
--caritas. Amalarius deals most elaborately with the
representational forms of this sense. The definition according
to Bede, which Amalarius follows, reads thus:

> Tertium pedem mensae requiramus. Dicit
> Beda in quo et supra: "Tropologica, id
> est moralis, locutio ad institutionem et
> correctionem morum, sive apertis seu figu-
> ratis prolata sermonibus, respicit." Fas
> est ut, postquam docti fuerint catecumini
> de purgatione baptismi, instruantur de
> moribus.[136]

The tropological sense has dynamic qualities because it
expresses in particular the relationship between God and man.
Accordingly, the fourth reading consists of God calling man,
i.e., here the neophyte is being called by God:

> Dicit lectio quarta: "Audite, audientes
> me, et comedite bonum, et delectabitur in
> crassitudine anima vestrae. Inclinata
> aurem vestram, et venite ad me, audite,
> et vivet anima vestra, et feriam vobiscum
> pactum sempiternum, misericordias David
> fideles."[137]

The interpretation and representation of the tropological sense
becomes even more complicated because it leads to an interplay
of two worlds and with that a three-fold situation is

created.[138] Amalarius expresses this interplay of the empiri-
cal-visible and mystical-invisible world by way of call and
response either in form of a dialogue or antiphonal chants. At
this point he returns to the meaning of the first sense which is
expressed in the first two readings whereby the second reading
of the two is followed by a song. The singing signifies at that
point the beginning of salvation. Moreover, in the third
reading man becomes an active participant in salvation history.
Amalarius himself draws a comparison between the two readings
from this point of view:

> Sicut primae duae lectiones propter histo-
> ricam narrationem concluduntur uno canti-
> co, sic ista una dilatatur in duobus,
> propter duas res sibi coniungentes, sci-
> licet mores bonos et caelestem patriam.[139]

Through the antiphonal singing between the lector and cantor the
dynamic relationship of both realms of man and of God, is given
expression and is stated as follows:

Dicit lectio:	"Omnes sitientes venite ad aquas."[141]
Canticum dicit:	"Sitivit anima mea ad Deum vivum."[142]
Dicit lectio:	Feriam vobiscum pactum sem- piternum, miseriocordias David fideles."[143]
Canticum:	"Deus fidelis et non est in eo iniquitas."[144]
Lectio:	"Et quomodo descendit imber et nix de caelo, et illuc ultra non revertitur, sed in-

                    ebriat terram, et infundit
                    eam."[145]

     Canticum: "Audiat terra verba oris mei,
                    expectetur sicut pluvia eloquium
                    meum, et descendant sicut ros
                    verba mea."[146]

The theme of the fulfilled earth represents a certain tangi-
bility of the spiritual realities into which the neophyte is
being initiated. From there the tropological situation leads
over into the anagogical sense.

     The fourth leg of the table symbolizes the fourth sense
which has mystical-anagogical significance and is given
expression only through singing. Amalarius, again citing Bede,
defines it as follows:

                    In quarto cantico teneamus quartum
                    pedem mensae. Beda in eodem: "Anagoge,
                    id est sensum superiora ducens, locutio
                    est quae de praemiis futuris et ea quae
                    in caelis est vita futura, sive mysticis
                    seu apertis sermonibus disputat."[147]

At the beginning of this sense, psalmody[148] continues the theme
of the preceding readings and the antiphonal songs:

                    Audiamus quid dicant catecumini post
                    ammonitionem doctoris: "Sicut cervus
                    desiderat ad fontes acquarium: ita
                    desiderat anima mea ad te, Deus . . ."[149]

Herewith the harmonic-organic unity which unites the mystical
sense directly with the realm of caritas finds striking
expression because the entire anagogical part is sung:

                    Totum anagogiam sonat. Id ipsum de-
                    precatur sacerdos: "Ut qui festa pascha-
                    lia agimus, caelestibus desideriis

accensi, fontem vitae sitiamus."[150]

This singing however points not only to the mystical realm but
moreover to the constant perseverance in good works which alone
brings access to this mystical realm. The anagogical sense
results as it were from the fulfillment of the earth. In other
words, the readings and the songs of the tropological sense flow
over into the anagogical sense. Amalarius himself expounds the
anagogical sense also from this point of view which can be
demonstrated in the following passage:

> Inter haec duo cantica non est lectio
> necessaria. Qui, ut praediximus, in
> bonis moribus moratur, restat ut caele-
> stia tantummodo sciat, quamvis propter
> convenientiam lectionis et duorum canti-
> corum sine altera lectione congrue coni-
> ungantur.[151]

Following this, the anagogical sense then leads over into the
baptismal ceremony, penetrated with light symbolism and into the
exultation of the Easter Vigil where Amalarius markedly fuses
the Gloria of the Incarnation with the brightness of the Easter
Night:

> Dicamus modo, "Gloria in excelsis Deo,"
> quia tanto lumine inlustrata est praesens
> nox, scilicet dominica resurrectione . . .
> Ubi notandum vocem ministrorum ad neo-
> fytos esse usque ad evangelium.
> Dicit lector ad eos: "Si consurrexistis
> cum Christo, quae sursum sunt quaerite,
> ubi Christus est in dextra Dei sedens."
> Habes lectionem de anagogico pede, in
> quo catecumini, accensi per verba cantici,
> "Sicut cervus" desiderabant apparere ante
> faciem Dei. Quod nunc habent in effectu,
> tunc habebant in desiderio. . .[152]

The anagogical sense brings the spiritual realities of the
Easter Vigil to full expression. After that there follows a

further dramatization of the Resurrection theme which will be dealt with later.[153]

Summary

Through the application of Bede's interpretation, Amalarius connects the fourfold sense of Scripture with the liturgy. The understanding of the application of the fourfold sense of Scripture during the Easter Vigil and from there to the entire liturgy as such is of great significance for the dramatic interpretation of the liturgy as shaped by Amalarius because it expresses Amalarius' entire cosmic view which is fed by various streams of tradition.[154]

The first historical sense of Scripture is divided into two readings, the first reading of which refers to the creation of man and his fall. It was pointed out that the first reading was not followed by a song because it dealt with man created by God but also separated from Him through the fall of sin. The second reading on the other hand refers to the historical manifestation of salvation, namely, the Exodus; but it has allegorical significance as well and therefore it is meaningfully followed by a song. The singing therefore becomes an expression of the motive of salvation.

The second sense of Scripture has purely allegorical meaning and refers exclusively to the sacramental-mystical character of the Church and therefore it has complex, typological meaning.

The third, the tropological sense, is for Amalarius of greatest significance because it expresses the reciprocal relationship of God and man and includes the concrete, empirical world here and now, the realm in which caritas is performed, the word of the Bible acted out. This relationship becomes allegorically accentuated by a following antiphonal song.

The antiphonal song of the tropological sense leads into the fourth, anagogical sense. It is exclusively sung. This symbolizes man's perseverance in caritas and from there it leads to exultation and joy of the Easter Vigil. It seems as if Amalarius here for the first time applied a systematic interpretation of the fourfold sense of Scripture to the liturgy, i.e., primarily to that of the Easter Vigil. And here seems to lie its most essential kernel, its <u>ratio</u>, by which the history of salvation is given expression in dramatic form. In its essence it is intricately interwoven with the gradual steps of the four senses of Scripture.

Liber II:[155] The second book of the <u>Liber Officialis</u> deals with regulations of the rubrics for the liturgical year, the number of readings, number symbolism signifying the four elements, the four seasons, the quadrennial times of fasting as well as the quadripartition of the Holy Office, <u>matutinum</u>, <u>meridianum</u>, <u>vespertinum</u>, <u>nocturnum</u>, the individual church offices such as bishop, presbyter, deacon, sub-deacon, acolyte as well as the signifying vestments and altar cloths. Since everything for Amalarius is symbolically interrelated, he wishes to penetrate into their meaning and their interrelationship, for nothing is without meaning. <u>"Neque hoc sine ratione est . . ."</u>, he says.[156] Through the allegorization of the historical events of the Old and New Testaments, the four elements and the four seasons are brought into relationship with each other. Herewith history and cosmology penetrate each other by way of allegory and receive from here their novel significance for salvation history, which finds expression and representation in the configurations of the liturgical drama.

Amalarius deals especially with the allegorical and functional meaning of the vestments and their particular signi-ficance in the interpretation of the liturgy. In the first book he had mainly explained the allegorical sense of Scripture in relation to the baptismal liturgy applying and transforming re-levant material from Bede, whereas in the second book he is rather dependent on Augustine's theory of signs.[157] The external rite corresponds to a deeper, interrelated, sense of the invisible realm. Amalarius says: <u>Omnia haec extrinsecus geruntur, signa sunt rerum intimarum.</u>[158] This deeper meaning can only be disclosed slowly, namely through representational forms. According to the Apostolic tradition the vestments have not only allegorical-symbolic meaning but also an educational, didactic function which helps to penetrate deeper into the meaning of truth. Amalarius makes the following significant statement:

> Quamvis haec spiritaliter intellegere debe-
> amus, tamen ammoniti sumus a supra memo-
> rato apostolico, ut mutationem vestimenti
> iuxta litteram compleamus. Nobis enim qui
> spiritu sumus renati, ante oculos bonum
> est frequentare quod in mentem transeat.
> Per lineam vestem, qua tantummodo utimur
> in sanctis, intellegimus subtilem ora-
> tionem, exutam ab omni carnali cogita-
> tione ante Dominum; locutio vero ad popu-
> lum alia debet esse, tamque grossa ut
> intellegi valeat a populo.[159]

The external sense of Scripture corresponds for him to the outer
part of the vestment and frequently vividly represented
repetition makes possible the growing knowledge of the deeper
spiritual sense of the liturgy which is at the same time of
cosmic significance. Amalarius makes here an essential statement regarding the aesthetic figurative manner of representation
of liturgical drama. The active inclusion of the faithful
receives from this point of view--as spectator--subjective as
well as objective representational dramatic significance.[160]

A further example which shows that Amalarius also differentiates between letter and spirit in the liturgy is a direct
reference to Augustin's De Doctrina Christiana and to the rules
of Tyconius. Through the following informative statement, Amalarius' conception of the liturgy can be unlocked even further.
He says:

> Inter regulas sacrae scripturae septem
> haec una ex illis constat, ut a littera
> transeamus ad spiritum, et a spiritu ad
> litteram. Ac ideo non abhorret a vero,
> quamvis de laneo vestimento accipiamus
> secundum spiritum, si secundum litteram
> perfecerimus mutationem vestimenti, quod
> et secundum litteram et secundum spiri-
> tum rite possumus intellegere.[161]

209

The outer cover of Scripture and liturgy signifies the spiritual reality which lies hidden beneath it. This vision comes close to that of a Narsai, or a Maximos, or the dynamic signum-res-schema of Augustine as well as the typological figurativeness of Hilary of Poitiers.[162]

Amalarius of Metz was, however, the first writer in the Western Church who systematically applied the allegorical exegesis of Scripture to the liturgy and to give it representational form. With that he externalized that which was already implied in the Roman-Franco world view, namely, the searching for the deeper sense which was contained in tangible reality. This vision, however, contradicted neither the Byzantine nor the Gallican liturgy nor the world view inherited by the Germanic peoples. Furthermore, this conception of the inner and outer senses also corresponds to the cosmic-negative theology of Amalarius' contemporary, John Scotus Eriugena, for whom a kernel of divine ratio was inherent in all manifestations of creation.[163] The above citation brings to expression the inner dynamics of the figurativeness of the liturgy in which each gesture and each movement is interrelated and becomes signified, assuming new meaning, and pointing time and again beyond itself.

Liber III:[164] The preface of the third book, Domino opitulante, is a summary of the one unified meaning of the Mass, which in a figurative and manifold manner is indicated and represented in the rite. Amalarius sketches here the spiritual as well as the eschatological significance and the dramatic-allegorical representational forms of the liturgy which lastly, in its real sense, is rooted in the First Liturgical Act and sign of the Last Supper. Again Amalarius stresses the commemorative significance which culminates in the anagogical sense. In summary, he gives the following view:

> Domino opitulante, intercedente beato
> Medardo confessore, cuius festivitas
> hodie apud nos celebratur, in guadio
> sanctorum, prompti sumus animo ad sus-
> cipiendum Dei munus, si tamen ipse dig-

natur purgare et serenare oculum, in quo
discamus de officio missae, quid rationis
in se contineat diversitas illa quae ibi
agitur, cum satis esset, sine cantoribus
et lectoribus et ceteris quae ibi agun-
tur, sola benedictio episcoporum aut
presbyterorum ad benedicendum panem et
vinum, quo reficeretur populos ad ani-
marum salutem, sicut primevis temporibus fiebat apud apostolos, ac ideo primo
decendum est de signis.[165]

Amalarius' particular desire and goal to penetrate to the bottom
and ultimate source of tradition is again intensely articulated
here.

In this third book, Amalarius deals in detail with the
dramatic-allegorical structure of the Mass which seems to have
grown out of his liturgical basic work, Missae Expositionis I et
II. Dramatic representation and personfication cristallize
explicitly around two themes and structural units:

1. Around the Liturgy of the Word (Synaxis):
    Here the Coming of Christ (Introit) and the
    Life of Christ (Lectio) are enacted and its
    representational forms are surrounded by
    a certain splendor.

2. Around the Offertory (Eucharist): Beginning
    with the Offertory, the Passion, Resurrec-
    tion and Ascension of Jesus are enacted
    concluding with the breaking of the bread
    and final benediction.[166]

The life of Jesus and the entire salvation history is unwinding
before our eyes from its beginning to the end. The roles of the
clerics become clearly disclosed as types (i.e., apostles, holy
women, Joseph of Arimathea, Nicodemus and the host of angels).
The Church community too has its active function and plays its
special roles in the course of the liturgical dramatization.
The significance and change of place become clearly manifested

211

in positional symbolism and in the movements of which the temporal layers constantly intersect and overlap in a fascinating way among themselves and with the spatial components. Gestures and positions have allegorical-dramatic, often complex, significance and meaning. Candles and censors as well as other sacred objects are drawn into the dramatic configurations and are often anthropomorphized and personified. Particularly conspicuous is the externalization of a spiritual process as well as the making-present of the supernatural realm through signifying gestures and dramatic representational forms. In contrast to the first book, the theme of the Easter Vigil is here represented by the configurations of the well-known variant, the holy women, as they also later appear in the quem quaeritis tropes. The final benediction receives representational significance because it refers to the Ascension of Jesus at Bethany. The dramatization of the suffering Job at the end of the third book deserves particular attention because Amalarius deals here with the different levels of representation of the historical and allegorical senses. Most conspicuous, however, are the figures of Joseph of Arimathea and Nicodemus as well as the working out of the burial topos. Neither of these two personifications nor the burial scene can be found in the documented Gallican liturgy nor do they seem to have been dramatized as singular themes in the tenth century. They betray the influence of the Byzantine liturgy, which was fed by Syriac influences, on the synthesis of Amalarius.

Liber IV:[167] The fourth book was added to the second edition of the Liber Officialis and deals with the daily and noctural offices as well as with the songs and readings of the different octaves. Amalarius stresses the purpose of this book as follows:

> In hoc quarto libello continentur mota
> ad investigandum, et, iuxta facultatem
> quam potui precari a misericordia Domini,
> scripta de cursibus diurnalibus et noctur-
> nalibus, sive in festis diebus seu coti-
> dianis, quatinus, considerato ordine com-
> positionis et numero psalmorum et lecti-
> onem ac responsoriorum convenienti qui-

212

busque temporibus. . . Necnon etiam aliqua
recapitulantur de superioribus libellis,
quae apertus inventa sunt a mea parvi-
tate post scriptos memoratos libellos.[168]

Here too Amalarius works in the manner of dramatic representations as well as with the interpretation of the
tropological sense. It again is obvious that the allegorical interpretation for Amalarius of Metz is no super-
ficial word game but rather a profound vision and interpretation of the cosmos.[169] The tropological sense assumes
thereby focal significance of human life because man's salvation
is determined from the situation of this sense which is
embodying the real situation of the Christian, that is to say,
the sanctification of his environment through good works
(caritas); that this is so, is signified by the transition from
the tropological sense to the anagogical sense. Psalmody is to
be understood as tropological because it relates to the good
works of man. Therefore its precedence is symbolically
significant. The reason for this is that psalm and reading
refer each to the works and teachings of Christ, the teaching of
whom is derived from his works. This theory of facere et docere
is justified by Amalarius from Scripture itself. He says:

> . . . Morem sanctae ecclesiae tenet
> cursus iste, ut primo operari studeat
> et postea docere. Hoc exemplum reliquit
> nobis Christus de quo dicit Lucas: "Quae
> coepit Iesus facere et docere." Psalmi
> pertinent ad opera, lectio ad doctrinam;
> unde, si Dominus dederit, apertius in
> sequentibus parati sumus dicere.[170]

In his further interpretation of the division of the songs,
Amalarius is dependent on Jerome. According to this Church
Father, each of the different songs has a different meaning.
Thus, the "psalm" refers to the sphere of man, to his good works
and his dialogue with God which follows from good works. The
"hymnus" on the other hand signifies the praise of God by the
Church Fathers, whereas the "cantica" reflect the contemplative
life through the anagogical sense. Amalarius says so

213

specifically:

> . . . ut psalmi sint in nostra locuti-
> one, quando psalmos cantamus; et ymni,
> quando ex lectione dictorum sanctorum
> patrum ad laudes Dei compungimur; et
> cantica, quando per cantum responsorii
> nostra mens sublevatur aliqua laetitia
> ad concentum supernae patriae.[171]

Following this, Amalarius justifies his own manner of representation with a citation of Jerome.[172] After this reference to
the authority of tradition, Amalarius deals with the tropological sense according to his own understanding and gives it
representational form by positional symbolism. He writes
explicitly as follows:

> Opus psalterii, quod manu percutitur, ut
> resonet, ad opera nostra pertinent; opera
> sanctorum sunt mores boni, quos exercemus,
> sive in profectione spiritalis itineris,
> sive in occisione carnalium voluptatum.
> Hi enim mores sine labore non possunt exer-
> ceri. Quapropter, quando psalmos canta-
> mus, solemus stare; ex statu corporis
> demonstramus effectum mentis nostrae, hoc
> est paratos nos esse, sive ad domandam
> carnem nostram, seu ad exercitium operis
> in causa nostra et fratrum.[173]

The activity and exertion of man for the greater glory of God is
given expression through the positional symbolism of standing.
This standing position belongs here exclusively to the
figurative expression of the tropological sense. This is an
important point for our study and overall interpretation of
liturgical drama because it refers in its representational form
to the dynamic relationship between God and man, i.e., it
basically expresses a sign-situation.

The psalm is followed by a sign which gives expression to
the majesty of God. In this connection, Amalarius makes one of

the most profound statements about the fourfold sense of
Scripture in connection with the liturgy:

> Post istam tropolgicam locutionem, id
> est quae de moribus disputat, subsequitur
> lectio, in qua illa reperiuntur quae sanc-
> tus Hieronimus deputavit ymnis, id est
> quae ad laudem Dei pertinent. Ibi maiesta-
> tem Domini invenimus, quomodo incircum-
> scriptu omnia in se contineat, . . . ibi
> facta eius, quomodo fecit caelum, et
> terram, et mare, et omnia quae in eis
> sunt. <u>In illa non deest historia, non
> deest allegoria, non deest tropologia,
> non deest anagogen, quamvis tropologia
> seorsum celebretur,</u> ut praetulimus in
> psalmis. In tropologia psalmorum nostra
> opera recolimus, et in tropologia lecti-
> onem aliorum. Non enim in Domini maiest-
> ate, sive in sua fortitudine, seu in bene-
> ficiis vel factis laboramus; quapropter
> solemus sedere in recitatione lectionis,
> aut silendo stare.[174]

The fourfold interpretation of the senses of Scripture is to be
understood essentially and basically: for Amalarius it belongs
to the structure of the cosmos itself. The fourfold senses,
according to Amalarius are not merely an external tool for the
exegete or for the liturgist but they are essentially con-
stitutive of creation itself. They belong, in his view, to
creation's primordial beginning. All searching for the meaning
and proper sense will therefore have to lead to the Creator and,
taking the liturgy as a point of departure, the image of the
cosmos will receive its ultimate meaning through Christ. Amalarius' searching for <u>ratio</u> is lastly to be understood, according
to his own definition, as a search for the most profound interpretation of the fourfold senses of Scripture. While man is
assigned an active role in his own empirical sphere which is
expressed during the singing of the psalms in a standing
position, he has a passive role, signified again by his sitting
or kneeling position, during the hymnus and the readings. It is

not until the transposition to the anagogical sense that once more an active participation is expressed.[175] The elevated voices refer to the spiritual-mystical realm which thus becomes also spatially related. Amalarius states this as follows:

> In responsoriis namque solemus vocem al-
> tius levare, quam in superioribus, id est
> psalmis et ymnis. Per altitudinem vocis
> altitudinem mentis monstramus, quae se
> erigit in gaudium supernae civitatis. Post
> bona opera et refectionem mentis de sacra
> scriptura, sequitur gaudium caeleste.[176]

From here onward the singing gives way to the anagogical <u>Gloria subsequitur in anagogico officio</u>[177] and thus, the <u>Gloria</u> of Christmas at Bethlehem mingles with the <u>Gloria-Alleluia</u> of the Easter joy and there unfolds, as it were, a telescoping vision of the anagogical mystical sense in which everything seems to fuse.[178]

The fourth book of the <u>Liber Officialis</u> gives further evidence that Amalarius himself was still familiar with the remnants of the Gallican rite because he refers to it in connection with the dramatic hymn of the "three young men in the furnace". This was, as has been pointed out earlier, an integral part of the Gallican liturgy. In the liturgy which Amalarius describes, the hymn appears on the Saturday before Septuagesima. He writes as follows:

> . . . Propter hoc sacramentum, ut opinor
> audivi cantare in vigiliis paschae in
> ecclesia Turonensi post lectiones
> <u>Benedicite</u> . . .[179]

From this indication it is presumed that at least remains of the Gallican rite were alive at Tours, which was a leading center under Alcuin, during the time of Amalarius. This knowledge about indigenous forms will most probably have influenced Amalarius in his mimetic reshaping of the liturgy.

At the end of book four, Amalarius summarizes once more the

meaning of the liturgy. He again proceeds from the First
Liturgical Act and emphasizes the commemorative character of the
liturgy:

> Manifestum est missam caelebrari prae-
> cipue in recordatione passionis Domini
> nostri Jesu Christi. In cuius commemo-
> ratione agatur, ex ipsis verbis quae in
> canone leguntur manifeste liquet: "Haec"
> iniquiunt, "quotiescumque feceritis in mei
> memoriam facietis. . .". Quae aguntur
> in caelebratione missae post initiatum
> canonem, Domini passionem et resurrecti-
> onem, ac in ascensionem recolunt, de
> quibus omnibus quae mihi occurrerunt
> tetegi, quando de officio missae scripsi.[180]

Amalarius again stresses at the end of the fourth book the
dramatization of the liturgy and with that he concludes the
corpus of the Liber Officialis. Again he applies the cover of
"inspiration" because he is describing a liturgical adaptation
from Byzantium, a rival political center to the Emperors of
Aachen. On the other hand, he seems to have found the ratio,
the deepest meaning of the figurative drama of the liturgy. His
words are as follows:

> Nuperrime monstratum est mihi, ut puto,
> ab eo qui quod aperit, nemo claudit, quid
> rationabiliter possit dici de corpore Do-
> mini posito in altari, et de calice ex
> latere eius . . . Altare crux Christi
> est ab eo loco ubi scriptum est in ca-
> cone: "Unde et memores sumus," usque
> dum involvitur calix de sudario diaconi,
> vice Joseph, qui involvit corpus Domini
> sindone et sudario . . . Panis extensus
> super altare corpus Domini monstrat ex-
> temsum in cruce . . . Vinum et acqua in
> calice monstrant sacramenta quae de la-
> tere Domini in cruce fluxerunt, id est
> sanguinem et aquam. . .[181]

In the Unde et memores sumus lies the essential constellation of
the dramatic structure from which the representational form is
ensuing as a whole: the making present of the life of Christ
with retrospective glances to the Old Testament of the past and
with eschatological anticipation to the future always initially
rooted in historical events and then representing in figurative
forms the manifold meaning of the entire cosmos.

The third edition of the Liber Officialis[182] appeared, with
the addition of the preface Postquam scripsi, after Amalarius'
journey to Rome around 831 A.D., approximately in 835 A.D.,
while he held the episcopal seat in Lyons; it should really be
classified with his later works. This edition refers to the
differences in the orders of prayer between the Frankish and
Roman churches. He deals with this phenomenon particularly in
his antiphonal. Amalarius describes this difference in the
following way:

> Postquam scripsi libellum qui a mea
> parvitate vocatur de ecclesiastico
> officio, veni Roman, interrogavique
> ministros ecclesiae sancti Petri quot
> orationes soliti essent celebrare ante
> epistolam missae per dies festos in
> quibus duas solempnitates caelebramus;
> . . . Responsum est mihi unam tantum.[183]

While Amalarius stresses his own capacities in the understanding
of liturgical matters, he justifies his searching for a unifying
sense, i.e., for ratio, of the liturgy:

> Hoc sciscitato, quia vidi apud plerosque
> diverso modo eundem ordinem agere, id est
> aliquos tres orationes, aliquos duas iuxta
> affectum uniuscuiusque animi, non me piguit
> scribere anquesitum meum super hac re
> a Romanis, et in fronte ponere memorati
> libelli meorum devotorum ad notitiam;
> . . . Insuper etiam qua mihi visa sunt
> rationi eiusdem ordinis congruere iuxta

capacitatem ingenioli mei.[184]

After Amalarius refers to the authorities of Augustine and Paul, he makes it clear that he is intending to reshape the orders of prayers according to his own feelings, insights and understanding. He states further:

> In omnibus quae scribo, suspendor verorum
> sanctorumque, ac piorum patrum iudicio,
> interim dico quae sentio.[185]

After this, Amalarius again clearly emphasizes the representational character of the liturgy which develops from the actual presence of the First Liturgical Act:

> Qua aguntur in caelebratione missae, in sacra-
> mento dominicae passionis aguntur, ut
> ipse praecepti dicens: "Haec quoties-
> cumque feceritis, in mei memoriam facie-
> tis."[186]

Following this, Amalarius then unifies the inner essence of the sacrament with the representational form itself. He continues to say:

> Idcirco presbyter immolans panem et
> vinum et aquam in sacramento est Christi
> panis, vinum et aquam. . . Sacramenta
> debent habere similitudinem aliquam
> earum rerum sacramenta sunt. Qua-
> propter similis sit sacerdos Christo,
> sicuit panis et liquor similia sunt cor-
> pori Christi.[187]

As the presence of Christ in the forms of bread and wine thus, the priest in his function becomes united with the image of Christ and from here flows the representation and making present of the entire salvation history with its complex interaction of spatial and temporal dimensions.[188]

After more than ten years, Amalarius confirms with this

219

preface to the third edition of his Liber Officialis, the success of his dramatic-allegorical manner of representation of the entire liturgy. He again summarizes the purpose and meaning of his liturgical reform program: To penetrate to the central meaning and sense of the liturgy according to tradition. Once he has penetrated to the basic liturgical meaning, he proceeds from there to unite the divergent forms of liturgical allegorical drama by way of a unifying sense, the profound meaning of which flows from the significance of the First Liturgical Act. Amalarius shows then that this Act is not an act in isolation but rather embracing the entire life of Christ, blending retrospectively back into the past of the Old Testament and then becoming permeated with eachatological anticipation, projecting into the future of all times. The world view of this imagination finds expression in the representational forms of the fourfold senses of Scripture. Amalarius' liturgical drama cannot be properly understood without consideration of the structure of the four senses of Scripture which are an essential integration of the entire configurations.

Late Works (831-852 A.D.)

Eclogae de ordine romano et de
quattour orationibus in Missa (823-850 A.D.)[189]

The work Eclogae cannot be dated with certainty. The most interesting aspects of this work are that they constitute a combination of Amalarius' initial works Missae Expositionis I et II as well as parts of book three of the Liber Officialis. In addition to the characteristic features of a cosmic vision from the beginning of creation to the resurrection concluding with the benediction and the kiss of peace before communion, it points to the deeper sense of ratio especially in relation to the quadruple number symbolism the significance of which is represented in the touching of the four sides of the chalice. Amalarius' allegorical synthesis of the four senses finds in this configuration its most meaningful expression.

The official title of this work is Eclogae de Ordine Romano. Yet, Amalarius nevertheless integrates in this work his

<u>Missae Expositionis Codex I et II</u> and thus the basic dramatic
structure[190] precedes the <u>Ordo Romanus</u>. This however means that
the whole text is composed of the Byzantine-Gallican-Frankish
liturgy. Does this mean under the cover of the <u>Roman Ordo</u>?

The dramatic structure of individual scenes as well as the
overall dramatization are most conspicuously worked out by which
the individual representational forms and scenes, <u>i.e.</u>, the
active and passive life, Christ's calling of his disciples, the
silent women, the fearful apostles, the burial scene with Joseph
of Arimathea and Nicodemus have over a long process become manifested as types and commonplaces. Moreover, the scene of the
two disciplines at the road of Emmaus is conspicuously
represented. With the clarity and coherence of the various
dramatic representational configurations, the lucid emergence
and manifestation of the <u>medulla res memorata</u>--<u>i.e.</u>,
<u>ratio</u>--has lastly been achieved by the mystical vision and
creative hand of Amalarius of Metz.

In contrast to <u>Missae Expositionis Codex I et II</u>, which has
only one manuscript, <u>Eclogae</u> has a total of 16 manuscripts which
points to a wide distribution and acceptance of this work. It
seems that Amalarius had reached the minds and religious
imagination of the Franks by his insight and manner of representational forms. This fact can be demonstrated by two further
writings, namely, <u>De Ordine totius missae expositione priore</u>
which is a meaningful and partly explanatory composition of <u>Exp</u>.
<u>I</u> and <u>Eclogae</u> and has for the most part been copied.[191] The
manuscripts of this work also point to a wide distribution and
reception of the dramatic allegorical liturgy. The other work,
<u>Ordinis totius missae expositio altera</u> is a commentary on
<u>Exp</u>.<u>II</u>.[192] These two works are not directly from Amalarius'
hand but as variants they evidence the great influence of
Amalarius. The reform of liturgical songs was the real purpose
for Amalarius' later works. If Pepin and Charlemagne had taken
effort in their reform of liturgical singing to eradicate even
the smallest differences between the practice of the Frankish
Church and the custom of Rome, then the later works of Amalarius
indicate that such unity, if it at all existed, cannot have been
of long duration. Right at the beginning of the <u>Prologus</u>, which
was meant as a preface to Amalarius' non-extant <u>Antiphonal</u> and

the <u>Liber de Ordine Antiphonarii</u>, Amalarius expresses his
concern about the song-forms and gives a detailed description of
the discrepancy of the different song phenomena within the
Carolingian Church itself as well as the differences between
Rome and Metz.

<u>Prologus de Ordine Antiphonarii (831-835 A.D.)</u>[193]

Amalarius describes at the beginning the different forms of
antiphonal singing which exist side by side in the vicinity of
his immediate home. He says:

> Cum longo tempore taedio affectus essem
> propter antiphonarios discordantes inter
> se in nostra provincia, moderni enim alio
> ordine currebant quam vetusti, et quid
> plus retinendum esset nesciebam, placuit
> ei qui omnibus tribuit affluenter, ab
> hoc scrupulo liberare me.[194]

This anarchy was an occasion for official renewal of church
singing and in 831 A.D. Amalarius was sent by Louis the Pious to
obtain an <u>antiphonal</u> from Rome. Pope Gregory IV (827-844 A.D.)
however, had to tell him that the <u>antiphonal</u> in question was to
be found with a certain Abbot Wala in the monastery of
Corbey.[195] Amalarius travelled to Corbey and, indeed, found it
there. After examining and comparing the antiphonal of Metz
with the works from Rome, Amalarius expresses great astonishment
about the difference which existed in the variant text of the
songs and between the mother and daughter churches in this
respect; he exclaims:

> Quae memorata volumina contuli cum
> nostris antiphonariis, invenique ea
> discrepare a nostris non solum in or-
> dine, verum etiam in verbis et multi-
> tudine responsorium et antiphonarum,
> quas non cantamus. Nam in multis ra-
> tionabilis statuta reperi nostra volu-
> mina, quam essent illa. Mirarbar quo-
> modo factum sit quod mater et filia

222

tantum a se discreparent.[196]

Furthermore, the _Antiphonal_ of Metz had originated in an
entirely different time than the copy from Rome. While the
Roman antiphonal indicates that it was written in the time of
Pope Hadrian, i.e., in the time of Alcuin, the copy of Metz was
of a much older form which was most likely extant from the song-
reform under Pepin; it could go back as far as the Gallican
time. Amalarius explicitly writes on this matter:

> Inveni in uno volumine memoratorum anti-
> phonariorum ex his quae infra continebant-
> tur, esse illud ordinatum prisco tempore
> ab Adrian apostolico; cognovi nostra
> volumina antiquiora esse aliquanto tem-
> pore volumine illo Romanae urbis.[197]

The side-by-side existence of old and new forms was still
further evident with the difference between fixed theories and
living practice at Metz. A further difference existed in the
sequence as well as in composition. Amalarius in this context
refers in particular to the modern singers who respectively co-
ordinate their antiphonal songs with the meaning and purpose of
the Church Fathers or the celebration of saints from which there
would come more meaningful unity and presentation. Here Ama-
lurius writes as follows:

> Ubi nostri moderni cantores rationa-
> bilius authenticis verbis statuerunt
> officia sua, dividendo antiphonas per
> ferias, necnon et responsorios, et in
> festivitatibus sanctorum antiphonas
> distribuendo singulis vigiliis suas
> . . .[198]

Amalarius then proceeds to discuss the relationship between
historia et ratio from whence comes the meaning of the liturgy.
This statement to which Amalarius constantly refers in his work
Liber de Ordine Antiphonarii is especially important for the
further understanding of the allegorical-dramatic
representational forms. He writes:

223

> Ubi ordo responsoriorum et antiphonarum
> in perspectis voluminibus dissonare vide-
> batur ab ordine librorum de quibus sumpta
> sunt, et a consonantia quae ratione ad-
> stipulatur, non dubitavi sequi in nostro
> antiphonario ea potius <u>quae historiae et
> rationi</u> istius vel illius festivitatis
> visa sunt congruere. (my emphasis)[199]

To be able to connect <u>historia et ratio</u> characterizes according
to Amalarius the more open-minded and modern singers which are
not to be found in Rome but rather in Metz.

Furthermore, the <u>prologus</u> discloses Amalarius' own
practical way of working from which there comes the official
antiphonal renewal. During the editing of the antiphonal Ama-
lurius marked the Roman part with an "R", that part which refers
to the custom at Metz, with "M", and his own creative revision
with "I.C.":

> . . . ibi scripsi in margine R, propter
> nomen urbis Romae; et ubi in nostro M,
> propter Metensem civitatem; ubi nostrum
> ingenium cogitavit aliquid posse rationa-
> bilius illis ordinare, I.C. propter[200]
> indulgentiam at caritatem.

This information about his manner of work discloses something
about Amalar's theories, namely, to combine the useful part of
the older traditions with a living practice and his own
imagination and concepts weaving it into a meaningful whole. In
the process of this revision, Amalarius prefers again the indigenous custom. He asks the singers, not to neglect the native
songs which he, Amalarius, had composed in favor of other songs:

> Idcirco precor cantores ut non prius
> despiciant nostra, quam discutiant ea
> iuxta ordinem librorum et rotunditatem
> rationis. Et si invenerint minus congru-
> ere ea ordini librorum et rationi alicui,

224

dent indulgentiam meae imperitae; sin
autem non despiciant edere nostra olera,
qua rubra testa illis ministrat.[201]

Proper sequence and a unifying sense mark Amalarius' contribution to the reform of antiphonal songs. In order to designate
the indigenous songs, Amalarius applies the organic metaphor of
a healthy herbal plant which is served in a red clay pot (. . .
edere nostra olera, quae rubra testa illis ministrat.)[202] Amalarius justifies this preference of the indigenous native custom
with a reference to a letter by Pope Gregory to Augustine in
connection with the missionary work in England in which the Pope
had recommended the continuation of the native cult forms within
the ecclesiastical structure.[203] With a reference to the native
custom, Amalarius concludes this short work as follows:

Ego secutus sum nostrum usum et posui
mixtim responsoria et antiphonas secundum ordinem temporum, in quibus solem-
nitas nostrae celebrantur.[204]

This short treatment gave particular insight into the discrepancies of the liturgical song forms as they existed among the
different forms in Metz itself and between Rome and Metz. It
demonstrated Amalarius' own theories in the revision and transformation of the liturgical drama by which he drew from his own
imagination and from indigenous traditions. Ratio in connection
with historia deepened the dimension of meaningfulness of the
liturgy in connection with the fourfold interpretation of
Scripture.

Liber de Ordine Antiphonarii (831-844 A.D.)[205]

In this work Amalarius emphasizes in particular the
existing difference between Rome and Metz:

225

Non enim sancta Romana [ecclesia] et
nostra regio uno ordine canunt respon-
sorios et versus.[206]

Again Amalarius stresses the essential relationship between
ratio et historia.[207] Their congruence should find particular
expression in the structure of the responsories. The dramatization of themes of the Old Testament constitutes a large part
of this work. There are scenes such as the three young men in
the furnace, the suffering Job, or those taken from the stories
of Tobias, Judith and Esther.[208] The representation of the three
Magi was also integrated.[208] This was a liturgical custom which
Amalarius probably had the occasion to observe in Constantinople.[209] It was Agobard of Lyons who later polemicized against
the renewal of the antiphonal reform by Amalarius. Agobard
later undertook his own revisions.[210]

Summary

The correspondence between Amalarius and Charlemagne
regarding his work De Scrutinio de Baptismo stands at the
beginning of the literary activity of Amalarius of Metz. The
letter of the Emperor indicated the leadership of Amalarius in
theological-liturgical matters. His work De Scrutinio de
Baptismo still belongs to the tradition of the more simple forms
of the Expositionis which were a didactic necessity under Alcuin
and Charlemagne modeled on those forms which were widely
distributed under the reform of Pepin. The early works Missae
expositionis Codex geminis I et II belong to a more subtle and
complex form of the Expositionis; the structure and dramatic
representational forms and their mystical orientation betray the
Byzantine influence upon the Gallo-Frankish liturgy. These two
small works form the basis of and key to Amalarius' later works
because he integrates them with the structure of the Ordo
Romanus.

From Amalarius' letters to Abbot Peter N. and Abbot Hilduin
as well as from the introduction of the individual editions and
books of the Liber Officialis it is possible to grasp the basic
forms of Amalarius' visions and theories which, in the course of

this study, became time and again evident. The driving forces
of his activity were pursuit of knowledge, his burning desire to
search for and disclose the deepest meaning and sense (ratio) of
the liturgical tradition, and his own creative propensities and
religious feelings.

Amalarius' most inner desire to penetrate into the deeper
sense of the liturgy, as it must have been inherent in the very
primary tradition, vibrates through his entire works. Out of
this tradition which is rooted in the First Liturgical Act of
Jesus Himself, Amalar re-shapes the Frankish liturgy and he
himself works creatively where this tradition is no longer
sufficient enough to proceed with a meaningful liturgical
reform.

The point of departure of his reform program may perhaps be
seen in connection with the incident at Iadhare and the subsequent dispute with his travel companions about the regulations
of the rubrics. But his real impetus had its source most likely
in his encounter with the Byzantine liturgy in Constantinople.
The representational forms of the Byzantine liturgy stood in no
contrast to the extant forms of the Gallican liturgy with which
Amalarius was familiar. The liturgy as celebrated in the Hagia
Sophia was most likely a welcome means by which Amalarius could
integrate the diverse forms and achieve a meaningful uniformity
of the Frankish liturgy.

The four books of the Liber Officialis deal with all parts
of the entire liturgical cycle. In the first book Amalarius
concerns himself with liturgical details of the entire Easter
cycle; the intensification and variations of the Passion themes
are most obvious in this text. In connection with the baptismal
liturgy Amalarius deals extensively with the four-fold interpretation of the allegorical senses of Scripture and its
figurative representational forms. In the second book Amalarius
takes the sign theory of Augustine as a point of departure and
concerns himself with the significance of number symbolism, the
individual church offices as well as with allegorical symbolism
of the vestments and the coverings of the altar; in this
connection he also discusses the rubrics. In the first book of
the Liber Officialis, Amalarius had taken Bede's work as a point

227

of departure, and expressed the allegorical interpretation in representational forms during the baptismal liturgy. And in the second book, Amalarius obviously takes Augustine's theory of signs as his framework, differentiating between letter and spirit in forms of the rite. Although he stands in a rich tradition, Amalarius is the first in the Western Church to formulate and apply the systematic interpretation of the allegorical sense of Scripture to the liturgy. The third book deals extensively with the details of the structure of the Mass the conception of which seems to have grown out of his two early works, the Missae expositionis geminus Codex I et II. The structural unity of the synaxis and of the Eucharist is clearly delineated in these texts and the manifold sense and dramatic manner of representation is most conspicuous. The fourth book deals with the nocturnal offices; it also contains the dramatization of different themes. The Ymnus trium puerorum is obviously a remains of the Gallican rite. Amalarius' treatment of the tropological and anagogical sense as well as his profound statement about the essential meaning of the four-fold allegorical sense of Scripture within the entire cosmic structure are a noted part of this book. At the end, Amalarius summarizes once more the commemorative character of the Mass. Here it is most obvious that the complex burial scenes with Joseph of Arimathea have become conspicuous features and that the figure of Joseph has become a central typus. It was also pointed out that Joseph of Arimathea betrays the Byzantine influence of Amalarius and that we are dealing here with a topos of the Eastern, particularly the Syriac-Byzantine, liturgies.

In the foreword of the third edition, which was written after more than ten years, Amalarius again summarizes the goals of his reform program. His motivation is here still similar to that of his first letter to Abbot Peter N., in which he expounded his dramatic-allegorical method. A similar crystallization of Amalarius' initial motivation is again manifest in his latest work, Eclogae.

The renewal of the antiphonal focuses primarily on the differences in chants within the Church of Metz itself and between the differences of the Frankish and Roman churches. The divergencies which Amalarius describes refer to the reading part, the orders of prayer, and to singing and chanting. But these parts are the more flexible ones of the liturgy, corresponding more intimately to expressions of religious feelings and the power of the imagination. The wide distribution of the reform program of Amalarius seems to verify that he had reached the heart (Gemüt), imagination and religious disposition of the Carolingians. It should also be pointed out that Amalarius with his own disposition towards openness and meaningful synthesis of old and new forms, shows a truly indigenous Gallican characteristic. We had observed this Gallican trait in our discussions of Hilary of Poitiérs, Caesar of Arles, and Germanus of Paris. This trait found also expression in the Gallican mixed liturgies and in the Alcuin-Supplement. Thus Amalarius had provided enough room in his liturgical program for the expressions of native piety and imagination. But at the Synod of Quirzy, his works were condemned as superstitionis fantasmata and subjected to rigorous negative judgement. To conclude our summary, we shall briefly elaborate on the condemnations of Amalar's writings.

The Reasons for Condemnation against Amalarius:
The condemnation of the work of Amalarius of Metz was summarized by Florus of Lyons as follows:

> Cumque in eorum (Patrum) auribus tam
> inepta et prophana novarum adinventio-
> num commenta, (ex Amalarii libris) re-
> citarentur, ipso quoque qui ea de cor-
> dis sui audicissima vanitate protu-
> lerat praesente, et res blasphemas re-
> ligiosus horreret auditus. . . Inter-
> rogant ubi haec legerit. Tunc ille,
> maximo constrictur articulo, rem qua
> neque de scripturis sumpta est, neque
> de catholicorum patrum dogmatibus
> tracta, sed nec ab ipsis etiam haere-
> ticis praesumpta, quia aliud quod
> diceret, penitus non habebat, in suo
> spiritu se legisse respondit. Sed mox
> tam superbam et fatuam responsionem
> veneranda synodus execrans: Dixit:

Vere ille fuit spiritus erroris. . .[211]

Although it is most likely that on the one hand, ecclesiastical
politics in the Carolingian Empire and theological obscurities
may have played a prominent part in connection with this condemnation, it is obvious on the other hand however that the very
same theological arguments of the Church Fathers in their
polemics against the pagan representational forms of the Roman
theatre—which we discussed in the first chapter of this
study—were of equal importance in the ecclesiastical
and theological disputes which evolved around the position of
Amalarius. But at this time these polemics were directed
against creative work within the ecclesiastical structure
itself, namely, against that which was expressed in the
liturgical works of Amalarius of Metz. I have argued, however,
that these liturgical dramatic works in their creative and
aesthetic constitution were sustained by a long tradition within
the Church itself. The main opposition against Amalarius of
Metz came from the liturgical center of Lyons whose main
representatives were Agobard and Florus.

It should also be considered in this connection that the
basic arguments for the condemnation of Amalarius' works were
perhaps to be found in the Synod of Paris. At this Synod the
iconoclastic controversy was at the center of discussions and
disputes. Agobard, Archbishop of Lyons, had composed a tractatus which polemicized against images and creative literary work
of Biblical material. Agobard, as the Church Fathers before
him, saw in poetic imagination nothing but the work of the devil
and he feared, as they did, a relapse into pagan idolatry.
Agobard says in this regard the following:

> Si enim sanctorum imagines hi qui daemo-
> num cultum, reliquerant, venerari iube-
> rentur, puto quod videretur eis non
> tam idols reliquisse quam simulacra
> mutasse. . . . .
> Nunc autem error invalescendo tam per
> spicuus factus est, ut idololatria
> vel anthropomorphitarum haeresi pro-
> pinquum aut simile set adorare figmen-

230

> ta, et spem in eis habere. At quae
> hujus erroris causa? Fides de corde
> ablata, tota fiducia in rebus visi-
> bilius collocata.[212]

That the condemnation of Amalarius could be explained from this
position is evident from the charges against him, which he had
summarized in the exposition <u>Embolis meorum opusculorum</u>, a work
that is not entirely extant. But it was in part reconstru-
ucted.[213] These negative statements shall conclude our long
analysis of the works of Amalarius of Metz.

Against Personification

> Calicem Domini vocat sepulchrum, pres-
> biterum Joseph ab Arimathia, archidea-
> conum Nicodemum, tanquam sepultores
> Christi, diaconos, retro acclines,
> apostolos, se in passione Domini velut
> contrahentes et occultare volentes, sub-
> diaconos, ad faciem erectos, mulieres
> libere astantes . . . .
> Diaconos, altari cum assistunt inclines,
> asserit significare apostolos in passio-
> ne Domini metuentes atque latitantes;
> subdiaconos mulieres cruci intrepide
> assistentes; presbyterum Joseph ab Ari-
> mathia; archidiaconum Nicodemum; cali-
> cem sepulchrum; oblationem dominici cor-
> poris dicit crucifixionem . . . manum
> trahentis, cum levatur, vitam contem-
> plativam; cum deponitur, activam. . . .[214]

Against new and allegorical Interpretations

> Cum ab altari sumitur evangelium,
> ipsum altare significat Hierusalem,
> unde evangelium processit. Locus
> altaris locum illum significat ubi

231

Iacob dormiens angelos vidit. Romanus
pontifex, cum sabbato ante palmas ele-
mosiam dat, mulierem significant quae
Dominum unxit. . . .[215]

Against mystical and tropological Interpretations:

. . . quam inepta et fatua et omni
risu digna confingit, quasi ei soli
licuerit post legem et prophetas,
post evangelia et apostolos, res
typicas et mysticas in ecclesia statuere, ita ut mysteriorum eius prae-
varicator habeatur qui, usu et consue-
tudine simplici, aliud quid celebrare
praesumpserit. Dicit se in talium
fantasiarum adinventionibus sancti
Augusti auctoritatem sequi, . . .[216]

Polemics against deceitful Fantasies and their wide Distribution:

. . . multiplicat vesaniam suam, sic
sentire, clamans omnem Germaniam, sic
totam Italiam, sic ipsam Roman; se
fuisse Constantinopoli, se apud
Histriam sive Lucaniam, et idcirco
in talibus singularis auctoritatis
existere. Nec ei sat est quod
ipse tantis implicatur erroribus atque
fantasiis, nisi et totum pene orbem
sui complicem infamet. . . .[217]

Mocking of Amalarius' Interpretation:

. . . antiphonarium Iohannis Apocalypsi comparat. Atque has omnes et
innumerabiles alias nenias per sanctum

dicit spiritum revelari sibi . . . Ex
quo manifeste et de prophetam et doctrinam vanissimam et risu dignam, heu!
miserabiliter deceptus, vult credi pro-
phetiam.[218]

Furthermore, at another place Florus stated that the books of
Amalarius and their deceitful drivellings had infected most of
the churches of the Franks.[219] Florus himself, however, had to
admit that Amalarius' liturgical reform program had been widely
distributed and had had great influence throughout the
Carolingian Empire.

     For Amalarius the empirical world was interconnected with
invisible realities. It was not so for Agobard; he saw them as
sharply divided, almost from a dualistic point of view.[220]
Amalar's vision of liturgical renewal was informed by a
figurative way of imagination which was similar to that of the
Gallican, Frankish and Germanic peoples. In this connection it
should also be taken into consideration that the conception of
an image (Bild)--bilidi--in the Old-High-German language
the development of which belongs to our period of study,
corresponded to a numinous or magic power. Similarly the word
zeihhan (Zeichen, sign) had also such a reference.[221] This then
seems to suggest that the sign-like figurativeness which was
inherent in Amalarius' works was in congruence not only with the
traditions of the metaphoric and iconic Weltanschauung of the
Syrians, Byzantines and Gauls and the signum-res-schema of
Augustine, but also with a Vorstellungswelt of the Germanic
peoples embedded in signs and runes and related to invisible
powers. Amalarius seems to have grasped this figurativeness and
dramatic potential inherent in the different traditions. His
genius then gave it synthetic expression in dramatic liturgical
forms. In the following chapter, I shall analyze the works of
Amalarius mainly by focusing on this essential shaping of
liturgical drama.

233

[1]Cf. above, pp. 55-121.

[2]Cf. above, pp. 94-121.

[3]Cyrille Vogel, "Le Développmmement historique du culte chrétien en occident résultants et próblems," in Problemi di storia della Chiesa, L' Alto Medievo 2 (Milano: Vitae Pensiero, 1973), pp. 73-97; "La reforme culturelle sous Pépin le Bref et sous Charlemagne," in Erna Patzelt and Cyrille Vogel, Die Karolingische Renaissance (Graz: Akademische Druck- und Verlagsanstalt, 1965), pp. 171-210; Theodor Klauser, "Die liturgischen Austauchbeziehungen zwischen der römischen und fränkischen Kirche vom achten bis elften Jahrhundert," Historisches Jahrbuch 53 (1933): 169-177, and W. S. Porter, Gallican Rite, p. 53; Mircea Eliade, A History of Relgious Ideas, Vol. III. Translated from the French (1983) by Alf Hiltebeitel and Diane Apostolos-Cappadona. (Chicago: University of Chicago Press, 1985), pp. 38-92 and 296-311; for a general discussion of "tradition" see Edward Shils, Tradition, (Chicago: The Univeristy of Chicago Press, 1981).

[4]Cf. Vogel, "Développement historique," p. 75, and Klauser, "Austauschbeziehungen," pp. 170-177.

[5]Cf. above, pp. 104-105.

[6]Vogel, "Développement historique," pp. 76-80; cf. also above, pp. 106-107.

[7]Vogel, "Développement historique," pp. 92-93.

[8]Cf. above, pp. 61ff.

[9]Vogel, "Développement historique," pp. 90-97.

[10]Ibid., pp. 77-78, 84-88.

[11]Klauser, "Austauschbeziehungen," pp. 172-73.

[12]Ibid., pp. 173-77 and Vogel, "Développement historique," pp. 75-80.

[13]Marie de Chantal Bunting, O.S.U., "Liturgy and Politics in Ninth Century Gaul," (Ph.D. Dissertation, Fordham University, 1967), pp. 51-94, and William D. Carpe, "The Vita Canonica in the Regular Canonicorum of Chrodegang of Metz" (Ph.D. Dissertation, University of Chicago, 1975), pp. 51-59.

[14]Cf. above, pp. 95ff.

[15]Capitularia Regnum Francorum.

[16]Wilmart, "Expositio," pp. 1015-16.

[17]Cf. above, pp. 97ff.

[18]Karolus Magnus Admonitio Generalis v. 23. März, 798, n. 80, cited by Klauser, "Austauschbeziehungen," p. 170, n. 2; see also Vogel, "Développement," pp. 83-84.

[19]Karolus Magnus Capitulare de imaginibus, 1.6. cited by Klauser, "Austauschbeziehungen," p. 170, n. 2; see also Vogel, "Développement," pp. 83-84.

[20]Karolus Magnus Epistola generalis, cited by Klauser, "Austauschbeziehungen," p. 170, n. 2.

[21]Cf. below, pp. 222ff.

[22]Cf. above, pp. 281-284.

[23]Vogel, "Développement," p. 88, n. 27.

[24]Ibid., pp. 74-74, 88-89, and Klauser, "Austauschbeziehungen," p. 178.

[25]Bernhard Meyer, "Alkuin zwischen Antike und Mittelalter," ZfkTh 81 (1959): 316-19. Regarding the Book of Cerne see the research done by Dumville, "Liturgical Drama," where he focuses on the questions of dating and authorship of the responsorio

paying particular attention to the dramatic side of this liturgical genre. See also above, p. 95, n. 131.

[26]Gerard Ellard, Master Alkuin Liturgist (Chicago: Loyola University Press, 1950), p. 120.

[27]Ibid.

[28]Vogel, "Developpement historique," pp. 89-92.

[29]Cf. R. Kottje, "Einheit und Vielfalt des kirchlichen Lebens in der Karolingerzeit," Zeitschrift fur Kirchengeschichte 3-4 (1965): 323-342.

[30]Until the end of the nineteenth century is was assumed that there had been two persons by the name of Amalarius, i.e., on the one hand there was thought to have been a liturgist named Symphosii Amalarii (Amalarius of Metz), the author of the Liber Officialis, and on the other hand an Amalarius Fortunatus, Bishop of Treves. However, these two names, Symphosius and Fortunatus are cognomens of the poet, which Amalarius most likely had given to himself. The extensive research done by Germain Morin, OSB, "La question de deux Amalaire," RB 8 (1891): 433-442 and "Amalaire, Esquisse biographique," RB 9 (1892): 337-351 has proved that there was only one Amalarius, namely, the writer and the bishop were one and the same person. Regarding this question see also Ioanne Michaele Hanssens, S. J., ed. Amalarii Episcopi: Opera Liturgica, 3 vols., Studi et Testi, 138. (Citta del Vaticano: Biblioteca Vaticana, 1948), 1: 61-62. This is the first critical edition of Amalar's works. After this it will be cited as: H.

[31]Otfrieds Evangelienbuch.

[32]Iohannis Scotti Eriugenae Periphyseon (De Divisione Naturae) Liber 1 et 2.

[33]H, 1: 341.

[34]H, 1: 59.

[35]De Libro de ordine antiphonarii 58., H, 3: 93-94.

[36]H, 1: 63.

[37]Leidradus Lugdunensis Epistula ad Karolum imperatorum. Scholars have assumed that the reference "unum de metensi ecclesia clericum" refers to Amalarius. See Morin, "Esquisse," pp. 339-40 and H, 1:63. Morin leaves the possibility open whether Florus and Amalarius could have met here for the first time. (Such a meeting would throw light on the later animosity of Florus against Amalarius).

[38]Ex Vita S. Anscharii,". . . Qua de re primitus etiam ibi ecclesiam per quedam episcopus Gallilae Amalharium nomine, consecrari fecit" . . . and ". . . Ex remoti Gallia partibus Ecclesiam ibidem consecraret," in Dom Bonquet, Recueil des historiens des Gauls, nov. ed. v. 6 (1870): 304, 593. Cf. H, 1: 64, n. 20.

[39]See especially A. Cabaniss, Amalarius von Metz (Amsterdam: North Holland Publication Co., 1954).

[40]H, 1: 235-251.

[41]Epistula Caroli imperatoris ad Amalarium prior, H, 1: 235-36.

[42]Epistula Caroli imperatoris ad Amalarium altera, H, 1: 251.

[43]H, 1: 65. Cf. Einhardus Annales, ad ann. 813.

[44]H, 1: 65, 66.

[45]H, 1: 255-81.

[46]H, 1: 65, PL, 101: 1287-88.

[47]Einhardus Annales, ad ann. 814, Annales Laurissenses

<u>minores</u>, ad. ann. 814, see also H, 1: 67, n. 29.

[48]H, 1: 67.

[49]Carl Josef von Hefele, <u>Conciliengeschichte</u>, 2nd augm. edition, 9 vols. (Freiburg, i. Br.: Herder'sche Verlags- buchhandlung, 1873-90), 4: 17.

[50]H, 1: 73.

[51]Ibid., p. 74.

[52]Ibid.

[53]Ibid., pp. 75-81.

[54]Ibid., pp. 80-81.

[55]H, 1: 56-57., see also Hefele, <u>Conciliengeschichte</u>, 4: 165.

[56]H, 1: 82.

[57]Florus, <u>De tribus epistolis libro</u> 40. See also H, 1: 57.

[58]H, 1: 82.

[59]Adolf Kolping, "Amalar von Metz und Florus von Lyons. Zeugen eines Wandels im liturgischen Mysterienverstandnis der Karolingerzeit," <u>ZfkTh</u> 73 (1951): 424-464. See also Bunting, "Liturgy and Politics," pp. 51-146, and Fischer, "Allegorese," pp. 1-3.

[60]See above, pp. 62-93 and p. 169.

[61]H, 1: 49-58.

[62]H, 1: 94-114, 239-338.

[63]See above, pp. 175ff.

[64]See above, pp. 169ff.

[65]See above, p. 176.

[65a]See above, pp. 97-103.

[65b]See above, pp. 89-92.

[66]H, 1: 229.

[67]Ibid.

[68]See above, pp. 167-172.

[69]H, 1: 229-231.

[70]H, 1: 229-230.

[71]H, 1: 230, and see above, pp. 142-144.

[72]H, 1: 230.

[73]Ibid.

[74]H, 1: 230.

[75]Ibid.

[76]Ibid.

[77]Ibid.

[78]Ibid., p. 231.

[79]Ibid., pp. 106-108.

[80]Missae Expositiones Geminus Codex, I, H, 1: 255-65.

[81]Ibid., pp. 255-56.

[82]Enarratio in ps. 89, l. Pl, 37: 1141. See also H, 1: 254. n.

[83]See above, p. 85.

[84]See above, pp. 89ff.

[85]See above, pp. 97ff.

[86]H, 1: 264-65.

[87]Ibid., pp. 259-61.

[88]See above, pp. 181ff.

[89]See above, pp. 55-107.

[90]H, 1: 269-81; Ordo Romanus II (Andrieu: Ordo V), PL, 78: 969-76 and M. Andrieu, Les Ordines Romani, 5 vols. (Louvain: Specilegium Sacrum Lovaniense Administration, 1948), 2: 207-238.

[91]Canonis Missae Interpretatione, H, 1: 284-338.

[92]See especially, H, 1: 295.

[93]Gregorius M., XL homiliae in evangelia, l. II. hom. 34.8, H, 1: 290-91, 293, 298, and Moralia 1 XXVII, c. 39, 65., H, 1: 291.

[94]H, 1: 108-14, 282.

[95]H, 1: 114-15, 339-358; see also G. Maier, "Amalarii Fortunati episcopi Trevirensis Epistula de tempore conse-crationis et ieiunii," Neues Archiv 13 (1888): 305-323.

[96]See above, pp. 173ff.

[97]H, 1: 342.

[98]Ibid.

[99] Ibid.

[100] H, 1: 348.

[101] H, 1: 342.

[102] H, 1: 348.

[103] Ibid.

[104] H, 1: 357.

[105] Liber Officialis, H, 2: 580 pages. Hereafter cited as LO.

[106] See the detailed discussion of this diffusion by Hanssens, H, 1: 120-202. The wide radius of the diffusion he describes as follows: Opus autem quo Amalarius amplissimam sibi famam acquisivit, est eius Liber Officialis. Hic certe cito ac latissime in multis regionibus divulgatus est. Primae editionis unde triginta codices superstites sunt, quorum unus et viginti textum operis integrum, tres eundem textum aliquantum abbreviatum, quinque excerpta tantum continent. Secundae editionis duodecim sunt codices, e quibus duo excerpta dumtaxat praebent. Tres codices textum mixtum complectunter id est libros I-III primae editionis et librum IV secundae. Tertia denique editionis quinque tantum sunt codices. Prima editio maxime in Gallia Belgica, in Germania inferiore et superiore, in Gallia Lugdunensi, in Franconia, Alemannia, Raetia, Anglia divulgata est; altera in Raetia, Franconia, Pannonia, Italia. Exempla mixta exarata sunt in Germania superiore, in Raetia occidentali, in Anglia. Tertia editio aliquantum in Gallia Belgica septentrionali viguit; unum exemplum Divione, alterum Lemovici exaratatum est. H, 1: 84.

[107] H, 1: 155-56.

[108] H, 2: 19.

[109] Ibid.

[110]Ibid.

[111]Ibid., p. 19.

[112]Ibid., p. 20.

[113]Ibid.

[114]LO 1., H, 2: 25-193.

[115]Ibid., p. 25 (De Civitate Dei 1. XIV., x. 8. 1-2., PL, 41: 411-12).

[116]Ibid.

[117]Ibid. (1 Cor., 12:7), p. 26.

[118]Ibid.

[119]Ibid.

[120]Ibid.

[121]The mythical point of departure of the liturgical drama cannot be considered in this present study. I shall pursue that problem in my post-doctoral research.

[122]LO 1., H, 2: 5-57.

[123]Ibid., p. 56.

[124]Ibid., p. 81. See above, pp. 55-56.

[125]LO 1., H, 2: 112.

[126]Ibid., p. 114 (De tabernaculi et vasis eius, 1. 1. 6 PL, 91: 410B.)

[127]See above, pp. 152-153.

[128]LO 1., H, 2: 114.

[129] Ibid.

[130] Ibid.

[131] Ibid. (Gen., 1: 26, 27).

[132] Ibid., p. 115.

[133] Ibid.

[134] Ibid., p. 116.

[135] Ibid. (Is. 4:1).

[136] Ibid., p. 118.

[137] Ibid., (Is. 55:2-3).

[138] Cf. above, p. 55.

[139] Ibid., pp. 118-19.

[140] ibid.

[141] Ibid., (Is. 55:1).

[142] Ibid., (Ps. 41:3).

[143] Ibid., (Is. 55:3).

[144] Ibid., (Ps. 91-16; Deut. 32:4).

[145] Ibid., (Is., 55:10).

[146] Ibid., (Deut. 32:2-3).

[146] Ibid., (Deut. 32:2-3).

[147] Ibid., 119-20.

[148] See above, pp. 202f.

[149] LO 1., H, 2: 199-20. (Ps. 41:2).

[150] Ibid., (Liber Sacramentorum 74: 326).

[151] LO 1., H, 2: 120-21.

[152] Ibid., p. 157 (Ps. 41: 2).

[153] See below, pp. 249-355.

[154] Cf. for example, above, pp. 55-107.

[155] LO 2., H, 2: 197-234.

[156] Ibid., Cf. LO, 1., H, 1: 342.

[157] Cf. above, pp. 138-140.

[158] LO 2., H, 2: 235.

[159] Ibid., pp. 237-38.

[160] Cf. Gadamer, Wahrheit, pp. 110-111.

[161] LO, 2., H, 2: 239.

[162] See above, pp. 79-84, 86-87, 136-149; 95-96, 131ff.

[163] Cf. above, p. 169.

[164] LO, 3, H, 2: 257-386.

[165] Ibid., p. 257.

[166] Cf. above, pp. 55-61.

[167] LO, 4., H, 2: 401-543.

[168] Ibid., p. 403.

[169]Cf. H, 1: 41.

[170]LO, 4., H, 2: 413.

[171]Ibid., p. 418.

[172]Ibid., pp. 418-19. Cf. above, pp. 135-136.

[173]LO, 4., H, 2: 419.

[174]Ibid., p. 419.

[175]Here might be a relationship to the pro-odos-epistrophe-scheme of John Scotus Eriugena which cannot be explored any further in this study.

[176]LO, 4., H, 2: 419-20.

[177]Ibid., p. 420.

[178]See above, pp. 206ff.

[179]LO, 4., H, 2: 464 (Dan. 3.), see above, pp. 98f.

[180]LO, 4., H, 2: 529.

[181]Ibid., p. 542.

[182]H, 2: 13-18.

[183]Ibid., p. 13.

[184]Ibid.

[185]Ibid., p. 14.

[186]Ibid.

[187]Ibid.

[188]Cf. the function of the _Pontifex Maximos_ in Roman culture; see above, pp. 1-10.

[189]_Eclogae de ordine romano et de quattour orationibus in Missa_. H, 1: 202-214 and H, 2: 229-265. See also V. E. Flicoteaux, "Un problème de litterature liturgique. Les Eclogae de Officio Missae d' Amalaire," _RB_ 25 (1908): 304-320.

[190]See below, pp. 262f. and H, 3: 229-31.

[191]H, 1: 217-223, and H, 3: 296-315.

[192]H, 3: 316-321.

[193]H, 1: 361-63, 200-201, 74-75.

[194]H, 1: 361.

[195]Ibid.

[196]Ibid.

[197]Ibid.

[198]Ibid.

[199]Ibid., 361-62.

[200]Ibid., p. 362.

[201]Ibid.

[202]Ibid.

[203]Ibid., p. 363. (Beda, _Historia ecclesiastica_, 1.1.25, _PL_, 95: 58$_C$-59$_A$).

[204]H, 1: 363.

[205]H, 3: 13-109.

[206] Ibid., p. 55.

[207] Ibid., pp. 51-52, 99, 103-104.

[208] Ibid., pp. 22-23, 100-102.

[209] Ibid., pp. 56-57.

[210] Ibid., p. 57.

[211] Florus Opusculum II, 6-7. PL, 119: 81_D-84_B. H, 1: 77-79.

[212] Agobard Liber contra eorum superstitionem qui picturis et imaginibus sanctorum adorationis obsequium deferendum putant, 19, 33. PL, 104: 199-228.

[213] Ibid., 1: 117-119, 366-390.

[214] Ibid., p. 388-390.

[215] Ibid., p. 389.

[216] Ibid.

[217] Ibid., p. 390.

[218] Ibid.

[219] Florus Liber Tribus Epistolas. See H, 1: 80-81.

[220] Cf. especially Fischer, "Allegorese," pp. 72-112.

[221] Elisabeth Karg-Gasterstädt, "Aus der Werkstatt des althochdeutschen Wörterbuchs, ahd. bilidi," Beiträge zur Geschichte der deutschen Sprache 66 (1941): 291-306. Edited by Elisabeth Karg-Gasterstädt und Theodor Frings, 14th ed. (Berlin: Akademie Verlag, 1962): 1028-1051.

CHAPTER V

AMALARIUS' DRAMATIC INTERPRETATION

OF THE LITURGY

In the preceding chapter the entire dramatic structure and the course of the unfolding of the dramatic plot was discussed. In the following analysis the principles of representation and the technical necessities by which Amalarius' work can be defined as drama, will be meticulously worked out. The fourfold division of the liturgical drama shall be the focus of our attention. This structure is as follows: 1. Introitus: Incarnation and the Second coming of Christ; 2. Lectio: Life and Works of Christ; 3. Offertorium: Passion of Christ; 4. Confractio-Benedictio: Resurrection and Ascension of Christ.[1]

Introitus: Incarnation and Second Coming of Christ

We have shown that the representational figurative forms of the life of Christ and the teachings of the work of salvation consist of a continuously unfolding plot. The narratives of the Incarnation, Life, Passion and Resurrection and Ascension constitute the web of this dramatic whole. The basic framework for the unfolding of the acts of the drama of salvation was laid out by Amalarius in his early work, Missae Ecpositionis Codex I et II.[2] It reaches from the Introit to the Ite Missa Est. Thus, the figurative representations are based on the historical events which began at Bethlehem and ended at Bethany. The space in which the plot is moving, that is the actual scope of the play, (its Spielraum) emerges from the inner organization, from the meaningful content of the entire signification (Sinnesganze). That space embraces the spheres of the visible and invisible realms as well as the three-dimensional realm of space and time. This space is, although in a certain sense limited, really limitless, ushering into the shores of infinity, as it were. This particular feature of limitlessness attributes to the activated plot a subtle mobility, a constant being in motion and inner tension which is unique to this liturgical drama.

Since Amalarius himself defines and describes a basilica,[3] we might imagine a basilica to be the exterior framework--the spatial center--for this liturgy. This framework, which externally limits and encompasses the plane of these visible and invisible worlds, is tangibly placed in the presbyterium in form of the elevated episcopal throne, the altar and ambo, as well as in the space assigned to the faithful--and acting--community in the nave of the church. During the performance of the liturgical drama, these different planes intersect. The result of this interaction is an intricate relationship out of which a harmonius representational whole emerges. The effect of this moving figurative formation is achieved by the principle of simultaneity. Naturally, it is not possible that all the nuances can either be brought into play or that they can be grasped at the outer level of their representational forms. It seems to me, however, that Amalarius has been very successful in the shaping of the stage on which the visible and invisible worlds are given form; this is most effectively done in the Introit which contains the essence of the plot. The principle of simultaneity shall therefore be examined on the basis of this example, the Introit.

In the Introit the essence of the liturgical drama micro-scopically unfolds in interrelated figurative representations. As a prelude before the opening of the actual drama it brings into focus the congregation of the Church in their double representatitional form:

> Duo audistis cur conveniat populus:
> unum ex antique traditione, ut iudi-
> cia rerum et cognitiones accipiat;
> alterum ex novo testamento, ut man-
> ducet.[4]

With this projection, the world of the Old Testament and the double meaning of the liturgy in relation to both the Old and New Testament is made present. The separate position of men and women at the right and left side of the church nave is also justified on the basis of tradition.[5] Then follows a meticulous description of the choir and its significance. The choir re-

presents at this point the prophets of the Old Testament.
Through the harmony of singing and through the positional
symbolism of the choir, most likely in form of a circle, the
community of believers is led by the prophets to the adoration
of one God:

> Hinc tractent cantores quid significet
> simphonia eorum; ea ammonent plebem ut
> in unitate unius Dei cultus perseverent.
> Etiamsi aliquis surdus affuerint, id-
> ipsum statu illorum in choro ordinatis-
> simo insinuant, ut qui auribus capere
> non possunt unitatem, visu capiant.[6]

The interrelationship between the singing and the forms of
representation which Amalarius had emphasized earlier, again
finds expression here. Through the activation of the faithful
community--as Israelites--and the chorus--as prophets--the
background of the world of the Old Testament has been created;
the drama of salvation begins to unfold. Now, the congregation,
in their role as Israelites, and in a standing position, are
expecting the arrival of Christ. Thus, the community of the
faithful, on the one hand being the spectators of the drama,
also assumes on the other an active role in the same drama.[7]

After the singing of the psalm has begun, a most peculiar
figurative formation begins to unfold before our eyes which can
only gradually be unlocked and not without empathy into the
Gemüt and imagination of the peoples of the early Middle Ages.

During the singing of psalms, Christ, personified by the
bishop, comes into the world, carried by a "fire carriage"
(currum):

> Praeconibus psallentibus, quando placuit
> Christo, domino psallentum, venire,
> ascendit super currum suum, et venit
> in mundum disponere eundem currum per
> loca congrua.[8]

This is an image of the triumphant Christ, which, through the

metaphor of the "fire carriage" (<u>currum</u>), stands on the one side
in direct relation to the Old Testament but symbolizes on the
other the eschatological expectations of the New Testament.[9]
Furthermore, according to Augustine, the Church is symbolized as
a carriage of victory (<u>Triumphwagen</u>) consisting of an infinite
number of saints and faithful believers. Amalarius gives
visible representational form to this image through the priests,
bishops and faithful which surround the bishop at his entrance
at the beginning of the <u>Introit</u>.[10] This configuration is
described as follows:

> Multitudo decem milium sanctorum est
> in ordinibus ecclesiasticis et in audi-
> toribus eorum. Septem gradus sunt ordi-
> natorum, octavus cantorum, nonus et deci-
> mus auditorum utrisque sexus.[11]

The interpretation of a three-dimensional realm is right here at
the beginning of the <u>Introit</u> implicated by way of a complex configuration. The metaphor of the Old Testament, the "fire
carriage" which carried Elias toward heaven, receives here
through Christ a new eschatological significance. This complex
configuration does not only contain the victory of the
Resurrection but it also points to the end of the world and the
final victory of Christ both which are believed to be near at
hand. The hierarchical order of the Church constitutes the new
form of the "triumph wagon". Therefore, the entrance of Christ
into the world as signified at the beginning of the <u>Introit</u>
should be interpreted from an eschatological point of view and
not, as it might seem to be plausible, in the sense of Christ's
Incarnation. This configuration not only includes the
expectations of the Israelites, it also embraces the
Incarnation-Death-Resurrection of Christ as well as the
eschatological expectation of His Second Coming. Although
neither the Anti-Christ nor the Last Judgment are mentioned
here, the thick metaphor of the <u>currum</u> provokes the entire
figurativeness of the drama of salvation which takes form from
here onwards. The three-dimensionality of space and time
becomes even more multi-layered and interwoven through the
conception of the three ages of the world, <u>ante legem</u>, <u>sub lege</u>,
<u>sub gratia</u>.[12]

252

From this first configuration of the _Introit_ emerges an episcopal procession which embodies the teachings of the New Testament. A censor for incense symbolizes the Crucified and opens the procession. The incense signifies here the teaching of the Crucified which, according to St. Paul, constitutes the primary precept of the doctrine of salvation:

> Veniente Domino, ducit secum prophetas,
> sapientes et scribas; hos in evangelio
> promisit se mittere ad invitandum popu-
> lum . . . Praevenit in turibulo thymi-
> ama, quod significant corpus Christi ple-
> num odore bono; hoc enim corpus primo
> necesse est praedicari in omnibus genti-
> bus.[13]

Following the censor are the scribes, the wise scholars and the prophets of the New Testament which are each respectively represented in this drama by the acolytes, subdeacons and deacons.[14] The scribes who have the task to expound and clarify the dark passages of Scripture are personified in the procession by the acolytes who are carrying burning candles and who follow immediately after the incense-censor. Next are the subdeacons who personify wisdom. It is only through wisdom that the teaching of Scripture can become intelligible and it is therefore reasonable that the subdeacons should precede the deacons. Then the deacons, representing the prophets of the New Testament, follow wisdom. This position signifies that prophecies must constantly be checked by wisdom. The bishop concludes the procession. He follows the Gospel Book which makes visible his unconditional following of Christ.[15] _Ante oculos habeat sepissime episcopus quod in mente semper oportet retinere._[16] The bishop dominates the configuration of the _Introit_ because he embodies simulataneously the follower, the custodian of the teachings, and the personfication of Christ. By way of positional symbolism and through simultaneous personfication of Christ by the incense censor, the Gospel Book and by the bishop, there emerges a simultaneity by which a telescoping effect of the manifoldedness of the configuration is achieved. This simultaneity constitutes the very meaningfulness of this liturgical drama.

In the configuration which follows, the transposition of the new doctrine of Christ is given form by way of Amalarius' representing both sides of this teaching--i.e, contemplative et activa--through positional symbolism: the contemplative side through praying and singing, the active side through good works. The former is mostly symbolized by way of sitting or kneeling, the latter by a standing position.

The seven deacons symbolize the heptagonal division of the Old and New Testament.[17] While they, with the bishops in their midst, go over to the altar, the subdeacons, who represent wisdom, instruct the choir, which is representing the prophets of the Old Testament, in the teachings of Christ. In the previous scene[18] positional symbolism signified that prophets ought to be examined by wisdom; now, the subdeacons, as personified wisdom, are instructing the choir personifying the prophets of the Old Testament. Thus, the previous representational form is being re-activated and simultaneously taking on new dimensions of meaning.

While the choir--the prophets--is instructed in the new teachings at the dawn of the Incarnation, the bishop is assuming a bowed position in front of the altar, imitating the form of a slave. This symbolizes the humble form taken on by Christ when he entered the world:

> Christum semet ipsum exinanivisse se
> et formam servi accepisse. Quapropter
> postquam praesentatus est ecclesiae,
> inclinatus stat usque ad impletionem
> suae humilitatis. . .[19]

The bishop, while remaining in a bowed position, personifying Christ taking on the form of a slave, is now turning to both sides on each of which the deacons are standing, offering the kiss of peace to them. Through this gesture the unity of the Old and the New Testament in Christ is taking on symbolic form because the seven deacons represent both Testaments. After this gesture the bishop goes over to the choir which personifies the

254

prophets of the Old Testament who have been instructed by wisdom until the coming and the teachings of Christ and bringing them peace also. Through this blessing the prophets come to full understanding of the meaning of the Incarnation. Because of this cognitive change and expansion, they, i.e., the choir, change from the songs of the Old Testament to the praise of the triune God of the New Testament singing jubilantly: "Gloria, Patri, et Filio et Spiritu Sancti".[20] This transposition to the New Testament is furthermore configuratively expressed when the choir, i.e., the prophets of the Old Testament, are moving towards the deacons, i.e, the prophets of the New Testament, and remain standing with them. Thus, the prophets of both Testaments are now standing in humble position together before the bishop, asking him to teach them how to prey: "Domino, doce nos orare".[21] The bishop, of course, personifies Christ.

In this configuration the inner disposition for repentance and humility, prayer and understanding through wisdom and faith in Christ, are brought into visible form. The movements of the subdeacons symbolize the enlightening of the prophets through wisdom leading to faith in Christ while the bowed position of the bishop and the deacons is making visible the humility of Christ, of the bishop, the apostles and the deacons. The singing, signifying here a higher level of consciousness and understanding indicates the era begun with the New Testament while the change of roles of the choir also signifies the transition to the New Testament, externalizing, as it were, the turning of heart and faith in Christ; the position of the subdeacons now expresses the unity of Christ, that is to say, the unity of both Testaments.

The active side of the new teaching is made visible through the sending of the disciples by Christ. They are personified by the deacons, who now, two by two, enter from both sides of the altar, step before the altar, kiss it and then return to the bishop. The altar receives through the kiss of peace a double meaning: on the one hand representing the geographical space surrounding Jerusalem into which the apostles are sent:

> Eodem modo vicissem duo et duo diaconi al-
> trinsecus vadunt osculari latera altaris.

> Per osculum eorum demonstratur pax quam
> eis commendavit Dominus: "In quamcumque
> domum intraveritis, primum dicite: "Pax
> huic domui".[22]

On the other hand, however, the altar signifies allegorically
the hearts of the believers. This latter meaning can be exemplified with the following citation:

> Altare vel, alio modo, mensa quae oscula-
> tur, corda electorum significat, sive in
> Hierusalem sive extra Hierusalem. . . .
> "Corda itaque sanctorum mensae Dei sunt"
> Postea revertuntur ad episcopum.[23]

But then Amalarius turns again to the exterior meaning by
referring to the returning of the apostles:

> . . . legimus fecisse missos illo
> tempore: Et reversi . . . apostoli nun-
> tiaverunt illi quae fecerunt . . . Sunt
> discipuli cum Christo; Christus solus
> orat.[24]

With the psalter, the foreplay of the Passion begins as follows:

> Dein, postquam tempus advenit praeconii
> dominicae passionis, cantores, ut ad memoriam
> reducant. Christi novissimam humiliationem,
> dicunt versum de psalterio. Psalterium
> ex inferiore parte habet in quo reboat.
> Sic et opus passionis Christi ab inferi-
> ore parte habet percussuram, a dulce-
> dinem resurrectionis . . .[25]

Thus, the psalter is of great dramatic significance in
foreshadowing the Passion.

Then, in a sudden turn, the figure of Christ becomes
identified with the role of the celebrant:. . . vadit Christus.
. . . The setting is Jerusalem. This shift indicates the

essential typographical congruence of the respective roles in
this liturgical drama:

> Adimpleto tempore praeconatus praeconum,
> vadit Christus ad Hierusalem, in qua est
> altare, quod osculatur in medio, quoniam
> ipse est de quo dicitur in Canticis can-
> ticorum, "Media caritate constravit prop-
> ter filias Hierusalem." . . .[26]

The way to Jerusalem--and here to the altar--symbolizes the love
of Christ, in the gesture of the kiss of peace, to the entire
world and all mankind:

> Osculatur altare, ut ostendat adventum
> Christi fuisse Hierusalem; osculatur
> evangelium, in quo duo populi ad pacem
> redeunt. . .[27]

Through a few steps, beginning with the deacons coming from the
altar, symbolic gestures and change of place, the action of the
drama undergoes a spatial expansion and a temporal compression
(Zeitbewältigung/Zeitraffung). This spatial expansion and
temporal compression having been achieved through symbolic-
allegorical gestures and movements, will from now on remain
before the eyes of the spectator, engage his imagination and
whole being and thus involving him actively into the entire
drama of salvation history.

With this setting of Jerusalem now having been established,
and with the chorus in the background setting the appropriate
mood, the story of the Passion begins to unfold before the eyes
of the believing congregation as they themselves simultaneously
are spectators and actors of the drama. The temporal compression as well as the spatial expansion into the invisible
realm which occurs here is really achieved through the changing
of place. The Book of the Gospel remains at the left side of
the altar symbolizing that the Word first came forth from
Jerusalem but was not accepted there. From the left side the
bishop, as Christ, moves to the right side of the altar which
here symbolizes the heavenly Jerusalem where Christ personified

by the bishop is now throning at the right hand of the Father:

> Dein transit episcopus ad dexteram
> altaris. Liquet omnibus quod semper
> Christus egit dexteram vitam postquam
> resurrexit a mortuis.[28]

The transposition to this part might at first seem to be too
sudden a turn. But at this point, the singing is of extreme
importance because the psalter not only prefigures the Passion
but also has a temporal-transpositional function. Thus, there is
therefore no discontinuity in the entire configuration. Furthermore, with this position of the bishop, the eschatological
orientation comes again to the fore. His image signifies here
not only the triumph of the Risen Christ but it also contains
the image of Christ as Eternal Judge not only of the Last Judgement but of the judgement over every individual here and now.
This configuration is therefore simultaneously a preparation for
the following Kyrie Eleison. And after the bishop has taken his
seat at the right side of the altar, there is again another
telescoping temporal shift, this time focusing on the present
Church. It is made visible through the deacons, who, as unconditional followers of Christ--and of the bishop--are standing at
the right and left side behind the bishop. The majority are on
the right side. In this position they represent respectively
the Old and the New Testaments. Amidst them stand the acolytes,
carrying burning candles indicating that teaching alone is not
enough; it will have to lead to good works (caritas).[29]

   With the Kyrie Eleison a dramatic turn has been achieved
which represents the transposition from the Old to the New
Testament. Through songs, motion, and positional symbolism, a
change in the configuration begins to take place which
henceforth will determine the drama until the fractio. The
complex background which has been staged here symbolizes an
immense width and breadth containing the multi-dimensions of the
visible and invisible realms. With the choir in the background,
the Gospel Book lying at the left side of the altar--symbolizing
the historical setting of Jerusalem--the bishop sitting at the
right side, representing the triumphant Christ and the Eternal
Judge at the right hand of the Father, there occurs a blending

of the image of the earthly and heavenly Jerusalem. Then, in front of this configuration, the deacons, subdeacons and acolytes are standing in central position, ready to preach the Word. The congregation in the foreground expresses readiness for penance and acceptance of the Word before Christ the Lord. Here the immediacy of the Gospel to be recited and enacted in representational form and the immediacy of the visible and invisible Eternal Judge become dynamically interwoven: it is the era sub gratia which had begun with the Law of the Old Testament and culminating now in the New Testament. With this complex configuration of the repenting Church, the plot of the Kyrie eleison begins to unfold.

Kyrie Eleison

With the Kyrie Eleison the motive of humility unfolds completely. The focus is again on the human situation: hic et nunc. It is no longer the people of Israel who at the opening scene represented the people in the nave of the Church imploring the mercy of God asking for the liberation from wrong teachings. It is again the choir who is assigned a major role, for Amalarius states thus:

> Potest et simpliciter intellegi de
> "Kyrie Eleison" necessario constitu-
> tum esse a praeceptoribus ecclesiae,
> ut cantores post finitam antiphonam
> deprecentur Domini misericordiam, quae
> deprimat inanem iactantium, quae solet
> sequi cantores . . . Qua de re possunt
> fallaciter depici per philosophiam et
> inanem fallaciam secundum traditionem
> hominum.[30]

In this scene, by way of songs and candle symbolism, human unworthiness and sinfulness is brought into the foreground but the possibility and reality of salvation is equally emphasized. In the development of this theme, light and positional symbolism of the candle play an important role. While the choir sings the Kyrie Eleison, the acolytes place the candles at both sides of the altar, letting one candle stand in the center. This con-

stellation is of multiple significance: it signifies the
enlightening through the Holy Spirit who instructs in humility
and in the performance of good works. It also signifies, in the
sense of memento mori, that man will turn to dust and ashes: ut
vere nos cognoscamus esse cincerem et pulverem.[31] Furthermore,
the standing, burning candle in the center signifies and makes
visible how Christ through prayer is present in the midst of the
community of believers:

> Cereus in medio stans eum designat qui
> dixit: "Ubi duo vel tres congregrati
> fuerint in nomine meo, in medio eorum
> sum."[32]

Thus, the one candle standing at the center in relation to the
surrounding candles, signifies in visible representational form,
the spiritual, inner life of prayer of the believer.

While the bishop now takes his seat, the meaning of the
entire constellation changes again. The position of the candles
which stand before the altar also changes. They are now being
placed into a straight line with the exception of the first
candle which remains standing at the center before the altar.
Amalarius explains this position as follows:

> Episcopo ascendente ad sedem, cereostata
> mutantur de locis suis in ordine unius
> linear, excepto primo, usque ad altare.[33]

This image makes visible the presence of the Holy Spirit and the
manifestation of good works through the gifts of that same
Spirit. The candle in front of the altar personifies Christ
from whom the Holy Spirit is proceeding. Here again, a double
representation of Christ can be observed: on the one hand in
the person of the bishop and on the other in the form of a
glowing candle. This double representation refers both to the
visible-hierarchical Church as well as to the invisible-mystical
Church. In this figurativeness, the spiritual sphere, i.e., the
transcendental and the immanent, becomes doubly interwoven and
reaching into the visible world. On the one hand, the candles
represent the faithfulness of the elected hearts which are

signifying the reality of the Holy Spirit, and on the other, they signify the manifestation of the undivided gifts of the Spirit in unceasing good works by the believer. The source of this strength is ultimately Christ from whom the Holy Spirit is proceeding. Thus, an interaction of the immanent and the transcendental realms emerges: the symbolic representation of the one spiritual reality leading to the transformation of the empirical world through prayer and good works. This complexity is stated thus:

> In donis memoratis duo debemus memorari,
> id est multifaria dona et unitatem spiri-
> tus. Per cereostata altrinsecus posita, us-
> que nunc distributa dona per corda elect-
> orum signantur; per compositionem unius
> lineae, unitas Spiritus Sancti in singu-
> lis donis; quae compositio examusin habet
> a primo cereo, quem diximus significare
> Christum, a quo procedit Spiritus Sanctus
> et in quo aeternaliter manet.[34]

Through singing which involves a higher level of consciousness and which makes prayer present, Amalarius seems to attempt to dramatize externally an interior process; the singing also has a counter-image in the candles which symbolize both the presence of Christ and human unworthiness. With the turning and movement of the bishop, his eyes directed towards heaven, the transcendental realm is invoked and thus gives an almost cosmic-spiritual dimension to the configuration. It is from this point of the Kyrie Eleison that the mood and transposition to the Gloria can follow smoothly.

If at the end of the Kyrie Eleison a spiritual unity is implied, then the Gloria leads to an almost cosmic unity breaking through all boundaries of space and time. Here, a great fusion of the figurative representations of the sicut erat in principio[35] is achieved. At this point not only Amalarius' mystical vision but above all, his dramatic skill by way of simultaneity finds its fullest expression.

Gloria

The celebrant begins to sing <u>Gloria in excelsis Deo</u> while
his eyes are searchingly directed towards the Eastern part of
the church--here perhaps the <u>presbyterium</u>--as if Christ where
there at His place; yet he could also be found everywhere else.
Thus Amalarius says:

> Sacerdos quando dicit: "Gloria in excel-
> sis Deo," orientes partes solet respicere,
> in quibus ita solemus Dominum requirere,
> quasi ibi propria eius sedes sit, cum
> potius eum sciamus ubique esse.[36]

Then the song of the angels begins to resound from the Eastern
part of the church--the place of which is Bethlehem where Christ
was born taking on the form of a slave. And with a few strokes
the church changes into the town of Bethlehem where the choirs
and voices of angels and men sing the <u>Gloria</u> at the Birth of
Christ. Meanwhile the choir and the community have assumed the
role of the hosts and choirs of angels singing at the splendor
of Bethlehem:

> Ipsum statum ex qualitate loci ubi angeli
> cecinerunt memoratum ymnum, possumus coni-
> ceri. Dominus qui ubique est, secundum
> formam servi in Bethleem est; quae Beth-
> leem nostram ecclesiam signat, quae est
> domus panis.[37]

In his work <u>Expositionis Missae Codex I et II</u>, Amalarius
identifies the bishop or celebrant with the first angel of
Bethlehem to announce the <u>Gloria</u> and peace on earth and the
singing church with the songs of the host of angels over the
manger and fields of Bethlehem. He says here:

> Non unus solus angelus cantavit, sed
> unus primo adjuisse dicitur, et subito
> cum eo factam esse multitudinem angelo-
> rum laudantium Deum. Sicque modo unus
> episcopus inchoat, et omnis ecclesia re-

sonat laudem Deo.[38]

The sounding of the <u>Gloria</u> breaks through the spatial and temporal boundaries of the congregation gathered in the physical building of the church. The searching of the celebrant also signifies the searching of the shepherds at Bethlehem. Thus, with the bishop or celebrant, the congregation is engaged in a double or even triple role: They belong in their role of personification to the host of angels, the searching shepherds and the streaming crowds on the roads to Bethlehem:

> Angeli ad orientem cecinerunt. De quo
> statu dicit Micha: 'Et tu turris gregis
> nebulosa filiae Sion, usque ad te veni-
> ent.' Turris quippe gregis . . . mille
> circiter passibus a civitate Bethleem
> ad orientem distat.[39]

Once Amalarius has engaged the entire church in this complex and manifold configuration, there is first a telescoping backward glance which at the same time foreshadows the end of the drama and of all times. Amalarius reminds us of the transposition of the bishop to the right side of the altar which symbolizes the Resurrection and Ascension of Christ to the right hand of the Father. Having done this, then the jubilation of the <u>Gloria</u> of Bethlehem begins to fuse with the Easter <u>alleluia</u> of Jerusalem and with the singing of the hosts of angels at the Ascension of Jesus Christ at Bethany, thus resounding the Great Peace of heaven and earth:

> Diximus superius transitum episcopi de
> altari in dexteram partem significare
> Christi transitum de passione ad aeter-
> nam vitam, ac ideo hoc in loco dicimus,
> 'Gloria in excelsis Deo,' cantandum,
> quoniam gloria ineffabilis in excelsis
> facta est, quando Christus transitu suo
> animas sanctorum copulavit consortio an-
> gelorum. Hoc gaudium adnuntiavit angelus
> in nativitate eius dicens: ' . . . quia
> natus est vobis hodie salvator.' Mani-

263

festum est quibus extitit salvator:
quando gloria resurrectionis eius caele-
brata est, tunc in terra pax hominibus
fuit, quibus dicebat: Pax vobis, Pax magna est, quando sub uno domino copulan-
tur caelestia et terrena.[40]

The peace which was announced at Bethlehem becomes that great
peace of the Resurrection--and at communion at the end of the
drama--a peace which united heaven and earth. The angels' song
over Bethlehem which resounded at the Birth of Christ in form of
a helpless child is now transformed into the triumphal song of
the Risen Lord at Jerusalem, who now has been given all power
over heaven and earth:

Ita factum esse post resurrectionem
suam denuntiat salvator dicens: 'Data
est mihi omnis potestas in caelo et
in terra.'[41]

And with this turn, the drama focuses again on the figure of the
bishop representing the enthroned Christ.

    This cosmic-mystical vision reveals not only an extra-
ordinary power of a rich religious imagination of existential
significance but also a dramatic skill of the principle of
simultaneity which is of great interest to us here. The
searching gaze of the celebrant leads to an initial tension and
spatial expansion while at the same time activating a change of
roles of the participants. This searching gaze could be
directed to the still vacant seat of the bishop implying the
question: where is Christ? It could broach the great
expectation of Christ at the verge of His coming; it could
symbolize the searching of the shepherds at Bethlehem; it could
also foreshadow the bishop's ascension to the episcopal throne
following the first benediction; and this then could simultaneously be a projection toward the end of the drama with the
representation of the Resurrection and Ascension of Christ.
Particularly significant for the dramatic action is the change
of place and the spatial expansion by way of directive
symbolism, here especially into the direction of the east. The

change of roles in this scene is manifold: The voices of the
chorus and those of the congregation change into those of the
hosts of angels, who then are singing simultaneously over
Bethlehem, Jerusalem and Bethany fusing mystically and
symbolically Birth, Death-Resurrection and Ascension. It is
most important to note that the harmony of singing expresses
here a fusion of heaven and earth--a new cosmogony as
it were--a reconciled world in which birth had conquered death.
Then, with a powerful image of the Risen Christ, figuratively
represented in the person of the bishop or celebrant, the
eschatological meaning of the image of which also rises, pre-
figuring simultaneously the Last Judgement and great cosmic
Resurrection. In summary, it can be said of this configuration
that dramatic simultaneity has been achieved by way of a few
suggestive glances and gestures, movements, change of roles and
singing, thus making possible the mystical experience of the
fusion of all things visible and invisible within the context of
this liturgical drama.

The Gloria is also a transition from the Great Peace to the
Dominus vobiscum of the primary prayer and to the bishop's
throne which follows immediately. Thus, again the image of the
enthroned Christ as Judge of the world dominates the entire
configuration.

De Prima Oratione

The primary prayer focuses on the one hand again on the
present church and on the other it stands in immediate relationship to the cosmic Birth-Resurrection-scene of the preceding
Gloria. With the kiss of peace and his prayer, Dominus
vobiscum, the bishop turns to the congregation who answers with
a loud "et cum spiritu tuo".[42] This gesture is foremost an
expression of community between the bishop and the faithful:

> Hac salutatione episcopi et respon-
> sione populi intelligemus unum debere
> esse affectum episcopi et populi,
> sicut hospitum unius domini.[43]

After this communal act of the first prayer, the bishop turns to the direction of the east, speaking the <u>Oremus</u>, and giving the blessing. This configuration also prefigures the final benediction at the end of the liturgical drama and with that simultaneously the Ascension of Christ at Bethany:

> Deinde revertitur episcopus ad orientem
> et dicit, 'Oremus'. Ac dein sequitur bene-
> dictio. Sic et Christus, ante quam ascenderet
> ad caelum, benedixit eos, sicut scriptum
> est in evangelio . . .[44]

Furthermore, with the primary prayer and the benediction there is a backward projection to the last scene of the <u>Introit</u> where the bishop ascended to the throne symbolizing the actual Ascension of Christ at Bethany. It is most interesting that the motive of the fire-carriage (<u>currum</u>) recurs again at this point. This interplay of constantly moving backward and forward of symbols and allegorical gestures shifts not only the focus to the opening scene of the <u>Introit</u>, including the world of the Old Testament, or to the prefiguration of the final benediction of the Ascension of Jesus at Bethany at the very closing scene of the liturgical drama, but here the eschatological meaning of the entire structure comes most conspicuously to the fore.

De Sessione de Episcopi

With the enthroned bishop now in the foreground, the following eschatological configuration emerges:

> Dein Christus ascendit in caelum, ut
> sedeat ad dexteram Patris. Episcopus,
> quia vicarius est Christi, in omnibus
> memoratis superius debet et hic ad memo-
> riam nobis intronizare Christi ascen-
> sionem et sedem. Quapropter ascendit
> in sedem post opus et laborem ministrii
> commissi. Christus, disposito curru suo
> per convenientia loca, id est presby-
> teros in suo ordine, diaconos in suo,
> subdiaconus in suo, ceterosque gradus
> in suis, necnon et auditores unumquem-

que in suo, ascendit ad sedem et sedet
. . . . De his qui ascenderunt secum,
aliqui sedent et aliqui stant.[45]

This configuration in its first symbolic layer symbolizes
the Ascension of Christ at Bethany. Simultaneously however the
elevated enthroned figure of the bishop assumes the symbolic
figurative meaning of Christ, now enthroned at the right hand of
the Father. Furthermore, the metaphor of the "fire carriage"
(currum) is also blending with this configuration. Thus the
hierarchical order of the Church is interwoven with the invisible kingdom of God. The congregation assumes in this connection a standing or sitting position respectively symbolizing
the active or contemplative life. This double image is still
carried further. As the bishop watches over the Church, so
Christ watches over his "triumph-carriage", the currum. From
the image of the ecclesiastical-hierarchical order develops the
anagogical image of the heavenly Jerusalem. It is stated here:

Dominus in alto caelorum sedens custodit currum suum, id est civitatem de qua
dicit psalmista: "Nisi Dominus
custodierit civitatem, frustra vigi-
lat qui custodit eam." . . . custodie-
bat, custos erat, vigilabat, quantum
poterat super eos quibus praeerat; et
episcopi hoc faciunt. Nam ideo altior
locus positus est episcopis, ut ipsi
superintendant et tamquam custodiant
populum.[46]

The position of the episcopal throne at the center of the
presbyterium assumes great significance at this point. Through
the symbolism of the center[47] a direct relation to the altar
emerges. On the one hand, the earthly historical Jerusalem is
symbolized by the altar and its spatial surroundings; on the
other hand the center of the altar becomes the connective link
to the heavenly Jerusalem. Furthermore, with the image of the
"fire-carriage" (currum), the opening scene of the Introit with
the world of the Old Testament, the arrival of Christ and His
overthrowing of Satan is brought back into play with all its

267

dramatic tensions. Then, simultaneously, the end of the scene prefigures the Benediction and ite missa est of the liturgical drama, and the Second Coming of Christ on the Day of the Last Judgment and His final triumph over the Anti-Christ. Thus another complex layer enters the dramatic interplay. In itself, this "figurative formation and transformation" symbolizes the visible and invisible world bringing to expression the deeper sense of Scripture and of liturgical drama. This deeper sense Amalarius understood as ratio.

Dramatic Analysis

The Introit can be defined as the foreplay of the liturgical drama. Amalarius created there a meaningful complex background for the unfolding of the plot. The staging began with the arrival of Christ in His currum culminating in the configuration of the enthroned bishop with all its complex combinations. Songs, gestures, positional symbolism, simultaneous personfications and movements, are obviously dramatic principles with which Amalarius achieved simultaneity. Out of this background emerged a formation and transformation of a figurative dramatic structure. Its beautiful aesthetic forms were subtly interrelated constituting a dynamic whole. From one sign and figurative form often another emerged; behind one image and configuration another was concealed. The representations of manifold mysteries were for Amalarius the expression of one Mystery the source of which and point of reference was grounded in Christ, in the one God, in ratio.

With this background having been established, the next act, the lectio, unfolds the life and works of Christ.

Lectio: Life and Works of Christ

The last scene of the <u>Introit</u> with the configuration of the enthroned bishop concluded with the anagogical <u>Gloria</u> and its cosmic-eschatological orientation. The beginning of the second act opens again with a retrospective blending into the world of the Old Testament.

Before the beginning of our analysis, I should point out that Amalarius followed two streams of tradition in the representations of liturgical drama one of which is obviously manifested in his earlier work, the <u>Missae Expositionis Codex I et II</u> and in the later <u>Eclogae</u>. The other can be found in the text of the third book of the <u>Liber Officialis</u>. While the former composition focuses on the New Testament, the latter one goes obviously back to the old tradition of the Synagoge and the young Church and is mainly derived from the traditional readings of the Old Testament. Amalarius specifies this:

> Usus lectionis et cantus sumptus est
> a veteri testamento, ut legitur in libro
> Esdrae. . . Lectio legis et prophetarum
> frequentabantur a populo antiquo. Unde
> scriptum est . . . : 'Et ingressi syna-
> gogam die sabbatorum, sederunt. Post
> lectionem autem legis et prophetarum . . . [48]

Since both streams of tradition existed side by side and since both of them are significant as dramatic variants, I shall analyze both of them. I shall begin with the variant of the <u>Liber Officialis</u> because its structure seems to be the more complex one. The entire readings consist of three parts, <u>i.e.</u>, firstly of the Old Testament readings; secondly of the <u>responsorium</u> with sequence-like expansions through <u>tractus</u> and <u>alleluia</u> and through a combination of <u>tractus/alleluia</u>; and thirdly of the Gospel.[49]

Lectio: Readings of the Old Testament[50]

Allegorical representational forms emerge most conspicuously out of the first part of the <u>lectio</u>. It is therefore important for the understanding of this liturgical drama as a whole that we focus our attention from the beginning on this phenomenon. Since reading and chanting are intricate components of the ensuing allegorical web of representational forms, I shall begin by analyzing their essential purpose and function.

The readings refer primarily to the Law of Moses. The function of the lector is described as follows:

> Lector legem Domini debet tradere audi-
> toribus, quasi incipientibus in scola
> domini exerceri; . . . audiant doctorem
> necesse est. Doctor et lector unum sunt.[51]

It is the task of the lector not only to recite but also to instruct: he is <u>doctor et lector</u>. The task of the cantor however is more diverse. He mainly takes on the role of the prophets; but since the prophets were the voices of the different manifestations of the Spirit from Moses to Christ, the task of the cantor will have to be all the more differentiated and flexible. Amalarius makes this clear by stating that:

> Cantor multa officio habet . . . Possumus
> etiam officio cantoris officium prophetae
> intellegere.[52]

With the introduction to the teachings of the Old Testament, <u>lector</u> and <u>cantor</u> complement each other with mutal interaction. Amalarius understands both roles as instrumental for the basics of the teachings of Christian doctrine.[53] Although both reading and chanting express the first step of the introduction, they have to be differentiated in the sense of scriptural exegesis and hermeneutics. The teachings from the Law of Moses thus correspond to the historical-allegorical sense, the songs of the prophets to the allegorical-tropological interpretation. The singing of the <u>cantor</u> therefore symbolizes a higher grade of the basic teaching because it leads into the fulfillment of the Law. Amalarius specifies the function of both parts correspondingly:

> Per lectionem praedicationem veteris
> testamenti, quae humilior est, possumus

intellegere; per responsorium novi testamenti, quae excelsior est. Haec duo prae-
dicamenta per Johannis vitam et Christi
designantur.[54]

From the inferior basis of the Old Testament the singing then
proceeds to culminate in the figure and voice of the last prophet before Christ, namely John the Baptist. From here it flows
into the figure of fulfillment of the New Testament: Jesus
Christ. This gradual structure is simultaneously made visible
by way of positional symbolism in ambo and tribunal.

Lector and doctor are limited in their teaching of the
written Word. Consequently, only the learned and purified
scribes can at first properly understand the meaning of the Law.
Therefore it will be the task of the cantors, according to the
law of the prophets, to awaken and to excite the less receptive
hearts of the believers and to disclose the deeper sense of
Scripture to them. Amalarius stresses these tasks:

Dent lectores sive doctores precium Domini,
id est verba legis, et recipiant scolasti-
cas mentes . . . . At si adhuc aliquis sur-
dus, obturatis auribus cordis, torpescit,
veniat cantor cum excelsa tuba more prophetarum, sonetque in aures eius dulce-
dinem melodiae; forsan excitabitur.[55]

The voice of the cantor is as that of the prophets, the call of
God to the Israelites who are personified here by the congregation gathered in the nave of the church.

Responsorium[56]

Following the first part, the choir begins to sing a song
of praise answering for those people of the congregation who
have understood the Word of the Law and have accepted it:

Cantores qui respondent primo canenti,
vocem auditorum proferunt, quos testi-
ficant laudare Deum.[57]

Through this antiphonal chanting the congregation is again, actively and figuratively, part of the liturgical drama. For those Israelites who have not yet understood the Law, the role of the prophets changes over into that of the preacher. And thus, the verse which follows the second song, takes on the form and purpose of a sermon and the cantor assumes thereby the role of the preacher. Amalarius explains this as follows:

> Lex enim scripta data set in tabulis.
> Scriptura enim pertinet ad lectoris
> officium; prophetia menti inscripta erat,
> quam voce fidenti prophetae proferebant;
> quod pertinet ad cantoris officium. Fidi
> praedicatoris officium gerit cantor, quem
> oportet post oboedientiam auditorum ver-
> sum cantare.[58]

With this interpretation Amalarius uses a complicated allegory, namely that of plowing, which, as it does in the case of plowing the earth, breaks open the hearts of the believers and yields that which was buried deeply in memory.[59] It is obvious from Amalarius' concluding explanation of lectio and responsorium that a figurative mode of imagination and representation and emotional orientation are to be considered essential means of introduction into the fuller understanding of the teachings of Christ. I shall cite this text of Amalarius in full:

> . . . Ideo scribuntur litterae, ut per
> eas memoriae reddatur quod oblivione de-
> letum est; simili modo ex pictura recor-
> damur quod interius memoriae commendari
> potest. Ita et responsorio ammonetur prae-
> dicator quomodo doctrinam, quae praeces-
> sit in lectione, exerceat. Primo, ut dul-
> cedine suae imitationis plurimos sibi as-
> ciscat; coniuncti corda multorum excitent
> ad conpunctionem et lacrimas; et ne se
> extollere debeat de opere praedicationis,
> pulsatur versu, quatinus ad memoriam
> sibi reducat de propriis causis iudican-

272

dum ante Dominum.[60]

This activation of memory, imagination, heart and soul and mind (Gemüt) through Word and Scripture, personification of the biblical figures, positional symbolism, song and gestures was most probably not without effect. Gestures and emotional eruptions within the congregation were also not unlikely to happen.[61]

In summary, the structure of lectio and responsorium is as follows: the first step is the teaching of the Law according to the historical-allegorical sense. It thus forms the fundament of salvation. The second step which corresponds to the allegorical-tropological sense, is signified by the voice of the cantor, who, according to the law of the prophets, unlocks the hearts of the faithful. As an answer to this call of God, the voices of the choir sing a hymnus, representing the people of God. The verse which then follows is a form of a sermon. The cantor assumes here the role of the preacher for those who have not yet understood.

This very complicated structure of a modulated responsorial chant is expanded even further by songs of sorrow and yearning of the tractus or by songs of joy of the alleluia. Within the framework of this structure, the tractus is sung in a simple tone in contrast to the modulations of the alleluia songs. This sequence-like expansion has its special meaning. Amalarius differentiates between three ways of this type of expression, the responsorium et tractus, the alleluia and the tractus-alleluia. I will briefly analyze them.

Responsorium et tractus.[62]

These two songs are combined through the allegorical symbol of the turtle-dove and pigeon sacrifice. The doves symbolize the active life of faith--the vita activa--because of their tendency to group together. Because of this characteristic they are symbolized in form of the responsorial song. The pigeons, on the other hand, tend to remain individually by themselves; they also prefer flying in solitude. Because of these two traits they are symbolic representational forms of the

273

speculative and contemplative life of faith--the _vita contemplativa_. They are thus symbolized by the modes of the _tractus_. In the chants of the _tractus_, contrition of heart, penance for sins, prayers, lamentations and general suffering are expressed; but these can also refer to mystical darkness of soul, suffering and yearning in solitude. This structure has also the capacity to express liberating joy in a cosmic-eschatological vision. Amalarius refers to Moses, Daniel and Ezechiel as examples of such manifestations of mystical solitude and visions:

> Moyses quasi tractum cantat tribulationis,
> qui 'solus ascendit ad Dominum, et ne
> idem populus feriatur, lacrimosis preci-
> bus impetrat'. Daniel tractum laetitiae
> cantat, quando solus fugientibus sociis,
> inter angelos remanet. Solus Iezechiel
> quadrigas, cerubin et supernae civitatis
> aedificia celsa miratur.[63]

It is possible that dramatic representations of these figures were performed during the chanting. Since Amalarius gives specific descriptions of the suffering Job during the offertory, it is perhaps safe to assume that this might not be an isolated instance of such representations.[64] Within the framework of the senses of Scripture, the _tractus_ might partly be interpreted as an extension of the tropological sense of the responsorium. Thus it would then lead further into the anagogical and mystical sense and vision.

Alleluia[65]

The _alleluia_ is foremost a song of praise and joy with a variety of modulations. It can become a tropological song of praise as well as an anagogical song of mystical joy with reference to the Birth and Resurrection of Christ.

Tractus et alleluia[66]

If _tractus_ and _alleluia_ are combined in an antiphonal chant, the only two consecutive verses may be sung in the simple tone of the _tractus_. The third verse on the other hand must be sung in the modulations of the alleluia:

> Post duos tribulationis tertius occurrit laetitiae, quoniam, post duos dies sepulturae, tertius occurrit resurrectionis.[67]

Thus the three verses symbolize the combination of the three days of the Death and Resurrection of Christ. Within the sacred drama, the _alleluia_ as well as the _tractus/alleluia_ are a transition to the Gospel which follows after these dramatic representational songs.

I have attempted to work out the sequence-like structure of the _lectio_ and the task of the _lector_ and _cantor_ in this context. The structure which leads to the proclamation and re-presentation of the Gospel is a very complicated but also a very flexible one. It is therefore capable of a variety of expressions and representations. Its structure is based on the allegorical mode of the interpretation of Scripture and is given representational form in the roles assumed by the _lector_ and _cantor_.

Dramatic Analysis

The _lectio_-structure of this edition of the _Liber Officialis_ is in essence spatially oriented. Out of this space-orientation and from their spatial relationships, dramatic forms emerge which have abundant possibilities for representational expressions. From the basic grade of the _lectio_, this part of the liturgical drama is in constantly increasing gradation structured in such a way that first Moses, the figure of the Old Testament, is represented by the _lector_. His figure will finally transform and culminate into that of Christ; the _cantor_ on the other hand will finally take on the representational form of John the Baptist. This gradation is expressed in the structure of the _lectio_ as well as in the interior structure of the basilica which is mainly expressed by the gradual elevation from the nave of the church to the ambo and then to the tribunal. The purpose of the _lectio_ is not only didactic in proclaiming the spoken Word. It also aims at objective form and beauty through symmetric structures and representations. Through the gradual inner structure of the reading part, which is also spatially related through the vision of the four senses of Scripture, there emerges space for movements in which the representational forms of salvation history can be given expression. The gradual structure of this architectural space of the church corresponds to the actual scope of the play (Spielraum) as we have indicated earlier.[68] It is most important to keep constantly before our eyes this constellation and interaction of exterior architectural space and the inner scope of the play and with that also the interplay between invisible and visible space because this manifold interaction belongs to the mode of being of that liturgical drama of the ninth century which concerns us in this study. Without such empathy we are unable to grasp its significant structure. Out of the web of interactions arises the following configuration: the congregation of the church, in sitting position, has now again resumed the role of the Israelites. Amalarius describes this position as coming from an old custom:

> Quamdie haec duo caelebrantur id est
> lex et prophetia, solemus sedere more
> antiquorum.[69]

In contrast to this position, lector and cantor are ascending to an elevated position, also according to an old custom: Lector et cantor in gradum ascendunt more antiquorum.[70] The cantor, most probably will be stationed on a higher step than the lector because the song of the prophets is more advanced in the course of salvation history than the actual biblical situation of the Old Testament. Furthermore, the tropological sense which is expressed in the song of the prophet, is structurally higher than the historical sense of the actual readings by the lector. The first part is being read by the subdeacon expressing the historical-literal sense of the law of the Old Testament. The figure of the subdeacon in elevated position thus assumes the contours of the teacher of the Old Law, namely Moses, as later the deacon, when reading the Gospel, is personifying Christ.

The vocal modulations of the responsorium with sequence-like expansion of tractus and alleluia contain within themselves

great dramatic possibilities because of their flexible
structure.[71] The songs express the diversity of the Spirit expressed through the different prophets and the dynamics of the
interaction between God and the Israelites in form of calling
and response. The responsorium is through the communal
symbolism and interaction of cantor and chorus a representation
of the active life of faith, the vita activa, while the tractus
with its moderate melody in correlation with a biblical figure
represents the mystical life, the vita contemplativa. Personifications such as Moses, Daniel, Ezechiel, or Tobias, Judith and
Job or other figures are implied in the dramatic structure. In
this "figurative transformation of a dramatic structure" which
emerges before our eyes, the focus is on figures of the Old
Testament, i.e., the people of Israel as a whole who first turn
away from God and then return to Him and those who represent
mystical solitude and jubilant joy in eschatological vision.
This configuration leads by way of its gradual structure, moving
within itself, to the Gospel which is the fullfillment of the
Law of the Old Testament. This culminative point which is
symbolized by the elevated position of the deacon in the
tribunal, is surrounded by great theatrical splendour.
Referring to Cyprian,[72] Amalar describes the position of the
deacon in the tribunal as follows:

> . . . quid aliud quam super pulpitum,
> id est super tribunal ecclesiae, opor-
> tebat imponi, ut, loci altioris celsi-
> tate subnixus, et plebi universae pro
> honoris sui claritate conspicuus, legat
> praecepta et evangelium Domini . . .
> Vox Domini confessa in his cotidie quae
> Dominus locutus est audiatur; viderit
> an sit ulterior gradus ad quem profici
> in ecclesia possit.[73]

Through the elevated position of the tribunal the configuration
now expands into a cosmic vastness; the perspective moves from
the past of the Old Testament into the future of the Last
Judgement of Christ at the end of time. In the background is
the image of Christ enthroned at the right hand of the Father
and personified by the figure of the bishop. With this dramatic

turn and double image of Christ in form of the deacon, and
bishop, the world of the New Testament now emerges.

Evangelium: De Diaconi
Ascensione in Tribunal[74]

The congregation changes its role again from that of the
Israelites to that of the crowds of Jerusalem: it changes from a
sitting to a standing position:

> Nunc revertamur ad ordinem. Usque nunc
> sedimus more veteris consuetudinis; . . [75]
> modo surgentibus est ad verba evangelii.

While the congregation and the priests remain in a standing
position, the celebrant fills an incense-censor symbolizing the
body of Christ, filled with the fire of the Holy Spirit. The
incense is thus symbolizing the good works which go out from
Christ:

> Turibulum Christi corpus significat, in
> quo est ignis, scilicet Spiritus Sanctus, [76]
> et ex quo precedit bonus odor. . .

After this the deacon asks for the priestly blessing expressing
his readiness to accept the Word of God. Amalarius gives the
following description of roles and scenes:

> Deinde vadit ad altare, ut inde sumat evan-
> gelium ad legendum. Altare Hierusalem
> potest designare . . . vel ipsius Domini
> corpus, in quo sunt verba evangelii, vide-
> licet bonae nuntiationis. Ipse praecepit
> apostolis praedicare evangelium omnis
> creaturae. [77]

Through these few steps the transition from John the Baptist to
the sending of the disciples has taken place indicating also a
change of scenes. The altar now represents Jerusalem from where
the Word of God first proceeded and from where the apostles
began to preach the Good News.

The deacon takes the Gospel-Book and carries it in his left arm. This signifies that he represents the feet of the Lord while the curved position of the left arm signifies the empirical world in which the Gospel is to be proclaimed. Amalarius says here:

> Diaconus qui portat evangelium, Christi, pes est. Portat evangelium in sinistro brachio, per quod significatur temporalis vita, ubi necesse est praedicare evangelium.[78]

With this most peculiar allegorical miniature representation of the world, the deacon turns with a gesture of communal symbolism to the congregation, then the people turn with him to the East, all bow down and make the sign of the Cross. This action signifies both, the handing down of the priestly blessings and the reception of the Word of God. While the congregation remains in a bowed position, the deacon walks towards the tribunal. Two candles which are carried before him represent the Books of the Law and the Prophets; an acolyte carrying an incense-censor, follows the candles, signifying the good works which preceded the teaching of Christ. It is basically a representation of the facere et docere.[79] While on the one hand the candles remain standing at the lower ambo, which was also the position from which the readings and songs of the Old Testament were recited, thus symbolizing its inferior position, the incense-censor on the other hand, is preceding directly ahead of the Gospel-Book which is now being carried to the tribunal. This configuration symbolizes that good works must precede the teachings of Christ as it had been the case in His life on earth. Thus the facere et docere again takes on figurative shape:

> Duo cerei qui portantur ante evangelium, legem et prophetas designat praecisse evangelicam doctrinam. turibulum vero opinionem bonarum virtutum procedentem de Christo. Ipsum turibulum in tribunal ascendit ante evangelium, ut ibi suavem

odorem ministret. Christi enim bona
opera praecesserunt evangelicam doctrinam, ut Lucas testatur in Actibus apostolorum: 'Quae coepit Jesus facere et
docere.'[80]

One can imagine how easily, in the eyes of the spectators, the
figure of the deacon in this elevated position, surrounded by
manifold allegorical symbolism would become interwoven with the
figure of Christ. Furthermore, the elevated position constituted a parallel position to the elevated episcopal throne,[81]
where the judge of all the world was emerging and presiding,
personified by the bishop. Amalarius also stresses the eschatological significance of this image at this point of the
liturgical drama:

Excellentior locus, in quo evangelium
legitur, eminentissimam doctrinam evan-
gelicae praedicationis atque manifesta-
tissimam auctoritatem iudicandi signat.
Status cereorum monstrat inferiorem
esse legem et prophetas evangelio.[82]

With a masterfully swift turn to the candles, Amalarius succeeds
in bringing the entire configuration of salvation history into
the scope of a visual perspective. No longer the Old Law of
Moses and the prophets but Christ, Who is the fulfillment of the
Law and Eternal Judge, dominates the scene and calls for
responsibility.

The extinction of the candles after the reading of the
Gospel symbolizes the end of the Old Testament and the dawn of
the new era with eschatological significance under the New
Testament. It is also the beginning of the public preaching of
the Word of God which until now was concealed in silence. This
silence of the Word of God is symbolized by the Gospel Book
which had quietly been lying at the altar after the bishop had
proceeded to his throne earlier in the drama.[83]

With epic anticipation Amalarius then points to the further
course of the liturgical drama. He states:

Praecedens officium praedicationem Christi
usque ad oram passionis demonstrat, et suorum praedicatorum usque in finem mundi, et
ultra. Sequens opus passionis Christi et
resurrectionis atque ascensionis in cae-
los, similiter suorum per confessionem,
atque suspirium in caelum, ubi audituri
sunt: 'Venite, benedicti Patris mei,
possidete paratum vobis regnum.'[84]

After the dismissal of the catechumens the fully initiated of
the Christian community will be drawn into the making-present of
the historical Passion and Resurrection. Their active participation in the liturgical drama will henceforth become even
more intensive.

Dramatic Analysis

The dramatic means which give representational form to the
Gospel consist especially in the changing of roles, the making
visible of inner dispositions through bodily objects such as the
incense-censor and candles; movements, gestures, steps and
chants which imply an expansion of space; communal symbolism and
the representation of the Old and New Testaments through certain
positional symbolism; parallelism of ambo and elevated episcopal
throne which symbolize simultaneously the teaching of Christ and
the tribunal of the Eternal Judgment.

Lectio: Missae Expositionis Codex I et II[85]

The tradition of this edition is in its first part of the
readings oriented towards the New Testament rather than to the
Old Testament as it was the case with the tradition represented
in the Liber Officialis and which I discussed in the preceding
pages. The focus in the Missae Expositione is first on John the
Baptist and then on Christ. These roles are assumed by the subdeacon and deacon. Both are in relationship to their roles
defined as follows: Of the deacon Amalarius says:

Christus enim minister fuit, qui dixit:

281

'Non veni ministrari sed ministrare.'
Johannes nempe subminister qui dixit:
'Hic erat quem dixit vobis: quia post
me venturus est. Ante me factus est
quia prior mea erat'. . .[86]

Then Amalarius defines the role of the subdeacon:

Videamus quae convenientia sit officio
apostolorum sive aliorum praedicatorum,
quorum dicta subdiaconi legunt in am-
bone, cum Iohanne . . Epistola quae
legitur ante evangelium, ministerio
Iohannis convenit.[87]

We may safely assume that with the figure of John the Baptist,
circumscription of time and place, i.e., the desert, the
vicinity of the River Jordan and the surroundings of the City of
Jerusalem were also implied in this configuration.

Responsorium

This part differs also in its orientation. It symbolizes
and represents the calling of the apostles by Christ. Here
Christ is personified by the cantor and the choir assumes the
role of the apostles. And again, Amalarius gives an exact
description of the roles:

Veniamus modo ad chorum apostolorum.
Responsorium in ecclesia cantatur, post
lectionem. Responsorium ideo dicitur,
eo quod uno cantate ceteri respondeant.
Cantavit unus Christus, id est vocavit
Petrum et ceteros apostolos et illi
responderunt, quia Christum imitati
sunt; et ideo responsorium convocationi
apostolorum convenit.[88]

In this configuration the positional symbolism is to be exactly
observed. The lector, who represents John the Baptist, dominates the ambo. The cantor, who personifies Christ, stands at

282

the tribunal, i.e. in the most elevated position. The chorus on the other hand, who represents the apostles, stands between lector (John the Baptist) and cantor (Christ), i.e. lower as the cantor and higher as the lector.[89]

After the responsorial song of the chorus which most probably also consisted of solo voices, representing the individual responses of the apostles, a verse which followed was sung in solo voice by the cantor. This song signifies the solitude of Christ in prayer as he had retreated in order to pray:

> Ipse idem qui inchoavit solus, solus
> versus cantat, quia Christus, qui
> apostolos vocavit seorsum, et pernoctans et
> solus orabat.[90]

Other themes were also represented such, as for example, Christ and Peter walking on the water. Amalarius describes this as follows:

> Vis audire ubi iterum responsorium:
> "Statimque Jesus locutus est, dicens:
> 'Habete te fiduciam, ego sum, nolite
> timere.' Audi et ubi respondeat chorus:
> 'Respondens autem Petrus dixit: Domine,
> si tu es, iube me veniere ad te.'" Am-
> bulabat Christus super mare, et fecit et
> Petrum ambulare supra mare.[91]

From such description it follows that a whole scene could easily develop through gestures and small movements. In the same manner, other Scriptural themes might have been performed. Amalarius justifies his representational forms as being based on Scripture itself for at the conclusion of the responsorium he says:

> Si quis vult investigare de vocatione
> apostolorum, legat evangelium, et ibi
> inveniet vocatos esse apostolos a Chris-
> to post praedicationem Johannis Baptistae.[92]

Such a statement in his own defense implies Amalarius' own creative vision of the liturgy, although it most likely received its impetus in Constantinople; but it also indicates the criticisms to which his works were subjected.

Alleluia

The _alleluia_ which follows the _responsorium_ signifies the exultation of Christ following the calling and sending of the 72 disciples:

> In ipsa hora . . . exultavit Jesus in
> Spiritu Sancto, et dixit: "Confiteor,
> tibi, Pater, Domini caeli et terrae . . ."[93]

The representation which gives form to this exultation of Christ in addressing and praising His Father, is the most beautiful and moving fulfillment of the anagogical sense of Scripture. It is the pinnacle of expression in the form of singing. Amalarius hastens to exhort the choir at the conclusion of the _alleluia_:

> O cantores, "cantate Domino canticum novum,
> quia mirabilia fecit." Mirabile opus, ut te
> vocaret, fecit, quando hoc quod totus mun-
> dus capere non potest, ad hoc contractum
> est, ut in uno homine totum maneret et
> tu haberes quod imitareris.[94]

Thus, the exultant song of Christ after the sending of his disciples to preach and to enact His Word represents the highest level of unification of the tropological and anagogical senses.

The edition of the _Missae Expositiones Codex I_ suggests that the Gospel was recited in singing, but in a simpler, less elaborate form more congruous with the themes of the Sermon of the Mount. The edition of Codex II, on the other hand, is again full of gestures and movements such as we observed and discussed in our study of the _Liber Officialis_.[95]

Summary

In our analysis of this section it could be noted that the orientation of the Old Testament in the _Liber Officialis_ is primarily based on spatial dimensions which are both horizontally and vertically related. The spatial structure which was built up in a gradual form emerges on the one hand from the exterior space of the basilica and on the other from the interior structure of the spiritual cosmos which is rooted in the allegorical visions and images emerging from Scripture. The temporal perspective rests in the image of the three ages. It begins with Moses and culminates in the figure of the Eternal King and Judge. Thus, within this blending of spatial and temporal dimensions there emerges before our eyes a figurative transformation of Biblical personages who, in a gradual process, culminate in the figure of Christ. The dramatic means essential for the formation of this entire configuration are as follows: personfication, positional symbolism, singing in all its modulations and variations, gestures and movements. The simultaneity, as the main dramatic means, emerges here particularly out of the manifold forms of positional symbolism and allusive gestures.

Missae Expositionis Codex I et II is mainly oriented towards the New Testament where the focus rests on the figures of John the Baptist and Christ. The spatial relationship is more rectilineal and is concentrated on the tribunal. From there it assumes horizontal direction. The horizontal orientation is especially indicated through the calling and sending of the disciples by Jesus Christ. The spatial limitlessness emerges here not so much from the eschatological orientation centered on the Eternal Judge but rather from the anagogical exultation of Christ. The transition to the Gospel seems also to be direct rather than gradual because Christ Himself is the Gospel. Songs, personficiation, and positional symbolism are the essential means of representation. These variations are dramatically most interesting because they indicate an unanticipated richness of imagination and dramatic representational possibilities of the early Middle Ages.

<u>Offertorium: Passion of Christ</u>[96]

De Oblatione Legali

After the catechumens have been dismissed, the enactment of
the Passion, beginning with the offertory, opens. As
previously, there is at first a blending back to the world of
the Old Testament:

> Primo ad memoriam reducenda est ob-
> latio legalis, ac deinde Christi,[97]
> postremo nostra.

During the opening of the offertory, the sacrifice of the Old
Testament is made present. This then will lead to the preparation for the sacrifice of Christ which simultaneously
includes the sacrifice of the Christian community and the entire
Church in its cosmic dimension. The offering of gifts which
begins in form of an offertory procession proceeding from the
background of the nave of the church, symbolize the preparation
of the sacrifice of the Old Testament and the people of the
Church for the sacrifice of Christ.

By means of change in place and roles the sacrifical rite
of the Old Law is made present. The altar now represents the
Mosaic altar, the celebrant is personifying the High Priest
according to the order of Melchisedech, while the congregation
is resuming the role of Israelites:

> Oblatio legalis habebet duo altaria, unum
> in introitu tabernaculi, alterum in ta-
> bernaculo. Altare in introitu praefi-
> gurabat praesens officium . . . Est et
> alterum genus sacrificii, quia duae sunt
> nostrae oblationes; una est per mortifi-
> cationem carnis, altera in oblatione
> bonorum operum; quae utraeque offerun-
> tur in introitu tabernaculi. In prae-
> senti vita mortificare carnem oportet
> et bona opera reddere . . . Et quod per

sacerdotis manum debeat offerri, manifestatur in Levitico . . .[98]

As there were two altars for the legal sacrifice of the Old
Testament, so the congregation now too makes a double sacrifice:
that of abstinence and mortification leading to purification of
heart which in turn will lead to good works. During the sym-
bolization of the purification of gifts, the Levites play an
important representational role. The choir takes over this
role. During the presentation of gifts, the Levites sing
according to the order of the House of David. The priestly line
of the Levites was assigned different tasks in the sanctuary of
the Temple; in this liturgical drama the chorus takes over these
responsibilities. The functional importance of the singing is
most interesting because it is related to the purification of
the gifts made worthy to be presented to God. The songs of the
Levites coincide allegorically with the motive of salvation;
they accompany therefore the entire offertory. Amalarius gives
the following explanation for this:

> Interim cantus celebratur in templo
> Domini, dicente eodem Paralipemenon:
> ". . . Cumque offerrentur holocausta,
> coeperunt laudes canere Domino, et
> clangere tubis, atque in diversis or-
> ganis quae David rex repererat concre-
> pare. Omni autem turba adorante, can-
> tores qui tenebant tubas, erant in
> officio suo, donec compleretur holo-
> caustum; cumque finite esset oblatio,
> incurvatus est rex, et omnes qui erant
> cum eo, et adoraverunt".[99]

Thus the Levites have a mediating role functionally connected
with the symbol of purification. The washing of hands of the
High Priest which follows, is also a symbol of purification
before the presentation of the sacrificial leading over to the
offertory which is at first the sacrifice of the Old Law:

> Sed ante quam ingrederentur sacerdotes
> ad holocausta, lavabant manus suas, ut

scriptum est in libro Exodi. . .[100]

The singing and washing of hands of the High Priest and the Levites have in their allegorical meaning of purification a transitional function and are therefore structurally important. From here Amalarius leads over into the New Testament:

Sufficiant ista interim de oblatione veteri; nunc videamus Christi oblationem.[101]

From this background of the Old Testament the figure of Christ is now slowly emerging.

De oblatione Christi

The structure of the background which has been sketched above indicates a preparation of the sacrificial gifts the meaning of which is twofold: On the one hand, the sacrifice of the Old Law is in itself a preparation for the sacrifice of the New Testament; on the other hand, the preparation for the sacrifice within the liturgical drama—the purification of heart of the faithful—which will culminate in the sacrifice of Christ takes on representational form at the beginning through the offertory procession of the congregation and the simultaneous preparatory actions around the altar. As the drama of the Passion proceeds, the various meanings will lucidly unfold.

Right at the beginning the significance of the spatial orientation is obvious. There is not only emphasis on the exterior space but the interior space is variously symbolized, i.e., the image of the exterior Mosaic altar will begin to have a counter image in the hearts of the believing persons; the external sacrifice will correspond to an interior sacrificial disposition, manifesting itself in contrition, repentance and good works. The singing of the Levites and the washing of hands of the High Priest are also external signs of an internal purification. Only purity of heart will lead to the acceptance of the gifts by the High Priest. As the drama proceeds, there will soon be an interplay of the various spatial layers both of the external and internal realms.

288

The dramatic background of the Old Testament has emerged with the means of change of place and roles, positional symbolism of the Levites and High Priest and especially through the spatially related movements of the offertory procession in the nave of the church. The next configurational setting, proceeding from this background, will be Jerusalem with the Passion of Christ as the central action.

The offertory of the sacrifice of Christ begins according to Amalarius with the Dominus vobiscum of the priest and ending after the secreta with a loud voice saying or singing per omnia saeculorum introducing the Preface. Amalarius brings the offertory preparation of Christ into focus by way of the dramatic means of change in place and roles and temporal compression. After the washing of hands (lavabo), which precedes the offertory, the altar becomes slowly the center of actions. The configuration of the Old Testament changes now into the surrounding of Jerusalem during Holy Week where the events of the Passion of Jesus Christ from their beginning on Palm Sunday until Holy Saturday will again take place. The physical motion of the offertory procession in the nave of the church and the movements of the celebrant at the altar contribute especially to the development of the following configuration: the figure of the High Priest personified by the celebrant transforms into the person of Christ, the altar signifying now the surroundings of Jerusalem and the Garden of Olives, the congregation changing its role to the crowds of Jerusalem while the choir retains its role as priestly Levites. The objects of the altar such as the linteum (which is the white covering of the altar), sindon and sudarium, assume from here on a very significant meaning and a particular function. They are the allegorical symbols of corporality and sensuality in need of purification. From this point onward they are essential symbolic-allegorical objects in the drama expressing the Passion.[102]

De oblatione nostra

From the figurative dramatic formation of the Old Testament there emerges now a new configuration, full of motion and movements involving the entire space of the church: out of the background of the nave of the church there comes, slowly moving,

289

the offertory procession, carrying its sacrifical gifts. In the
foreground of the altar, the celebrant, after completing the
washing of hands as the High Priest, begins to move slowly from
the side to the center, and then to the entrance of the altar.
In this process, the figure of the celebrant representing the
High Priest becomes interwoven with the figure of Christ. With
this change of role, the scene and entire configuration changes
into the site of Jerusalem on Palm Sunday: Christ coming from
the Garden of Olives moving towards the singing offertory procession who now has assumed the role of the hosanna-shouting
crowds of Jerusalem. Amalarius gives the following description:

> Christus enim venire dignatus est Hieru-
> salem die palmarum, et ibi expectare diem
> immolationis suae. Omnis retro immola-
> tio illum praefigurabat; in illo consum-
> mata est omnis immolatio. In eo die des-
> cendit Dominus de monte Oliveti, venien-
> te ei obviam turba multa.[103]

This is an exact description of roles, scenes, time and place:
Christ emerges as the protagonist, the circumscription of place
refers to Jerusalem with the Mount of Olives in the background,
the time is Palm Sunday. The crowds receive Christ both with
their songs and with their sacrifical gifts; the latter is an
old custom of the Israelites but also corresponds to an old
tradition in the Byzantine and Gallican Church.[104] The hosanna-
song itself is the most important gift. These sacrifical gifts
including the singing, encompass the entire hierarchical Church
and not only the sacerdotal order. The presentation of gifts at
the entrance of the altar corresponds to the blessing of fruits
according to an old custom. This presentation is also related
to the hosanna-song which is here the blessing of the crowd over
Jesus Christ, their Messiah. Amalarius continues his most interesting description:

> Non est dubium quin salutaret eam secun-
> dum morem bonum antiquae traditionis, quem
> etiam nostra, non solum perita ecclesia,
> sed etiam vulgaris tenet. Solet sibi ob-
> vianti aliquod bonum optare cause salu-

tationis, et praecipue propterea dicimus
Dominum salutasse turbam venientem sibi
obviam, quoniam talis erat consuetudo
Iudaeorum, ut Augustinus in psalmo Saepe
expugnaverunt me: "nostis enim . . .
quando transitur super operantes, est
consuetudo ut dicatur illis: Benedictio Domini super vos, et magis ista consuetudo erat in gente Iudaeorum. Nemo
transiebat et videbat aliquod opus in
agro, vel in vinea, vel in messe . . .
non licebat, transire sine benedictione."[105]

This particular blessing of the gifts which to Amalarius' time
was obviously a remains of an old custom of the Gallican Church
must be differentiated from the actual presentation of bread and
wine for the offertory. Amalarius points to this difference and
to the transition from one to the other:

Haec consuetudo manet usque hodie in
nostra ecclesia; quando transitum faci-
mus de uno officio ad alterum, quasi
nuper introeamus ad operarios, saluta-
mus eos verbis benedictione plenis.[106]

The dramatic effect of this configuration lies in the
spatial relationship between the slowly approaching Christ and
the singing crowds of Jerusalem. The priest, in the figure of
Christ, coming slowly down the altar which is here the Mount of
Olives and the people of Jerusalem represented by the offertory
procession in the nave of the church, moving towards each other.
This movement of the calmly walking Christ is standing in
contrast to the hosanna-singing crowds, perhaps even accompanied
by gestures and movements. Furthermore, the external movement
corresponds to an internal one: on the one side the calmness of
Christ corresponds to His inner disposition of prayer, on the
other side, the excitement of the crowds expresses yet wordly
joy and attachment. This combination of the sacrificial gifts
of the Old Testament with the hosanna-songs of Palm Sunday
deserves attention because it seems to be structurally significant. At this point, it seems to be the expression of the

historical sense of the liturgical drama. Both, gifts and
songs, are in need of purification through the hands of the
priest personifying Christ. From Amalarius' further
explanations we can infer that we are dealing here with a most
significant layer of singing. He says that the Oremus-prayer
should have a specifying effect so that Christ could be
recognized and accepted:

> Postea dicit sacerdos, "Oremus". Nisi
> Christi virtus corda replessent tur-
> barum ad orationem, non ei canerent tam
> magnificas laudes. Oratione enim sere-
> natur cor ad cognoscendum Dominum.[107]

The following allusion to the cleansing of the Temple implies
that with the loosely structured offertory part it might have
been possible that it came to emotional eruptions or to representations of that scene in the Temple of Jerusalem. Exactly
at this point there follows the insertion of the symbol of
purity, namely, the white altar linen, indicating the transition
to the offering of gifts at the altar because purity of heart
and thoughts are pre-dispositions for prayer and singing in the
Temple:

> Puritas lintei quod ponitur in altari,
> puritatem mentium eorum signat, qui
> Domino cantabant. Eandem puritatem qua
> repleverat corda cantantium, requirebat
> in templo, quando eiecit inde vedentes et
> ementes . . .[108]

But we must also differentiate between two layers of songs:
namely, the purified and the unpurified. The purified songs of
the Levites also suggest this meaning. The symbol of purity as
symbolized by the linen-cover is here also in congruence with
the acceptance of the offerings by the priest or deacon.
Amalarius himself also differentiates between these two layers
of songs:

> Dum enim sacerdos suscipit oblationes,
> cantores cantant. Quamdiu enim turba

cantabat. "Osanna in excelsis", Christus
vota eorum suscipiebat.[109]

Structurally it seems that we are dealing with the second layer
in the allegorical framework of the liturgy; therefore, the
expansion of the songs by the Levites should be interpreted in
the allegorical-tropological sense.

The acceptance of the offertory gifts which includes the
hosanna-songs, takes place at the entrance of the altar. After
the acceptance of the gifts, the returning to the altar
symbolizes Christ's entry into the Temple of Jerusalem where He
will be praying and offering Himself to the Father:

> Oblatione suscepta, sacerdos redit ad
> altare, ut in eo disponat . . . obla-
> tiones coram Domino, quas illi immo-
> laturus est in sequentibus missae.
> Christus enim, post accepta vota cantan-
> tium, Hierusalem et templum Domini in-
> travit, in quo erat altare, ibique se
> praesentavit sibi Deoque Patri ad immo-
> lationem futuram.[110]

In the next configuration, the figure of the silently
praying priest at the altar interweaves easily with the image of
the praying Christ in the Temple of Jerusalem. This image
signifies also the deeper spiritual sense which is inherent in
the offering which will be following soon. This deeper meaning
of Christ's Passion and sacrifice is still concealed from the
apostles, disciples and the people of Jerusalem. It lies yet
concealed in Christ Himself as it lies concealed in the forms of
bread and wine at the altar. At the depth of this sign-theory,
Amalarius writes according to St. Augustine:

> Agnus paschalis latebat in Christo, qui
> immolandus erat. Hoc erat secretum apo-
> stolis, erat secretum ceteris fidelibus
> qui cum eo erant, erat secretum populo
> Iudaeorum, usque ad diem caenae, quo ipse
> apertius manifestare dignatus est pas-

sionem suam; usque ad illum diem proten-
ditur secreta sacerdotis.[111]

And with the signified concealment of the meaning of the
offertory and mystery of the Passion, the preparation of the
gifts in which the congregation is included, comes to an end
leading into the configurations of the actual offering of the
Passion. The preparation of offertory gifts coming down from
the Old Testament become intricately interwoven with Christ's
preparation for His passion. The initial configurations underwent an expansion and deepening of meaning which had not yet
reached its fulfillment. Again Amalarius achieves this by a
skillful dramatic turn in which he projects the Hosanna-chants
of the prefatio into the offertory songs of the congregation
while the movements of the celebrant after the primary washing
of hands begin to signify Christ's entry into Jerusalem. By now
the entire expanded configuration is a blending of the historical, allegorical and tropological sense of Scripture but not yet
of the anagogical-mystical sense.

The sindon is the leading allegorical-tropological symbol
in the transition to the offertory because it signifies penance
and purification which are a predisposition of the heart for the
unification with the sacrifice of Christ.

> Interim ponitur sindo in altare. Sindone,
> quam solemus corporale nominare, admone-
> tur omnis scilicet populus, et ministri
> altaris, nec non et sacerdos ut sicut
> illud linteum castigatum est ab omni na-
> turali viriditate et humore. . . ita in-
> tentio offerentium simplicitate niteat
> coram Deo.[112]

Then follows the presentation of bread and wine. Amalarius
again emphasizes the two layers of the song pointing to the
deeper meaning yet concealed in the forms of bread and wine.
Here the connection between the image of the Son of Man praying
in the Temple and offering Himself to the Father and the
offering at the altar is established in the drama. As the

294

apostles, the women and disciples of Jerusalem were still
ignorant of the sacrifice to come, so the congregation does not
have the full understanding of the offering either. Amalarius'
constant search for a deeper meaning--for ratio--is
manifested again when he says:

> Dein transit sacerdos ad suscipiendas
> oblationes. Interim cantores, cantant
> more antiquorum, ut iam praetulimus,
> sive turbarum, quae cantabant Christo
> venienti Hierusalem. Populus dat ob-
> lationes suas, id est panem et vinum,
> secundum ordinem Melchisedech. Panis,
> quem offert, et vinum exprimunt omnia
> desideria pia intrinsecus latentia, sive
> sint pro immolatione seu pro hostia viva.
> Quod foris agitur, signum est illius
> quod intrinsecus latet.[113]

The two layers of singing during the visible sacrifice emerge as
structurally very important parts,[114] at the same time, the
significance of the invisible sacrifice is moving more and more
into the foreground. The offerings are laid on the altar in
memory of the first seven deacons: "disponente diacono oblates
super altare more primorum septem diaconorum."[115] The subsequent, second washing of hands is at first, in the sense of
the order of the Old Testament, a symbol of penance and purification. But at this point in the drama, the washing of hands
also symbolizes the tears of Christ which He shed shortly before
His death in Jerusalem and also shortly before He had raised
Lazarus from his death.[116] Structurally, the tears of Christ in
connection with Lazarus, risen to life again, have anticipating
significance implying Christ's own death and resurrection, which
will shortly take place within the framework of the liturgical
drama. The offering of incense has at this point retrospective
as well as foreshadowing meaning. It symbolizes the sacrifice
of Aaron on the one side and the invisible sacrifice of the
angels which is to take place during the following prefatio, on
the other. Here the censor represents again the body of
Christ[117] as it did during the act of the Introit.

The mixing of water and wine in this offertory scene does
not, as one would anticipate, point to the Crucifixion but is
rather the foreshadowing of the Resurrection. Amalarius interweaves here a custom of the Levites of the Old Testament who had
to present the water in the Temple with the organic metaphor of
the mystical-cosmic body of Christ. Amalarius writes in
summary:

> Omnis populus, intrans ecclesiam, debet
> sacrificium Deo offerre; at cantores, qui
> sunt de genere levitarum propter instan-
> tem necessitatem cantandi non habent li-
> centiam huc illucque discurrendi, ut sin-
> guli offerent cum ceteris; statutum est
> eis, ut penitus non sint extorres a sacri-
> ficio, custodire aquam, et hanc unum of-
> ferre pro ceteris. Populus offert vinum,
> cantores aquam. Sicut vinum et aqua
> unum fiunt in calice, sic populus et can-
> tores in corpore Christi. Cantores more
> levitarum antiquorum, qui omnia necessa-
> ria tabernaculi providebant, quaerant
> aquam ad fontem, et servent eam cooper-
> tam usque ad tempus sacrificii, et tunc
> eam offerant.[118]

The water in connection with the Levites, is a special symbol of
purification. Furthermore, it seems that the mediating Levites
in their offering of the water remain to be functionally important in the structure of the liturgy.

After the mixture of water and wine the deacon puts the
chalice at the altar, while the sudarium which symbolizes
exertion, suffering and sweat, is placed at the right side
because its symbolic function is to cleanse away all the rest of
impurity which has remained yet:

> Postea ponit calicem in altari diaconus,
> et sudarium suum in dextro cornu altaris;
> est habile ad hoc, ut, quicquid acces-
> serit sordidi, illo tergatur . . .[119]

The sudarium symbolizes and foreshadows in its positional symbolism at the right side, the Passion and Death of Christ.

The concluding orate fratres is a plea for the acceptance of the sacrifice through the hands of the celebrant at which time the prayer of the people blends with the songs of the levites and priests. This blending of prayer and singing is very informative and structurally significant. I shall discuss this combination below. Amalarius summarizes the actual offertory as follows:

> Quo facto, revertitur ad populum sacer-
> dos, et precatur ut orent pro illo, qua-
> tinus dignus sit universae plebis obla-
> tionem offerre Domino. Praesentes ado-
> rationes praelibatae sunt in Paralipe-
> menon. ubi orat tuba, cantantibus levitis.
> Post holocaustem nempe incurvatus est
> rex et populus. Audivi dicere quod plebs
> eadem ora tres versiculos cantet pro
> sacerdote: Mittat tibi Domini auxi-
> lium de sancto et duos sequentes.[120]

This configuration has at first cosmic-eschatological meaning followed by a retrospective glance into the Old Testament while stressing the bowed position of the king during the prayers of the acceptance of the offerings. What is of particular interest to us here is the ending of the singing with a blending of prayers. We have noticed above[121] that during the blessings of the gifts, Christ had exhorted the singing crowd of Jerusalem and the people of the Church, to pray so that they may recognize Christ by way of a calm and quiet disposition of soul. Thus, the singing, in the same way as with the physical offertory gifts, was in need of purification in order to be acceptable to God. Through prayer not only the gifts were purified but also the hearts of the faithful. Thus, the calmness of prayer led to further deeper sacrifical readiness. Therefore, the blending of the prayers of the congregation with the purified singing of the Levites, is, as it seems to me, now possible, whereas the initial singing of the congregation expressing the historical

sense of Scripture did not fall together with the allegorical-
tropological songs of the Levites. Now, however, after the
prayers of the believing congegration have undergone purification and turning of heart, they have reached a different level
in the structure of the four senses, namely that of the allegorical-tropological sense.

In contrast to the previous configurational part of the
reading, Amalarius does not exactly define the song-structure of
the offertory part. But from his repeated mentioning and his
various applications it can be inferred that the singing had
dramatic and allegorical significance. That there were dramatic
representations within the configurational framework of the
singing and that there were several layers of singing containing
different meanings, is evident from Amalarius' statements in the
appendix to the third book of the Liber Officialis. Such a
possiblity is furthermore indicated by Amalarius' long explanation surrounding the dramatic representation of the figure of
the suffering Job, where he deals especially with the diverse
purposes and differentiation of meaning of the historical and
allegorical senses. Because of its significance we shall
briefly deal with this part in the following discussion:

De offerenda vir erat in terra

> Interim occurrit mihi repetitio verborum
> quae est in versibus offertori "Vir erat".
> Nollui praetermittere quod senso de illa,
> quam vis ordo rerum teneat post scriptio-
> nem nativitatis sanctis Iohannis nati-
> vitatem Christi scribere. In offertorio
> non est repetitio verborum; in versibus
> est. Verba historici continentur in offer-
> torio; verba Iob aegroti et dolentis con-
> tinentur in versibus. Aegrotus cuius an-
> helitus non est sanus neque fortis, solet
> verba inperfecta saepius repetere. Offi-
> cii, auctor, ut affectanter nobis ad memo-
> riam reduceret aegrotantem Iob, repetivit
> saepius verba more aegrotantium. In of-
> fertorio, ut dixi, non sunt verba repe-

298

tita, quia historicus scribens historiam
non aegrotabat.[122]

It is evident from this citation that Amalarius differentiates
between the song of the offertory procession, which, as he
indicates, refers to the historical sense--verba historici
continentur in offertorio--and the verses which follow the
offertory songs representing also the figure of the suffering
Job: verba Job aegroti et dolentis. The modulated verses thus
present the allegorical-tropological sense whereas the suffering
and pain of Job are dramatically presented in personified form.
After this description, there follows an exact description of
the roles: Aegrotus cuius anhelitus non est sanus neque fortis,
solet verba inperfecta saepius repetere. The soft melodies of
the modulated songs most likely continued with mimetic gestures
giving formal representation of the suffering Job in congruence
with the purification theme of sin.

This appendix gives further evidence of the extraordinary
mobility and flexibility of the offertory part and the significance of the singing as a dramatically structural means. It
further strengthens our hypothesis that the fourfold senses of
Scriptural exegesis were also given expression in representational forms of the liturgy. This will become even more obvious
during the following part of the Canon. Given the overall
flexibility and improvisional character of the offertory, it is
plausible to assume that there were various representational
forms during this part of the liturgical drama.[123]

Secreta

The secreta or silent prayer which concludes this part
follows the blending of songs and prayers at the end of the
offertory. The offerings, including the singing, are now worthy
as a sacrifice: In hac primo nominatur hostia sive sacrificium,
oblatio.[124] The position of the celebrant, praying silently and
solitarily, now personifies Christ praying in the Temple. The
song which follows is conjointly sung by celebrant and congregation signifying the purified and elevated heart now worthy to
be joined to the altar of sacrifice:

In sequenti namque oratione clamat populum ut quod ipse iam habet, habeat et
ille, hoc est sursum cor, ac deinde ut
gratias agant Deo pro serenitate mentis.[125]
Igitur haec necessario extollitur voce.

In the following part, the singing develops to its pinnacle culminating in the antiphonal songs of angel voices and voices of
men. Structurally the secreta is important because of its positional and communal symbolism. It is also a transition from
the visible to the realm of the invisible sacrifice. This realm
becomes activated during the Canon. Christ is the center of
these two realms: here visibly that of the Israelites and the
transformed Christian congregation and there the hierarchy of
angels and saints. Both hierarchical orders merge and unite in
one sacrifice at the altar of Christ. The Christian congregation after having undergone an act of purification now takes
part in the invisible sacrifice, although on a different level.

Dramatic Analysis

The essential dramatic characteristics in this part are
again its spatial relationship and the intersection of the
different temporal dimensions. From this basic groundwork
emerge first the Biblical figures of the High Priest, the
Levites, and the people of Israel. After this setting has been
established, the figure of Jesus emerges in the surroundings of
Jerusalem with the Garden of Olives in the background. The
singing remains an essential structural means for the expression
of the four senses of Scripture. The outstanding dramatic
effect of these offertory configurations lies in the movement of
the mutal approaches of Christ and the crowds of Jerusalem.
These representational forms gradually assume the contours of
the present congregation in the church, the figure of Christ
merging closer with the figure of the priest. As they move
towards each other different emotional movements are expressed
through modulated songs and prayers and gestures. The linen
coverings of the altar such as the linteum, sindon and sudarium
now begin to emerge in their specific allegorical significance
and dramatic function. The transition from the historical
singing of the congregation, separated yet from the songs of the

300

Levites, symbolize the lower and higher grades in the process of salvation; I would argue that this transition is a movement within the structure of the four senses of Scripture.

The per omnia saecula saeculorum at the end of the secreta concludes the part of the visible sacrifice of the faithful. The following antiphonal exhortation of the sursum-corda of the celebrant and the positive response by the congregation in form of the habemus ad Dominum leads over into the praefatio. This tropological unity of priest and congregation seems to be a counter image of the anagogical sanctus-hymnus, the antiphonal song of the blending of angelic and human voices at the end of the praefatio.

The Canon, as the visible sacrifice, contains a threefold layer of the invisible realm: firstly, the invisible sacrifice of the angels which is given expression in the praefatio and the sanctus; secondly, the sacrifice of the saints and the elect which is alluded to in the prayers of the Te igitur; and thirdly the universal sacrifice of Christ during the time of the Consecration. This part is especially unified through the symbol of the patena.[126]

De ymnus ante passionem Domini

The Praefatio and the entire Canon, in order to be properly interpreted, must be seen in relation to Amalarius' earlier work, De Canonis Missae Interpretatione,[127] because this work is an essential interpretation of the invisible world which is now being symbolically enacted within the surroundings of the altar. At the beginning of this part, Amalarius refers to the angels being present at the sacrifice of Christ:

> Ymnus ideo dicitur, quia refertus est
> gratiarum actione et laudibus angelorum,
> praeparatio, quia parat fratrum mentes
> ad honestatem decentem conventum sanc-
> torum angelorum, qui solent adesse con-
> secrationi corporis Christi, et ad ip-
> sam reverentiam tantae consecrationis;
> ac ideo excelsa voce cantatur. . .[128]

301

The high-pitch singing of the angel voices reflects the anagogical sense, the highest grade of the allegorical structural layers. The prefatio was still a tropological preparation for this hymnus before the Passion. The singing is here again an important means of dramatic expression because it symbolizes the blending of the visible and invisible sacrifice.

After the altar has undergone an additional expansion to include the presence of the invisible angelic sacrifice, Amalrius makes a turn toward the concrete representation of the historical Last Supper; this occurs through a change of place and certain allegorical functions of the altar objects and vestments. Amalarius says:

> Praesens officium illud tempus nobis ad
> memoriam reducit, quando Christus in caena
> ascendit in cenaculum magnum stratum et
> ibi locutus est multa cum discipulis, et
> ymnum retulit Deo Patri, quem Iohannes
> commemorat, usque dum exiret in montem
> Oliveti . . . Iuxta hunc sensum, altare
> est mensa Domini, in qua convivabatur
> cum discipulis; corporale, linteum quo
> erat ipse praecingtus; sudarium labor de
> Iuda proditore.[129]

The altar now assumes also the contours of the room of the Last Supper in Jerusalem, the Mount of Olives being in the background; sindon and sudarium signify more and more the expression of humility, the pain of suffering and the exertion of the world of salvation. The sindon becomes the sign of humility; it also symbolizes the towel with which Christ girded himself prior to the washing of the feet of the apostles, whereas the sudarium signifies in this scene the betrayal of Judas.

With the contours of the Last Supper, the presence of the altar moves more and more into the foreground. Through the sursum corda the members of the congregation also become drawn into the expanded room of the Last Supper which extends into the

nave of the church. This expansion not only includes the
external space, it includes simultaneously the internal tropological space of the hearts of the believers. As I discussed
earlier, the exterior altar of sacrifice has a counterpart in
the internal altar symbolized by the heart of the believer.
Amalarius makes this double image again very clear:

> Hunc ordinem sequitur sacerdos: cum suis
> auditoribus ascendit in cenaculum, quando
> dicit: "Sursum corda;" . . . Illud in-
> tendendum est in omnibus officiis immo-
> lationis tali nomine censendum esse
> visibile altare, quale est cor offerentium.[130]

With this spatial blending of the external and internal altars,
a deepending of the tropological sense occurs which soon will
usher into the anagogical sense of the Resurrection, already
present in the invisible world.

Sanctus-Hymnus

The sanctus-hymnus which now follows exemplifies a most
fascinating representation of the interaction and blending of
the visible and invisible realms. The sanctus-sanctus-sanctus
of the angelic world irrupts into the visible realm of the concrete altar and there it is immediately joined by the hosanna
songs of human voices which symbolizes on the one hand the songs
of the Israelites of Jerusalem on Palm Sunday, and on the other
the purified songs of the congregation of believers in the nave
of the church. This profound antiphonal singing embraces and
resounds into the entire space of the church. Amalarius gives
this description:

> Idem ymnus horum duorum ordinem voces
> continet: ordo angelorum dicit: "Sanctus,
> sanctus, sanctus Domini Deus sabbaoth,
> pleni sunt caeli et terra gloria tua;"
> ordo hominum dicit: "Osanna in excel-
> sis, benedictus qui venit in nomine Do-
> mini." Quam partem ymni cantavit tur-

303

ba die psalmarum praecedens Dominum
Hierusalem.[131]

At the first level of meaning an image of a blending of human
and angelic voices emerges in order to be united in the
sacrifice of Christ, which will be leading to the Resurrection.
Amalarius then expands this image at the end of the sanctus-
hymnus into a vision of the Gloria at the beginning of the
Incarnation of Christ. He summarizes this as follows:

> . . . Angelorum concentus, dicendo:
> "Sanctus . . .," maiestatem divinam
> introducit; turbarum vero Domini in-
> carnationem, dicendo: "Benedictus . .
> . .".[132]

Song and configuration achieve a blending of the historical-
tropological and anagogical sense resulting simultaneously in a
retrospective glance and anticipating vision of cosmic breadth.
It anticipates a fusion of the Gloria at Bethlehem, the Hosanna
at Jerusalem, the never-ceasing Sanctus of the angelic powers,
descending and ascending from and to the Throne of the Most
High, and the joyful Alleluia-song of Easter.

After this description of the sanctus-hymnus, Amalarius
focuses again on the altar; this time he includes the presence
of the angels into the empirical dimension of the world of
salvation. He does this with the aid of the sudarium which
signifies the exertion of the angels in the work for the per-
fection of men:

> Iam diximus de altari quid significet.
> Dicendum est sudario. Sudarium ia-
> cens in altari significat laborem quem
> habent angeli in ministerio humano, sive
> perfecti viri, qui non cessant orare
> pro nostra fragilitate; corporale vero
> intentionem non fictam.[133]

After this description of the reality of the angels, the
positional symbolism of the sacerdotal order around the altar

304

begins to emerge according to St. Luke: the subdeacons stand, because of their lower ranks, in front of the priests; the deacons, who are of higher rank, are standing in a lower position behind them:

> Stant interim episcopi, sive sacerdotes,
> seu diaconi post pontificem; subdiaconi
> vero facie eius. Ibi illud adimpletur
> quod in memorato cenaculo dixit Dominus
> discipulis secundum Lucam: ". . . Vos
> autem non sic, sed qui maior est in
> vobis, fiat sicut iunior, et qui prae-
> cessor est, sicut minister.[134]

The sacerdotal hierarchy after having been positioned in a specific order, assume a supine posture expressing both adoration and humility before the majesty and Incarnation of God. The altar with its manifold meaning and the positional symbolism of the priesthood--signifying both the visible and invisible church hierarchies--moves now clearly into the foreground where the act of the Passion is beginning to concentrate. Amalarius points out that the room of the Last Supper was a room in the house of Joseph of Arimathea[135] the meaning of which immediately foreshadows the entire story of the Passion until the burial scene. This is a most interesting factor because Joseph of Arimathea develops into a dominant figure after the Crucifixion and during the burial scene. Since the tomb, into which the dead body of Jesus was laid belonged to Joseph of Arimathea, Amalarius establishes a most meaningful connection between the room of the Last Supper and the tomb of the Resurrection. Amalarius then gives a description of the courageous women during the Passion and Resurrection contrasting them with the fearful apostles and disciples:

> Hos credimus designari per subdiaconus
> qui in facie stant, sicut ille stetit, sive
> per praesentiam suam seu per ministerium,
> cuius erat cenaculum, sive mulieres, qua
> perseveraverunt in passione Domini. De
> quibus Gregorius in Moralibus scribit:
> "Sed cum ad crucis oram ventum est, eius

305

> discipulos gravis ex persecutione Iudae-
> orum timor invasit; fugerunt singuli;
> mulieres astiterunt. Quasi ergo, con-
> sumpta carne, os Domini pelli suae ad-
> hesit quia . . . mulieres invenit. Ste-
> tit equidem aliquandiu Petrus, sed ta-
> men post territus negavit; stetit etiam
> Iohannes, cui ipso crucis tempore dic-
> tum est . . . Mulieres autem non solum
> non timuisse, neque fugisse, sed etiam
> usque ad sepulchrum stetisse memorantur
> . . . [136]

According to this description, in which Amalarius depends on the allegorical interpretation of Gregory the Great, it seems likely that the subdeacons might also have assumed the role of the holy women during the Passion.[137] (The representational variant of the holy women is most interesting since in the tradition of the Quem quaeritis tropes they have been associated mainly in their representational role at the Resurrection).

The supine position of the subdeacons, signifying a change in meaning, constitutes a transition to the next part of the drama where it remains the most dominant means of expression of the yoke of sin, of humility, of fear and silence. This configuration is the most essential basis of the praefatio. The other most significant dramatic means of the praefatio and the sanctus were on the one hand antiphonal singing of celebrant and congregation at the beginning of the praefatio and on the other during the sanctus of angel and human voices. A similar pinnacle of fusion in the drama was achieved by Amalarius through the skillful application of the principle of simultaneity as we could observe at the end of the Introit during the Gloria. Positional symbolism and the allegorical-symbolic meaning of sindonis and sudarii turn into major means of dramatic expression. Jesus, the protagonist, stands, in the figure of the celebrant, at the center of the altar, whereas the act of Judas' betrayal is allegorically alluded to by the sudario lying at the altar. The spatial relationships are being concentrated around the altar and through the irruption of the angelic world they become transcendentally expanded.

306

The "Te Igitur" and "Hanc Igitur"

This part of the liturgical drama stretches from the Te
igitur to the Hanc igitur prayers and is defined by Amalarius as
the sacrifice of the elect (electi) and saints.[138] Here the
story of the Passion from the Last Supper to the Burial of Jesus
is enacted:

> Celebratio huius officio ita currit,
> ut ostendatur quid illo in tempore
> actum sit circa passionem Domini et
> sepulturam eius, et quomodo nos id
> ad memoriam reducere debeamus per ob-
> sequium nostrum, quod pro nobis
> factum est.[139]

The verb ostendatur used by Amalarius in this text is significant because it indicates the representational character of the
liturgy.

The emphasis is on the theme of sin; the scene is in the
Garden of Olives. As indicated above, the supine positional
symbolism dominates this part of the drama; it expresses the
burden of sin, humility and fear. Sindon and sudarium remain to
be meaningful leitmotives of humility, degradation, agony and
exertion in the work of salvation. The action is now concentrated around the altar. With the exterior space thus
confined, Amalarius concentrates on the interior space of the
hearts of the believers which finds a visible counter image in
the altar of sacrifice. Furthermore, the imagination comes into
play in making present the Life and Passion of Jesus which
emerges from the kernel of the Liturgical drama, the representation of the First Liturgical Act of Jesus.

After the sanctus, the symbolism of the supine position
moves into the foreground the meaning of which had previously
changed from adoration to fear, sadness and shame but also to
endurance and courage, particularly with respect to the representation of the holy women by the subdeacons. Amalarius gives
this description:

307

> Perseverant retro stantes inclinati, us-
> que dum finiatur omnis praesens oratio,
> id est dum dicatur post orationem domini-
> cam: "Sed libera nos a malo . . " Ipsi
> stant inclinati, donec liberentur a
> malo. Hi enim sunt apostoli, qui magna
> tribulatione erant oppressi; ante quam
> audirent Domini resurrectionem, non se
> audebant erigere, ut confiterentur se
> esse Christi discipulos. Hi, quamvis in
> passione non forent praesentes, tamen
> perseverant post Christi resurrectionem
> in temptationibus.[140]

The deacons standing behind the celebrant, personify at this
point the frightened apostles while the same posture in front
signfies sadness and courage, especially of the holy women.
This important description given by Amalarius reads as follows:

> At qui facie stant, signant discipulos
> occultos propter metum Iudaeorum, sive
> mulieres, quae poterant in facie per-
> sistere. Sua declinatione subdiaconi
> mestitiam eorum signant, de quibus dicit
> idem qui supra in eodem (Beda): "Non
> autem ideo solus mulierum planctus eum
> sequebatur, quia non innumerus etiam
> praesentium virorum coetus de eius erat
> passione mestissimus . . "[141]

The subdeacons in their supine position and in their various
roles dominate now the configuration; they relate essentially to
the Passion of Christ. The following meditation indicates with
which intensity and figurative reality the Passion of Christ was
experienced during this liturgical drama:

> Qui poterant non dolere, quando eum
> quem nimio amore dilexerunt et noverunt inno-
> centem, ab impiis comprehendi, ligari,
> duci ante eos, flagellari, spui in faciem,

crucifige viderunt?[142]

This intense experience of sin and suffering expressed in and
aided by visual representations, preceded the outburst of joy at
the Resurrection at the end of this liturgical drama. It is
probable, that gesticulating and other emotional outbursts, such
as sobbing and wailing also occurred among the people of the
congregation who were drawn into this cosmic drama as actors and
as spectators. Amalarius alludes to such manifestations in his
later work Eclogae[143] where he, referring to this part of the
drama, makes the following remarks:

> . . . quoniam discipuli et mulieres
> sequentes erant Dominum usque ad
> locum crucificionis, non solum se-
> quentes, sed et plagentes . .. Mu-
> lieres flebant . . . sed ipse Dominus
> ostendit non super illo debere
> flere, sed super ipsis quae pecca-
> trices erant.[144]

The supine position and other gestures connected with fear and
sadness, suffering and shame express primarily the heavy burden
of the "yoke of sin". Amalarius interprets this as a symbol of
sin-consciousness but also as an awareness of the deliverance of
sin. Therefore he interprets this position in the tropological
sense of Scripture:

> Et quid vis dicere quale ministerium
> habeant subdiaconi, quando stant incli-
> nati, si pro suis peccatis non orant
> et plorant? Per tropologiam subdia-
> coni inclinati sunt, quia declinaverunt,
> . . .[145]

Since Eclogae seems to be primarily a backward glance of Amalarius and the summary of his own work, it is dramatically very
informative because it contains exact descriptions of roles.

With this supine position in front of the altar where now
fear, sadness and sin primarily dominate, the background for the

309

scene in the Garden of Olives emerges slowly. The three prayers of the Te igitur, Memento mori, and Et communicantes between the Te igitur and Hanc igitur circumscribe the scene in the Garden. These three prayers signify the prayers of Christ in His agony in the Garden of Olives; the silent prayer of the celebrant now symbolizes the God-forsakenness of the Son of Man.[146] During the monolog-like representation of the prayers, the image of the celebrant, standing before the altar with his head bowed, easily interweaves with the figure of Christ in the Garden of Olives; the deacons who stand behind the celebrant in supine position become easily transformed into an image of the sleeping apostles during the agony of Christ. Amalarius interprets these three prayers as follows:

> Primo vice Christi sacerdos tres ora-
> tiones exercet, sicut Dominus fecit,
> postquam exivit in montem Oliveti ante
> traditionem suam, id est pro universali
> ecclesia, et pro specialibus fratribus,
> et pro coro sacerdotum.[147]

It should be mentioned here that this scene in the Garden of Olives with the three prayers of Christ is already a topos of the liturgical drama because in Missae Expositionis Codex II this same scene becomes enacted after the gospel before the episcopal ascension to the throne and in connection with three incense-censors signifying the three prayers. We are obviously dealing here with a representational variant of the same theme. It is described as follows:

> . . . Ideoque statim post candelabra
> aliquotiens portatur unum, aliquo-
> tiens duo, aliquotiens tria . . .
> Quibus non desunt mysteria secreta:
> si unum portatur, Christus corpus
> significat; si duo portantur, ostendit
> Christum venisse et passum pro duobus
> populis; si tria, ostendit orationes
> ipsas quas ipse Dominus fecit ante
> passionem suam in montem Oliveti.[148]

Here the incense-censor personifying Christ and the monolog-like
agonizing prayers of Christ, intensify the dramatization. The
text of the Missae Expositionis II is held even more vividly:

> Primo oravit: "Pater mi, si possibile
> est, transeat a me calix iste, id est ut ip-
> sa gens qua carnem adsumpsi, non me
> occidat. "Secundo oravit . . . . :
> "Pater mi, si non potest hic calix
> transire, nisi bibam illum, fiat
> voluntas tua, id est si aliter gentes
> salvari non possunt, nisi ad tempus fiat
> deminutio Iudeorum, fiat voluntas tua, ut
> secundum prophetias ips me crucifigant,
> ut plures salvi fiant . . .[149]

Amalarius' own imagination speaks out of the words of Christ
when he expands the actual text of the biblical prayer. The
same can later be observed with the text of the Last Supper.[150]

    Sindon and sudarium also signify the scene in the Garden of
Olives and receive from there more intense allegorical meaning.
In the Liber Officialis, Amalarius states that:

> In hac oratione (Te igitur) designat
> sindo quantum caput pertinet, humili-
> tatem Christi, quam assumpsit ex terre-
> no habitu; in qua oravit Deum Patrum.
> Sudarium vero, quod iacet in cornu al-
> taris, laborem suum, quem sustinuit in
> oratione, sicut Lucas dicit: "Et factus
> est in agonia et prolixius orabet; et
> factus est, sudor eius sicut guttae san-
> guinis decurrentis in terram."[151]

The allegorical meaning of sindon and sudarium, expressing the
Passion and Agony of Christ, is deepening more and more, the
sindon symbolizing the utmost degradation while the sudarium
expresses the sweat of anxiety. The configuration of the
priest, praying silently in supine position and the objects of
the altar, i.e., sindon and sudarium signify the God-for-

311

sakenness of the Son of Man to which the prophet Jeremiah refers, the text of which Amalarius is citing in this connection:

> Ego Deus approprinquans et non Deus
> longe. Si absconditus fuerit homo in
> absconditis, ego ergo non videbo eum?
> Nonne caelum et terram ego impleo?[152]

Then, at the end of the sacrifice of the elect (Hanc-igitur), the handing over of Christ into the hands of his adversaries is represented as follows:

> De corporali et de sudario dictum est,
> quantum ad corpus pertinet . . . Christus,
> postquam oravit pro membris suis, dixit
> discipulis suis: "Surgite, eamus, ecce
> adpropinquabit qui me traditurus est."
> . . . In hac oratione significat dignatus
> est orare pro suis, sed etiam tradi in
> manus impiorum; sudarium vero laborem
> quem sustinuit ex traditore.[153]

Amalarius' repeated reference to sindon and sudarium indicates the importance of these altar objects in their allegorical-symbolic function for the provocation and intensification of the scene in the Garden of Olives. They appear over and over again in this function. While the scene of the handing-over of Jesus is especially signified through these two objects at the altar, this scene becomes even more complex through allusive gestures and movements which might take place during Holy Week. Since this scene of the handing-over of Jesus after His agony is a dramatically important variant, I shall cite the text from the first book of the Liber Officialis:

> "Statim duo diaconi nudant altare sindone
> quae prius fuerat sub evangelio posita, in
> modum furantis." Altare, ut heri diximus
> Dominum nostrum significat, in quo nostras
> oblationes Patri offerimus; vestimenta,
> apostolos et omnes sanctos. Congruum est

ut subtus evangelium aliquid iaceat propter honestatem. Quo sublato, rapitur
quod subiectum fuit, quia, dedito Christo
inter manus iniquorum, apostoli, more
furum fugerunt et latuerunt. Quod enim
significat, altare, hoc et evangelium.
Potest in hac sindone intelligi speciali-
ter Iohannes, qui et audivit: "Ecce mater
tua," et postea propter metum Iudaeorum se
occuluit more furum.[154]

The specific description of modum furantis becomes dramatically
significant because it describes the exact mode of acting, i.e.,
it expresses the hatred of the enemies of Christ as well as the
fear of the apostles. Most obvious is the anthropomorphization
and personfication of the altar as the figure of Christ. This
personfication, of course, is given even more plastic expression during the scene where Christ is captured and robbed
of His garments--i.e., when all covers have been taken from the
altar in a furious manner. Thus, the altar robbed of its
garments, standing bare, symbolizes Christ, humiliated and
deserted by His apostles and followers.[155] Whether or not this
configuration was only part of the drama during Passion Week or
was also enacted during ordinary times, must remain hypothetical. The flexible character of the dramatic liturgy, however,
implies that such variations were probably also performed during
the general course of the liturgical year.

The sacrifical meaning of the Te igitur includes the external and internal altar of sacrifice, i.e, the altar of
sacrifice has a counter image in the hearts of the believers.
This allegory of the heart becomes a symbol of inner space which
then expands and converges with the realm of transcendental
space of the cosmos. Amalarius betrays here the influence of
Augustine:

"Sacrificium ergo visible invisibilis
sacrificii sacramentum, id est sacrum
signum est." . . . "Quocirca, sicut

orantes atque laudantes ad eum diri-
gimus sacrificantes voces, cui res
ipsas in corde quas significamus, of-
ferimus, ita sacrificantes non alteri
visibile sacrificium offerendum esse
noverimus, quam illi cuius in cordi-
bus nostris invisibile sacrificium nos
ipse esse debemus.[156]

The interplay of the external visible altar with that of the
internal and transcendental invisible altars contributes to the
unity and vividness of this drama.

Dramatic Analysis

The significance of the dramatic means in this part lies in
the supine position expressing fear, sadness, the hiding of the
apostles but also courage and perserverance; it also symbolizes
the burden of the yoke of sin. The dramatization of the scene
in the Garden of Olives is effectively achieved by the
circumscription of the tripartite prayers of the Te igitur, the
bowed silent position of the celebrant and the manifolded
allegorical meanings of the sindon and sudarium expressing the
agony of suffering and degradation inherent in the work of
salvation. The principle of simultaneity is mainly expressed in
positional symbolism with its various roles and manifold
meanings representing the hiding of the fearful apostles, the
courageous women, humility and the burden of the yoke of sin.
In terms of the allegorical interpretation this part is
essentially tropological.

De Institutione Dominica

The sanctus has been the invisible sacrifice of the angels,
the Te igitur the sacrifice of the saints, but the Qui pridie
becomes the universal sacrifice of Christ which had been fore-
shadowed in the First Liturgical Act of Jesus at the Last
Supper.[157] It is at the center of the descending and ascending
movement of the invisible powers:

Immolato priore sacrificio, quod con-

314

stat orationibus perfectorum, et est
coniunctum sacrificio angelorum, descen-
ditur ad universale sacrificium, immo-
lationem scilicet Christi, quod caelebra-
tur ante Nobis quoque peccatoribus. Etenim Christus pro peccatoribus descendit
ad immolandum . . .[158]

At the center of the altar of sacrifice there is now a representation of the death of Jesus Christ on the Cross — an expression of the consequences of the gruesome reality of sin. In
order to relate the Last Supper to the death of Christ on the
Cross and the death of mankind to sin, a retrospective glance is
necessary. We recall that after the Hanc-igitur-prayer which
had been related to the handing-over of Christ to His adversaries during the Quam oblationem, tu Domino, Amalarius focused
again on the configuration of the Last Supper primarily through
the principle of simultaneity. This was expressed by way of
connective symbolism: i.e., the deacons and subdeacons remaining
continuously in supine position, the allegorical-symbolic
function of the sindon and sudarium and the changes of place
around the altar at which time the altar received a different
representational meaning. From the scene of the Garden of
Olives, the altar has been transformed into the room of the Last
Supper and soon it will represent the dimension of Golgotha.
But with this constellation of the Upper Room, the altar not
only becomes intricately interwoven with the First Act of the
Last Supper but also with the Spoken Words at the time of the
institution. Thus, both Act and Word of Christ are at the
center from which initially the entire course of the liturgical drama proceeded and they remain the source out of which
Amalarius shapes his version of the drama:

Hic concrepant verba dominicae mensae
cum toto officio missae . . . Sindo
iacens in altari signat linteum quo
erat Dominus praecinctus, et sudarium
laborem quem assumpsit in lavatione
pedum, sive quem sustinuit pro labore
Judae; altare mensam Domini.[159]

315

It should be noted that with the change of scenery the meaning
of the sindon and sudarium also changes. Here they signify
humility and service in connection with the washing of feet of
the apostles by Jesus at the Last Supper and the entire work of
salvation. The contours of the room of the Last Supper are the
essential background out of which emerges the next configuration: Golgotha: the Crucifixion of Jesus, the Christ.

De Ascensione Christi in Crucem

After the pronouncement of the Words which will make
present the Body and Blood of Jesus Christ, the prayer for the
memory of Christ's work of salvation, the Unde et memores sumus,
becomes the source, the well-spring and point of departure of
the act of making present not only the First Liturgical Act but
the entire Life of Christ because for Amalarius, this making-
present hinges essentially on the pronouncement of the words of
Jesus Christ Himself.[160] Thus the actual Eucharistic presence
of the Lord extends into and fuses with the representational
forms of the drama. Here lies the kernel of the liturgy; but
Amalarius' dramatic vision proceeds also from this Act and from
these Words. His following statements are most important for
our understanding of this liturgical drama:

> In sacramento panis et vini, necnon etiam
> in memoria mea, passio Christi in promptu
> est. Dixit ipse: "Haec quotiescumque
> feceritis, in mei memoriam facietis," id
> est quoties hunc panem et calicem bene-
> dixeritis, recordamini meae nativitatis
> secundum humanitatem passiones ac plebis:
> "Unde et memores sumus . . ."[161]

Significant is the relationship of the phrase "in memoria mea"
with the speaking of Christ's". . . in mei memoriam facietis."
The presence of Christ in the forms of bread and wine
corresponds to the interiorization of the actual present memory
of Christ in the heart of Amalarius and of all Christians. It
becomes a mystical presence and beholding of the image of the
Lord: in a memory which extends into the present. From this
conception, Amalarius fuses, as it were, his own words with

316

those of Christ's when he says: "<u>. . . id est quoties hunc panem
et calicem benedixeritis recordamini meae nativitatis secundum
humanitatem, passionis ac resurrectionis</u>." The dramatic-allegorical enactment springs forth (<u>entquillt</u>) from the fullness of
the mystical presence in connection with the power of the
imagination; thus, the external figuration leads to further
cognitive beholding of the truth of faith. Not only in the
forms of bread and wine but in <u>memoria</u>, in the presence of
memory (<u>Sich-Erinnern</u>), there lies the meaning, the ratio of the
Liturgical Act, the <u>in promptu est</u> and its actual representation. Out of this fusion of <u>ratio</u> and <u>memoria</u> there emerges
the image of the Cross with the dead body of Christ. Amalarius
places this process almost plastically before our eyes:

> Sicut in superioribus Christi corpus
> est in sacramento panis et vini, atque
> in memoria mea, ita in praesenti ascendit
> crucem. Cordis sacrificio intendit Deus.
> . . . De donis Dei ac datis hostiam
> puram, hostiam sanctam, hostiam immacu-
> latam, offerimus, quando caritate accensi
> hostiam offerimus de corde puro, et con-
> scientia bona, et fide non ficta.[162]

In connection with the external altar of sacrifice there appears
again the counter image of the interior altar of the heart; but
both altars, the external and internal one, have another counter
image in the altar of the Most High, the place to which the
sacrifice of Christ and that of the Christian congregation is
carried on the hands of the angels. The externalization of the
interiorized image of Christ is taking form in the figure of the
celebrant, who, standing with his head bowed, is praying in
front of the altar. For the quiet, perhaps Germanic spectator
and meditator, there slowly grow the contours of the dying Lord,
hanging on the Cross. The angels belong to the realities of the
Throne of the Most High and to that of the altar below. With
the inclusion of the transcendental realm the image of the altar
of sacrifice, the Golgotha of Jesus Christ, becomes limitlessly
expanded and the imagination mingles with--and perhaps
augments--the formulated truth of faith. Amalarius
continues:

Dein precatur ut suscipiantur, dicendo:
"Supplices te rogamus, omnipotens Deus,
iube haec perferri per manus angeli tui
in sublime altare tuum, in conspectu
divinae majestatis tuae, ut, quotquot
ex hac altaris participatione sacro-
sanctum Filii tui corpus et sanguinem
sumpserimus: ". . . Precatur sacerdos, ut praesens oblatio ita sit accep-
ta in conspectu divinae maiestatis qua-
tinus sumpturi eam simul fiant caelestes
et gratia Dei repleti. Mira et magna fides
sanctae ecclesiae, quae suis oculis videt
quod mortalibus deest, videt quid credere
debeat quamvis nondum videat quod in specie
est; credit sacrificium praesens per angelorum
manus deferri ante conspectum Domini . . . [163]

At this point, we have to remember that the heavenly throne is
also concretely represented in the form of the episcopal throne.
After Amalarius has sufficiently focused on the invisible throne
of the Most High with the presence of the angels, he is shifting
back to the visible world of the external configuration of the
liturgical drama. Through personification, gestures, change of
place, _sindon_ and _sudarium_, the God-forsakenness of the
Crucifixion scene arises and the death of Christ on the Cross
becomes imminent:

Nempe Christus oravit in cruce incipiens
in psalmo, "_Deus, Deus meus_," usque ad
versum: "_In manus tuas commendo spiritum meum_." Postea, inclinato capite,
emisit spiritum. Sacerdo inclinat se,
et hoc quod vice Christi immolatum est,
Deo Patri commendat. Sancita est passio
Christi pro nobis usque at istum ab eo
loco ubi dicit: "Unde et memores
sumus."[164]

The altar now signifies the Cross of Christ. _Sindon_ and

318

sudarium are physical signs of His agony and passion. In this position, his head remaining bowed the priest becomes the imitated figure of Christ, dying on the Cross:

> Altare praesens altare est crucis: in
> isto nos peccatores qui ex gentibus
> venimus, reconciliati sumus Deo ad
> offerenda ei sacrificia. Sindo in isto
> humilitatem illam signat, qua humiliatus
> est Christus Patri usque ad mortem. . .
> Sudarium vero laborem passionis.[165]

The altar which has been transformed into the symbol of the Cross forms now the vast cosmic background of the configuration, the imagination transcending the external structures as the beholding eyes meditate Christ, dying, hanging on the Cross represented in the figure of the priest, motionlessly standing, his head bowed, in front of the altar. Sindon and sudarium increase in their meaning; they symbolize sweat, passion, pain and degradation; the angels, present at the altar, now carry the soul of Christ, so it was imagined, to the Throne of the Most High. This complex configuration of the Crucifixion is the pinnacle where all ascending, descending and horizontal movements of the preceding acts come to a still-point.

At this cosmic still-point and quietness of everything, focusing on the Cross, a most interesting movement and expansion of the visible space occurs. Amalarius calls our attention to the subdeacons who have, since the sanctus, been standing in supine motionless position, before the priest and altar; they had represented the holy women, disciples and crowds of Jerusalem. However, after the priest had bowed his head, signifying the death of Christ, the women and disciples begin to assume an erect position. This erection symbolizes a certain relief, a release of anxiety and knowledge that at least now the enemies and traitors of Jesus had no longer any power over the life and body of Christ. The following citation is particularly informative from the dramatic point of view because it deals with role description and the dramatic significance of spatial relationships. This circumscription of the scene gives evidence with which sense of reality and intensity, by means of the

319

allegorical function of the altar-objects the drama of the
Passion was experienced. Amalarius' own description of this
scene is as follows:

> Inclinata subdiaconorum usque mode mesti-
> tiam demonstrat eorum discipulorum quibus
> licitum erat perseverare in praesentia
> Christi. Quando flagellabatur et omnia
> illa agebantur quae de eius erant secta-
> tores; at postquam emisit spiritum, scien-
> tes non iam habere persecutores unde
> rabiem suam amplius in Christi corpus
> expleant, ut ipsi dicit in evangelio
> . . . consolantur aliquo modo, et
> erigunt se, aspicientes in dilectum
> sibi corpus, quousque pendet in cruce,
> maxime cum vident multa miracula fieri.
> Unde conturbari poterant persecutores,
> et obsequentes solari.[166]

Amalarius stresses again how the priest, standing with his head
bowed, represents the dead Christ hanging on the Cross; the
subdeacons, personifying the disciples and holy women, are now
standing in meditation before the Cross; the Christian
congregation is representing on one level also the Jewish crowds
of Jerusalem, thus assuming a double role as spectators of this
great drama. Through the erection of the subdeacons, now
standing quietly before the cross-altar and with the inclusion
of the Christian congregation into the expanded configuration,
there emerges a spatial expansion going beyond the spatial
confines of the basilica which resembles a cosmic, panorama-like
image of the universe. One could ask here the question whether
the allegorical representations of the historical events which
leave enough playground for the imagination could not have been
as effective both in their confined staging and imaginative expansion as the later passion-plays in a broader liturgical
context and cycle?

A most peculiar action occurs when the deacons wash their
hands in a supine position. Since they have been representing
the apostles, this could perhaps still be seen in connection

with the apostles' hiding in fear and perhaps to their shedding
of tears. It indicates the significance of this particular
posture within the drama.[167]

De Corpore Domini
post emissum spiritum

In the following configuration the image of Christ, being
dead, still hanging on the Cross combined with the motive of
death to sin continues to dominate the scene. However, the subdeacons standing before the Cross represent now the universal
sinners. Amalarius summarizes their significance at the end as
follows:

> Moraliter. Possumus subdiaconus nos
> peccatores intellegere; qui faciem, id
> est conscientiam peccatorum nostrorum,
> sacerdoti ostendimus, ut nostram con-
> fessionem offerat Deo. Quo peracto non
> ilico saltum facimus in locum magistro-
> rum, sed post diutinam humiliationem,
> fervore crescente Spiritu Sancti, dilan-
> tantur corda nostra, quasi patena ad
> suscipienda sacramenta ecclesiae.[168]

This double image of the Crucifixion, the death of Christ and
the death to sin of the Christian contributes substantially to
the proper understanding and experience of the Resurrection.
The patena, which receives dramatic functional significance, is
for the first time brought into view; allegorically it signifies
the image of the heart, now filled with the Spirit; dilantur
corda quasi patena. The mentioning of water and blood flowing
out the side of Christ intensifies the theme of liberation from
sin because it is brought into relationship with the conversion
of the Roman captain who opened the side of Christ. Amalarius
describes this image as follows:

> Christus iam emisit spiritum exivit
> ab eius latera sanguis et aqua; sine
> his sacramentis nemo intrat ad vitam
> aeternam . . . "Ille sanguis in re-

321

missionem fusus est peccatorum; aqua
illa salutare temperat poculum haec
et lavacrum praestat et potum". . . .
"Hic secundus Adam, inclinato capite,
in cruce dormivit, ut inde formaretur
ei coniux, quod de latere dormientis
defluxit".[169]

The celebrant, his head bowed, now personifies Christ, sleeping
on the Cross--in cruce dormivit--while the chalice standing at
the right side of the altar, gathers the water and blood flowing
out of the side of Christ. The interweaving of imagination and
concrete representational form with the realities of faith most
likely intensified the deep experience of these events and
probably provided rich soil for the Germanic-Frankish-Gallic
heart and soul (Gemüt).

In this scene in which the symbol of death to sin is
dominating, there is also the first enactment of a gentile conversion, that of the Roman captain of the court of Pilate who
pierced the side of Jesus with his lance. He became the link,
the coniux, to the pagans who were redeemed by the death of
Christ; the conversion of the Roman soldier was not the result
of contrition but of his love for Christ:

Nisi futurum esset ut sacramento sangui-
nis et aqua inficeretur gentilitas, non
ilico se centurio mutaret ad tantam com-
punctionem, ut aperte clamaret ex intimo
cordios affectu: Vere hic homo iustus
erat.[170]

The role of the captain is then taken over by the celebrant at
which time the conversion and the change of role are symbolized
through a change in the tone of voice. The change in the tone
of voice apparently symbolized the stab of the lance at the same
time of which the conversion of the captain took place:

Hanc mutationem designat sacerdos per
mutationem vocis, quando exaltat vocem,
dicende: "Nobis quoquo peccatoribus".[171]

322

This scene is further intensified and the horizon of the image
of the Cross is further expanded when Amalarius cites Beda,
drawing into the field of the imagination the women, disciples
and crowds of Jerusalem, who, from a distance, had witnessed the
Crucifixion and the conversion of the Roman captain:

> . . . "Notanda distantia gentis et gentis.
> Et gentiles quippe, moriente Christo,
> Deum timentes aperta confessionis voce
> glorificant . . . Interim "stabant
> autem omnes noti eius a longe, et mu-
> lieres quae secutae erant eum at Gali-
> laea, haec videntes."[172]

The panoramic scene of the Crucified begins to expand further
and further into cosmic dimensions in which gentis et gentis--
peoples and nations of all ages--emerge before the beholding eye
of the spectators. In Amalarius' liturgical vision the locality
of the church transcends into universal dimensions--time and
again with different dramatic means and on different levels.
Amalarius then returns to the immediate scene under the Cross,
to the closest relatives and friends of Jesus of Nazareth who
are represented by the subdeacons keeping their eyes steadily on
the movements and activities of the scene of the Crucifixion:

> Hos amicos et proximos ad memoriam nobis
> ducunt subdiaconi, erecti et intuentes in
> presbyteri opus.[173]

Thus, the subdeacons in their configuration before the cross-
altar, activate memory, imagination and vision of the believing
spectator. Amalarius clearly differentiates between vicinity
and distance, between the immediate followers of Christ, those
who follow Him in a distant time, those who follow Him in Ama-
lurius' own time, and the followers of Christ of all times. The
differentiation in roles refers to the subdeacons on one hand
and the congregation in the nave of the church on the other.
Spatial relationships, temporal intersecting and changes in
roles are most obvious dramatic means in this scene.

While the women and disciples in quiet meditation are not taking their eyes from the Crucified, the apostles filled with fear, are still hiding somewhere. Out of the stillness of this configuration--the women and disciples quietly looking on and the hiding apostles represented by the deacons, still in supine position--there arises the figure of <u>Joseph Arimathea</u>. For this most fascinating depiction Amalarius uses the basic text of St. Luke:

> His ita intuentibus, venit "vir nomine
> Joseph, qui erat decurio, vir bonus et
> justus: hic non consenserat consilio
> et actibus eorum, ab Arimathia civitate
> Iudeae. . .; hic accessit ad Pilatum,
> et petiit corpus Iesu, et depositum in-
> volvit sindone, et posuit eum in monu-
> mento exciso, in quo nondum quisquam
> positus fuerat."[174]

Amalarius then adds his own interpretation and circumscription to the theme of the deposition from the Cross and the burial of Jesus:

> Qui quamvis ex numero foret occultorum
> discipulorum, tamen in promptu omnes
> transcendit, scilicet et discipulis et
> apostolos. Discipulis tantummodo a longe
> stantibus et intuentibus, apostolis veri
> latentibus in abditis, Ioseph mercatus
> est sindonem, ut depositum corpus Iesu
> involveret.[175]

With the liturgical-dramatic expression of this Biblical text, Amalarius, however, stands in the long tradition of the Syrians and Byzantines.[176] Nevertheless, Amalarius enriches this <u>topos</u> of the burial of Christ in his own creative way. This empha- sizes the importance of the role of Joseph of Arimathea after the Crucifixion. At the same time, Amalarius uses his figure to bring about a turn in the liturgical drama. It consists of Joseph's breaking through of the paralyzing barriers of fear and the ban of the stand-still which occurred at the time of the

324

death of Jesus. Amalarius describes this situation most effectively when he remarks regarding Joseph: "Qui quamvis omnes
transcendit." Joseph's departure to Pilate and the purchase of
the burial linen brings movement, although very gradually, into
the configuration. A change in meaning of the configuration
occurs when after the deposition from the Cross the allegorical
shift is to the burial scene in the Garden of Joseph where the
tomb in which Jesus is to be laid, is located. There is both
motion and stillness in this configuration: the apostles are
still hiding and afraid, the women and disciples are quietly
looking on. From the midst of this silence there now arises
Joseph of Arimathea, causing motion and movement. The pur-
chasing of the burial shroud and his meeting with Nicodemus, are
made present through the arising of Joseph and walking toward
the altar. This configuration with its slowly expanding movements is extending into the background behind the altar. Thus
the absence[177] of Pilate and the shopkeeper in front of the
scene alludes to their presence in the back. This imaginatively
and concretely expanding background however develops slowly into
the preparatory scene for the embalment of Jesus in which the
women are the main actors, although first only in the background, i.e., behind the altar.

The actual deposition from the Cross and the burial of
Jesus is symbolized by gestures, movements and by the allegorical significance of sindonis and sudarii. The archdeacon
personifies Joseph of Arimathea as it is stated by Amalarius:

> Hunc Joseph ad memoriam ducit archidia-
> conus, qui elevat calicem de altari, et
> involvit sudario, scilicet ab aure ca-
> licis usque ad aurem. Sicut ille dia-
> conus primatum tenet inter ceteros dia-
> conus, qui levat calicem cum sacerdote,
> ita iste Joseph tenuit inter ceteros
> discipulos qui meruit corpus Domini de
> cruce deponere et sepelire in monumento
> suo; idem deputatur retro stare cum apos-
> tolis quoniam timore Iudaeorum occultus
> erat.[178]

The celebrant on the other hand represents Nicodemus who historically was helping with this deposition from the Cross. Amalarius specifies this:

> Sacerdos qui elevat oblatam praesentat
> Nichodemum, de quo narrat Iohannes
> dicens: "Venit autem et Nichodemus, qui
> venerat ad Iesum nocte primum, ferens
> mixturam myrrae et aloes . . . Acce-
> perunt ergo corpus Iesu, et ligaverunt
> eum linteis cum aromatibus sicut mos
> Iudaeis est sepelire".[179]

Both of these descriptions are concerned with the exact description of roles each of which is assigned to the celebrant and archdeacon respectively. The gesture of the sign of the cross also takes on dramatic significance. The celebrant, here personifying Nicodemus, makes twice the sign of the cross over the form of bread. This signals the deposition from the Cross within the liturgical drama. But this double sign of the Cross also signifies that Christ suffered and died for both, pagans and Jews. The elevation of the forms of bread and wine, which follows the signs of the Cross, then represents the actual deposition from the Cross:

> Sacerdos facit oblata duas cruces iuxta
> calicem, ut doceat eum depositum esse
> de cruce, qui pro duobus populis cruci-
> fixus est. Christi depositionem de cruce
> monstrat elevatio sacerdotis et diaconi.[180]

As soon as the archdeacon notices that the celebrant is making the signs of the cross, he walks to the altar to elevate the chalice. The elevation of the forms of bread and wine, which signifies here the deposition from the Cross, is lasting until the pronouncement of the "Per omnia saecula saeculorum" which also concludes the Canon. During all this time, the altar symbolizes the Cross. However, immediately following the Amen and the completion of the deposition from the Cross by placing the bread and wine again on the altar, the altar is transformed into the tomb of Christ located in the Garden of Joseph of Arimathea;

the space around the altar becomes the burial site in the Garden of Joseph. The covering and wrapping of the chalice with the sudario begins to signify now the burial or entombment of the Lord. The sudarium transforms now into its very meaning: the sweat rag with which the head of Christ was covered and which later was found in the empty tomb whereas the altar linen, the sindon, now symbolizes the shroud in which the corpse of Jesus was wrapped and which also was found after the Resurrection. Amalarius based his interpretation on Scripture itself:

> Sudarium super caput Iesu notum
> est fuisse, narrante eodem Iohanne quod
> videret Petrus "linteamina posita et
> sudarium quod fuerat super caput Jesu."
> Oblata et calix dominicum corpus sig-
> nant,. . .[181]

The sudarium activates the memory of Christ's agony and per-spiration of blood. The burial scene then is expanded through the holy women who had followed the funeral procession in Jerusalem:

> . . . "Supra legimus, inquiens, quia
> stabant omnes noti eius a longe, et
> mulieres quae secutate erant eum. His
> ergo notis Jesu, post depositum eius
> cadaver ad sua remeantibus, solae mu-
> lieres, quae artius amabant, funus sub-
> secutate, quomodo poneretur inspicere
> cupiebant.[182]

It should be noted that in the following scene, the subdeacons represent only the holy women because only women followed the remote burial of Jesus and afterwards went to their homes to prepare the ointment for the embalment which within the present framework takes place in the background of the altar.

Amalarius now proceeds to link the external silence and the empty burial scene around the tomb to the internal space of the heart of the believer in which death to sin and the tomb of Christ find a parallel. It is in the inner space of the heart

that sin has become buried through penance, fasting and other
abnegations. Once more, <u>sindon</u> and <u>sudarium</u> are signs of
abnegation, humility and purity as they had been at the
beginning of the offertory. Thus, the connection between the
offertory and the death of Christ is established:

> . . . Paenitentia sepeliuntur peccata
> nostra. Altare paenitentum est altare
> holocausti; altare holocausti signat
> cor eorum quibus necesse est carnales
> motus consummare fervore Spiritus Sancti.
> Sindo est ipsa castigatio carnis per iei-
> unia et vigilas . . . ceu quoddam linum,
> ad candorem, ut fiat de eo corporale, in
> quo possit qui pura eum mente susceperit.
> Sudarium est ipsa intentio, qua festinat
> omnes venientes motus temptationum pristi-
> narum tergere, ante quam oculos sau-
> tiant.[183]

It is important to keep in mind constantly this double image of
outer and inner space because otherwise it is not possible to
grasp and interpret the manifoldedness of ninth-century
liturgical drama. The allegory of the heart in relation to
inner space is assuming even more significance with the event of
the Resurrection.

The burial scene which we had encountered earlier,
especially in the Syriac and Byzantine texts, has now been fully
developed in the liturgy of the West by Amalarius of Metz. It
is an old <u>topos</u> which Amalarius obviously has reshaped in view
of his own insights and creative imagination. As his source,
however, Amalarius is not citing Byzantium but rather Bede.
Amalarius had, however, already pointed to the traits of Joseph
and the significance of this figure in the exposition of his
liturgical drama. Bede says the following about Joseph of
Arimathea:

> "Magnae quidem Joseph ista dignitatis
> apud saeculum, sed maioris apud Deum
> meriti fuisse laudatur, ut et per iusti-

tiam meritorum sepeliendo corpore domi-
nico dignus foret, et per nobilitatem
potentiae saecularis idem corpus acci-
pere possit. . ."[184]

But Ephraim the Syrian, depending on Tatian, had already
elaborated on the special characteristics of Joseph of Arimathea.[185]   And Amalarius, out of this tradition, most likely by
way of his sojourn in Constantinople--and not only through Bede
--activates fully the dramatic potentiality of this figure which
gives the impression of a typus, not petrified or static but
augmented and invigorated coming from a long tradition.

Dramatic Analysis

Through a few movements, gestures, change of place, spatial
relationships with enough scope for play of the imagination, a
new scene has developed which is preparing for the Resurrection
in the Garden of Joseph.[186]   It is the towering figure of Joseph
of Arimathea who shatters the boundaries of fear and silence.
The raising up and movement of the archdeacon, who personifies
Joseph, receive a dramatic function because at first this movement signifies Joseph's walk to Pilate and the purchase of
linen. The signs of the Cross are simultaneously connected with
the change of role of the celebrant who assumes the role of
Nicodemus; the signs of the cross also signalize that Nicodemus
is occupied with the Cross and the deposition of the body of
Christ and the subsequent burial preparations and carrying to
the tomb. Thus, the signs of the Cross have important functions
within the course of this liturgical drama. When after the
elevation, the forms of bread and wine are placed back on the
altar, the altar is being transformed into the tomb of Christ;
the covering of the chalice specifying the covering of the head
of Christ with the sudario (sweat rag), while the altar linen
(sindon) becomes the shroud in which the dead body of Christ is
being wrapped. The subdeacons represent in this scene the holy
women only because the women had been the only persons following
Christ to His distant burial place, located in the Garden of
Joseph. The disappearance of the holy women, represented by the
subdeacons, into the backgrund, foreshadows now the
Resurrection.

The remaining _altar holocausti_ symbolizes the interplay between outer and inner space. As the barren altar so the heart, barren of all sin and wordly attachment, is ready to receive the Risen Christ.

Amalarius repeatedly focuses on Joseph of Arimathea and the significance of the _sindon_ and _sudarium_. Nicodemus is mentioned only once, _i.e._, in connection with the purchase of the linen and ointments. And these seem to have been more important than the figure of Nicodemus himself. On the other hand, it is the celebrant who assumes the role of Nicodemus. Once more Amalarius summarizes the essence of the preceding scene:

> Haec oratio "Nobis quoque peccatoribus"
> tenit usque "Per omnia saecula saecu-
> lorum." Usque ad istum locum quantum
> pertinet ad exequias sepulturae Christi,
> altare crucem praestat; quantum ad nos-
> tram mortificationem, altare holocausti.
> Sindon et sudarium sunt quae supra memo-
> ravi.[187]

The burial scene does not, however, end with Joseph of Arimathea but rather leads over into the silence of the Sabbath and the preparations for the embalment of Christ's body in the tomb. The following _Pater noster_ is structurally the expression of that silence of the Sabbath before Easter. This prayer is of functional significance within the course of the drama. Again, there arises a double-image of silence and movement. Silence penetrates the foreground of the scene, the activity for the embalment takes place in the background leading to the Re- surrection. During this transition it is the _patena_ which receives primarily dramatic-allegorical significance.

De Officio quod Memorat Requiem Domini in Sepulchro[188]

Pater noster

The _pater noster_ which now follows is a transition from the Passion and Death to the Resurrection. It enacts in repres-

entational form the praying during the silence of the Sabbath
following the Burial of Christ. The seven supplications of the
Our Father express retrospectively the seven days of the Passion
Week and foreshadow the seven gifts of the Holy Spirit to be
poured down on the Day of Pentecost. This relationship of the
pater noster to the Sabbath-silence of Holy Saturday comes from
an older tradition which Amalarius reshapes dramatically. In
his own treatment of the Prayer of the Lord, he states:

> In recordatione septimae diei,quando
> Christus quievit in sepulchro, agitur
> dominica oratio, quae septem petitiones
> continet. In quo septimo die laborant,
> apostoli tristitia ac metu Iudaeorum, et,
> ni fallor, orabant, ut liberarentur a
> malo et consecuti sunt quod orabant, re-
> surrectionem Domini.[189]

The representation and enactment of the Sabbath-silence is
achieved through the position of the deacons and subdeacons.
The subdeacons retreat from their position in front of the altar
which still symbolizes the tomb of Christ; in doing this, they
change their upright position to a supine one. This does not
signify that they are to be leaving the burial site but rather
it indicates the preparation for the embalming and prayer in
silence. Amalarius is quite specific about this change in
position:

> Subdiaconi, qui stant usque modo in
> facie sacrificii, et nunc recedunt,
> ministeria feminarum ad memoriam nobis
> ducunt, quae recesserunt de monumento,
> sepulto Domino. Non etim ita reces-
> serunt a sepulchro, ut abessent minis-
> terio Domini, sed sabbato siluerunt;
> quo transacto paraverunt aromata, ut
> ungerunt corpus eius. Eo modo prae-
> sentes subdiaconi recedunt a praesentia
> sacrificii, ut sabbato quidem, hoc est
> quamdiu septem petitiones dominicae ora-
> tionis dicuntur, sint in silentio et in-

331

clinati, sicut erant apostoli illo in
tempore et sanctae mulieres.[190]

Again we have here an exact description of roles and a specific
designation of space. But this part is furthermore significant
because of the double configuration of silence which on the one
hand still implies the yoke of sin and death and the burden of
fear and sadness but which on the other hand expresses the inner
disposition of prayer, calmness and stillness. The supine
position symbolizes the three aspects of sin, fear and prayer.
In the background, however, there is motion and activity in preparation for the embalming of Christ's body which signifies the
dawn of the Resurrection. In this complex configuration there
lies a certain tension. This tension, shortly before the
turning point within the drama, is of extreme importance because
it will break the ban of death and will be leading to the joy of
a new creation. Amalarius closes his description of this positional change by mentioning the patena. The patena in its
polysemous meaning stands in special relationship to the preparation of the ointment for the embalment on the eve of the
Sabbath and the walking of the women to the tomb to embalm the
dead body of Christ. It symbolizes the alabaster-vessel in
which Mary Madgalena carried the ointment to the tomb. In contrast to the calmness which is signified by the supine position,
the patena indicates at first the external movements connected
with the embalment but soon it assumes a more complex meaning:
it also symbolizes the purified heart and its dilated inner
space to be filled with the presence of Christ. Amalarius concludes his transition to the Resurrection the visible representation of which begins with the fractio of the bread and
communion as follows:

> Qui postea satagunt cum patentis ad
> requirendum corpus Domini circa altare,
> ut mulieres quaesierunt corpus Domini
> circa sepulchrum.[191]

This description is most interesting for our study because the
movements in carrying the patena around the altar signify the
searching of the women for the body of Jesus around the tomb in
the Garden of Joseph at the dawn of Easter.

De Praesentatio Patenae

Since Amalarius himself devoted a whole chapter to the
patena, the dramatic-allegorical function of this object is most
conspicuous. We shall therefore examine this text meticulously.
Although Amalarius cites as his source the Ordo Romanus II
(A:V), its basic meaning comes obviously from the Byzantine
liturgy of Germanos of Constantinople.[192]

According to the Ordo Romanus II (A:V), the patena has from
the beginning of the prefatio the following significant meaning:
During the sursum corda, at the beginning of the Canon, an
acolytus enters from the right side of the altar, holding the
patena, wrapped in a cloth, before his breast. Then a subdeacon
moves toward the acolytus, accepts the patena, goes in front of
the altar and is waiting there silently until the subdiaconus
regionarius is accepting it. During the prayer, "Et ab omni
perturbatione securi"--the continuation of the sup-
plication of the pater noster--the archdiaconus turns
around, kisses the patena and is then handing it on to the
second diaconus.[193]

Amalarius changes this part of that edition of the Ordo
Romanus creatively reshaping its allegorical-dramatic and
functional form. He begins by connecting the patena with the
burial scene:

> Mea humilitas dicit quod sibi videtur
> rationi congruere, relinquens arbitrio
> magistrorum quid potissimum tenendum
> sit. Videtur mihi ut ea ora praesen-
> tanda sit patena, qua circa mysteria
> passionis Domini satagebant discipuli
> vel mulieres. Postquam enim ivit ad
> mensam, studuerunt circa mysteria pas-
> sionis. Sequens vero subdiaconus in
> medio canone, id est cum dicitur, Te
> igitur, suscipit eam ab acolyto, usque
> dum suscipiatur a subdiacono regionario.
> Suscipitur enim, cum dicitur, "per om-
> nia saecula saeculorum". Regionarius

333

suscipit illam finito canone, id est
ubi dicitur: "Per omnia . . .", et
tenet illam usque ad susceptionem
diaconi. Potest etiam intellegi simpliciter recessio subdiaconi de facie
pontificis accessio ad patenam.[194]

It is evident that Amalarius relates the _patena_ at the beginning
of the Canon to the burial scene of Jesus:

. . . praesentanda sit patena qua
circa mysteria passionis Domini sata-
gabant discipulis vel mulieres. Postquam enim ivit ad mensam, studuerunt
circa mysteria passionis.[195]

Amalarius is not only bringing the _patena_ into relationship with
the general activity in preparation of the ointment for the
embalment; the _patena_ is the very object, the _alabaster-vessel_
in which Mary Magdalena had prepared the ointment for the
embalming of the body of Christ in which she carried it to the
tomb in the Garden of Joseph of Arimathea. _"Sicut alabasterum_
in quo portavit unguentum Maria Dominum . . .".[196] The _patena_
has yet another meaning: it also symbolizes allegorically the
believing and converted heart. With this signification the
allegorical-tropological sense of the _patena_ is leading over
into the anagogical sense of the Easter joy represented by the
expanded heart. Amalarius elaborates on this expansion, a mode
which in itself is inherent in the form of the _patena_ made of
golden material:

Patena dicitur eo quod patet; corda ampla
significat. Sicut alabastrum in quo portavit unguentum Maria ad unguendum Dominum, significavit cor eius, in quo erat
fides sine impostura; ita et patena potest corda sanctarum feminarum desig-
nare, quae patebant latitudine carita-
tis in obsequio Christi.[197]

Such a specific designation of the _patena_, first its

general connection with the activity of the embalment preparation for the burial, then signifying an alabaster-vessel and
additionally its allegorical representation of the heart,
purified and dilated by sacrifice and penance, is dramatically
very important because it serves as a connective link to the
other previous scenes. It gives also dramatic unity to the
Canon and is, since it refers to the Resurrection, at the same
time foreshadowing the Easter event. In order to make a
detailed analysis, retrospection is necessary at this point. We
recall that the sacrificial gifts of the faithful as well as the
sacrifice of the angels at the beginning of the praefatio were
related to the Week of the Passion. Furthermore, the washing of
hands--lavabo--after the offertory signified the tears which
Christ had shed before His death. Then, shortly before the
praefatio, i.e., after the washing of hands, the patena, carried
by an acolyte is brought to the altar. Although Amalarius does
not specify this in any way, the delivery of the patena at that
point might be interpreted according to Scripture. It might
symbolize the annointing of Christ by Mary Magdalena at Bethany
an event which falls between the Resurrection of Lazarus and
Palm Sunday. This hypothesis seems to be justified because in
the first book of the Liber Officialis, where Amalarius deals
with the liturgical structure of Septuagesima, the Week of the
Passion does not begin with Palm Sunday but rather with the
Saturday before that Sunday which refers to the ointment in
Bethany.[198]   Thus, my hypothesis that the patena, as an
alabaster-vessel, would also signify the annointing at Bethany
which, according to Christ's own words, foreshadows His death
and burial, is not unfounded. Furthermore, the themes of Passion
Week, especially that of the Palm Sunday liturgy, are also drawn
into the general structure of the dramatic celebration--in fact,
they constitute the essence of its more or less flexible
structure which provides room for additional expansion and
insertions

We should once more recall the position of the subdeacons
and deacons. The subdeacons are standing before the celebrant.
After the acolyte, at the beginning of the sursum corda, has
entered from the right side of the altar, a subdeacon--the
subdiaconus regionarus--moves out of the row and turns away from
the celebrant in order to accept the patena from the acolyte.

This takes place during the Te igitur. Amalarius himself
assigns dramatic significance to the acceptance of the patena by
the subdeacon when he concludes the interpretation of this text
with the following statement: "Potest etiam intellegi
simpliciter recessio subdiaconi accessio ad patenam."[199] This
turn is dramatically considered especially important because of
the double meaning of the patena: It activates in the memory of
the believer Christ's own words at the annointing in Bethany:
this then takes on representational form, visually foreshadowing
Christ's Burial and Resurrection.

By its very purpose and form, the patena contains within
itself the sign of motion and dilation. It symbolizes as an
alabaster-vessel the physical activity of the preparation for
the Sabbath, the embalment, and the walk to the tomb all of
which occur in the stillness of the Sabbath. But since the
patena also signifies the counter image of the heart, the inner
space, it also symbolizes the quiet work of prayer and the Holy
Spirit which precedes the Resurrection; the work of the Holy
Spirit is alluded to especially by the seven supplications of
the pater noster.

While the deacons and subdeacons in supine position
silently pray together the seven supplications of the pater
noster, the patena remains at that time in the background
signifying the preparations for the embalment; the manner of
silently praying in this position still expresses fear and
sadness. And as we recall, this supine position is also a
symbol of hiding, and thus it becomes again a representation of
the apostles and disciples hiding behind closed doors out of
fear of the Jews. The room alluded to as the hiding place is
the room of the Last Supper in the house of Joseph of Arimathea,
as Amalarius had indicated earlier.(This is also the room in
which the apostles and disciples gathered at the time of the
festivities for Pentecost).

To summarize this complex configuration: with the patena
remaining in the background, the preparations for the embalment
are signified. The silent prayer again is an expression of fear
and sadness while the supine position continues to be a symbol
of hiding and thus remains to be a representational form of the

336

apostles and disciples hidden behind closed doors out of fear
for the Jews. The room is that of the Last Supper, the upper
room in the house of Joseph of Arimathea.

By this time, the patena with its allegorical meaning of
the alabaster-vessel has sufficiently anticipated the Resurrection at the empty tomb. The supine position has signified
the yoke of sin and death, sin and fear and the silence of sadness but also perseverance in prayer. When the seventh supp-
lication of the pater noster is being prayed, i.e., the sed
libera nos a malo (deliver us from evil), the tension between
silence and activity has reached its culminative point: during
the Resurrection the burden of sin has been taken away, mankind
has been delivered from evil, and now the deacons and subdeacons
slowly raise up to an upright position. Thus, this movement to
an upright position from a long endured supine one, becomes a
visible sign of the Resurrection, the lifting of the ban of
death and the burden of sin. It is the turning point of the
drama. It is the making visible of an invisible process, the
"raising up" of the Resurrection. This positional symbolism of
the upright position becomes after a long time--since the
sanctus--a silent but most effective means for the expression of liberation and freedom. Parallel to this silent
raising, there is the eager searching of the women at the tomb,
where the Resurrection has become visibly manifested. Amalarius describes this double image of the dramatic situation of
the Resurrection as follows:

> Subdiaconus regionarius accipit patenam,
> finito canone, quia laetitiam dominicae
> resurrectionis mulieres primo audierunt.
> Illae huc illucque discurrebant ferventi
> studio circa sepulturam Domini. Stant
> diaconi stantque subdiaconi inclinati,
> usque dum audiant: "Sed libera nos a
> malo. . .". Septima petitiones domini-
> cae orationis finis signatur totius
> tristiae ac perturbationis apostolorum,
> quam habebant de Domini morte.[200]

This movement which breaks out of this silence and becomes

dramatically represented, can only be understood when it is seen in connection with the motif of the yoke of sin which was presented so elaborately earlier in the drama. Here especially Amalarius' masterful dramatic handling of visibly representing the liberation from sin, connecting interior and exterior space, is once more evident. He again distinguishes carefully between the different roles and emphasizes that deacons and subdeacons in their supine position represent the apostles and disciples in their fear and sadness but not, in this scene, the holy women, who, as a matter of fact, were during that time engaged in the activities of the preparation for the embalment and were later walking to the tomb. This activity of the women is therefore a situation contrary to that which is expressed in the representational form of the supine position of the subdeacons expressing hiding in silence and fear of the apostles. But now, Amalarius distinguishes again carefully between the deacons and subdeacons because the disciples who are personified by the subdeacons are the two disciples of Emmaus who had spoken in sadness with Christ about His Death and whose sadness disappeared only after the Breaking of the Bread. The image of fear and sadness of the disciples and apostles before the event of the Resurrection is taken from the basic Scriptural text:

> Quid illo tempore, hoc est quando
> Christus quivit in sepulchro, apostoli
> agerent, non legitur aperte, sed ex
> Iohannis evangelio metum eorum cognos-
> ciumus, qui dicit: "Cum esset ergo sero
> die illo una sabbatorum, et fores essent
> clausae, ubi erant discipuli congre-
> gati propter metum Iudaeorum." Ex quo
> discimus tristitia demonstratur per diaco-
> norum declinationem. Discipulorum vero
> tristiam cognoscimus ex Domini sermone,
> qui dicit . . . ad duos qui ibant in die
> resurrectionis in castellum Emaus . . ."[201]

Here again, Amalarius has given an exact description of roles, designation of place as well as a specific meaning of positional symbolism which signifies fear, sadness and silent prayer.[202]

338

By way of positional symbolism of the <u>pater</u> <u>noster</u> the
Christian congregation becomes again actively drawn into the
liturgical drama; the congregation also experiences the libera-
ation from the slavery of sin by raising together with the
deacons from the bowed position:

> Publica est nobis et communis oratio,
> et, quando oramus, non pro uno, sed
> pro toto populo oramus, quia totus po-
> pulus unum sumus.[203]

Liberation from sin because of awareness of sin and guilt
includes finally the entire Church:

> Orat et nunc sancta ecclesia, quasi in
> septima die, quando, iam quiescentibus
> animabus sanctorum, instat ieiunando,
> vigilando, orando, certando in cari-
> tate, ne abrumpatur periculis huius mundi
> a spe caelestium gaudiorum.[204]

The predominant historical-allegorical-tropological significance of the offertory part, <u>i.e.</u>, the third act, has now
given way to the anagogical sense. This sense is mainly expressed by positional symbolism connected with movements and
songs. The significance of the <u>patena</u> remains dramatic-
allegorical.

Dramatic Analysis

After the <u>sanctus-hymnus</u>, where the voices of angels and
men had been fused and at which time the singing was still an
essential structural means, the <u>gestus allegoricus</u> assumes
essential significance. By means of movements, gestures,
position, various changes in roles, the objects of <u>sindon</u> and
<u>sudarium</u>, the different symbolic meanings and representations of
the altar and its immediate surrounding, the entire Passion,
deposition from the Cross and the burial in the tomb became
dramatically enacted. The spatial relationship shifts from
cosmic expansion to the inner space of the heart the repres-
sentational expression of which is first the altar and then in

connection with the Resurrection, the patena. Most obvious is
also the dramatic significance of the change in voices by which,
for example, the conversion of the Roman captain was signified.

Confractio et Benedictio: Resurrection and
Ascension of Christ[205]

De Praesentatione subdiaconorum ut
suscipiant Corpus Domini de Altari

Patena

    The patena remains the main link to the Resurrection scenes
which in all their manifestations are given dramatic representation during the distribution of Communion. The leading scene
is thereby the Resurrection at the empty tomb which is initiated
by the subdeacons who stand in a position ready to accept the
Bread. In his introduction to this part, Amalarius gives the
following dramatic description:

> Hoc officium ad memoriam ducit devotis-
> simus mentes, quae se ipsas praesenta-
> verunt in exequiis sepultura Domini. Prae-
> sentantibus se sanctis mulieribus ad se-
> pulchrum Domini, inveniunt spiritum re-
> disse ad corpus, et angelorum visionem
> circa sepulchrum, ad adnuntiant aposto-
> lis quae viderant.[206]

Again we have here an exact description of scenery, of roles,
designation of place, movement, the walk to the tomb, the
searching for the dead body of Jesus at the tomb, the encounter with the angels and the annunciation of the message of
Easter. In the shaping of the scene, Amalarius is dependent on
Bede:

> . . . "Quomodo, inquit, posito in sepul-
> chro corpore salvatoris, angeli adsti-
> tisse leguntur, ita etiam caelebrandis
> eiusdem sacratissimi corporis mysteriis
> tempore consecrationis assistere sunt

340

credendi, monente apostolo: Mulieres
in ecclesia velamen habere propter angelos. Cum timerent autem et declinarent
vultum in terra, dixerunt ad illas:
'Quid queritis viventum cum mortuis?
Non est hic, sed surrexit'.[207]

A most interesting phenomenon referred to in Bede's text are the
wings of the angels which he compares with the veils of women:
Mulieres velamen habere propter angelos. Such a description
raises several questions. The first question which comes to
mind is whether the angels during this scene were personified by the subdeacons or symbolized in any other form. As I
have shown above, the wings of the angels belong to the earliest
motives and representations of spiritual and invisible realities
of the dramatic-liturgical tradition which has been grouping
around the burial and Resurrection scenes.[208] The second
question is whether they are represented in any other symbolic
form than that of the anagogical angel voices. As I have shown,
Amalarius considers the angels as essential realities surrounding the altar.

In the first book of the Liber Officialis, there is a description of a representational variant of the Resurrection scene
at the tomb, which is signified by an angel's song. This Res-
surrection scene is a variant which represents the women not
joyfully or jubilantly but rather fearfully running away from
the tomb, remaining silent while the angels are announcing the
Resurrection with their songs. Since this variant reflects
again the unique flexible mode of the liturgical drama, we shall
partially insert this text here:

Ecce finitum est sacrificium neofytorum.
Deinde Christi resurrectio ad memoriam
reducitur et angelorum allocutio ad fe-
minas et feminarum affectus . . . Illis
locutus est angelus dicens: "Nolite ex-
pavescere. Jesum quaeritis Nazarenum
crucifixum; surrexit, non est hic." In
sequentibus manifestur affectus mulierum:
"At illae exeuntes, fugerunt de monu-

341

mento, invaserat enim eas tremor et
pavor; et nemini, quicquam dixerunt; time-
bant enim."[209]

Here emerges a counter image to the courageous women who had
remained with Christ under the Cross; according to Mark's
narrative, they are fearful and running away from the tomb: In
sequentibus manifestatur mulierum. . ., Amalarius compares, as
Bede does, the different Scriptural accounts of Mark, Luke and
Matthew, closing then with a citation from Bede:

. . . nisi intellegamus ipsorum angelorum nemini ausas fuisse aliquid dicere,
id est respondere ad ea quae ab illis
audierant, aut certe custodibus, quos
iacentes viderunt.[210]

Following this variant, Amalarius gives a description of Bede's
dramatic representational form of the Resurrection scene involving this time the representation of angels and the songs of
angels:

Reducendo ad memoriam silentium et sacrificium mulierum, in tempore sacrificii
silent cantores. Eorum sacrificium erat
tunc, quod ferebant unguentum ad ungen-
dum corpus Domini. "Sanctus, sanctus,
sanctus," cantant, quod est angelorum
cantus, quia angeli non tacerunt de
eius resurrectione, sive iste qui modo
locutus est in Marco, sive illi quos
Iohannes narrat, "sedentes unum ad
caput et unum ad pedes."[211]

Amalarius' elaboration indicates with what sense of reality the
presence of the angels was experienced around the altar.
Nothing might therefore have been more natural as to give them
dramatic representational form also in this area. This particular Resurrection scene representing angelic songs at the
empty tomb establishes an integral connection to the anagogical
santus-hymnus of the offertory part. It is not until the Agnus

342

Dei that the women come again to the foreground. This is the scene where Mary Magdalena encounters the Gardener in the Garden of Joseph where the tomb is located.[212] Amalarius summarizes the allegorical enactment of the Resurrection by the angels' song at the end of this treatment of the drama of the Easter Vigil. His repeated reference to this part indicates the significance of this edition:

> Sacerdos, vicarius Christi, implet offi-
> cium suum. Dubitantibus apostolis de sua
> resurrectione, timentibus mulieribus nihil
> dicentibus, angelorum concentus clamat
> Christum resurrexisse a mortuis. Christus
> ipse per suam gloriosam apparitionem mani-
> nifestum se facit quibuscumque vult.[213]

This interpretation by Bede, dependent on Mark, seems to have been preferred during the Easter Vigil. It is therefore not impossible that during the course of the liturgical cycle this variant of the Resurrection scene was also performed; it is furthermore evident that the reality and presence of angels belonged essentially to the religious experience within the liturgical drama and therefore this expression sought forms of expression and representation. Whether this was achieved through allegorical symbolic gestures, power of imagination, or visible representations such as the wings of angels, the figures of subdeacons or deacons, must remain hypothetical. Could it also perhaps not be possible that the angels' wings--and with that the angels--were already a topos of earliest times in Christian liturgy that they no longer needed to be explained and specifically represented?

In the third book of the Liber Officialis, Amalarius again returns to the patena and focuses on the eagerly searching women at the tomb:

> Post haec praesentat se subdiaconus cum
> patena sua ad sepuchrum Domini. Quam
> accepit a subdiacono sequente qui ad
> memoriam, ut supra diximus, reducit sanc-
> tarum feminarum studissimum affectum

343

circa sepulturam Domini.[214]

The <u>patena</u> has here that double significance of the alabaster-
vessel and the believing purified heart which is prepared to
receive the Risen Christ, as we had discussed earlier.
Particular attention must be paid to the eager searching for
Christ at the empty tomb because we are dealing here again with
a skillful dramatic move by Amalarius. This searching is being
enacted by means of slow or rapid walking around the altar:
<u>Studiosissimum affectum circa sepulturum Domini</u>. Furthermore,
bodily gestures or movements such as turning around, bowing down
and above all the searching glance of the eyes--such as we could
already observe during the <u>Gloria</u> scene--might also have
signified the searching for the body of Christ. These gestures
and movements of searching, however, initiate the transition to
the backward glance, to the <u>Gloria</u> scene of the first act, the
<u>Introit</u>. But in the context of the configuration of the fourth
act--the <u>Confractio et Benedictio</u>--this retrospection
established the relationship between the <u>Gloria</u> above the
manager in Bethlehem at the Birth to Life, to the <u>alleluia</u> at[215]
the tomb of Jerusalem after Death and Rebirth to New Life.

Pax Domino et Fractio

After Amalarius has elaborately introduced the <u>patena</u>, the
celebrant, who personifies Christ, speaks with the elevated host
the <u>Pax Domini</u> and places simultaneously the form of Bread upon
the <u>patena</u>. This represents both the appearance and acceptance
of the Risen Lord. The <u>patena</u> receives in this part the significance of the believing heart, especially of the holy women.
It retains this meaning henceforth:

> Postquam sacerdos dicit: "Pax vobis,"
> ponuntur oblatae in patena. Postquam
> enim Christus sua salutatione laetifi-
> cavit corda discipulorum, vota femina-
> rum completa sunt percepto gaudio re-[216]
> surrectionis.

From this point onward, the liturgical drama assumes historical-anagogical orientation.

   With the above image of the Resurrection, the Pax Domini,
the immediate scene of the Resurrection at the empty tomb, comes
to an end but is at the same time extended first into the wider
surroundings of Jerusalem and then to the entire creation of the
cosmos. This motive of a new creation is developed simultaneously with the breaking of bread and the mixture of wine:
"... atque spiritu vivificante vegetari hominum novem . . ."[217]
The cosmic expansion is signified by the touching of the four
sides of the chalice:

   Ideo tangit quattour latera calicis, quia
   per illum hominum genus quattour climatum
   ad unitatem unius corporis accessit et
   ad pacem catholicae ecclesiae.[218]

Here, in the chalice of the New Covenant, the fourfold sense
inherent in Scripture as well as in creation, and the kernel of
ratio converge and fuse. From here they receive their deepest
meaning. In his later refined work, Eclogae, Amalarius again
emphasizes the touching of the four sides of the chalice,
saying:

   Sane et illud rational congruit ut, (quia)
   quattour sensus sunt in capite, per quattour partes labia calicis tangantur, sive
   quia per quattour partes mundi Christi resurrectio seperatur. Inde scriptum est:
   "A quattour ventis veni, et insuffla super
   interfecto isto, et revivescant."[219]

The mixture of bread and wine becomes the point of convergence
of the new creation initiated by the Resurrection; the inner
space expands into a spiritual cosmos of the entire creation
resulting again in the fusion of both spheres, the visible and
invisible.

   After the allegorical touching of the four sides of the
chalice, Amalarius makes a backward move to the peace of the
Gloria, as he had done at the end of the Introit; the Gloria had

345

prefigured the Peace of Resurrection through the song of the
angels over Bethlehem. Amalarius says now:

> . . . tunc data est pax quam promiserunt
> angeli in sacratissima nocte dicentes:
> "Gloria in excelsis Deo et in terra pax
> hominibus bonae voluntatis."[220]

Through the searching at the tomb and through the <u>Pax Domini</u>,
Amalarius established the relationship to the foreplay of the
<u>Introitus</u> and then combined the birth to life with the birth to
a new life which was brought about through death. After this
retrospective glance and interblending, Amalarius comes back to
the present scene:

> Eandem sacerdos nunc ad memoriam revocat
> dicens: "Pax Domini sit semper vobiscum;"
> eandem populus insequitur per basia
> blanda.[221]

Then Amalarius leads the movement of the drama with the <u>Agnus
Dei</u> to the extended scene of the breaking of the Bread of Life
which most likely belongs to the oldest forms of Resurrection
scenes. Already in his earlier work, <u>Missae Expositionis, Codex
I</u>, Amalarius elaborated extensively on this scene.[222] Later he
gives a variant of it in the first book of the <u>Liber
Officials</u>,[223] and finally he expands it to a larger scene in the
third book of the <u>Liber Officialis</u> which includes the entire
sacerdotal order.[224] The final summary of it appears in his
later work <u>Eclogae</u>.[225] This scene of the <u>Agnus Dei</u>, in
interrelationship with the scene of the bread has obviously
grown out of one of the first historical scenes of the
Resurrection, namely Jesus walking with the two disciples of
Emmaus. This scene is already defined as a <u>typus</u> by Amalarius.
I shall therefore briefly discuss this scene below.

Agnus Dei

According to Scripture, the scene of the breaking of Bread
primarily signifies that the Risen Christ, after He had appeared
to the women, and subsequently to Simon Peter, had appeared on

several occasions to the other apostles and disciples under the sign of the breaking of Bread. The scene which follows and which Amalarius again shapes according to the Ordo Romanus II is therefore extremely significant and interesting because it is full of motion in contrast to the "standing-still" and calmness of the preceding scenes before the enactment of the Resurrection. In this scene, the clerus represents the apostles and disciples:

> Sequitur in libello memorato: "Sed archi-
> diaconus pacem dat episcopo prior, deinde
> ceteri per ordinem, et populus. Tunc pon-
> tifex rumpit, oblatam ex latera dextro, et
> particulam quam rumpit, altare relinquit,
> reliquas vero oblationes point in patenam
> quam tenet disconus;". . . [226]

The archdeacon gives the Kiss of Peace, first to the bishop, then to the entire sacerdotal order, and finally to the entire congregation. After that the Pontifex breaks a piece out of the right side of the Bread--the prima sancta--which is later remaining at the altar; the rest he places on the patena which is being held by the deacon. From here emerges the double image of the presence of Christ: at the altar and in the hearts of the believer which is symbolized by the patena.

The inclusion of the bishop in this configuration is of greatest significance because he, as a representational figure, has appropriated additional meaning. In this scene, the bishop represents Christ as enthroned at the Right Hand of the Father, as the Risen Lord immediately after the Resurrection appearing among the women, disciples and apostles, and especially Simon Peter whose official envoy he also represents.

After the breaking (fractio) of the Bread there is almost a repetition of the passing around of the patena as it was described at the pater noster scene. The meaning of the patena at that time was very complex. After the Resurrection however its meaning has been condensed to signifying mainly the believing heart of the women, disciples, apostles and all believers:

347

> . . . et post pauca: "Tunc acolyti
> vadunt dextra levaque per episcopos
> circa altare; reliqui descendunt ad
> presbyteros, ut fragant hostias; pa-
> tena praecedit iuxta sedem, ferentibus
> eam duobus subdiaconibus regionariis ad
> diaconus ut fragrant,". . .[227]

The figure of the acolyte who is entering from the right side is
familiar. He accepts the patena from the bishop and takes it to
the priests who are breaking the Bread. The priests and deacons
are representing here the apostles who had previously been
hiding. The two subdeacons (diaconi regionarius) who take the
patena into the vicinity of the enthroned bishop seem to signify
the two disciples of Emmaus who later break the Bread with the
apostles and disciples and thus recognized the Risen Christ as
their Lord.

After the fractio is concluded, the Pontifex takes the host
with the mixture of Bread and Wine. Again, the archdeacon is
given the chalice:

> "Expleta confractione, diaconus minor,
> levata de subdiacono patena, fert ad
> sedem, ut communicet pontifex; qui dum
> communicaverit, de ipsa quam momorderat,
> ponit inter manus archidiaconi in calicem.[228]

With the mixture of Bread and Wine the Resurrection scenes have
been completed.

The background of the scene of the breaking of Bread
emerges through the antiphonal song of the Agnus Dei through
which this scene receives additional dramatic significance. The
Agnus Dei seems, in connection with the breaking of Bread, to
have been the original re-enactment of the Resurrection scene.
This scene was given special treatment by Amalarius and it is
very important for the history of drama. We will therefore
discuss this scene in detail.

Amalarius develops this scene in the third book of his

348

<u>Liber Officialis</u>, first on the basis of the <u>Liber Pontificalis</u>.
He mentions at the beginning: "<u>His statuis ut tempore confrac-</u>
<u>tionis domini corporis Agnus Dei a clero et populo de-</u>
<u>cantetur.</u>"[229]

Amalarius then proceeds to discuss the antiphonal song in
connection with the Emmaus scene: the singing tells the story
of the Resurrection:

> Antiphona sequens, id est vox reciproca,
> iura fraternitatis custodit, ut unusquis-
> que alterius utilitati studeat, et curet
> provocare ad gaudia resurrectionis. Quem
> typum gesserunt illi duo, qui Dominum cog-
> noverunt in fractione panis, et ilico
> perrexerunt Hierusalem, et invenerunt con-
> gregatos XI et eos qui cum ipsis erant,
> dicentes: "Surrexit vere Dominus, et
> apparuit Symoni; et ipsi narrabant quae
> erant in via, et quomodo cognoverunt eum
> in fractione panis." Illi nempe canta-
> verunt antiphonam vicissem narrando de
> resurrectione Domini.[230]

This scene is a <u>typus</u> deeply rooted in the beginning of its
tradition. The antiphonal singing has a triple function: the
first is an expression of communal symbolism; the second has
anagogical significance; the third brings the manifestations of
the Risen Lord into representational form. In the <u>Eclogae</u> it is
stated also that the scene of the breaking of the Bread refers
to the Emmaus scene: "<u>Fractio oblatarum illam fractionem</u>
<u>significat quam Dominus duobus fecit in Emaus</u>".[231] The actual
key for this extraordinary dramatic part is to be sought in
<u>Expositio Codex I</u>, <u>i.e.</u>, that text which Amalarius had composed
on his trip returning from Constantinople and shortly after his
impressions he had received in the Hagia Sophia. This text has
preserved an extraordinary liveliness. The dramatic figures
emerge with the antiphonal singing of the narrative:

> . . . postquam dixit: "Pro vobis et pro
> multis effundetur" adiunxit: 'In remissi-

349

onem peccatorum.' Intende, dilecte frater,
qualibus verbis cantores in eadem hora
ostia oris et cordis pulsent: "Agnus
Dei, dicentes qui tollis peccata mundi,
miserere nobis.". . . Quis est occisus,
dilecte, in remissionem peccatorum, nisi
agnus Dei innocens, qui ut catulus leonis
recubuit et ut leo vicit, resurrectione
sua destructa morte nostra?[232]

The experience of the forgiveness of sins and of the new life in
Christ pulsates (pulsent) and streams out of the singing voices
and configurations symbolized by the choir. It is moreover
obvious that the choir with the retrospective theme of the
burden of sin again assumes choric function. Amalarius cites
Scripture in his defense as follows:

Audi, si te delectat, quae convenientia
sit evangelii cum praesenti officio. Ipse
die qua Christus resurrexit a mortuis,
ambulantibus duobos in via, apparuit
illis, et interrogavit illos quos sermones invicem proferrent. Respondens
unus, cui nomen Cleophas, inter alia
dixit ei: "De Jesu Nazareno qui fuit
vir propheta potens in opere et sermone
coram Deo et omni populo; quomodo tra-
diderunt eum summi sacerdotis et prin-
cipes nostri in damnationem mortis, et
crucifixerunt eum. Nos autem sperabamus
quia ipse esset redempturus Israhel."[233]

This description suggests that the personification of the
disciples walking on the road to Emmaus joined by the Risen Lord
belongs to the representational forms of antiphonal singing.
Amalarius himself partakes in the doubting and questioning of
the two disciples: "Eorum dubitatio, quam habeat de Christi
resurrectione, nostra dubitationem signat. . ."[234] However, he
then refutes such doubts on the basis of Scripture, perhaps for
didactic reasons. Amalarius also elaborates the point further
by saying that the nature and purpose of antiphonal chanting is

to simultaneously narrate and represent the events of the Resurrection:

> Sed bonus magister in fractione panis
> dubitationem abstulit et confirmationem
> intulit; et cantores non statim silent,
> sed adhuc cantant post Agnus Dei antiphona
> ad complendum. Ut bene nosti, antiphona
> vox reciproca dicitur. Quod illi duo fe-
> cerunt qui venerunt, in mansione non certe,
> sed ad undecim congregatos statim per-
> gentes antiphonam retulerunt.[235]

These statements indicate that there seem to have been further enactments of additional manifestations of the Risen Christ. This probably is the reason why Amalar expands the Agnus Dei scene in the third book of the Liber Officialis bringing together the different traditions and remodeling them according to his own view, understanding and imagination. At the end of the Missae Expositionis Codex I, he refers specifically to such individual manifestations:

> Potest et ista antiphona quae ad complen-
> dum dicitur, quae ideo cantatur, sicut
> nobis videtur, ut digne conservetur sacra-
> mentum sumptum in cordibus sumentium, con-
> venire illi loco evangelii, ubi dicit:
> "Undecim discipuli abierunt in Galilaeam,"
> postquam eis dicit: "Pax vobis . . .
> Abierunt in Galilaeam, in montem ubi eis
> constitutum erat, et ubi videntes eum
> adoraverunt; quidam autem dubitaverunt."
> Qui mons apud nos usque hodie permanet.[236]

The dramatic significance of this part lies in the interaction of song and representational forms: ". . . quid ideo cantatur, sicut nobis videtur." The modulations of the songs were probably very important during these figurative representations in order to signify the different layers of allegorical meaning. The extraordinarily flexible structure of this concluding part of the liturgical drama made further expansion very likely. The first book of the <u>Liber Officialis</u> supports such a hypothesis because during the Easter Vigil, the <u>Agnus Dei</u> has such a variant: <u>i.e.</u>, the Risen Christ appearing to Mary Magdalena in the Garden of Joseph of Arimathea in the person of a gardener:

> Vice mulierum iterum, "<u>Agnus Dei</u>" reticent cantores. "Agnus Dei," dicit, "qui tollis peccata mundi, miserere nobis." Maria dicebat hortoloano: "Domino, si tu sustulisti eum, dicito mihi ubi posuisti eum." Quem credebat furto sublatum, non credebat tollere peccata mundi, ac propterea audivit, quando voluit Dominum tangere: "Noli me tangere, nondum enim ascendi ad Patrem meum."[237]

On the basis of these documentations one might plausibly assume that between the <u>Agnus Dei</u> and the <u>Final Benediction</u> it came to the representation of the entire story and acts of the Resurrection.

Benedictio

With the <u>Final Benediction</u> a connection is established to the eschatological configuration of the <u>Introit</u>. In this process the altar is being transformed into the surroundings of Bethany:

> Etenim Dominus ante ascensionem in caelos duxit discipulos in Bethaniam, ibique benedixit eos, et ascendit in caelum. Hunc morem tenet sacerdos, ut, post omnia sacramenta consummata, benedicat populo atque salutet. Dein revertitur ad orientem, ut se commendet Domini ascensioni.[238]

The deacon now speaks the <u>Ite missa est</u> which has exclusively eschatological orientation. It signifies the angel's saying to the apostles: <u>Hic Jesus qui assumptus est a vobis in caelum . . .</u>". In <u>Eclogae</u> the <u>Ite missa est</u> has exclusively this restricted meaning referring only to the words of

352

the angels. The Christian congregration representing the
apostles and disciples who are returning to the Temple:

> Hoc ait sancta ecclesia more apostolico,
> qui erant adorantes Iesum, et regressi
> sunt Hierusalem cum gaudio magno.[239]

In the Liber Officialis, the final blessing is more oriented
towards the eschatological meaning and breaking into a certain
cosmic limitlessness with Amalarius exclaiming:

> O utinam quando audimus a diacono:
> "Ite missa est mens nostra ad illam
> patriam tendat, quo caput nostrum
> praecessit, ut sibi simus desiderio,
> ubi desideratus cunctis gentibus nos
> expecta cum suo tropheo; quatinus sic
> desiderando aliquando ad eum pervenire
> possimus, qui ita Patrem supplicat pro
> nobis: "Volo Pater, ut ubi ego sum,
> ibi sit et minister meus."[240]

With the last blessing (de ultiore ultima benedictione) the
Christian congregration assumes the role of the militant soldiers
of Christ. This blessing is particularly part of the liturgical
drama of Lent:

> . . . in qua milites Christi commendatur
> pugnae contra antiquum hostem. Si omni
> tempore necesse est paratum esse belli-
> cosum adversus insidias sive impetus
> inimicorum, quanto magis in procinctu.[241]

With the configuration, expressing the tropological-anagogical
sense, the liturgical drama comes to an end. But the connection
to the Introit, in eschatological expectation, remains and will
at the beginning of the next performance of the liturgical drama
open the act of the Incarnation in a cosmic telescoping vision--
within the sign of ratio and the essentially allegorical world
structure of the four senses of Scripture.

Dramatic Analysis

In the fourth act, an immense temporal compression and spatial expansion occurs. The most significant means of representation within this scope are the patena, gestures, movements, antiphonal chants, personfication, multiple roles, and change of place. It is evident that variants of the Resurrection theme were performed in conclusion before the final blessing to represent the entire story of the Resurrection in visible forms.

Summary

Our detailed analysis of the liturgical-dramatic mode of representation of Amalarius of Metz justifies the conclusion that the liturgical drama of the early Middle Ages, which was deeply embedded in the actual course of the liturgical year, can claim to be a unique literary genre, i.e., a form of drama within the corpus of early Christian literature and in its own right. Its essential components which justify such a definition are: the life and acts of the protagonist Jesus, the biblical stories and the teaching of salvation history. These constitute the basic material of the plot. Other characteristic features are: spatial expansion and temporal compression dramatic objects such as: altar, linen cloth, sindon and sudarium, candles, incense censor, antiphonal chants, silence, gestures, movements, signs, positional, directive and communal symbolism, all of which assume multiple significance and meaning, and over-all manifold allegorical-symbolic structure. All of these contribute to the shaping of the different configurations from the beginning to the end of the drama.

The special merits of Amalarius in the shaping of this drama were as follows: Firstly, he fully integrated the allegorical mode of interpretation, combined with Augustine's theory of signs, into the liturgy; secondly, he integrated, aided by his own imagination and vision, the different liturgical traditions, i.e., those of the Byzantine, Gallo-Frankish-Germanic churches and the Roman forms which were laid down in the Ordo Romanus. The leitmotives of sindon and sudarium, the double-structure of the sanctus-hymnus, as well as the figures of

Joseph of Arimathea and Nicodemus bespeak the influence of his Byzantine experience and observations under the cover of "inspiration". Amalarius appears to have combined them with the remains of the Gallican liturgy which were partially preserved in the frame of the <u>Ordo Romanus</u> and which were most likely still alive in local customs—although perhaps only in dispersed forms.

This liturgy, as it emerged before our eyes in its very dramatic mode and uniqueness of configurational structure, was not only nourished by Patristic sources but also by the tradition of the Roman theatre and the imagination of the Germanic peoples, rooted in a mysterious-figurative <u>Weltanschauung</u>. Amalarius' liturgical world which was disclosed by his texts as we studied them indicates an immense richness of a figurative, allegorical enactment of the story of Jesus of Nazareth—his teachings and his actions, culminating in the Act of His Last Supper, the drama of His Passion, Death, Resurrection and Ascension—in the form of a liturgical drama the entire fulness of which we are no longer able to recapture.

355

FOOTNOTES

[1] It should be pointed out here that the structure of the Roman Missale, as we know it today, is based on this structure, but the length and dramatic build-up are only potentially there. The present units, particularly the Introit, are only remains of what was once an elaborate drama of the life of Christ and salvation history.

[2] Cf. above, pp. 184-188.

[3] LO 3., H, 2: 261. Ecclesia est convocatus populus per ministros ecclesiae ab eo facit unianimes habitare in domo. Ipsa domus vocatur ecclesia, quia ecclesiam continet. Ipsa vocatur Kyria, qui est dominicalis . . . Ipsa vocatur basilica, id est regalis, a basilio. Basileus rex dicitur, quasi basis populi; laos populus dicitur, basilaus basis populi . . .

[4] Ibid., p. 262.

[5] Ibid., pp. 262-64.

[6] Ibid., p. 267.

[7] Cf. Gadamer, Wahrheit, pp. 103-104 for a discussion of the inclusion of the spectator as the "fourth wall". Cf. also G. W. F. Hegel, and his discussion of the people becoming transformed into the very hero of the play, in his Phänomenologie des Geistes. Edited by J. Hoffmeister. (Hamburg: Verlag von Felix Meiner, 1956), pp. 471-548.

[8] LO 3., H, 2: 274.

[9] Cf. the Old-High German Muspilli where the currum of the fire carriage of Elias appears and where the basic material is taken from the description of the final combustion of the world, the Ragnarök, of the Nordic Edda sagas. Cf. Snorri Sturluson, The Prose Edda. Transl. from the Icelandic by J. L. Young. 1951. See also: Bernard McGinn, Visions of the End: Apocalyptic Traditions in the Middle Ages. (New York: Columbia University Press, 1979).

[10]LO 3., H, 2: 274.   (Augustin, Enarration in Ps. LXVIII, 24., PL, 36: 828-29).

[11]LO 2., H, 2: 274.

[12]Cf. above, pp. 99, n. 155 and 103, n. 165.

[13]LO 3., H, 2: 274-75.   (Matth. 8: 23-34; 1 Cor., 2:2).

[14]LO 2., H, 2: 274.

[15]Ibid., p. 275.

[16]Ibid.

[17]Ibid.

[18]Ibid., p. 275; cf. also above, p. 253.

[19]LO 3., H, 2: 278.

[20]Ibid.

[21]Ibid., p. 279.

[22]ibid., p. 280 (Luc., 10:5).

[23]Ibid. (Homilae in Ezechiel, 1.2. hom. 9.8. PL, 76: 1047B).

[24]LO 3., H, 2: 280.

[25]Ibid., p. 281 (Cant. 3:10).

[26]LO 3., H, 2: 281.

[27]Ibid., p. 281.

[28]Ibid., pp. 281-82.

²⁹Ibid., p. 282.

³⁰Ibid., pp. 283-84.

³¹Ibid., p. 285.

³²Ibid., p. 285 (Matth. 18:20).

³³LO 3., H, 2: 285.

³⁴Ibid., pp. 285-86.

³⁵In Expositionis Missae Cod. II, Amalarius dealt explicitly with the multi-structure of the sicut erat thus indicating the temporal compression apparent at this point: "in quo versu varietas multiplicium temporum demonstratur, id est, 'sicut erat in principio'", praeterium; "et nunc," praesens; "et semper," futurum aeternum; "secula seculorum," longitudo magna. H, 1: 267.

³⁶LO 3., H, 2: 286-87. (Luc., 2:13).

³⁷Ibid., p. 287.

³⁸Exp. Miss. Cod. I., H, 1: 258.

³⁹LO 3., H, 2: 287 (Mich., 4:8).

⁴⁰Ibid., (Luc., 2: 10-11, 24:36), With his "...copulantur caelestia et terrena", Amalarius expresses his vision in an inveterate widely disseminated cosmognic symbol of the history of religions namely, of the marriage of heaven and earth bringing forth a new creation. Cf. Mircea Eliade, Patterns, pp. 39-123.

⁴¹Ibid., (Matth. 28: 18).

⁴²LO 3., H, 2: 288.

⁴³Ibid., p. 289.

358

[44]Ibid., (Luc. 24:50).

[45]LO 3., H, 2: 290-91.

[46]Ibid., p. 291 (Augustine, Enarratio in ps. 126, 3. PL, 37: 1669).

[47]Regarding the symbolism of the center which can unfortunately not be dealt with in this thesis, see Eliade, Myth Eternal Return, pp. 12-17.

[48]LO 3., H, 2: 292-93. (Act., 13: 14-16).

[49]Cf. above, pp. 97-103.

[50]LO 3., H, 2: 292-94.

[51]Ibid., p. 294.

[52]Ibid., p. 292.

[53]Ibid., pp. 294-95.

[54]Ibid., p. 293.

[55]Ibid., p. 295.

[56]Ibid., pp. 294-99.

[57]Ibid., p. 296.

[58]Ibid.

[59]Ibid., pp. 297-98.

[60]Ibid., p. 299.

[61]Cf. above, pp. 63-64.

[62]Ibid., pp. 299-302.

[63]Ibid., p. 301. (Exod., 19, 32; Dan. 6; Ez., 1, 10, 40-48).

[64]Cf. below, pp. 298-299.

[65]LO 3., H, 2: 301.

[66]Ibid., p. 302.

[67]Ibid.

[68]Cf. above, pp. 249-250.

[69]LO 3., H, 2: 293.

[70]Ibid., p. 305.

[71]Cf. above, pp. 273-274.

[72]LO 3., H, 2: 306. (Epistula 34, ad clerum et plebem de Clerico lectore ordinato 4.5. PL, 4: 323BC-324AB).

[73]LO 3., H, 2: 307.

[74]Ibid., pp. 306-311.

[75]Ibid., p. 307.

[76]ibid., p. 308.

[77]Ibid.

[78]ibid., p. 309.

[79]Cf. above, pp. 212-213.

[80]LO 3., H, 2: 310 (Act., 1:1).

[81]Cf. above, pp. 266-267.

[82]LO 3., H, 2: 310-11.

[83]Ibid., and see also above, pp. 256-257.

[84]Ibid., p. 311. (Matth. 25: 34).

[85]Cf. above, pp. 203-204.

[86]Miss. Exp. Cod. I et II. H, 1: 258 (Matth., 20: 28. Jo. 1: 15).

[87]Ibid., pp. 258-259.

[88]Ibid., p. 259.

[89]Ibid., pp. 275-76.

[90]Ibid., p. 259.

[91]Ibid., pp. 259-60 (Matth. 14:28).

[92]Ibid.

[93]Ibid., pp. 260-61 (Luc., 10: 21).

[94]Ibid., p. 261. (Ps. 97:1).

[95]H, 1: 274-281.

[96]LO 3., H, 2: 311-59.

[97]Ibid., p. 311.

[98]Ibid., pp. 311-12. (Num., 15: 2-3).

[99]LO 3., H, 2: 213 (2 Par., 29, 25, 27-29; cf. below, pp.295-296).

[100]LO 3., H, 2: 313. (Ex., 30: 18-20).

[101]LO 3., H, 2: 313.

361

[102]Cf. above, pp. 74-78, 79-80, 100-102.

[103]LO 3., H, 2: 314.

[104]Cf. above, pp. 84ff. and 97ff.

[105]LO 3., H, 2: 314. (Enar. in ps. 128, 13. PL 37: 1695).

[106]LO 3., H, 2: 314.

[107]Ibid., p. 314-15.

[108]Ibid., p. 315.

[109]Ibid., (Matth., 21:9; Marc., 11:10).

[110]LO 3., H, 2: 315.

[111]Ibid., p. 316.

[112]Ibid., p. 317.

[113]Ibid., p. 327.

[114]It seems obvious that the two layers of singing signify a deepening of meaning and understanding. It is carried here on a deeper level than was expressed in the Byzantine and Gallican liturgies. Cf. above, pp. 191-192.

[115]LO 3., H, 2: 318.

[116]Ibid., (Beda, de Tabernaculo, 1.3.14 PL, 91: 496-97).

[117]LO 3., H, 2: 310.

[118]Ibid., pp. 320-21.

[119]Ibid., p. 321.

[120]Ibid., p. 322. (II. Par., 29: 28-29; Ps. 19: 3-5.) Cf. below, pp. 330ff.

[121]Cf. above, pp. 290-291.

[122]LO 3., H, 2: 373.

[123]In Liber de ordine antiphonarii, H, 3: 102-04, Amalarius deals with the different biblical figures, especially with Job, Tobias, Judith and Esther, the three young men in the furnace, etc. The description which Amalarius gives there is as follows: "Job de gentili populo electus est, Tobias in captivitate meruit probari et probatus inveniri, utrique propter cornam patientiae flagellati, utrique probati inventi per patientiam. Idcirco memoria eorum coniunctim et in uno mense celebratur . . . idcirco responsorii de Iob et Tobia infirmis in septembri mense canuntur, ut aegrotantes in eo discant iuxta exemplum beatorum patrum Iob et Tobia flagella Dei patienter tolerare. . . " (p. 102).

[124]LO 3., H, 2: 323.

[125]Ibid.

[126]Ibid., pp. 323-324, 331-35, 337.

[127]H, 1: 291-338. Cf. above, p. 188-189.

[128]LO 3., H, 2: 323-24.

[129]Ibid., p. 324.

[130]Ibid., pp. 324-25.

[131]Ibid., p. 327.

[132]Ibid., p. 329.

[133]Ibid., p. 327.

[134]Ibid., (Luc., 22:25-27).

[135]Ibid., pp. 327-28.

[136] Ibid., p. 328.

[137] Ibid., (Gregorius, M. Moralia, 1. XVI, 49, 57. PL, 75: 1068B-1069A).

[138] LO 3., H, 2: 329-337. (The use of the word electi was later used against Amalarius when his works were condemned. It seems, however, that this word should be interpreted as saints or the chosen ones rather than in the sense of "pre-destination").

[139] LO 3., H, 2: 355.

[140] Ibid., pp. 329-30.

[141] Ibid., p. 330. (Beda, In Lucae evangelium expositio, 1.6.22. PL, 92: 599).

[142] LO 3., H, 2: 330-31.

[143] Cf. above, pp. 220-222.

[144] Eccl., H, 3: 253 (Luc. 23:28).

[145] Ibid.

[146] LO 3., H, 2: 331-32. (Jer. 23: 23-24).

[147] LO 3., H, 2: 333.

[148] Miss. Exp. Cod. II, H, 1: 274.

[149] Ibid.

[150] Cf. below, p. 316.

[151] LO 3., H, 2: 336. (Luc., 22: 43-44).

[152] Ibid., pp. 331-32. (Jer., 23: 23-24).

[153] Ibid., pp. 336-37. (Matth. 26: 46).

[154] LO 1., H, 2: 96. (Ordo Romanus I., Suppl., 34 [Andrieu: I]). Michael Andrieu, Les Ordines Romani du haut moyen age, 5 vols. Specilegium Sacrum Lovaniense, 11, 23, 24, 28, 29 (Louvain: Specilegium Sacrum Lovaniense Administration, 1931-61). 2: (1948): 3-108.

[155] Most conspicuous is the motive of the garments in this scene. For the motive of the undivided garments, cf., the Gallican liturgy, above, pp. 102-103.

[156] LO 3., H, 2: 334-35 (Augustin de Civitate Dei 1.X.c.5. and c.19. PL, 41: 282, 297).

[157] LO 3., H, 2: 337-359.

[158] Ibid., p. 337.

[159] Ibid., p. 339.

[160] Cf. above, pp. 213ff.

[161] LO 3., H, 2: 340.

[162] Ibid., p. 340.

[163] Ibid., pp. 341-42.

[164] Ibid., p. 342.

[165] Ibid.

[166] Ibid., pp. 342-43.

[167] Ibid., p. 343.

[168] Ibid., p. 350.

[169] Ibid., p. 344. (Augustin in Ioannis evangelium tractatus, 120.2. PL, 35: 1953.)

^{170}<u>LO</u> 3., <u>H</u>, 2: 344.

^{171}Ibid., p. 345.

^{172}Ibid., (Beda <u>In Luc.</u>, 1.6.23. <u>PL</u>, 92: 620C.)

^{173}<u>LO</u> 3., <u>H</u>, 2: 345.

^{174}Ibid., (Luc., 23: 50-53).

^{175}<u>LO</u> 3., <u>H</u>, 2: 345-46.

^{176}Cf. above, pp. 64-94.

^{177}Cf. above, pp. 74-75.

^{178}<u>LO</u> 3., <u>H</u>, 2: 346.

^{179}Ibid., (John., 19: 39-40).

^{180}<u>LO</u> 3., <u>H</u>, 2: 346-47.

^{181}Ibid., p. 347. (John., 19: 6-7). Cf. regarding the <u>topos</u> of the shroud, above, pp. 69, 102, 104.

^{182}<u>LO</u> 3., <u>H</u>, 2: 347. (Beda <u>In Luc.</u>, 1.6.23., <u>PL</u>, 92: 622B)

^{183}<u>LO</u> 3., <u>H</u>, 2: 348.

^{184}Ibid., p. 346. (Beda, <u>In Luc.</u>, 1.6.23, <u>PL</u>, 92: 621A).

^{185}Cf. above, pp. 66ff. and 321ff.

^{186}It is not possible to deal in this work with the thick symbolism which developed around the figure of Joseph of Arimathea and his Garden linking both the Garden of Eden and the New Garden of Paradise. See for this especially the works of Professor Mircea Eliade.

^{187}<u>LO</u> 3., <u>H</u>, 2: 347.

[188]Ibid., pp. 350-57.

[189]Ibid., p. 357. (Cyprianus *Liber de oratione dominica*, 27-28, PL, 4: 537C-538A).

[190]Ibid., p. 349.

[191]Ibid., p. 349-350. (*Ordo Rom.*, II, 11. PL, 78: 974C-975A; A:V) Andrieu, *Les Ordines*, 2: 193-227.

[192]Cf. above, pp. 89-92.

[193]Cf. above, pp. 330ff.

[194]LO 3., H, 2: 351.

[195]Ibid.

[196]Ibid., p. 352.

[197]Ibid.

[198]LO 3., H, 2: 56-7.

[199]LO 3., H, 2: 351.

[200]Ibid., p. 353.

[201]Ibid., pp. 353-54. (Luc. 24: 17).

[202]Cf. above, p. 330.

[203]Ibid., p. 355.

[204]Ibid., p. 357.

[205]Ibid., pp. 359-72.

[206]Ibid., p. 359.

[207]Ibid., pp. 359-60. (Beda, In Luc., 1.6.24, PL, 29: 623C-624A).

[208]Cf. above, pp. 68ff and 72ff.

[209]LO 1, H, 2: 159-60. (Marc., 16: 6-8).

[210]Ibid., p. 160. (Beda In Marci evangelium expositio 1.4.16., PL, 92: 297AB).

[211]LO 1., H, 2: 160.

[212]Ibid., p. 161.

[213]Ibid.

[214]LO 3., H, 2: 360.

[215]Again, as I indicated above, pp. 329f., n. 186, a study of the interrelationships of the dominant symbols, here the manger and the tomb, in the context of the history of religions would most likely render rich results and would further the understanding of Christian liturgical drama.

[216]Ibid., p. 361.

[217]Ibid., p. 362.

[218]Ibid., p. 362.

[219]Eclogae, H, 3: 260.

[220]LO 3., H, 2: 362.

[221]Ibid.

[222]Miss. Exp. Cod. I., H, 1: 263-64.

[223]LO 1., H, 2: 161.

[224]LO 3., H, 2: 364-65.

[225] Ecl. H, 3: 258-59.

[226] LO 3., H, 2: 362-63 (Ordo Rom., II, 12-13, PL, 78: 975A-C; A:V).

[227] LO 3., H, 2: 363.

[228] Ibid., p. 363.

[229] Ibid., p. 363. (Liber Pontificalis LXXXVI. edit. Duchesne, p. 376).

[230] Ibid., p. 365.

[231] Ecl., H, 3: 258.

[232] H, 1: 263 (Matth. 26-28).

[233] Ibid., (Luc., 24: 13-21).

[234] H, 1: 263.

[235] Ibid., p. 264.

[236] Ibid.

[237] LO 1., H, 2: 161. (Joh., 20: 12-17).

[238] LO 3., H, 2: 368.

[239] Ecl., H, 3: 264.

[240] LO 3., H, 2: 370 (John, 17: 24, 12: 26).

[241] Ibid., p. 371.

369

CHAPTER VI

GENERAL SUMMARY, CONCLUSION AND PROSPECTUS

Summary

As an introductory basis for our investigation we studied in the first chapter the religiosity of the Roman tradition which concentrated primarily around the Emperor and the Cult of Victory. It was then pointed out how the Roman theatre dedicated to Venus was deeply rooted in the religious origin and cult of the Roman state. Proceeding from this basis of Roman religiosity, we then analyzed various Patristic texts from both the Fathers of the Western and of the Eastern Church. In addition to these texts, we also examined various documents of decrees from Church Councils and Synods. As a result of our textual analysis we were able to show that the denunciation of the theatre by the Church Fathers was rooted in the general polemics of the Church against idololatria. The theological groundings for this negative disposition were especially demonstrated on the basis of three major texts by Tertullian. We were further able to show that the tradition of this theology had already begun with the Apologists, who conceived the pagan gods to be fallen, apostatic angelic powers. In their view, these fallen angels had succeeded in deceiving poets, philosphers and Emperors alike with their lies, declaring themselves to be gods and ensnaring mankind into their adoration. Therefore, the entire pagan culture was from the religious point of view of the early Church saturated with one great idololatria at the root of which were the fallen angelic powers. Consequently, this culture was for the doctors of the early Church an expression not of the world of truth as created by God but one of perversion and falsehood, i.e., the work of the fallen angelic powers. We then pointed out that the Christians belonged to the heretics of the Roman state constituting a danger for its sacred tradition. The relentless negation of the theatre by the Church Fathers should therefore, I argued, not only be considered as primarily a moral exhortation but it should also be viewed as part of a great religious conflict. This conflict between Roman and Christian religions --between Romanitas and Christianitas--found public expression culminating in the struggle surrounding the Altar of Victory. The 3rd Relatio of Symmachus and the letters 17, 18 and 57 of Bishop Ambrose of Milan are further evidence of this official conflict over the right religion. We then called attention to the fact that in the polemical writings of the Church Fathers, a dialetic of two theatres began to emerge. They exhorted about a theatrum daemonicum and a theatrum infictitium et spirituale. During this conflict the Roman theatre of the daemons, as it was described from the time of the Apologists onward, found its positive spatial counterparts in the architecture of churches and basilicas as well as in the aesthetic-objective representational forms of the Christian drama of salvation representing a realization of the true world of God. The result of our research of the first chapter placed the Church Fathers and their negative attitude toward the Roman theatre into a different perspective. This aroused my curiosity and my further research led me to explore the liturgical texts which had developed since the First Liturgical Act of Jesus; these texts began to formalize around the Jewish synaxis and Christian Eucharist. Thus I have been trying to attempt to shed light, from a different perspective, on the complexity of the two phenomena which were studied in our investigation: the polemics of the Church Fathers against the Roman theatre on the one hand and that of the simultaneous development of the Christian liturgical drama on the other.

In our second chapter we explored the Judaeo-Christian liturgical tradition. Beginning with the tradition of the text of the Last Supper—the First Liturgical Act of Jesus—I analyzed various liturgical texts in chronological order until 750 A.D. I was able to show that the peregrinatio of a Spanish woman named Aetheria, belongs to the earliest documents which describe the representations of the events of the Passion at the very historical sites of their occurrences. Then we were able to document from the various Church Orders descriptions of configurational representations of the First Liturgical Act of Jesus and a positional symbolism signifying a hierarchical invisible order. It was obvious that fans of linen or peacock feathers received spiritual meaning, alluding to wings of the cherubim. Sindon, linteum and sudarium had also, since the fourth century, symbolic-dramatic meaning, representing the shroud in which Jesus was buried. Especially illuminating was the material of the <u>Mystagogical Catechism</u> of Theodore of Mopsuestia and Narsai in which the art of narration combined with the power of the imagination of the Syrians seem to have enriched the dramatic representations of the Passion and Resurrection. Local customs and mystical experiences found integral expressions in these representational configurations. Furthermore, it seemed to me that Tatian's <u>Gospel-Harmony</u> (<u>Diatessaron</u>) had fundamentally influenced the structure of the liturgical dramatic tradition. The allegorical-dramatic evidence of the above variants of which appear in the Byzantine liturgy, in the Gallican texts and later with Amalarius in the Carolingian Empire, can be summarized as follows: <u>sindon</u>, <u>linteum</u> and <u>sudarium</u>, symbolizing the Passion, the Burial and Resurrection of Jesus; the altar in its manifold meaning and signification representing the historical Jerusalem, from which the actual Word of Jesus proceeded, the Cross, the Tomb, the Heavenly Jerusalem, Paradise of the new creation, the heavenly throne of the Most High; personification of angels by deacons, symbolizing freedom in the service of Christ; positional symbolism corresponding to the constellation of the Last Supper, the Deposition from the Cross, the burial site in the Garden of Joseph of Arimathea; a <u>gestus</u> <u>allegoricus</u> which consisted of complex and subtle gestures which could evoke the entire Passion story, the harrowing of hell, the fear of the apostles and disciples, the searching of the angels and of the women, the working of the Holy Spirit; Jews and other figures and themes which would not be positively in congruence with the history of salvation were alluded to by their very absence; the <u>topos</u> of the burial scene in relation to Joseph of Arimathea and Nicodemus; songs, candles, incense censor, and other objects. All these means of representation were evidence of a rich liturgical drama in the Syriac traditions of Edessa and Nisibis. The sermons of Saint Chrysostom were most informative about the liturgy in Antioch as he described and denounced the theatrical manners and behavior of the worshippers; such manners had obviously been transposed from the theatre of Antioch to the church in that city. These texts especially bespeak the close affinity between the Roman theatre and the Christian liturgical drama in its earliest stages of development. My analysis showed further that the Byzantine liturgy, based on several traditions,

373

was very complex. In the liturgy of Constantinople (and later Ravenna), the structure of the Greek drama, Syriac figurativeness, allegorical scriptural exegesis of the Alexandrians, the hierarchical structure of the world-view of Ps.-Dionysius the Aeropagite and the vision of Roman political universalism were fused together in a great coherent configuration of a liturgical drama. Most conspicuous in this liturgy were complex spatial dimensions which were interpreted to be essential dramatic components because they were the means by which the dimensions of salvation history were primarily represented. The intricacy of interior and exterior spaciousness seems to have distinguished this Byzantine liturgical drama from the Syriac representational forms. The liturgical dramatic texts of the Patriarch Germanos of Constantinople especially reflected a structure deeply embedded in a figurative Weltanschauung. From the texts of the Western liturgies, the Gallican Missae Expositionis was most informative; it also indicated a unique flexibility of this liturgy. Although this liturgical text belonged to the radius of the liturgy of the Eastern Church, it obviously reflected its own Western trait and point of view which was based on law, sacrifice and merit. The Gallican Missae Expositionis was in contrast to the Byzantine and Syriac liturgies not so much mystically oriented as much as it had primarily an eschatological orientation. The long and frequent triumphal songs of this liturgy were combined with figurative representations. The second chapter then concludes with a brief discussion of the texts of the Roman liturgy such as the libelli and the first sacramentaries, i.e., the Leoniamun, Gelasianum, and Gregorianum and their relationship to the Gallican mixed liturgies. The abundant source material of this chapter is evidence for the dramatic mode of the liturgy the source of which is the plot of the First Liturgical Act, the narrative of the Life of Jesus and the entire cosmological scope of salvation history.

In the third chapter of this study, I attempted to explore the traditions of the allegorical mode of interpretation of the four senses of Scripture because they seemed to be an integral part of the dramatic liturgy. The study of this perplexing phenomenon which signifies a complex and manifold structure of the cosmos closely interwoven with the world of signs, necessarily had to remain an initial attempt. In this chapter our approach was also chronological. Selected texts of Greek and Latin Patristic sources with special consideration of Augustine's signum-res-schema were analyzed in this chapter.

The fourth chapter introduces the liturgical reform of Pepin, Charlemagne and Alcuin. It then gives a biographical sketch of Amalarius of Metz and discusses his works in chronological order. Through the analysis of Amalarius' early works, Missae Expositionis Codex I et II (which he composed during his journey from Constantinople), it became evident that there existed an affinity between the structure of this liturgy and that of the Byzantine and Gallican liturgies which I had examined in chapter two. The subsequent, careful study of his main work, the Liber Officialis, indicated that it was based on the very structure of the Missae Expositionis. It was also obvious that Amalarius was a gifted person with poetic and artistic propensities. He was able to weave together, in a poetic-mystical vision, different traditions and new modes of perception which resulted in an aesthetic configurational form of liturgical drama. In this endeavor, Amalarius was driven by a burning desire to penetrate into the essence of ratio, the ground of all things, and to lay open in representational form the sense and meaning of the First Liturgical Act. It deserves attention that Amalarius, under the cover of inspiration, molded together the structure and images of the Syriac-Byzantine liturgies, particularly the topoi-complex of the burial scene of Joseph of Arimathea and Nicodemus with the remains of the Gallican liturgy and those of the Ordo Romanus. Furthermore, we were able to show that his original contributions consisted in his vision of the four senses of Scripture as inherent in the cosmos from the beginning of creation and the integration of this fourfold vision into the entire structure of the liturgical drama. Amalarius' viewpoint was neither in conflict with his impressions he had gained in Constantinople because the Byzantine liturgy, in its figurativeness, signified already an allegorical vision nor with the signum-res-schema of St. Augustine. Amalarius' view could furthermore be related to the tradition of an organic Weltanschauung such as that of the Franks and Germanic peoples who tried to penetrate beneath the surface of the signs of their runes and of nature into the

375

deeper meaning of the cosmos. In this connection I also dealt briefly with the etymology of the German words Bild and Zeichen --bilidi and zeihhan--which correspond in the Old-High-German language to numinous cosmic powers. The last part of this chapter dealt with the condemnation of Amalarius which was primarily directed against the allegorical-figurative mode of his liturgical drama. I raised the question whether the disposition of Amalarius' opponents at the School of Lyons could not have had deeper theological reasons rather than only political ones. The source of their polemics against Amalarius could have been the iconoclastic controversy. Such a viewpoint would place Agobard, the main exponent of the School of Lyons, into the tradition of the polemics of the Church Fathers against the theatre and idololatria. At this time, however, such a controversy was carried out within the structure of the Church itself.

The fifth chapter is a detailed analysis of the dramatic-allegorical mode of Amalarius. I mainly examined his earliest work Missae expositionis Codex I et II, his great work Liber Officialis and his later work, Eclogae de Ordine Romano. From the study of the world of these texts of Amalarius of Metz, a liturgical drama emerged which was of unique aesthetic form. Nourished by a rich tradition of Eastern, Gallican and partly Roman liturgies, it had been transformed into a harmonius whole interwoven with the figurativeness of allegory. It was evident that in its structure and in its figurative language this liturgical drama showed a close affinity with other works of Old-High-German literature of that same period. The rich figurative variants of the liturgical-dramatic material and the skillful mastery of the principle of simultaneity with which interrelationships of his entire allegorical vision were specifically worked out and discussed. We were further able to show that there was a close relationship and interaction between singing and representational forms.

Conclusion

Out of the Act and Words of the Last Supper combined with the biblical material and the figure of Christ, a new dramatic reality had developed which renewed itself in a transformed

structure of configurational forms in constantly moving interrelationships of subtle nuances, symbolic-allegorical allusions,
personifications, double and multiple roles, gestures, songs,
silence, positional, communal and directive symbolism, change of
place and above all spatial expansion and temporal compression.
We argued that these means of representation were in congruence
with the long stream of tradition of liturgical drama which we
discussed in chapter two.

In such representational forms of liturgical drama it seems
that _mimesis_ not only unfolded as the highest form of worship--
as Lactantius had already indicated--but moreover, that
mimesis was essentially the very aesthetic expression, the
creative factor in the shaping of liturgical drama. From this
inner relationship between plot and _mimesis_ arose a form of
liturgical drama which can claim, I have argued, to be a genre
of its own within the Christian literary corpus. The _Quem_
Quaeritis tropes and the subsequent individual Passion and
Easter plays which developed after that are, I would further
argue, only partial themes of a dramatic whole which expressed
the entire drama of salvation. Perhaps these later plays,
beginning with the _Quem-Quaeritis_ tropes, are an expression of
another epoch. They do, however, not merit to be considered as
the beginning of modern Western drama _per se_ but rather they
should be viewed and studied in a larger cultural context and
within the stream of tradition of the Roman theatre. But even
if such a claim for a unique definition of liturgical drama
would need further verification, then I think that it could be
successfully submitted to other aesthetic criteria. For
example, Aristotle in his _Poetics_ considered the _mythos_ to be
the most essential part of drama. In modern times, Brecht in
his aesthetics of the epic theatre comes closest to the description of the components for liturgical drama as I found them in
our study. Furthermore, he considered gestures, the V-effect
and an audience as essential to epic theatre. Yet, already
Augustine considered the _gestus allegoricus_ as an important
means for the actor in the Roman theatre. It is also
significant that the oldest extant plays, the texts of which
were discovered in Egypt, are also of epic-liturgical nature.

Whether one proceeds to let liturgical drama speak out of

377

its own aesthetic norms attempting to grasp it from within its own structure as I have tried to do in our present study, or whether one wishes to methodically apply other external criteria, i.e., those of Aristole or Brecht, the result of our study justifies the proposition that liturgical drama of the ninth century in Western Christendom, as it has been preserved in the works of Amalarius of Metz, be considered as a unique aesthetic achievement, based on a rich dramatic tradition. For this reason, the history of drama deserves to be studied from different perspectives as it has hitherto been the case.

Prospectus

During our journey through these different textual traditions of liturgical drama another dimension began to disclose itself. I began to see liturgical drama also in connection with the first extant expressions of Old-High-German (and old Saxon) literature, especially the Gospel-Harmonies, based on Tatian's Diatessaron, and other literary fragments of that corpus. Content, metaphors, symbols and structures of these precious texts would perhaps be more fully accessible if liturgical drama were considered to be an integral part of Old-High-German literature.

Furthermore, it has been long argued that the Germanic peoples had no drama and no theatre. For this reason, at the closure of this study, I would like to draw another perspective into the discussion: We have noted that singing belonged to the most essential structural means of liturgical drama. It is therefore most interesting that recent results of scholarship consider Shamanistic rites as the origin of the theatre on the grounds that music, songs, dialogues, personification, an audience and numinous powers are its very components. But most important, Shamanistic rites belong also to the Germanic religious and spiritual heritage; also singing is inherently a trait of Germanic nature. A hypothesis that there might be an affinity between liturgical drama and Shamanism and that on the grounds of this affinity the Germanic peoples might have had their own indigenous theatre might not be too far-fetched. Further studies, research and re-thinking of this problem from the viewpoint of the history of religions and hermeneutics might

378

shed a different light on the possibility of a Germanic
dramatic-theatrical tradition which perhaps was transformed and
continued in the tradition of the liturgical drama of Amalarius
of Metz.

APPENDIX

This is an additional text of the topos of the deposition
from the Cross with Joseph of Arimathea as the main actor as
preserved in Eclogae: De ordine romano, H, 3: 257-58:

. . . Cum ipsam crucem videt diaconus
facere et incipere, calicem exaltare
vadit, et tent calicem simul cum epis-
copo exaltatum, usque dum dicit: "Per
omnia saecula saeculorum", et postea ponit
calicem in altare, et involvit eum sudario. Nempe Joseph, accepto corpore
posuit illud in monumento suo. Hunc prae-
sentem diaconum propter conveniens minis-
terium in typo ponimus Joseph, sive gene-
raliter in typo erorum qui casto corde
mysteria Christi suscipiunt. Diaconus
siquidem, qui tenet calicem exaltatum cum
pontifice, ponit illum in altare, quia
Joseph deposuit de cruce corpus dominicum,
et posuit in monumentum. Diaconus sicut
dicimus, involvit cum sudario calicem,
quoniam Joseph involvit in sindone munda.
In ipso altari, id est in sepulchro,
corporale iacet. Per quod intellegitur
ipsum linteum maius quo totum corpus
Domini tegebatur in sepulchro. Et per
illud quod aliquam partem calicis tegit,
sudarium intellegimus quod aliquam partem
capitis Domini tegebat, et aliquam non
tegebat, sicut mos Iudeis est facere. Et
remanet in altari, id est in sepulchro, hoc
opus, usque dum tria capitula compleantur,
id est prologus de oratione sequenti,
"Pater noster" et "libera nos," quaesumus,
"Domine." Etenim tres dies in sepulchor Dominus
quievit.

SELECTED BIBLIOGRAPHY

Series of Critical Text Editions

Corpus Christianorum seu nova Patrum Collectio (=CC).
Turnhouti, 1953.

Corpus Scriptorum Ecclesiasticorum Latinorum (=CSEL). Wien,
1866.

Corpus Scriptorum Christianorum Orientalium (=CSEO). Louvain,
1951.

Liber Pontificalis. MGH, A.D. 500-1500. Berlin, 1898.

Mansi, J. D. Sacrorum Conciliorum, Nova et Amplissima
Collectio (=Mansi). 31 vols. Florenz-Venedig, 1757-98.
Neudruck und Fortsetzung herausgegeben von L. Petit and
J. B. Martin. 60 vols. Paris, 1844-64.

Migne, J. - P. Patrologiae Cursus Completus: Series Latina
(=PL). 221 vols. Paris, 1857-66.

————. Patrologicae Cursus Completus: Series Graeca
(=PG). 162 vols. Paris, 1857-66.

Monumenta Germaniae Historica. Berlin, 1821- (=MGH).
Abteilungen:
Auctores Antiquissimi. (=Auct. ant.)
Capitularia Regum Francorum. (=Cap.)
Concilia Aevi Karolini. (=Conc.)
Epistolae. (=Ep.)
Scriptores. (=SS)
Poetae Avi Karolini. (=Poet.)
Scriptores Rerum Merovingicarum.
(=SS rer. mer.)

Recueil des historiens des Gauls et de la France. 24 vols
Paris, 1738-1904.

Sources Chrétiennes. Paris, 1942-

383

Translations

Ancient Christian Writers: The Work of the Fathers in
Translation. Edited by Johannes Quasten et al.
New York: Newman Press (Bookshop) 1946-

Ante-Nicene Fathers: Translation of the Writings of
Fathers down to A.D. 325. Edited by Alexander Roberts
and James Donaldson. American Reprint of the
Edinburgh edition. Revised and chronologically arranged
with brief prefaces and occasional notes by A. C. Coxe.
Grand Rapids, Michigan: Wm. B. Eerdmans Publishing Co.,
1950.

The Apostolic Fathers: A New Translation and Commentary. 6 vols
Robert M. Grant, general editor. New York and Camden:
Nelson and Sons, 1964-68.

Bibliothek der Kirchenväter (=BKV^2). Herausgegeben von O.
Bardenhewer, Th. Scherman (ab Band 35 von J. Zellinger)
und C. Weymann. 83 Bde. Kempten und München, 1911-

Bibliothek der Kirchenväter (=BKV). Herausgegeben von F. X.
Reithmayer, fortgesetzt von V. Talhöfer. 79 Bde. Kempten,
1869-88.

The Fathers of the Church: A New Translation. Editorial Director
Ludwig Schopp. New York: CIM Publishing Co., Inc., 1948-

Hefele, Carl-Joseph von, et Leclercq, Henri. Histoire des
Conciles. Nouvelle traduction corrigée et augmentée. 22
vols. Paris: Letouzey et Ané, 1908-52.

Loeb Classical Library. Edited by J. E. page and W. H. D. Rouse.
New York: Macmillan Co., 1913-

384

Lexica and Dictionaries

Althochdeutsches Wörterbuch. Bearbeitet und herausgegeben von
Elisabeth Karg-Gasterstädt und Theodor Frings. Berlin:
Akademie-Verlag, 1962.

Arndt, W. F. and Gingrich, F. W. A Greek-English Lexicon of
New Testament and Other Early Christian Literature. 13th
edition. Chicago: University of Chicago Press, 1971.

Atlas zur Kirchengeschichte: Die christliche Kirche in
Geschichte und Gegenwart. Herausgegeben von Hubert Jedin
et al. Freiburg: Herder, 1970.

Catholic Encyclopedia. 6th edition.

Dekkers, Eligius. Clavis Patrum Latinorum. Editio altera.
Steenbrugis: Abbatia Sancti Petri, 1961.

Dictionnaire d'Archéologie Chrétienne et de Liturgie. (=DACL).
15 vols. Publie par Fernand Cabrol et Henri Leclercq.
Paris: Letouzey et Ané, 1907-51.

Encyclopedia Britannica. 1971 edition.

Graff, E. G. Althochdeutscher Sprachschatz. (=Graff). 6 Bde.
Reprographischer Nachdruck der Ausgabe Berlin, 1940.
Darmstadt: Wissenschaftliche Buchgesellschaft, 1963.

Grimm, Jacob und Grimm, Wilhelm. Deutsches Wörterbuch. 16 Bde.
Leipzig: Verlag von S. Hirzel, 1854-1938.

Jerusalem Bible. (=JB). 1966 edition.

Kluge, Friedrich. Etymologisches Wörterbuch der deutschen
Sprache. 20. Auflage bearbeitet von Walter Mitzka.
Berlin: Walter de Gruyter & Co., 1967.

Kobler, Gerhard. Lateinisch-Althochdeutsches Wörterbuch.
Göttingen: Musterschmidt Verlag, 1971

Krumbacher, K. Geschichte der byzantinischen Litteratur von Justinian bis zum Ende des ostromischen Reiches. 2 Bde., 2. Aufl. New York: Burt Franklin, 1958.

Lewis, C. T. and Short, C. S. A Latin Dictionary. Revised and enlarged edition. Oxford: At the Clarendon Press, 1966.

Lexikon fur Theologie und Kirche. (=LThK). Zweite vollig neubearbeitete Auflage. Herausgegeben von Joseph Hofer und Karl Rahner. Freiburg: Verlag Herder, 1957-65.

Liddell, H. G. and Scott, R. A. A Greek-English Lexicon. New 9th edition. Oxford: At the Clarendon Press, 1968.

Manitius, M. Geschichte der lateinischen Literatur des Mittelalters. 3 Bde. Munchen: C. H. Beck, 1911-31.

McKenzie, John L. Dictionary of the Bible. Milwaukee: The Bruce Publishing Co., 1965.

Rahner, Karl und Vorgrimler, Herbert. Kleines Theologisches Worterbuch. Freiburg, i. Br.: Herder Bucherei, 1967.

Reallexikon fur Antike und Christentum: Sachworterbuch zur Auseinandersetzung des Christentums mit der antiken Welt. (=RAC). Herausgegeben von Theodor Klauser et al. Stuttgart: Hiersemann Verlag GMBH, 1950-

Die Religion in Geschichte und Gegenwart: Handworterbuch fur Theologie und Religionswissenschaft (=RGG). 3. vollig neu-bearbeitete Auflage. Herausgegeben von Kurt Galling et al. 6 Bde. Tubingen: J. C. B. Mohr (Paul Siebeck), 1957-62.

Schmid, Wilhelm und Stahlin, Otto. Geschichte der griechischen Literatur. Handbuch der Altertumswissenschaft, Nr. 7. Munchen: C. H. Beck, 1929.

Primary Sources

Agobard of Lyons. Contra libros quattour Amalarii abbatis. PL, 104: 339-350.
Liber de correctione antiphonarii. PL, 329-340.
Liber contra eorum superstitionem qui picturis et imaginibus sanctorum adorationis obsequium deferendum putant. PL, 104: 199-228.

Amalarius of Metz. Amalarii Episcopi Opera Liturgica Omnia. (=H). 3 vols. Edited by Ioannes M. Hanssens. Citta del Vaticana: Biblioteca Apostolica Vaticana, 1948.
Epistula ad Petrum abbatem Nonantulanum. H, 1: 227-31.
Epistula ad Carolum imperatorem de scrutinio et baptismo. H, 1: 236-51.
Missae expositionis geminus codex. Cod. I et II. H, 1: 254-81.
Canonis missae interpretatio. H, 1: 283-338.
Epistula ad Hilduinum abbatem de diebus ordinationis et quattour temporum. H, 1: 339-58.
Prologus antiphonarii. H, 1: 359-63.
"Embolis opusculorum meorum". H, 1: 365-90.
Liber Officialis. H, 2: 580 pp.
Liber de ordine antiphonarii. H, 3: 13-109.
Eclogae: De ordine romano. H, 3: 225-65.
Versus marini. MGH: Poeta 1: 426-28.

Ambrosius De Abraham. PL, 14: 441-524.
De Cain et Abel. PL, 14: 333-380.
Enarrationes in Psalmo 36. PL, 14: 1011-56.
Enarrationes in Psalmo 118. CSEL, 62.
Expositio in evangelium Lucam. CC, 14.
De Sacramentis et de Mysteriis. CSEL, 73: 1-116.

Anscharii Vita. Recueil des Historians des Gauls et de la France. 6: 304, 598.

Andrieu, Michel. Les "Ordines Romani" du Haut Moyen Age.

(=<u>Andrieu</u>). 5 vols. Spicilegium Sacrum Lovaniense 11, 23, 24, 18, 29. Louvain: Spicilegium, Administration, 1931-61.

Aristoteles <u>Erste Analytik</u>.
  <u>Poetik</u>.
  <u>Rhetorik</u>.
  <u>Aristoteles: Die Lehrschriften</u>. Herausgegeben, ubertragen und in ihrer Entstehung erlautert von Dr. Paul Gohlke. Paderborn: Verlag Ferdinand Schoeningh, 1951.

Arnobius <u>Adversus Nationes</u>. <u>CSEL</u>, 4.

Augustinus <u>De Civitate Dei</u>. <u>CC</u>, 47-48.
  <u>Confessiones</u>. <u>CSEL</u>, 33 .
  <u>De Consensu Evangelistarum</u>. <u>CSEL</u>, 43.
  <u>De Doctrina Christiana</u>. <u>CC</u>, 31.
  <u>De Epistola 120</u>. <u>CSEL</u>, 24.
  <u>De Genesi ad Litteram, liber imperfectus</u>. <u>PL</u>, 34: 330-46.
  <u>De Genesi Contra Manichaeos</u>. <u>PL</u>, 34: 173-220.
  <u>De Genesi ad Litteram. Libri duodecimus</u>. <u>PL</u>, 34: 246-466.
  <u>Johannes Tractatus</u>. <u>PL</u>, 35: 1977-2062.
  <u>De Magistro</u>. <u>CSEL</u>, 77: 3-55.
  <u>Enarratione in Ps. 103</u>. <u>CC</u>, 40.
  <u>Sermo 241</u>. <u>PL</u>, 38: 1133-35.
  <u>De Trinitate</u>. <u>PL</u>, 42: 819-1098.
  <u>De Utilitate Credendi</u>. <u>CSEL</u>, 25: 1-48.
  <u>De Vera Religione</u>. <u>CC</u>, 31.

Basileios Magnos <u>Liturgia</u>. <u>PG</u>, 31: 1630-56.

Barrow, R. H., Editor. <u>Prefect and Emperor: The Relations of Symmachus, A. D. 384</u>. With translation, introduction and notes. Oxford: At the Clarendon Press, 1973.

Beda Venerabilis <u>De Tabernaculo vasis eius</u>. <u>PL</u>, 91: 393-498.

Bourque, E. Étude sur les Sacramentaries Romains. Studi di Antichitita Cristiana. vols. 20, 25. Citta del del Vaticano: Pontificio instituto di archeologia cristiana, 1949, 1958.

Brecht, Bertolt. Kleines Organon für das Theater; mit einem Nachtrag zum Kleinen Organon. Frankfurt A.M.: Suhrkamp Verlag, 1961.

Brisson, Jean-Paul. Hilaire de Poitiérs, "Traité de Mystéres." texte etabli et traduit avec intro- duction et notes. Sources Chrétiennes. Paris: Les Editions du Cerf, 1943.

Caesarius de Arles Sermones 61.3, CC, 103-04.

Carolus Magnus Capitulare de imaginibus, MGH, Conc., Epistola generalis (786-800). MGH Cap. 1: 80-81.
Admonitio generalis (23. marzo, 798). MHG Cap. 1: 52-66.

Cassianus Conlationes. PL: 49.

Cassiodorus Variarum. MGH auct. ant. 12.

Cavallin, Samuel J. Vita Sanctorum Honorati et Hilarii Episcoporum Arelatensium. Skrifter ut givna av vetenskaps-Societetem Lund.

Chrysostomus In illud vidi Dominum. PG: 56: 98-107. Adversus eos qui ecclesia relicta ad circenses ludos et theatra transfugerunt. PG, 56: 263-270.

Cyprianus De Spectaculis (Novatian). CSEL, 3: 1-13. Epistola. PL, 4: 194-452.

Clement of Alexandria Stromata. In Ante-Nicene Fathers: Translation of the Writings of the Fathers down to

A.D. 325. Edited by A. Roberts and J. Donaldson. Grand
Rapids, Michigan: Wm. B. Eerdmans Publishing Co., 1950.
Praedagogus. BKV^2
Protreptikos. BVK^2

Connolly, R. Hugh. Didascalia Apostolorum. The Syriac Version
translated and accompanied by the Verona Latin Fragment
with an introduction and notes. Oxford: At the
Clarendon Press, 1929.

Connolly, R. Hugh. The Liturgical Homilies of Narsai. Translated
from the Syriac with an Appendix by Edmund Bishop. Text
and Studies. Vol. 8, no. 1. Cambridge: At the
University Press, 1909.

Cooper, James and MacLean, A. J. The Testament of our Lord.
Edited and translated. Edinburgh: T. T. Clark, 1902.

Dix, Gregory. The Apostolic Tradition of St. Hippolytus of
Rome. Edited and translated. 2nd edition. Reissued by
Henry Chadwick. London: S.P.C.K., 1968.

Egeria. Diary of a Pilgrimage. Translated and annotated by
George Gingras. Ancient Christian Writers Series. New
York: Newman Press, 1970.

Einhardus Annales (ad ann. 814). MGH, SS. 1: 201.

Ellison, A. Die Tragödie, "Das Leiden des Erlösers" (Christos
Paschon) angeblich vom heil. Gregorius von Nazianz. Aus
dem Griechischen ubersetzt. Leipzig: Verlag von Otto
Wiegand, 1855.

Eucher of Lyons Formulae Spiritalis Intelligentsiae. CSEL, 31:
1-62.

Falls, Thomas B. Justinus Martyr: The First Apology. The
Fathers of the Church: A New Translation. New York:
Christian Heritage, 1948.

Fisher, C. D. Cornelii Taciti Annalium. Adnotatione critica

instruxit. Oxford Classical Texts. Oxford: At the Clarendon Press, 1966.

Florus de Lyons. Opuscula adversus Amalarium. PL, 119: 7-96.

Funk, Francis X. Didascalia et Constitutiones Apostolorum. Paderborn: Ferdinand Schoeningh Verlag, 1905.

Gamber, Klaus. Ordo Antiqua Gallicanus. Der gallikanische Messritus des 6. Jahrhunderts. Regensburg: Verlag Friedrich Pustet, 1965.

Germanos Patriarch von Konstantinopel Historia Ecclesiastica et Mystica Contemplatio. PG, 98: 383-454.

Giesebrecht, W. Zehn Bucher frankischer Geschichte von Gregorius von Tours. Ubersetzt und herausgegeben von W. Giesebrecht. (Geschichtsschreiber der deutschen Vorzeit, vol. 8-9). Leipzig: Duncker, 1878.

Goethe, Johann Wolfgang von. Werke. Hamburger Ausgabe in 14 Banden. Textkritisch durchgesehen und mit Anmerkungen versehen von Erich Trunz. 2. Aufl. Hamburg: Christian Wegner Verlag, 1966. Bd. 1: Gedichte und Epen.

Grant, Robert M. Theophilus of Antioch: Ad Autolycum. Text and translation from the Greek. Oxford Early Christian Texts. Oxford: At the Clarendon Press, 1970.

Gregorius I. Moralia in Job. PL, 75: 515-PL, 76: 782. Dialogi. PL, 77: 150-430.

Gregorius Nazianzenus Orationes. PG, 35: 395-1251.

Gregorius Nyssenus Epistolae. PG, 46: 999-1108.

Hadrian I. Epistola ad Carolus Magnus. MGH, Ep., 3: 626.

Hieronymus Prologus de Homiliae in Jeremiam et Ezechielem.

————. Commentaria in Ezechielem. PL, 25: 16-490.

Hippolytos Traditio Apostolica 16.12.

Irenaeus Adversus Haereses. BKV[2]

Isidore de Séville De Viris Illustribus. PL, 83:
    1081-1106.
    De Ordine Creaturarum de Paradiso.
    PL, 83: 913-54.
    Ecclesiasticis Officiis. PL, 83: 737-826.
    Etymologiarum. PL, 82: 74-727.
    Sententiarum. PL, 83: 537-738.

Isidori Pelusiotae Epistola 123: Explicatio Ecclesiasticae
    initiationis. PG, 78: 264-66.

Itinearium Egeria (Peregrinatio Aetheriae). 5. verbesserte und
    erweiterte Auflage herausgegeben von Otto Prinz.
    Heidelberg: Carl Winter Universitätsverlag, 1960.

Juvenal Satires. Loeb Classical Library.

Klein, Richard. Der Streit um den Viktoriaaltar: Die dritte
    Relatio des Symmachus und die Briefe 17, 18, und 57
    des Mailänder Bischofs Ambrosius. Einführung, Text,
    Übersetzung und Erläuterung. Texte zur Forschung, Nr. 7.
    Darmstadt: Wissenschaftliche Buchgesellschaft, 1972.

Klose, Dietrich. Cicero in Catilinam. Herausgegeben und
    übersetzt von D. Kose. Stuttgart: Reclam, 1972.

Lactantius Divinae Institutiones. CSEL, 19.

Liber Pontificalis. MGH, 1: 51.

Lietzmann, Hans. Das Sakramentarium Gregorianum nach dem
    Aachener Uexempler. Münster, i.W.: Aschendorff'sche
    Verlagsbuchhandlung, 1921.

Leidrad of Lyons. Epistula ad Carolum imperatorum. MGH, ep. 2:
    541-3.

LeLoir, Louis. Saint Ephrem Commentaire de l'évangele concordant. Version Armenienne traduit. CSEO, 145. Scriptores Armeniaci. t. 2. Louvain: Imprémerie Orientaliste, L. Durbecq, 1954.

Maximos Confessor Mystagogia. PG, 91: 657-718.

McCauley, Leo P. and Stephenson, Anthony. The Works of Saint Cyrille of Jerusalem. Edited and translated. 2 vols. The Fathers of the Church: A new translation. Washington: Catholic University Press of America, 1969.

Morin, Germain. Editor. Sancti Caesarii episcopi Arelatensis Opera Omnia. 2 vols. Maretioli, 1937.

Mingana, A. Theodore of Mopsuestia: Commentary on the Lord's Prayer and on the Sacraments of Baptism and the Eucharist. Woodbroke Studies Nr. 6. Christian Documents edited and translated with a critical apparatus by A. Mingana. Cambridge: W. Heffer and Sons, Ltd., 1933.

Mohlberg, Leo C., Herausgeber. Missale Gothicum: Rerum Ecclesiasticarum Documenta, Series Maior: Fontes 5. Roma: Casa Editrice Herder, 1961.

Mohlberg, Leo C., Eisenhöfer, L. und Siffrin, P., Herausgeber. Missale Gallicanum Vetus. Rerum Ecclesiasticarum Documenta, Series Maior: Fontes 3. Roma: Casa Editrice Herder, 1958.

———. Missale Francorum. Rerum Ecclesiasticarum Documenta Series Maior: Fontes 2. Roma: Casa Editrice Herder, 1957.

Mone, J. Lateinische und griechische Messen aus dem 2. bis 6. Jahrhundert. Frankfurt A. M.: C. B. Lizius, 1851.

Moss, C. "Jacob of Serugh's Homelies on the Spectacles of the Theater," Le Muséon. Revue d'Études Orientales 48 (1935):

393

87-112.

Munier, Charles. Les "Status ecclesia antiqua." Edition-études critiques. Bibliotheque de l'institute de droit Canonique de l'université de Strassbourg. Paris: Presses Universitaire de France, 1960.

Muspilli. Bruchstücke einer althochdeutschen alliterierende Dichtung vom Ende der Welt. Herausgegeben von J. A. Schmeller, München, 1832.

Handschrift, Form und Sprache des Muspilli. Herausgegeben von Cola Minis. Philologische Studien und Quellen. Heft 35. Berlin: Erich Schmidt Verlag, 1966.

Oelman, F., Ed. Heraclitus Questiones Homericae. Leipzig: Teubner Verlag, 1910.

Ordo Romanus I. PL, 78: 937-968. (Andrieu: Ordo I.)

Ordo Romanus II. PL, 78: 569-978. (Andrieu: Ordo V.)

Origenes Contra Celsum. BKV^2
    In Joannem. PG, 14: 9-740.
    De Principiis. In Ante-Nicene Fathers:
    Translation of the Fathers down to A.D.
    325. Edited by A. Roberts and J. Donaldson. Grand
    Rapids, Michigan: Wm. B. Eerdmans Publishing Co.,
    1950.

Otfrieds Evangelienbuch. Herausgegeben von Oskar Erdmann. Fortgeführt von Edward Schröder. 5. Aufl. besorgt von Ludwig Wolff. Altdeutsche Textbibliothek, Nr. 49. Tübingen: Max Niemeier Verlag, 1965.

Pease, Arthur Stanley. Cicero Naturam Deorum. Critical annotated edition. 2 vols. Cambridge: Harvard University Press, 1955-58.

Philo of Alexandria. De Opeficio Mundi. Loeb Classical Library.
                      De Migratione Abrahami. Loeb Classical

Library.
De Vita Comtemplativa. Loeb Classical
Library.
Quod omnis probus liber sit. Loeb
Classical Library.

Piédagnel, Auguste et Paries, Pierre. _Cyrille de Jerusalem:_
Catechéses Mystagogiques. Introduction, texte critique,
et notes. Sources Chrétiennes. Paris: Le Editions du
Cerf, 1966.

Plinius _Epistula, 10_. Abgedruckt bei Carl Mirbt. _Quellen zur_
Geschichte des Papsttums. 4. Auflage. Tübingen: J. C. B.
Mohr (Paul Siebeck), 1924.

Plato _Apology_.
Protagoras.
Republic.
Timaeus.
Platos Collected Dialogues. Edited by E. Hamilton and H.
Cairns. Bollingen Series 71. 4th edition. New York:
Bollingen Foundation, 1966.

Prinz, Otto. _Itinerarium Egeria_. (Peregrinatiae Aetheriae) 5.
verbesserte und erweiterte Auflage herausgegeben von O.
Prinz. Heidelberg: Carl Winter Universitätsverlag, 1960.

Prudentius _Peristephanon_. _CSEL_, 61: 291-431.

Pseudo-Dionysius der Aeropagite. _Die Himmlischen und_
Kirchlichen Hierarchien. BKV

Richardson, Cyril C. _Early Christian Fathers_. Edited and newly
translated. The Library of Christian Classics. New York:
Macmillan Company, Paperback, 1970.

Rufinus Tyrannius Aquileia. _De Benedictionibus Patriarcharum_.
_CC_, 20: 189-222.

Quasten, J., Editor. _Expositio Antiqua Liturgicae Gallicanae_
Germano Parisiensi ascripta. Opuscula et Textus. Münster,

i.W.: Aschendorffsche Verlagsbuchhandlung, 1934.

Raabe, Richard. Die Apologie des Aristides. Aus dem Syrischen
übersetzt. Leipzig: J. C. Hinrich'sche Buchhandlung,
1892.

Salmon, Pierre. Editeur. Le Lectionnaire de Luxeuil. (Paris, Ms.
la, 9427). 2 vols. Collectanae Biblica Latina, No. 7 and
9. Roma: Abbaye Saint Jerome, 1944-53.

Salvianus De Gubernatio Dei. MGH, auct. ant., 1: 108.

Schoedel, W. R., Athenagoras, Legation and De Resurrectione.
Edited and translated with an introduction. Oxford
Classical Texts Series. Oxford: At the Clarendon Press,
1972.

Sethe, Kurt. Dramatische Texte zu altägyptischen
Mysterienspielen. Untersuchungen zur Geschichte der
Altertumskunde Ägyptens. Bd. 10. Leipzig: J. C.
Hinrich'sche Buchhandlung, 1928.

Sheldon-Williams, J. P. Ioannis Scotti Eriugenae: Periphyseon
(De Divisione Natura). 2 vols. Edited and translated with
an introduction. Scriptores Latini Hiberniae, no. 7.
Dublin: The Dublin Institute for Advanced Studies, 1968-
72.

Sidonius Carmina. PL, 58: 639-748.

Simson, Bernhard. Jahrbücher des fränkischen Reiches unter
Ludwig dem Frommen. Leipzig: Verlag V. Duncker und
Humblot, 1874-76.

Sophronios Patriarch von Jerusalem Commentarius Liturgicus
PG, 87: 3981-4004.

Sozomenus Ecclesiastical History. A History of the Church in
Nine Books from A. D. 324-440. Translated from the Greek
by Edward Walford. London: Samuel Bagster and Sons,
1846.

Stern, Henri. Le calendier de 354. Institute Francais d'
        Archéologie de Beyrouth Bibliotheque Archéologique et
        Historique, no. 55. Paris: Imprémerie Nationale,
        Librarie Orientaliste Paul Geuther, 1953.

Stoicorum Veterum Fragmenta. Edited by H. Arnim. Leipzig:
        B. G. Teubner, 1905-24.

Tatianus Diatessaron. Übersetzt und herausgegeben von Erwin
        Preuschen. Heidelberg: Carl Winter Universitäts-
        buchhandlung, 1960.

Taylor, John H. "Sancti Aureli Augustini, 'De Genesi ad
        Litteram, Liber Duodecimus.'" Edited with an
        introduction, translation and commentary. Ph.D.
        Dissertation, St. Louis Univeristy, 1948.

Tertullianus Apologeticum. CSEL, 69.
                De Baptismo. CC, 1: 277-95.
                De Paenetentia. CC, 1: 321-40.
                Adversus Marcion. CC, 1: 437-726.
                De Puditia. CSEL, 20: 30-58.
                De Idololatria. CSEL, 20: 30-58.
                De Spectaculis. CC, 1: 227-53.

Thompson, T. On the Sacraments and on the Mysteries. Edited with
        an introduction and notes by J. H. Strawley. Revised
        edition. London: S. P. C. K., 1950.

Troeltsch, Ernst. Gesammelte Werke. 1. Band. Die Soziallehren
        der christlichen Kirchen und Gruppen. 2. Neudruck der im
        Verlag J. C. B. Mohr (Paul Siebeck) 1922 erschienenen
        Ausgabe. Aalen: Scientia Verlag, 1965.

Varro De Lingua Latina. Loeb Classical Library.

Secondary Sources

Abresmann, Rudolph. O. S. A., "The 'Daemonium Meridianum' and
    Greek Latin Patristic Exegesis," Traditio 14 (1958): 17-
    31.

Alt, H. Theater und Kirche in ihrem gegenseitigen Verhàltnis.
    Berlin: Plahnsche Buchhandlung, 1840.

Altaner, Berthold und Stuiber, Alfred. Patrologie. Siebte,
    völlig neubearbeitete Auflage. Freiburg: Verlag Herder,
    1966.

Altheim, Franz. Römische Religionsgeschichte. 2 Bde. Baden-
    Baden: Verlag für Kunst und Wissenschaft, 1951-53.

Allgeier, Arthur. "Der Einfluss des Manichäismus auf die
    exegetische Fragestellung bei Augustin," in Aurelius
    Augustinus. Festschrift der Görresgesellschaft zum 1500.
    Todestag des Heiligen Augustinus. Herausgegeben von M.
    Grabmann und Joseph Mausbach. Koln: Verlag J. P. Bachem,
    GMBH, 1930.

Altweiler, A., "Hilarius, Bischof v. Poitiérs," Lexikon für
    Theologie und Kirche 5 (1960): 337.

Amiet, A. "Le prologue 'Hucusque' et la table des Capitula du
    Supplement d'Alcuin au sacramentaire grégorien,"
    Scriptorum 7 (1953): 177-209; 9 (1955): 76-84.

Arnold, C. F. Caesarius von Arelate und die gallikanische
    Kirche. Leipzig: J. C. Hinrich'sche Buchhandlung, 1894.

Auerbach, Erich. Mimesis. Translated by W. Trask. Garden City,
    New York: Doubleday & Company, Inc., Anchor Books, 1957.

Axton, Richard. European Drama of the Early Middle Ages. London:
    Hutchinson's University Library, 1974.

Bardy, G., "L'Inspiration des Péres de l'église," Recherches de

Théologie Ancienne et Médiévale 31 (1964): 5-31.

Baumstark, Anton. _Comparative Liturgy_. Revised by Bernard
    Botte. English edition by F. L. Cross. London: A. R.
    Mowbray & Co., Ltd., 1958.

———. "Nichtevangelische syrische Perikopenordnungen des
    ersten Jahrhunderts." _Liturgische Quellen_ No. 1, 1.2.
    (1921).

———. _Vom geschichtlichen Werden der Liturgie_. Freiburg,
    i. Br.: Herder & Co., GMBH Verlagsbuchhandlung, 1923.

Baynes, Normann H., _Byzantine Studies and Other Essays_. London:
    The University of London, the Athlone Press, 1960.

Berg, K., _Die Werke des hl. Caesarius von Arles als liturgie-
    geschichtliche Quelle_. Dissertationsteildruck, Pontifica
    Universitas Gregoriana. Birkeneck:
    Buchdruckerlehrwerkstätte, 1946.

Bieber, Margaret. "Kuchenformen mit Tragödienszenen," _Programm
    zum Winckelmannfeste der Archäologischen Gesellschaft_ 75
    (1915): 1-31.

———. _Die Denkmäler zum Theaterwesen im Altertum_.
    Berlin und Leipzig: Walter de Gruyter and Co., 1920.

Bishop, Edmund. "The Liturgical Reforms of Charlemagne: Their
    Meaning and Value," _Downside Review_ 38 (1919): 1-16.

———. "The Genius of the Roman Rite." in _Liturgica
    Historia_. Oxford: At the Clarendon Press, 1918.

Bishop, W. C. "The African Rite." _Journal of Theological
    Studies_ 13 (1922): 250-77.

Blair, Peter Hunter. _The World of Beda_. New York: St. Martin's
    Press, 1971.

Bornert, R., O. S. B. "Éxplication de la liturgie et inter-

prétation de l'Ecriture chez Maxime le Confesseur."
Studia Patristica 10 (1970): 323-27.

Boshof, Egon. _Erzbischof Agobard von Lyon: Leben und Werk._
Köln und Wien: Bohlau Verlag, 1969.

Bourke, Vernon J. _Augustin's Quest for Wisdom._ Milwaukee: The
Bruce Publishing Company, 1945.

Brand, C. E. _Roman Military Law._ Austin: University of Texas
Press, 1968.

Braun, Joseph. _Der christliche Altar._ München: G. Koch & Co.,
1924.

——. _Liturgisches Handlexikon._ Regensburg: J. Kosel
und F. Pustet Verlag, 1924.

Braunfels, Wolfgang. _Karl der Grosse._ 5 Bde. Düsseldorf: L.
Schwann Verlag, 1965-68.

——. _Die Welt der Karolinger und ihre Kunst._ München:
G. D. W. Calloway, 1968.

Brightman, F. E. "The Historia Mystagogia and other Greek Commentaries on the Byzantine Liturgy." _Journal of Theological Studies_, 9 (1908): 248-67, 387-97.

——. _Liturgies Eastern and Western._ London: At the
Clarendon Press, 1896.

Brinkmann, H. "Die Eigenformen des mittelalterlichen Dramas in
Deutschland." In _Studien zur Geschichte der deutschen
Sprache und Literatur._ 2 Bde. Düsseldorf: Pädagogischer
Verlag Schwann, 1965.

——. "Das religiöse Drama im Mittelalter," _Wirkendes
Wort_, 9 (1959): 257-74.

Brody, Alan. _The English Mummers and their Plays: Traces of
Ancient Mystery._ Philadelphia: University of Pennsylvania

Press, 1969.

Brown, Peter L. M., <u>Augustine of Hippo: A Biography</u>. Berkeley: University of California Press, 1967.

——. <u>The World of Late Antiquity A. D. 150-750</u>. History of European Civilization Library. New York: Harcourt: Brace Jovanovich, Paperback, 1971.

——. <u>Religion and Society in the Age of Saint Augustine</u>. London: Faber and Faber, Ltd., 1972.

——. "Aspects of the Christianization of the Roman Aristocracy." <u>The Journal of Roman Studies</u>. 61 (1971): 80-101.

Burkitt, F. C. "The Early Syriac Lectionary System," <u>Proceedings of the British Academy</u> 10 (1921-23): 301-338.

Burkitt, F. C. "The Old Lectionary of Jerusalem." <u>Journal of Theological Studies</u> 24 (1923): 415-425.

Bunting, Marie de Chantal, O. S. U. "Liturgy and Politics in Ninth Century Gaul." Ph. D. Dissertation, Fordham University, 1967.

Büttner, H. "Bonifatius und die Karolinger." <u>Hessisches Jahrbuch für Landesgeschichte</u> 4 (1954): 21ff.

Cabaniss, Allen. <u>Amalarius von Metz</u>. Amsterdam: North Holland Publication Co., 1954.

——. "The Personality of Amalarius." <u>Church History</u> 20 (1951): 34-41.

——. <u>Liturgy and Literature</u>. University City, Alabama: University of Alabama Press, 1970.

Cabrol, Fernand. <u>Les Origines Liturgiques</u>. Paris: Letouzey et Ané, 1906.

——. "Le Book of Cerne. Les Liturgies celtiques at gallicanes et la liturgie romaine." Revue des questions historique 56 N.S. 32 (1904): 210-222.

——. "Mozarabic." Dictionnaire d'Archéologie Chrétienne et de Liturgie 12 (1935): 390-491.

——. "Charlemagne et al liturgie." Dictionnaire d'-Archéologie Chrétienne et de Liturgie 3 (1913): 807-823.

Capelle, Bernard. S. Beda Venerabilis. Romae: S.E.L.E.R. Herder, 1936.

Cargill, Oscar. Drama and Liturgy. New York: Columbia University Press, 1930.

Carpe, William D. "The Vita Canonica in the Regula Canonicorum of Chrodegang of Metz." Ph.D. Dissertation, The University of Chicago, 1975.

Carpenter, Marjorie. "Romanos and the Mystery Plays of the East." Philological Studies in Honor of Walter Miller. The University of Missouri Studies 11, No. 3 (1936): 21-51.

Casel Dom. "Das Mysteriengedächtnis der Messliturgie im Lichte der Tradition." Jahrbuch für Liturgiewissenschaft 6 (1926): 113-204.

——. "Neue Zeugnisse für das Kultmysterium." Jahrbuch für Liturgiewissenschaft 13 (1933): 99-171.

——. "Glaube, Gnosis, Mysterium" Jahrbuch für Liturgiewissenschaft 15 (1941): 155-305.

Casper, E. Geschichte des Papsttums. 2 Bd. Tübingen: J. C. B. Mohr (Paul Siebeck), 1930-33.

Chambers, E. K. The Medieval Stage. 2 vols. Oxford: At the Clarendon Press, 1903.

Chadwick, O. John Cassian: A Study in Primitive Monasticism. 2nd edition. Cambridge: University Press, 1968.

Charles, Lucille, H., "Regeneration through Drama at Death." Journal of American Folklore 59 (1946).

Theochardis, Georgios J. "Beiträge zur Geschichte des Byzantinischen Profantheaters im 4. und 5. Jahrhundert, hauptsächlich auf Grund der Predigten des Johannes Chrysostomus, Patriarchen von Konstantinopel." Ph.D. Dissertation, München, 1942.

Cochrane, Charles N. Christianity and Classical Culture: A Study of Thought and Action from Augustus to Augustine. Oxford: At the Clarendon Press, 1940; revised 1944; reprint edition: Oxford: Oxford University Press, 1957, 1968.

Collins, Fletcher, Jr. The Production of Medieval Church-Music-Drama. Charlottesville: University of Virginia Press, 1972.

Connolly, R. H. "Jacob of Serugh and the 'Diatessaron'", Journal of Theological Studies 8 (1907): 581-590.

Cornford, Francis M. The Origin of the Attic Comedy. Edited with a foreword by Theodore Gaster. 1st edition 1914. Garden City, N.Y.: Doubleday & Company, Inc., Paperback, 1961.

Cottas, Vénétia. Le Théatre a Byzance. Paris: Librairie Orientaliste Paul Geunther, 1931.

Courcelle, Pierre. Recherches sur les Confessiones de S. Augustine. Paris: E. De Boccard, 1950.

Craig, Harden. English Relgious Drama of the Middle Ages. Oxford: At the Clarendon Press, 1955.

Creizenach, W. Geschichte des neueren Dramas, 5 Bde. Halle, a. S.: Max Niemeyer Verlag, 1893-1916.

Cullman, Oscar. Urchristentum und Gottesdienst: Abhandlungen zur Theologie des Alten und Neuen Testaments. Zweite vermehrte und veränderte Auflage. Zürich: Zwingli Verlag, 1950.

Curtius, Ernst Robert. European Literature and the Latin Middle Ages. Translated by W. Trask. New York: Harper & Row, Publishers, 1953; Paperback, 1963.

Danielou, J. Bible et Liturgie. Paris: Edition du Cerf, 1951.

Dawson, Christopher. The Making of Europe. Cleveland and New York: World Publishing Company, 1970. Meridian Book. First Printing, 1956.

Delhaye, Ph. "Les idées morales de Saint Isidore de Séville." Recherches de Théologie ancienne et médiévale 26 (1959): 17-49.

Dix, Dom Gregory. The Shape of the Liturgy. Westminster: Dacre Press, 1945.

Dolger, F. "Europas Gestaltung im Spiegel der fränkisch-byzantinischen Auseinandersetzung des 9. Jahrhunderts. In Byzanz und die europäische Staatenwelt. Ettal: Buchkunstverlag, 1957.

Dörrie, Heinrich. "Spätantike Symbolik und Allegorese." In Frühmittelalterliche Studien 6 (1973): 1-12.

Doerries, H. Das Selbstzeugnis Kaiser Konstantins. Abhdl. d. Ak. d. Wiss. in Göttingen. Phil. hist. Kl. 3. F. Nr. 34. Göttingen: Vandenhoeck & Ruprecht, 1954.

Duchesne, Louis. Christian Worship: Its Origin and Evolution. A Study of the Latin Liturgy up to the Time of Charlemagne. Translated by M. C. McClure. 5th edition. London Society for Promoting Christian Knowledge. New York: The Macmillan Co., 1919.

————.Fastes Episcopaux de Anciénne Gaule. 3 vols.
    Paris: E. de Boccard, 1915.

Duchrow, Ulrich. Sprachverstándnis und Biblisches Hóren.
    Tübingen: J.C.B. Mohr (Paul Siebeck), 1965.

Dumézil, Georges. La Religion Romaine Archaïque.
    Bibliotheque Historique Collection les Religions de
    Humanité. Paris: Payot, 1966.

Dumville, David N. "Liturgical Drama and Panegyric Responsory
    from the Eight Century? A Re-examination of the Origin
    and Content of the Ninth-Century Section of the Book of
    Cerne." Journal of Theological Studies, N.S. Pt. 2. 23
    (1972): 374-406.

Dunn, E. C. Editor. The Medieval Drama and its Claudien
    Revival. Washington: Catholic University of America,
    1970.

Eadie, E. C., Editor. The Conversion of Constantin. European
    Problem Studies. New York: Holt, Rinehardt and Winston,
    Paperback, 1971.

Edwards, Otis Carl, Jr. "Barbarian Philosophy: Tatian and the
    Greek Paideia." Ph.D. Dissertation, University of
    Chicago, 1971.

Ehrhardt, Arnold A. T., Politische Metaphysik von Solon bis
    Augustin. 3 Bde. Tübingen: J. C. B. Mohr (Paul Siebeck),
    1959.

Elbogen, Ismer. Der jüdische Gottesdienst in seiner geschicht-
    lichen Entwicklung. 4. Auflage. Hildesheim: Georg Olms
    Verlagsbuchhandlung, 1962

Eliade, Mircea. Patterns in Comparative Religion. 4th Edition.
    Translated by Rosemary Sheed. Cleveland: World Publishing
    Company: Meridian Books, 1967.

————. The Myth of Eternal Return or, Cosmos and History.

Bollingen Series Nr. 46. Orginally published in French:
Le "Mythe de éternel retour: archétypes et répetition."
Paris: Librarie Gallimard, NRF, 1949. Translated by W.
Trask. Princeton: Princeton University Press, 1954.
Published under the title: Cosmos and History. New York:
Harper Torchbooks, Paperback, 1959. 2nd printing with
corrections, Princeton, 1965. First Princeton/Bollingen
Paperback, 1971.

————. Shamanism. Translated by W. R. Trask. New York:
Panetheon Books, 1964.

Ellard, Gerard. Master Alkuin Liturgist. Chicago: Loyalo
University Press, 1950.

Federer, Alfred. "Kulturgeschichtliches in den Werkendes heil.
Hilarius v. Poitiérs." Stimmen aus Maria Laach 81 (1911):
30-45.

Fendt, L. Einführung in die Liturgiewissenschaft. Berlin:
Alfred Töpelmann, 1958.

Fischer, Ursula. "Karolingische Denkart: Allegorese und
Aufklärung. Dargestellt an den Schriften Amalars von
Metz und Agobard von Lyons." Ph.D. Dissertation,
Göttingen, 1957.

Flanigan, Clifford C. "The Roman Rite and the Origins of the
Liturgical Drama." University of Toronto Quarterly 43
(1974): 263-84.

Fletcher, Angus. Allegory. The Theory of a Symbolic Mode.
Ithaca: Cornell University Press, 1964; paperback, 1970.

Fortescue, A., "Cherubicon." Dictionnaire d'Archéologie
Chrétienne et de Liturgie 3 (1921): 1281-86.

————. "Liturgie." Catholic Encyclopedia, 1910
edition. s.v.

Funk, Francis X., Die Apostolischen Konstitutionen: Eine

<u>literar-historische Untersuchung</u>. Rottenburg, a.N.:
    Verlag von W. Bader, 1891.

Gadamer, Hans-Georg. <u>Wahrheit und Methode</u>. 3. erw. Auflage.
    Tübingen: J. C. B. Mohr (Paul Siebeck), 1972.

Gamber, Klaus. <u>Domus ecclesiae</u>. Regensburg: Pustet Verlag,
    1968.

Gamer, Helena M. "Mimes, Musicans and the Origins of the
    Medieval Religious Plays." <u>Deutsche Beiträge</u> 5 (1965): 9-
    28.

Gardiner, Harold C., S. J. <u>Mysteries End</u>: <u>An investigation of
    the Last Days of the Medieval Religious Stage</u>. New
    Haven: Yale University Press, 1946.

Gams, Pius Bonifatius. <u>Die Kirchengeschichte von Spanien</u>.
    Regensburg: Druck und Verlag von Joseph Manz, 1874.

Geertz, Clifford. <u>The Interpretation of Cultures</u>: <u>Selected
    Essays</u>. New York: Basic Books, 1973.

Geiselmann, J. R. <u>Die Abendmahlslehre an der Wende der
    christlichen Spätantike zum Frühmittelalter</u>. München:
    Max Hueber Verlag, 1933.

Geyser, Joseph. "Die erkenntnistheoretischen Anschauungen
    Augustins zu Beginn seiner schriftstellerischen
    Tätigkeit." In <u>Aurelius Augustinus</u>. Die Festschrift der
    Görresgesellschaft zum 1500. Todestag des Heiligen
    Augustinus. Herausgegeben von M. Grabmann und Joseph
    Mausbach. Köln: Verlag J. P. Bachem, GMBH, 1930.

Gibbon, Edward. <u>The Decline and Fall of the Roman Empire</u>. 2
    vols. First printed in London 1776-78 in 6 vols. New
    York: Modern Library, n.d.

Goodspeed, Edgar J., <u>History of Early Christian Literature</u>.
    London: George Allen and Unwin, Ltd., and Toronto:
    University of Toronto Press, 1942. Revised and enlarged

by Robert M. Grant. Chicago: The University of Chicago Press, Phoenix Book Paperback, 1966.

Goppelt, Leonard. _Typos_. Gütersloh: Verlag C. Bertelsmann, 1939.

Grant, Robert M. _The Letter and the Spirit_. London: S.P.C.K., 1957.

————. _Augustus to Constantin: The Thrust of the Christian Movement into the Roman World_. New York: Harper and Row Publishers, 1970.

————. "The Chronology of the early Greek Apologists." _Vigilae Christianae_ 9 (1955): 25-33.

Griffe, E. "Aux origines de la liturgie gallicane." _Bulletin de littérature écclesiastique_ 52 (1951): 17-43.

————. _La Gaule Chrétienne_. 2 vols. Paris: Editions Picard & Co., 1947-57. 2nd vol. revised and augmented. Paris: Letouzey et Ané, 1966.

Gregoire, H., _et al_. _Persécutions dans l'empire romain_. 2nd ed. Lettres et de sciences morals et politiques, Mémoires, Académie Royale de Belgique. Bruxelles: Palais des Académies, 1964.

Haendler, G. _Epochen Karolingischer Theologie: Eine Untersuchung über die Karolingischen Gutachten zum Byzantinischen Bilderstreit_. Berlin: Evangelische Verlagsbuchhandlung, 1952.

Haller, Johannes. _Das Papsttum: Idee und Wirklichkeit_. 5 Bde. 2. Auflage. Esslingen am Neckar: Port Verlag, 1962.

Hanson, John Arthur. _Roman Theater-Temples_. Princeton Monographs in Art and Archaeology, No. 33. Princeton: Princeton Univeristy Press, 1959.

Hanson, R. P. C. <u>Allegory and Event</u>. London: SMC Press, 1959.

Hardison, O. B., Jr. <u>Christian Rite and Christian Drama in the Middle Ages</u>: <u>Essays in the Origin and Early History of Modern Drama</u>. Baltimore: Johns Hopkins University Press, 1965.

————. "Gregorian Easter Vespers and Early Liturgical Drama" In <u>The Medieval Drama and Its Claudien Revival</u>. Edited by E. C. Dunn. Washington: Catholic University of America Press, 1970.

Harnack, Adolf. <u>Mission und Ausbreitung des Christentums in den ersten drei Jahrhunderten</u>. Vierte, verbesserte und vermehrte Auflage. 2 Bde. Leipzig: Hinrich'sche Buchhandlung, 1924.

Hatlen, Theodore W. <u>Drama: Principles and Plays</u>. Edited with an introduction by Th. Hatlen. 2nd edition. Englewood Cliffs, N.J.: Princeton Hall, paperback, 1975.

Hauck, Albert. <u>Kirchengeschichte Deutschlands</u>. 5 Bde. Leipzig: J. C. Hinrich'sche Buchhandlung, 1903-06.

Hefele, Carl Joseph. <u>Conciliengeschichte</u>. 2. verbesserte Auflage. Freiburg, i. Br.: Herder'sche Verlagsbuchhandlung, 1877.

Hegel, G. W. F., <u>Phänomenologie des Geistes</u>. Edited by J. Hoffmeister. Philosophische Bibliothek 114. Hamburg: Verlag von Felix Meiner, 1952), pp. 471-548.

Heiler, Friedrich. <u>Altkirchliche Autonomie und Päpstlicher Zentralismus</u>. München: Verlag von Ernst Reinhardt, 1941.

Heinemann, I. <u>Altjüdische Allegoristik</u>. Breslau, 1936.

Heitz, Carol. <u>Recherches sur les rapports entre architecture et liturgie a l'époque carolingienne</u>. Paris: S.E.V.P.E.N., 1963.

Helgeland, Joh. "Christians and Military Service," Ph.D. Dissertation, The University of Chicago, 1973.

Herzog, Reinhart. *Die allegorische Dichtkunst des Prudentius*. Dissertation Kiel, 1964. Zetamata, Nr. 42. Monographien zur klassischen Altertumswissenschaft. München: C. H. Becksche Verlagsbuchhandlung, 1966.

Hill, Dorothy. "The Temple above Pompey's Theatre." *The Classical Journal* 39 (1944): 360-65.

Hoffmann, Dietram. *Die geistige Auslegung der Schrift bei Gregor dem Grossen*. Münster-Schwarzacher Studien, Bd. 6. Münster-Schwarzach: Vier-Türme-Verlag: 1968.

Holl, Adolf. *Die Welt der Zeichen bei Augustin: Religionsphänomenologische Analyse des 13. Buches der Confessiones*. Wiener Beiträge zur Theologie, Nr. 2. Wien: Verlag Herder, 1965.

Holmes, T. Scott. *The Origin and Development of the Christian Church in Gaul*. London: Macmillan & Co., 1911.

Huhn, Joseph. "Bewertung und Gebrauch der Heil. Schrift durch den Kirchenvater Ambrosius," *Historisches Jahrbuch der Görresgesellschaft* 77 (1958): 387-96.

Hutton, William H. *The Church of the Sixth Century*. London and New York: Longmans, Green and Co., 1897.

Hunnigher, B. *The Origin of the Theater*. The Hague: M. Nijhoff, 1955.

Jackson, B. D. "Theory of Signs in St. Augustine's 'De Doctrina Christiana.'" in *Augustine: A Collection of Critical Essays*. Edited by R. A. Markus, Garden City, N. Y.: Doubleday & Co., Inc., Anchor Book, 1972.

Jaeger, Werner. *Early Christianity and Greek Paideia*. Cambridge, Mass.: Harvard University Press, 1961.

Jones, A. H. M. The Later Roman Empire 284-602: A Social, Economic and Administrative Survey. Oxford: Basil Blackwell, 1964.

————— . Constantine and the Conversion of Europe. Revised edition. New York: Collier Books, 1962.

Jürgens, Heiko. Pompa Diaboli: Die lateinischen Kirchenväter und das antike Theater. Tübinger Beiträge zur Altertumswissenschaft, Nr. 46. Stuttgart: Verlag W. Kohlhammer, 1972.

Jungmann, Joseph A. Die Stellung Christi im liturgischen Gebet. Münster, i.W.: Aschendorff Verlag, 1925.

—————. The Mass of the Roman Rite: Its Origin and Development Translated by F. Brunner. 2 vols. New York: Benzinger, 1951-55.

—————. Early Liturgies to the Time of Gregory the Great. Translated by F. Brunner. Notre Dame, Indiana: University of Notre Dame Press, 1959.

Kallis, A. "Griechische Väter." In Reallexikon für Antike und Christentum s.v. "Geister" (Dämonen), Bd. 9, Nr. 68-69 (1974-75): 700-15.

Karg-Gasterstädt, Elisabeth. "Aus der Werkstatt des althochdeutschen Wörterbuchs, ahd. bilidi." Beiträge zur Geschichte der deutschen Sprache 66 (1942): 291-308.

Kelly, John N. D. Early Christian Creeds. London and New York: Longmanns Green and Co., 1950.

Kindermann, Heinz. Theatergeschichte Europas. 3 Bde. Salzburg: Otto Muller Verlag, 1957. Bd. 1: Das Theater der Antike und des Mittelalters.

Kirby, Ernest Theodore. Ur-Drama: The Origins of the Theater. New York: New York University Press, 1975.

Klauser, Theodore. Kleine Abendländische Liturgiegeschichte.
  Bonn: Hanstein, 1965.

Klauser, Theodore. "Die Austauschbeziehungen zwischen der
  römischen und fränkischen Kirche vom achten bis elften
  Jahrhundert." Historisches Jahrbuch 53 (1933): 170-177.

Klein, Richard. Symmachus: Eine tragische Gestalt des
  ausgehenden Heidentums. Impulse der Forschung Nr. 2.
  Darmstadt: Wissenschaftliche Buchgesellschaft, 1971.

Köhne, Joseph. "Die Schrift Tertullians 'über die Schauspiele'
  in kultur-und religionsgeschichtlicher Beleuchtung."
  Ph.D. Dissertation, Breslau, 1929.

Kolping, Adolf. "Amalar von Metz und Florus von Lyons."
  Zeitschrift für katholische Theologie 73 (1951): 424-64.

Korger, Mathias A. "Grundprobleme der Augustinischen
  Erkenntnislehre. Erläutert am Beispiel von 'De Genesi ad
  Litteram.'" Recherches Augustiniennes 2 (1962): 33-57.

Kottje, R. "Einheit und Vielfalt des kirchlichen Lebens in der
  Karolingerzeit." Zeitschrift für Kirchengeschichte 3-4
  (1965): 323-342.

Krause, W. Die Stellung der frühchristlichen Autoren zur
  heidnischen Literatur. Wien: Verlag Herder, 1958.

Kretzmann, P. E. The Liturgical Element in Earliest Forms of
  Liturgical Drama. University of Minnesota Studies in
  Language and Literature, No. 4. Minneapolis: University
  of Minnesota Press, 1916.

LaPiana, George. "The Byzantine Theater," Speculum 11 (1936):
  171-211.

Lasko, Peter. The Kingdom of the Franks: North-West Europe
  before Charlemagne. Library of Medieval Civilization.
  New York: McGraw-Hill, paperback, 1971.

412

Leclercq, Henri. "Germain-de-Prés (Saint)". Dictionnaire d'
Archéologie Chrétienne et de Liturgie VI (1924): 1102-
1150.

List, Johannes. Studien zur Homelitik Germanos I. von
Konstantinopel und seiner Zeit. Texte und Unter-
suchungen zur Byzantinischen-Neugriechischen Philologie,
Nr. 29. Athen: Verlag der Byzantinischen-
Neugriechischen Sprache, 1939.

Longworth, Robert. The Cornish Ordinalia: Religion and
Dramaturgy. Cambridge, Mass.: Harvard University Press,
1967.

Lot, Ferdinand. The End of the Ancient World and the Beginning
of the Middle Ages. First published in 1927. Translated
into English 1931. Published with new material in the
United States by Glanville Downey, 1961. New York:
Harper and Row, Publishers, Harper Torchbook paperback,
1965.

Lubac, Henri de. Exégése Médiévale: les quartre sense de l'
Ecriture. 2 vols. Paris: Aubier, 1959.

————. "Typologie et allegorisme." Recherches de
science religieuse 24 (1947): 180-226.

Maas, Fritz. "Von den Ursprüngen der rabbinischen Schriftauslegung." Zeitschrift für katholische Theologie 52
(1955): 145.

Macaigne, R. L'Église merovingienne et l'État pontifical.
Paris: E. de Boccard, 1929.

Mahr, Augustus Carl. Relations of Passion Plays to St. Ephrem
the Syrian. Columbus: Wartburg Press, 1947.

Malden, R. H. "St. Ambrose as an Interpreter of Holy Scripture."
Journal of Theological Studies 16 (1914-15): 509-522.

Malnory, A. Saint Cesaire eveque d'Arles 503-43. Paris:
    E. Bouillon, 1894.

Markus, R. A. "St. Augustine on Signs." In Augustine: A Col-
    lection of Critical Essays. Edited by R. A. Markus.
    Garden City, N. Y.: Doubleday & Co., Anchor Books. 1972.

Marrou, Henri I. Saint Augustine et la fin de la culture an-
    tique. Paris: E. De. Boccard, 1938.

Manley, John. "Literary Forms and the New Theory of the Origins
    of Species." Modern Philology 4 (1906-1907): 383-97.

Mayer, Bernard. "Alkuin zwischen Antike und Mittelalter."
    Zeitschrift fur katholische Theologie 81 (1959): 306-50.

McNalley, Robert E. The Bible in the Early Middle Ages.
    Woodstock Papers, Nr. 4. Westminster, Md.: The
    Newmann Press, 1959.

McNeill, John T. The Celtic Churches: A History A.D. 200-1200.
    Chicago: University of Chicago Press, 1974.

Meril, E. du. Origines Latines du theatre modernes, 1849.

Michael, W. F. "Das dt. Drama und Theater vor der Reformation."
    Deutsche Vierteljahresschrift 31 (1957): 106-153.

Mirgeler, Albert. Ruckblick auf das abendlandische Christentum.
    Mainz: Mathias Grunewald Verlag, 1961.

Momigliano, Arnaldo. The Conflict between Paganism and
    Christianity in the Fourth Century: Essays. Oxford:
    At the Clarendon Press, 1963.

Morin, Germain. "La question de deux Amalaire," Revue
    Benedictine 16 (1899): 419-421.

Morin, Germain. "Amalaire, equisse biographique," Revue
    Benedictine 9 (1892): 337-351.

————. "Encore la question des deux Amalaire," <u>Revue Bénédictine</u> 11 (1894): 241-43.

Murphy, F. X. "Rufinus Tyrannius v. Aquileja." <u>Lexikon für Theologie und Kirche</u> 9 (1964): 91-92.

Müller, Albert. "Das Bühnenwesen in der Zeit von Konstantin bis Justinian." <u>Neue Jahrbücher für das klassische Altertum</u> 23 (1909): 36-55.

Müller, H. F. "Pre-history of the Medieval drama, the Antecedents of the Tropus and the Conditions of their Appearance." <u>Zeitschrift für Philologie</u> 4 (1925): 545-

Mullins, Sr. Patrick Jerome. <u>The Spiritual Life according to St. Isidore de Seville</u>. Ph.D. Dissertation. The Catholic University of America. Studies in Medieval and Renaissance Latin, Languages and Literature. Vol. 13. Washington: The Catholic University of America Press, 1940.

Murray, Gilbert. <u>Euripides and His Age</u>. London: Thornton Butterworth, Ltd. 1927.

Murin, Michael. <u>The Veil of Allegory</u>. Chicago: The University of Chicago Press, 1969.

Nat, P. G. van der. 'Apologeten und lateinische Väter.' s.v. "Geister (Dämonen)." In <u>Reallexikon für Antike und Christentum.</u> Vol. 9. Nos. 68-69 (1974-75): 715-61.

Nikel, G. <u>Der Anteil des Volkes an der Messliturgie des Frankenreiches</u>. Forschungen zur Geschichte des innerkirchlichen Lebens. Innsbruck: Druck und Verlag F. Rauch, 1930.

Nicoll, A. <u>Masks, Mimes and Miracles</u>. New York: Cooper Square Publications, 1963.

Noldechen, E. "Tertullian und das Theater." <u>Zeitschrift für katholische Theologie</u> 15 (1895): 161-203.

415

————. "Tertullian und das Spielwesen," <u>Zeitschrift</u>
<u>für wissenschaftliche Theologie</u> 37 (1894): 91-125.

Oesterley, W. E. <u>The Jewish Background of the Christian</u>
<u>Liturgy</u>. Oxford: At the Clarendon Press, 1925.

Ogilvy, J. D. A., "Mimes, Scurrae, Histriones: Entertaining of
the Middle Ages." <u>Speculum</u> 38 (1963): 603-19.

Ostrogorski, G. <u>Geschichte des Byzantinischen Staates</u>. 2. Aufl.
München, C. H. Beck, 1963.

Otto, W. <u>Die Karolingische Bilderwelt</u>. München: Selbstverlag
des kunsthistorischen Seminars der Universität München, in
Kommission bei Max Huber, 1957.

Pascal, R. "On the Origins of the Liturgical Drama of the Middle
Ages." <u>Modern Language Review</u> 36 (1941): 187-201.

Patzelt, E. und Vogel, C. <u>Die Karolingische Renaissance</u>. Graz:
Akademische Druck-und Verlagsanstalt, 1969.

Pélland, Giles. <u>Cinq etudes d'Augustin sur le debut Génese</u>. Recherches théologie Nr. 8. Paris: Desclee, 1972.

Pepin, J. <u>Mythe et Allégorie les origines grecques et les con-</u>
testationes judeo-chrétiennes. Paris: Presses Universitaires de France, 1947.

Piganiol, A. <u>L'Empire Chrétien</u>. Paris: Presses Universitaires de
France, 1947.

Porter, W. E. <u>The Gallican Rite</u>. Alcuin Club Edition. London: A.
R. Mowbray & Co., Lt. and New York: Morehouse Gorham Co.,
1958.

Potter, Robert. <u>The English Morality Plays</u>: <u>Origin</u>, <u>History</u>
<u>and Influence of a Dramatic Tradition</u>. London: Routledge
and Kegan Paul, 1975.

Probst, F., "Die Antiochische Messe nach den Schriften des heil. Johannes Chrysostomus dargestellt." Zeitschrift für katholische Theologie 7 (1883): 250-307.

Quasten, Johannes. "Oriental Influences in the Gallican Liturgy." Traditio 1 (1953): 55-78.

Rado, P. "Verfasser und Heimat der Monemessen." Éphémerides liturgicae 42 (1928): 58-65.

————. "Das älteste Schriftauslegungssystem der alt-gallikanischen Kirche." Éphémerides liturgicae 45 (1931): 9-25; 100-15.

Rahner, Hugo. "Pompa diaboli: Ein Beitrag zur Be-deutungsgeschichte des Wortes πομπη pompa in der urchristlichen Taufliturgie." Zeitschrift für katholische Theologie 55 (1931): 239-73.

Reich, Hermann. Der Mimus. 1 Band in 2 Teilen. Berlin: Weidemannsche Buchhandlung, 1903. 1. Bd. 1. Tl.: Die Theorie des Mimus.

Reine, Francis J. The Eucharistic Doctrine and Liturgy of the Mystical Catechese of Theodore of Mopsuestia. Ph.D. Dissertation. Catholic University of American Studies in Christian Antiquity, Nr. 2. Washington: The Catholic University of America Press, 1942.

Ricoeur, Paul. The Symbolism of Evil. Translated by Emerson Buchana. Boston: Beacon Press, Paperback, 1967.

Ricoeur, Paul. "Philosophy and Religious Language." The Journal of Religion 54 (1974): 71-85.

Robbins, Frank E. The Hexameral Literature. A Study of Greek and Latin Commentaries on Genesis. Ph.D. Dissertation. Chicago: University of Chicago Press, 1912.

Roetzer, Wunibald. Des heil. Augustinus Schriften als liturgiegeschichtliche Quellen. München: M. Hueber

Verlag, 1930.

Sahre, R. "Amalarius von Metz." Enzyklopadie für pro-
testantische Theologie und Kirche 1 (1896): 428-30.

—————. "Amalarius von Trier." Enzyklopädie für pro-
testantische Theologie und Kirche 1 (1896): 430-31.

Salaville, Pére Séverin. An Introduction to the Studies of
Eastern Liturgies. Adapted from the French with a preface
and some additional notes by M. T. Barton. London: Lauds
& Sons, Ltd., 1938.

Satre, Jean-Paul. The Psychology of Imagination. 2nd edition.
Translated by Bernard Frechtman. New York: Washington
Square Press, Inc., 1968.

Saunders, Catherine, "Altars on the Roman Comic Stage." Transactions of the American Philological Association 42
(1913): 91-103.

—————. "The Site of Dramatic Performance at Rome in
the Times of Plautus and Terrence." Transactions of the
American Philological Association 44 (1913): 87-97.

Schade, L. Die Inspirationslehre des heil. Hieronymus. Biblische
Studien Nr. 15. Freiburg, i. Br.: Herder'sche Verlagsbuchhandlung, 1910.

Scholz, Heinrich. Glaube und Unglaude in der Weltgeschichte.
Leipzig: J. C. Hinrich'sche Verlagsbuchhandlung, 1911.

Schneider, F. Rom und der Romgedanke im Mittelalter. München:
Drei-Türme-Verlag, 1926.

Schwietering, J. "Über den liturgischen Ursprung des mittelalterlichen Spiels." Zeitschrift für deutsche Altertumswissenschaft 62 (1925): 1-20.

Seibel, Wolfgang. Fleisch und Geist beim heil. Ambrosius. Ph.D.
Dissertation München. Münchener Theologische Studien Nr.

2. Systematische Abteilung Bd. 14. München: Kommissions Verlag Karl Zink, 1958.

Séjourne, Dom Paul. Saint Isidore de Séville. Études de Théologie Historique. Paris: Gabriel Beauchesse, 1929.

Siegfried, Carl. Philo von Alexandrien als Ausleger des Alten Testaments. Jena: Verlag von Hermann Dufft, 1875.

Simpson, Otto von. Sacred Fortress: Byzantine Art and States-craft in Ravenna. Chicago: University of Chicago Press, 1948.

Smalley, Beryl. The Study of the Bible in the Middle Ages. Oxford: Basil Blackwell & Mott Ltd., 1952. Paperback, second printing. Notre Dame, Indiana: University of Notre Dame Press, 1970.

Smolden, William L. "The Origins of the Quem Quaeritis Trope and the Easter Sepulchre Music Dramas as Demonstrated by their Musical Settings." In The Medieval Drama edited by Sandro Sticca. Albany: State University of New York Press, 1972.

Southern, R. W. The Making of the Middle Ages. New Haven and London: Yale University Press, paperback, 1969.

Staiger, Emil. Die Kunst der Interpretation: Studien zur deutschen Literaturgeschichte. Zürich: Atlantis Verlag, 1953.

Steuart, Dom Benedict. The Development of Christian Worship. London: Yale University Press, paperback, 1969.

Sticca, Sandro. Editor. The Medieval Drama. Albany: State University of New York Press, 1972.

Stiglmayer, J. "Eine syrische Liturgie als Vorlage des Ps. Aeropagiten." Zeitschrift für katholische Theologie 35 (1909): 383-85.

Strauss, Gerhard. Schriftgebrauch, Schriftauslegung und Schriftbeweis bei Augustin. Beiträge zur Geschichte der biblischen Hermeneutik. Tübingen: J. C. B. Mohr (Paul Siebeck), 1959.

Stumpfl, R. Kultspiele der Germanen als Ursprung des mittelalterlichen Dramas. Berlin: Junker und Dünnhaupt, 1936.

Szondi, Peter. Theorie des modernen Dramas. 4. Auflage. Frankfurt, A.M.: Suhrkamp Verlag, paperback, 1967.

Tate, J. "The Beginning of Greek Allegory." Classical Review 41 (1927): 214-15.

Taylor, Lili Ross. "The 'Sellisternium' and the "theatrical pompa.'" Classical Philology 30 (1935): 122-30.

Thibaut, J. B. L'anciénne liturgie gallicane, son origines et sa formation en provence aux V et VI siecles sons l' influence de Cassian et de Césaire d'Arles. Paris: Maison de la bonne presse, 1929.

Thompson, Alexander H., Editor. Bede: His Life, Times and Writings. Essays in Commemoration of the Twelfth Century of His Death. Introduction by Lord Bishop of Durham. Oxford: At the Clarendon Press, 1935.

Thum, B. "Beda," in Lexikon für Theologie und Kirche 2 (1958): 93-94.

Tisdel, F. M. "The Influence of popular Customs on the Mystery Plays." Journal of English and Germanic Philology 5 (1803-05): 323.

Tunison, J. S. Dramatic Traditions of the Dark Ages. Chicago: University of Chicago Press, 1907.

Vööbus, Arthur. History of the School of Nisibis. CSCO vol. 260. Subsidia t. 26. Louvain: Secretariat du Sorpus SCO: 1965.

—————. The Statutes of the School of Nisibis. Edited, translated and furnished with a commentary. Papers of the Estonian Theological Society in Exile. Stockholm: ETSE, 1962.

—————. History of Asceticism in the Syrian Orient: A Contribution to the History of Culture in the Near East. CSCO 183, 197, Subsidia t. 14, 17. Louvain: Secretariat du Corpus SC), 1958, 1960.

—————. Literary, Critical and Historical Studies in Ephrem the Syrian. Papers of the Estonian Theological Society in Exile, Nr. 10. Stockholm: ETSE, 1958.

—————. Neue Angaben uber die textgeschichtlichen Zustande in den Jahren ca. 326-340. Ein Beitrag zur Geschichte des altsyrischen Tetraeevangeliums. Papers of the Estonian Theological Society in Exile. Stockholm: ETSE, 1951.

—————. Liturgical Traditions in the Didache. Papers of the Estonian Theological Society in Exile, NR. 16. Stockholm: ETSE, 1958.

—————. "Regarding the theological Anthropology of Theodore of Mopsuestia." Church History 33 (1964): 115-124.

—————. "Theodore of Mopsuestia." In Encyclopedia Britannica s.v.

—————. "Theological Reflections on Human Nature in Ancient Syrian Traditions." In The Scope of Grace: Essays on Nature and Grace in Honor of Joseph Sittler. Edited by Philip Hefner. Philadelphia: Fortress Press, 1964.

Vogel, Cyrille. "Le développment historique du culte chrétien en occident. Resultate et problems." In Problemi di storia delle Chiesa l'Alto Medioevo. Milano: Vita et Piensero, Pubblicazione delli Universita Cattolica del

Sacro Curo, 1973.

————."La reforme culturelle sons Pépin de Bref et sons Charlemagne." In E. Patzelt and C. Vogel, <u>Die karolingische Renaissance</u>. Graz: Akademische Druck- und Verlagsanstalt, 1965.

————. "Les éxchanges liturgiques entre Rome et les francs jusqua l'époque de Charlemagne," dans <u>Le chiese nei regni dell'Europa occidentale ei Loro Rapporti con Roma sino a alto 800</u>. Les Settimane di studi del centro italiano di Studi sull' alto medioevo 7. Spoleto: Presso la sede del centro, 1960.

Vogt, J. <u>Zur Religiösität der Christenverfolger im Römischen Reich</u>. Sitzungsberichte der Heidelberger Akademie der Wissenschaften. Phil. Hist. Kl. Jhrg., 1962. I. Abhndl. Heidelberg: G. Winter Universitätsverlag, 1962.

————. "Constantin der Grosse," <u>Reallexikon für Antike und Christentum</u> 3 (1967): 306-379.

Walls, A. F. "A Note on the Apostolic Claim in the Church Order Literature." <u>Texte und Untersuchungen</u> 64 (1957): 83-92.

Wasselynck, René. "Les 'Morals in Job' dans le ouvrages de moral du haute Moyan age latin." <u>Recherches de Théologie Anciénne et Médiévale</u> 31 (1964): 5-31.

Waszink, J. H. "Varro, Livy and Tertullian on the History of Roman Dramatic Art." <u>Vigilae Christianae</u> 2 (1948): 224-242.

Weber, P. <u>Geistliches Schauspiel und kirchliche Kunst in ihrem Verhåltnis erlåutert an einer Ikonography der Kirche und Synagoge</u>. Stuttgart: Ebner & Seubert, 1894.

Weismann, Werner. <u>Kirche und Schauspiele im Urteil der lateinischen Kirchenväter unter besonderer Berücksichtigung von Augustin</u>. Cassiciacum 27. Würzburg: Augustinus Verlag, 1972.

Wey, Heinrich. Die Funktion der bösen Geister bei den griechischen Apologeten des zweiten Jahrhunderts nach Christus. Winterthur: Verlag P.S. Keller, 1957.

Wickham, Glynne. The Medieval Theaters. London: Weichenfels und Nicolson, 1974.

Wiegand, Fr. "Das Homiliarium Karls des Grossen auf seine ursprungliche Gestalt hin untersucht." Theologische Studien und Kritiken 75 (1902): 188-205.

Wilmart, A. "La réforme liturgique de Charlemagne." Éphémerides liturgicae 45 (1931): 186-207.

———. "Expositio Missae." Dictionnaire d'Archéologie Chrétienne et de Liturgie vol. 5, pt. 1 (1922): 1014-1027.

Wilmart, A. "Germain de Paris (lettres attribuees a saint). Dictionnaire d'Archéologie Chretienne et de Liturgie VI (1924): 1049-1102.

Winterfield, Paul von. Deutsche Dichter des lateinischen Mittelalters. München: C. H. Beck Verlag, 1922.

Woerdemann, Jude. "The Source of the Easter Play." Orate Fratres 20 (1945-46): 262-71.

Wolfson, Harry Austryn. Philo. 3rd. printing revised. Cambridge, Mass.: Harvard University Press, 1962.

Woolf. Rosemary. The English Mystery Plays. Berkeley and Los Angeles: University of California Press, 1962.

Young, Karl. The Drama of the Medieval Church. 2 vols. Oxford: At the Clarendon Press, 1933.

———. "Officium Pastorum. A study in the Dramatic Developments with the Liturgy of Christmas." Transactions of the Wisconsin Academy of Sciences 17

(1914): 299-395.

————. "The Dramatic Associations of the Easter
Sepulchre." University of Wisconsin Studies in Languages
and Literatures 7 (1920).

Addenda to English translation of works citations and translations of which were previously quoted in German:

The Basic Works of Aristotle, translated and with an introduction by Richard McKeon. New York: Random House, 1968.

Origen Contra Celsum, translated with an introduction and notes
by Henry Chadwick. Cambridge: At the University Press,
1953.

St. Irenaeus, The Demonstration of the Apostolic Preaching with
an introduction and notes by J. A. Robinson. London
Society for the Promotion of Christian Knowledge. New
York: Macmillan, 1920.

Additional Works Cited and Consulted

Aldernick, Larry Jon. "Crisis and Cosmogony: Post-Mortem Existence in the Eleusian and Orphic Mysteries". Ph.D. Dissertation: The University of Chicago, 1975. (Appendix: Translation of <u>Dervi Papyrus</u>, a commentary on Orphic Writings.)

Brinkmann, Henning. <u>Mittelalterliche Hermeneutik</u>. Darmstadt: Wissenschaftliche Buchgesellschaft, 1980.

Eliade, Mircea. <u>A History of Religious Ideas. III</u>. Translated from the French by Alf Hiltebeitel and Diane Apostolos-Cappadona. Chicago: University of Chicago Press, 1985.

——. <u>Images and Symbols</u>: <u>Studies in Religious Symbolism</u>. Translated from the French by Philip Mairet. New York: Sheed and Ward. A Search Book, 1969.

——. <u>Symbolism, the Sacred and the Arts</u>. Edited by Diane Apostolos-Cappadona. New York: Crossroads, 1985.

——. <u>Briser le Toit de la Maison: La Créativité et ses Symboles</u>. <u>Les Essais</u>. Paris: Edition Gallimard, 1986.

Gregoire de Nazianze, <u>La Passion du Christ</u>, <u>Tragédie</u>. Introduction, Texte Critique, Traduction, Notes et Index by Adre Tuilier. Paris: Les Editions du Cerf, 1969. (Sources Chrétiennes, 149).

McGinn, Bernard. <u>Visions of the End: Apocalyptic Traditions in the Middle Ages</u>. New York: Columbia University Press, 1979.

Meier, Christel. "Überlegungen zum gegenwärtigen Stand der Allegorieforschung, mit besonderer Berücksichtigung der Mischformen." <u>Frühmittelalterliche Studien</u> 10 (1976): 1-69.

425

Murray, Robert. Symbols of Church and Kingdom: A Study in Early Syriac Tradition. Cambridge: Cambridge University Press, 1975.

Ohly, Friedrich. Schriften zur Mittelalterlichen Bedeutungs- forschung. 2. Aufl. Darmstadt: Wissenschaftliche Buch- gesellschaft, 1983.

Ricoeur, Paul. Conflict of Interpretations: Essays in Her- meneutics. Translated from the French by Kathleen McLaughlin. Evanston: Northwestern University Press, 1974.

———. The Rule of Metaphor: Multidisciplinary Studies in the Creation of Meaning in Language. Translated from the French by Robert Czerny with Kathleen McLaughlin and John Costello, S. J. Toronto: University of Toronto Press, 1977.

Schnusenberg, Christine C. "Das Verhältnis von Kirche und Theater: Dargestellt an ausgewählten Schriften der Kirchenväter und liturgischen Texten bis auf Amalarius von Metz (775-852 A.D.)", Ph. D. Dissertation: The University of Chicago, 1976.

———. Das Verhältnis von Kirche und Theater: Dargestellt an ausgewählten Schriften der Kirchenväter und liturgischen Texten bis auf Amalarius von Metz (A.D. 775- 852). Bern-Frankfurt-Las Vegas: Peter Lang, 1981. (Europaisde Hochschulschriften, Reihe Theologie, Vol. 141).

Shils, Edward. Tradition. Chicago: University of Chicago Press, 1981.

Sturluson, Snorri. The Prose Edda. Translated from the Icelandic by J. L. Young. Berkeley: University of California Press, 1951.

Turner, Victor. The Forest of Symbols. Ithaca, N.Y.: Cornell University Press, 1967.

426

About the Author

Christine C. Schnusenberg received her B. A. (1967) from Creighton University, Omaha, Nebraska; her M.A. (1968) and her Ph. D. (1976) from the University of Chicago, Department of Germanic Languages and Literatures; she is presently completing a post-doctoral project which has been guided by Professors Mircea Eliade and Paul Ricoeur, Committee on Social Thought, the University of Chicago; there she is also holding a position as editorial-archival assistant to Professor Edward Shils.